Tall Ships
of the Piscataqua

1830-1877

The Portsmouth Marine Society
Publication Fifteen

Published for the Society by

Peter E. Randall
P U B L I S H E R

Tall Ships of the Piscataqua

1830-1877

by Ray Brighton

A publication of
The Portsmouth Marine Society
Box 147, Portsmouth, NH 03801

Frontispiece:
Lithograph of Portsmouth waterfront, from the Navy Yard, 1854.

ISBN 0915819-14-7

Other Portsmouth Marine Society Publications:
1. *John Haley Bellamy, Carver of Eagles*
2. *The Prescott Story*
3. *The Piscataqua Gundalow, Workhorse for a Tidal Basin Empire*
4. *The Checkered Career of Tobias Lear*
5. *Clippers of the Port of Portsmouth and the Men Who Built Them*
6. *Portsmouth-Built, Submarines of the Portsmouth Naval Shipyard*
7. *Atlantic Heights, A World War I Shipbuilders' Community*
8. *There Are No Victors Here, A Local Perspective on the Treaty of Portsmouth*
9. *The Diary of the Portsmouth, Kittery and York Electric Railroad*
10. *Port of Portsmouth Ships and the Cotton Trade*
11. *Port of Dover, Two Centuries of Shipping on the Cochecho*
12. *Wealth and Honour, Portsmouth During the Golden Age of Privateering, 1775-1815*
13. *The Sarah Mildred Long Bridge, A History of the Maine-New Hampshire Interstate Bridge from Portsmouth, New Hampshire, to Kittery, Maine*
14. *The Isles of Shoals, A Visual History*

Contents

Appreciation   xvii

Down to the Sea in Ships   1

The 1830s   11

The 1840s   81

The 1850s   159

The 1860s   267

The 1870s   299

Notes   359

Index   369

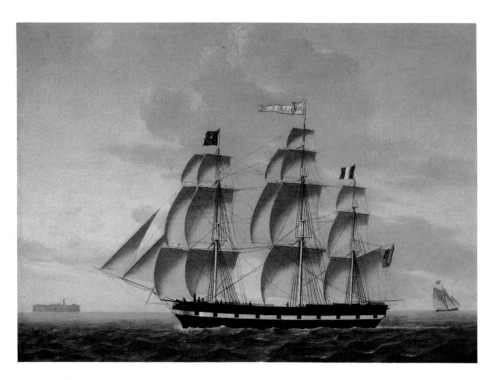

(above) Built in 1831 by Samuel Badger, Apollo, *spent its final days as a store ship in San Francisco. (below)* Issac Newton *was built in 1836 by George Raynes. Courtesy Peabody Museum.*

(left) Thomas Perkins, *was built in Portsmouth by Frederick W. Fernald in 1837. (below) Samuel Badger built* Huron *in 1837. Courtesy Peabody Museum.*

(above) Venice *was built in 1841 by George Raynes. Courtesy Portsmouth Historical Society. (below)* Pontiac *was built by Samuel Badger in 1838. Courtesy Peabody Museum.*

(above) The Samoset, *constructed in 1847 by Fernald and Pettigrew, was built for the Tuckers of Wiscasset, Maine. Courtesy Jane Tucker. (below)* Siam *built by George Raynes in 1847, was abandoned at sea in 1873. Courtesy Peabody Museum.*

(above) Levi Woodbury, *built by Fernald and Pettigrew in 1851, was named for a leading national political figure of the day. (below)* Samuel Badger, *shown entering Malta, was launched in 1852 and named for its builder. Courtesy Peabody Museum.*

Daniel Marcy and other prominent Democrats had Fernald and Pettigrew build the Frank Pierce in 1852. They named the vessel for the fourteenth president of the United States. Courtesy Mariners' Museum.

(above) The first Granite State *was constructed in 1853 by Samuel Badger. Courtesy City of Portsmouth. (below)* Othello, *was built in 1855 by Tobey and Littlefield for the Tuckers of Wiscasset. Courtesy Peabody Museum.*

(above) The Alice Ball, *built by Tobey and Littlefield in 1857, was lost off Honolulu in 1872. Courtesy California State Park System, Monterey State Historic Park. (below)* Santee *was built by Tobey and Littlefield in 1860 and lost off the coast of Ireland in 1870.*

(above) Grandee, *with Hong Kong in the background, was built in 1873 by Tobey and Littlefield. Courtesy Peabody Museum. (below)* Frank Jones *built by John Neal in 1873, was named in honor of the Portsmouth industrialist and congressman.*

(above) The white-hulled Paul Jones, *built by William Fernald in 1877, was the last full-rigged, three-masted vessel launched on the Piscataqua. Courtesy Peabody Museum. Fernald also built in 1875 the* Chocorua, *named for the New Hampshire Indian chief.*

Figurehead of the Grandee. *Courtesy Peabody Museum.*

Appreciation

ONCE UPON A TIME, I would have entitled this section "acknowledgments," but that really doesn't go far enough in expressing my debt of gratitude. However, it's easy to single out one person who added much to whatever worth this book may have. I'm under deep obligation to Jane S. Tucker, of Castle Tucker, Wiscasset, Maine. Miss Tucker is a descendant of the shipowning Tucker dynasty, and she is its faithful chronicler. The Tuckers, their lives, and their ships have been her life-long avocation. Miss Tucker abstracted dozens of pages of ships' logs, and combed through family correspondence in seeking pertinent passages. Unfortunately, all too much of her valuable material couldn't be used here. However, enough has been to give me cause to dedicate *The Tall Ships of the Piscataqua* to Jane S. Tucker, along with the fervent hope that some day, a lover of ships will come along and tell the story of the entire Tucker fleet—hopefully soon.

Once again credit must be given to the late George Nelson, a former customs officer in the District of Portsmouth, for the labor of love he performed more than 50 years ago in compiling a record of all the vessels of any rig, built in the district between 1789 and 1877.

Then there's Richard Winslow III, a fellow traveler through the dusty pages of Portsmouth history, who was indefatigable in making contributions to this work—even I was crying, "Cease and desist—enough is enough!"

Peter E. Randall, the Portsmouth Marine Society's publisher, was ever-ready with timely advice, and a pillar when it came to the final showdown on photography.

In the early going, Joseph P. Copley, the New Castle historian, can give adequate thanks to the dedicated Reference staff of the Portsmouth Public Library. And then there's that wonderful, limited staff of the Portsmouth Athenaeum. Anything within its power, that staff will produce. Frankly, thanks have to go to librarians everywhere: from Key West, Florida, to Monterey, California; to Boston and New York and the Library of Congress. The friendly help of the staff at the British Newspaper Library, in Colindale, London, England, was heart-warming, as was the help of the Central Reference Library staff, Leicester Square, London.

And the people who are in charge of the famed clipper *Cutty Sark*, at Greenwich, England, were helpful.

Then, a diver in Key West, Florida, Ray Maloney, happily shared photos of articles recovered from the wreck of the *Issac Allerton*, a Port of Portsmouth vessel wrecked on Washerwoman Shoal, south of the Saddlebunch Keys. Maloney even invited me down to dive on the wreck. Although, at seventy-five, I felt compelled to decline.

And, as has been the case since the first books I've written, I am indebted to Betty J. Nelson for her laborious work in reading copy and especially in reconciling the footnotes.

Also, those in the Portsmouth Marine Society's stable of authors should always give thanks to Joseph G. Sawtelle for his continuing, tireless support of writing about the Port of Portsmouth. Those of us who love the New Hampshire seacoast's history are deeply indebted to Joe Sawtelle.

Ray Brighton

This venerable house stood on Raynes Avenue at the junction with Maplewood. It was built in three sections. Nathaniel Meserve built the first part; George Boyd added to that; and George Raynes added still another section. The house was razed about 50 years ago to make way for a lumber yard. Photo courtesy of Strawbery Banke, Inc.

I   Down to the Sea in Ships

FOR NEARLY FOUR CENTURIES, the inhabitants of the Piscataqua River Valley have been sending their men down to the sea in vessels built out of timbers cut in the forests that once abounded along the seacoast of New Hampshire. Majestic white oaks once spread their antlered strength wherever the eye could see. Tall pines, so coveted by the British Navy in the eighteenth century, provided masts for the warships that kept the French at bay. If the reader drives from Portsmouth to New Castle, and glances off to the right, he or she will see The Pool, where ships once anchored to be loaded with tall sticks for the Royal Navy. At this juncture, it's impossible to appreciate, fully, what the mast commerce meant to the Province of New Hampshire and the Port of Portsmouth.

Basically, what happened to the trade of the Port of Portsmouth was the gradual decline in export materials from the interior of the state. What did Portsmouth really have to offer, once beaver pelts, mast pines, and other timbers became scarce? True, there was that magical product called "dun fish"—a cod specially cured and brought in from the Isles of Shoals. But how many quintals of dun fish, or any other kind of fish, does it take to keep a seaport thriving? In local seafood restaurants, there would be little call today for dun fish, but in its time it was a popular delicacy. When Tobias Lear, a Portsmouth native who was secretary to George Washington, came home on a visit, he took back to Mount Vernon several quintals of it.

It's encouraging to see history repeating itself for the Port of Portsmouth. By way of example, fishing was a major industry for the Port of Portsmouth in the early days. In the nineteenth century it

1

faded, but now once more fishermen are working out of the Piscataqua, as a visit to Pierce Island and the State Fishing Pier will attest.

Oil tankers come and go with great frequency, filling the huge storage tanks that line the riverbanks. This, too, repeats history, although on a much grander scale than the 1840s, when whaling vessels like the *Triton*, *Ann Parry*, and *Pocahontas* would come in from several years spent in the Indian and Pacific oceans. Whale oil lighted the homes of the seacoast until manufactured gas took over, and then electricity.

Also, the casual observer has but to stand at the intersection of Market and Deer streets to view one of the oldest importing businesses in the Port of Portsmouth—salt. In older times, locally owned ships went to places like St. Ubes, Portugal, Cadiz, Spain, or Liverpool to load salt as a return cargo. Today, one shipment of salt unloaded at Granite State Minerals more than surpasses the imports of an entire year 140 years ago. And the use to which the salt is being put has changed significantly in the last 30 years. When shipbuilding was a major industry along the Piscataqua, salt was used in large quantities to season the green timbers being framed into vessels. And, of course, many tons annually were used in the salting of fish for export. To a lesser extent that goes on today at the State Fish Pier. However, as motorists well know, the bulk of imported salt here in New England goes toward keeping snow and icy highways safe—although it raises havoc with the metal in automobiles.

No one knows who constructed the first seagoing vessel out of native materials. The Pilgrims, when they came in 1620, brought with them a prefabricated shallop, which they assembled for fishing and exploration of the coast. In all probability it was in this shallop in 1623 that Myles Standish, the military leader of Plimouth Plantation, paid a visit to David Thomson, then squatting at Odiorne's Point.[1] Thomson gave the visitors some foodstuffs, but such visits were rare among the very early settlers, who hadn't yet ventured very far inland. Slowly, the roads—if they could be called that—connecting the shoestring of settlements along the coast became more defined. For example, late in the seventeenth century, when Richard Waldron, the boss of the Dover settlement, ordered three Quaker women whipped as they passed from town to town en route to the Puritan Commonwealth, there were rough cart paths. Judge Samuel Sewall of Boston followed the same paths when he used to come through Portsmouth to preside over courts in the District of Maine in the early 1700s.[2]

However, when it came to the movement of goods between the coastal communities, vessels had high priority throughout the eighteenth century and passed their peak only with the coming of the

railroads in the 1840s. The inland towns sent their goods as directly as they could to the seaports. The early vessels were, for the most part, constructed upriver from Portsmouth, near the mouths of the Piscataqua's tributaries. *Port of Portsmouth Ships and the Cotton Trade* (Ray Brighton, 1986) sketches the stories of 202 of those vessels, as listed in the Customs Records of the Portsmouth District between 1789 and 1829. But it's recognized that the building of vessels, of one type or another, had long preceded the establishment of the governmental machinery of the United States in 1789. For example, the Portsmouth Athenaeum has on display a model of the ship *Elizabeth*, built in Durham in 1756 for Captain Nathaniel Adams, father of the nineteenth-century Portsmouth historian, Nathaniel Adams. But the *Elizabeth* was a late arrival on the Port of Portsmouth's shipbuilding scene.

It's known for certain, through British Admiralty records, that two warships were built on the Piscataqua in the 1690s. They were the *Falkland* and the *Bedford Galley*. The Royal Navy's contractor, John Taylor, brought artisans from England to build them.[3] The friction between these new artisans and the members of the closed society of the early Port of Portsmouth indicates that a strong shipbuilding fraternity already existed in the Piscataqua Basin. But it didn't take long for the newcomers to become assimilated; probably a few marriages worked wonders, and their descendants were the mechanics who built the vessels in the eighteenth and nineteenth centuries.

While the Royal Navy's avid interest stimulated shipbuilding to some degree, the demands of trade were the foundations of the industry. The Piscataqua ports, like Dover, Berwick, and Exeter, traded local goods to the Caribbean for rum, sugar, and other items. While they lasted in any quantity, beaver pelts were in high demand, along with fish and lumber products. Thus was established the famed "Triangle Trade." Every effort was made by the Mother Country to run a closed shop on commerce. The colonies could trade back and forth along the Atlantic Coast, and to the West Indies, and there was some direct trade with England—all of which slowly gave rise to a great mercantile class.

One of the first of these titans was George Boyd of Portsmouth, who eventually established himself in his long since vanished mansion on the North Mill Pond. Boyd not only traded directly with England, but also with the West Indies. Much of his business was done in his own vessels. He built three-masted, square-rigged ships on the North Mill Pond in a yard that had seen the construction in 1749 of a third British warship, HBM *America*. He also had ships built in yards at Hampton and Amesbury. Boyd made trips to England in the furthering of his business interests. One such venture was in 1769, and another in 1774, when it was reported:

> Last Monday [April 18] sail'd for London in ship *Felicity* Henry Nutter commander, Colonel George Boyd passenger, who has perhaps fixed out more ships, brigs &c in the course of 10 years than ever before done by any one man in the province in the same space of time—No less than 12 ships, two brigs within a year past—It may be said of him, that he is the most lucky Genius of the present day in a mercantile Way, though not bred a merchant, & has acquired a handsome fortune.[4]

George Boyd's career, loaded with intrigue and mysterious disappearances, can't be reported here, but it is a story that should be pursued by someone. However, there's space enough to say that George Boyd was not only a sharp merchant, but also a shrewd observer of the political scene. In letters now in the collections of the New Hampshire Historical Society, he constantly warned his English agents that the government of George III was fast bringing about revolution. Boyd, who had moved far enough up in the social life of the provincial capital to be a drinking companion of those in the inner circle, went to England during the Revolutionary War. He tried to return in 1787, but he died at sea a few days from home. His son, William, continued the business until 1816, when he moved to New Orleans.

Besides his son, Boyd had plenty of successors in the post-revolutionary Port of Portsmouth. These mercantile firms came back to life on all sides and continued to prosper. Among them, of course, were the Sheafes—Thomas, James, and Jacob. They had their warehouses and wharves along the river, and their ships sailed the Seven Seas. The ships they employed were built along the Piscataqua. Another of the major dynasties was that of the Ladds—Henry and Alexander. Their father, Eliphalet Ladd, had his start as a privateer during the

Revolution. In Exeter, in 1793, he built the first Piscataqua merchant vessel to have three decks, a feat not equaled until 1849, when Fernald and Pettigrew built the *Empire State*. Not only that, Ladd's big ship, the *Archelaus*, was the largest merchantman launched until 1833, when George Raynes put the first ship *Rockingham* in the water. Eliphalet Ladd moved his base of operations to Portsmouth, and his sons kept the business prosperous. They had ships built for them in Dover, Durham, and Exeter.

It would be well to note here that the town of Portsmouth's role in actual ship construction early in the nineteenth century was minor. Out of the 202 ships built here between 1789 and 1829, only 14 of them were launched in Portsmouth waters. Durham alone put 46 hulls in the water, although most of them came down the Piscataqua to Portsmouth to be rigged for sea duty. In those days, the upriver yards dominated shipbuilding. In a way, it's hairsplitting to minimize Portsmouth's production. After all, William Badger built 50 or more ships on the island that bears his name, only a couple of stones' throws from Portsmouth, and many of the workmen, as well as ship chandlers, came from Portsmouth.

Why the upriver yards dominated the early shipbuilding industry is really quite simple: they were near the sources of timber. In the backwoods of the three towns already mentioned, plus Somersworth, Newmarket, and Eliot, there was an abundance of white oak, the favored wood. Sawyers working in the forests behind those towns could float their lumber down the tributaries of the Piscataqua at little expense. The skilled artisans traveled from yard to yard as their particular skills were needed.

But times were changing. Slowly, the size of vessels increased, and that made it more and more difficult to get the ships out into the main river. Then, in 1820–1821, a syndicate built the Portsmouth Bridge, spanning the Piscataqua in the general vicinity of the present-day Sarah Long Bridge. Naturally, the bridge proprietors had to make provision for the passage of vessels. But the draw, with the river's seven-knot current, was difficult to navigate, and there were no steam tugs around to help. By the end of the 1820s, the shipyards upriver were virtually dormant. True, as late as 1832 and 1833, Berwick put two ships in the water, and Dover saw the launching of the *Oronoco* in 1837. The *Oronoco* was the last ship from above Portsmouth Bridge until 1847, when the Hanscoms launched the *Elizabeth Hamilton* from their yard, on the premises of present-day Green Acre.

William Badger, the famed "Master Badger," died in 1829, bragging that he had launched a hundred ships and would be back to launch a hundred more. But it is almost as if his passing, along with

THE REMARKABLE
FEJEE MERMAID.

WHICH was exhibited in most of the principal cities of
America in the years of 1840, '41 and '42, to the wonder
and astonishment of thousands of Naturalists and other scientific
persons, whose doubts of the existence of such an astonishing
creation were entirely removed, has been purchased at immense
cost and added to the mammoth collection of the
BOSTON MUSEUM
Situated on TREMONT ST. *near Court street* — BOSTON,
which comprises specimens of all that can instruct or amuse
of the
WONDERS OF NATURE AND ART
collected from all quarters of the Globe, to the number of nearly
HALF A MILLION ARTICLES
all of which in addition to the splendid
Theatrical Performances
of Tragedies, Comedies, Dramas, Operas Spec-
tacles, Burlettas, Farces, &c.
given every evening and Wednesday and Saturday afternoons
by performers of acknowledged talent, and with Orchestral,
Scenic and Stage arrangements that
CANNOT BE SURPASSED,
are to be seen for the unprecedented small charge of
ONLY 25 CENTS!

the decline in upriver building, marked the end of one era, and the
beginning of a new. Not only did Samuel Badger, William's nephew,
come out from under the great man's shadow, but two other younger
men were launching careers in shipbuilding. They were Frederick
William Fernald and George Raynes. In 1833, Raynes took over the
yard where George Boyd had built vessels in the 1760s, and he even
acquired the mansion, near the shipyard, in which Boyd had lived.
Fernald started out about five years behind both Raynes and Samuel
Badger, but he was soon the third man in the domination of Port of
Portsmouth shipbuilding for the next two decades. Raynes and Fernald died within days of each other in 1855, and are buried across the
lane from each other in Union Cemetery. Badger outlived them by
only a couple of years.

It was the good fortune of this trio of builders to come on the
scene when world commerce was about to explode. While the older
business houses, like the Ladds, Sheafes, and Havens, were phasing
out, newer ones were becoming active. One such was the firm formed

by Ichabod Goodwin and Samuel E. Coues. However, with the coming of the 1840s, demands from urban centers, such as Boston, New York, and Philadelphia, were steadily increasing. It was a slowly developing process, spurred by various influences throughout the world. At no point in time did the builders declare that outside buyers would have their undivided attention; yet this was nearly true, and became more so as the years passed.

Frederick W. Fernald, using plans prepared by a marine architect who has yet to be positively identified, built the racy *Thomas H. Perkins*. In hindsight, it's tempting to speculate that the *Thomas H. Perkins* could have been the first Piscataqua clipper. The ship was very narrow, but was she a clipper? Anyway, the *Portsmouth Journal* gave the vessel full marks for being of "avant-garde" construction.

By the by, there will be little discussion of clippers in this volume. Those glamorous vessels were described in *Clippers of the Port of Portsmouth* (Ray Brighton, 1985). There were 28 of them, and their names still echo down the years—the *Sea Serpent*, the *Dashing Wave*, and the *Typhoon*, for example.

The three principal builders—Fernald, Raynes, and Samuel Badger—kept pace with the demands for ships, and in the 1840s the demand grew rapidly for larger and larger vessels. The cotton mills in England, along the Mersey River, were insatiable in their consumption of raw cotton. Adding to the pressure was the rising tide of Irish immigration. The Potato Famine drove Irish families by the thousands out of the Emerald Isle. They came to the United States mostly in what were called packet ships, and various packet lines serviced the industry in Boston, New York, and Philadelphia. During the 1840s, 36 square-rigged ships were built in the Port of Portsmouth, and the rate of construction kept on unabated as the 1850s began. In that decade, 77 square-riggers, including the 28 clippers, were launched by the various firms. Gertrude Pickett aptly described the 1850s as the heyday of Portsmouth shipbuilding.[5]

The three original firms weren't long without competition. Beginning in 1853, Stephen Tobey and Daniel Littlefield were operating a shipyard on Noble's Island. Their first venture, the *Brother Jonathan*, was built for Richard Hawley Tucker of Wiscasset, Maine, patriarch of the prosperous shipping family. The Tuckers were already owners of two other Piscataqua ships, the *Alliance* and the *Samoset*, and they continued to buy more. Boston and New York firms kept the shipyards busy until the last couple of years of the 1850s, when the market became drugged with excess shipping.

An added stimulus in the early 1850s was, of course, the discovery of gold in California and Australia. Neither British nor American

JOHN M. DAVIS,

Shipwright & Caulker,

No. 111 Market Street, Portsmouth, N. H.

VESSELS of 200 tons or less, taken on blocks, new keels affixed, and all desired repairs made.

WHARVES, BRIDGES, &c., repaired in the most thorough manner, and on satisfactory terms.

CARTS, WHEELS, &c., made or repaired to order—an experienced wheel builder being employed by me.

All Work warranted to give Satisfaction.   † 21

shippers could get enough vessels. It was a boom of unprecedented proportions, until the supply exceeded the demand.

Another building company joined Tobey & Littlefield on Noble's Island. Daniel Moulton was the master shipwright. Then Elbridge G. Pierce came to Portsmouth from Maine and began operations on Pierce Island. When the "Big Three" laid down their tools, others took their places. George Raynes Jr. continued building in his father's yard and, after his failure, William F. Fernald worked there. John Neal built a pair of ships in the yard of his father-in-law, the late Samuel Badger. William Pettigrew, long associated with Frederick W. Fernald, teamed up with Captain Daniel Marcy to build ships in Portsmouth's South End, near the old South Mill.

Commerce in the Port of Portsmouth had ebbed to a low level, a situation in which the coming of the railroads played a major role. It would seem that that was inevitable, as nothing was being produced in the New Hampshire hinterland that could maintain a lively trade. Toward the end, the big ships going out of the Port of Portsmouth, never to return, were taking out cargoes such as ice, hay, or apples.

The Civil War brought Piscataqua shipbuilding almost to a standstill. Confederate raiders, like the CSS *Alabama*, made commerce hazardous, and cotton-producing states had no cargoes to offer. Steadily, despite all the noble sentiments deploring the dwindling demand for sailing ships, steamers, made of iron and steel, were capturing the world's trade routes. The yards on the Piscataqua produced 14 big ships in the 1860s, and only seven in the 1870s. In 1877, the last two big square-riggers were launched on the river. An era had come to an end.

Charles H. Salter was one of Portsmouth's most outstanding shipmasters in the heyday of sail. He commanded the clipper Typhoon *on a record run between Portsmouth and Liverpool. Courtesy of the Portsmouth Historical Society.*

II *The 1830s*

THE OPENING OF THE DECADE OF THE 1830s sharply marked the opening of a new era in Port of Portsmouth shipbuilding. When William Badger, "Master Badger" to nearly two generations on the Piscataqua, died in 1829 on the island that bears his name, the high tide of upriver shipbuilding had already run out. The tidewater ports, Berwick, Dover, Durham, Exeter, and Somersworth, would thereafter contribute only schooners, sloops, and the like. Three more square-riggers were built upriver during the 1830s. The last was the *Oronoco*, 636 tons, built at Dover in 1837. Two others, both built at Berwick, preceded the *Oronoco*. They were the *Berwick* and the *Pactolus*.

One of the major reasons for the decline of ship construction upriver was Portsmouth Bridge, a structure built in 1820–1821, and spanning the Piscataqua between Noble's Island in Portsmouth and the Kittery shore. The draw for the passage of vessels was narrow, and the current was swift, requiring great dexterity in maneuvering vessels through. And it should be noted that the size of the three-masted square riggers was ever increasing.

Another weighty factor in the transition from the upper reaches to the lower was that the skilled craftsmen needed in ship construction were becoming concentrated in the growing towns nearer the open sea. All through the shipbuilding period, these artisans moved from shipyard to shipyard, even the Portsmouth Navy Yard, when their particular trade was needed.

Still one additional factor was the matter of building materials. As the decades passed, the Port of Portsmouth depended more and more on supplies from other areas. New Hampshire white oak still played an important role, but ships needed other materials, too,

11

and oak could easily be cut and transported to Portsmouth or Kittery rather than to the yards upriver.

As noted in chapter 1, with the passing of Master Badger, two highly skilled ship constructors were already at work, and a third would join them before the end of the decade. Samuel Badger had served a long apprenticeship under Uncle William in the Badger's Island yard, but, as noted in *Port of Portsmouth Ships and the Cotton Trade* (Ray Brighton, 1986), the old man had left stipulations in his will that prevented Samuel Badger from expanding the yard. George Raynes was ready when 1830 dawned and lost little time in getting production under way. Frederick William Fernald, the third in the troika of great shipbuilders, began his career in 1835.

George Raynes was the first of the trio to put a three-masted square-rigger into the water. The construction of his first ships was done in a small yard that had been operated on the North Mill Pond in Portsmouth by Jacob Remick. The latter eventually moved to Kittery, where he continued to build vessels of lesser size than did the ambitious George Raynes. Because it will be the pattern in this volume to discuss the ships as they were launched, the beginning for the 1830s will be with the ship *Alexander*.

Alexander

SPECIFICATIONS: 1830. George Raynes. Portsmouth. Billet head, square stern. Burthen, 398 tons. Length, 114 feet; beam, 28 feet; depth, 14 feet. Two decks. Original owners—Samuel Pray, William Neal, and John Ball, all of Portsmouth.

When the *Alexander*, the inaugural vessel in the 1830s decade of Port of Portsmouth shipbuilding, went down the ways, she was the first of 35 square-riggers George Raynes would create. Raynes had built a brig, the *Planet*, 129 tons, in 1828, and that vessel was followed by three schooners before he began work on the *Alexander*. Raynes advertised for timber late in July 1830, saying that the timber should be "suitable for a ship of 600 tons." He also specified that timber he was seeking should "be good white oak." Would-be suppliers were directed to "enquire of George Raynes, near Portsmouth Bridge."[1] That last confirms that the Remick shipyard was nearer the outlet of the North Mill Pond than the former Meserve-Boyd yard Raynes later acquired.

It must be noted that the *Alexander*, although undoubtedly built in 1830, wasn't launched until January 1, 1831, and the *Journal* reported: "LAUNCH. — A superior ship of more than 400 tons, built by Mr. George Raynes for Messrs. Pray & Neal, at the ship yard near Portsmouth Bridge, will be launched this day, Jan. 1, precisely at 1 o'clock P.M."

The owners lost no time putting the *Alexander* to work. She sailed from the Port of Portsmouth on February 14, 1831.[2] She was headed to New Orleans to load cotton for Liverpool, but went aground on the Bar at New Orleans on March 8, and had to throw off her ballast to get free. She finally loaded and made her first passage to Liverpool, returning from that port to New York. Details of the *Alexander*'s career are lacking. However, George Nelson, in a compilation of Custom Records, notes that the *Alexander* was sold in Liverpool in 1866, and renamed the *Emily Caroline*—which indicates, if nothing else, that Raynes built ships to last.[3]

Nestor

SPECIFICATIONS: 1831. George Raynes. Billet head, square stern. Burthen, 396 tons. Length, 119 feet; beam, 27 feet; depth, 13 feet. Two decks. Original owners—Samuel Pray, William Neal, S. H. Sise, T. J. Rice, and Alexander Rice.

Even her name was auspicious. Certainly the *Nestor* lightly bore the burden of being named for a figure in Greek mythology. Nestor was the "wise king of Pylos; husband of Eurydice and father of Antiochius."[4] However, it's more probable that the immediate inspiration for the name came from the sobriquet often applied to John Quincy Adams, son of the second president, John Adams. John Quincy Adams, who had served as the sixth president and then in the U.S. House of Representatives, was known in political circles as "Old Nestor."

The *Nestor*'s master was Shadrach H. Sise, one of the owners, and he took her to Savannah to load cotton. A news item on March 17, 1832, reported she had sailed from Savannah with 1,517 "round bales of cotton," and it was hailed as a "great cargo."[5] That cargo went to Liverpool, and she came into her home port in August with a load of salt. During the next few years, the *Nestor* voyaged constantly around the triangle: from a northern U.S. port to a cotton port, to either Liverpool or Le Havre, France, and then back to Portsmouth or Boston.

In August 1837, the *Nestor* sailed from New York for New Orleans, carrying 212 passengers. Out of that number 162 died of yellow fever before October 4. By the nineteenth only 10 of the 212 still

Drawing of the Nestor, *built in 1831 by George Raynes. Courtesy Peabody Museum.*

lived.[6] Presumably the dead were buried at sea, and the *Nestor*'s captain must have had the funeral rites well mastered by that time. When the *Nestor*, literally a death ship, arrived in New Orleans, she took on cotton for Liverpool.

In 1839, the *Nestor* was one of eight ships seized at New Orleans in a cotton-brokering scandal, but she cleared out in May for Le Havre.

Capt. John G. Moses was in command of the *Nestor* in 1840. Captain Moses became one of the Port of Portsmouth's foremost mariners and shipowners. In the latter part of his life he made annual trips to Europe in connection with his shipping interests. In 1848, the *Nestor* was chartered in the New Line of packets under John A. Russell. When the Gold Rush began in 1849, the *Nestor* was pressed into service to the West Coast. In 1853, the *Nestor* scored a financial coup for the consignee of her cargo in San Francisco. The *Portsmouth Journal* reprinted on October 8, 1853, an article it had copied from the *San Francisco Herald*:

> ADVANTAGES OF A SLOW VESSEL. — We understand the cargo of flour brought by the Nestor, which got into port the day before yesterday, the 24th, was sold some time ago for $15, providing it arrived before the 21st, by which time

it would have been upwards of 80 days to make the passage from Valparaiso to this port. In the meantime for a $5 advance on each sack, making the pretty sum of $10,000 by the operation, always providing that the Nestor was not over 80 days on the passage.

She held back, however, greatly to the satisfaction of the consignee, and did not get into port until the 24th, three days after the contract had expired by limitation.

In other words, the price of flour had risen, and the gamblers made out.

In 1841, the *Nestor* was condemned and sold in London.[7] But a few months later, she was in Havana. According to Nelson, she wound up her days as a guard ship in the Chincha Islands, off Peru.[8]

Apollo

SPECIFICATIONS: 1831. Samuel Badger. Kittery Foreside. Billet head, square stern. Burthen, 412 tons. Length, 120 feet; beam, 27.4 feet; depth, 13.7 feet. Two decks. Owners, as of March 10, 1832—John Haven and Robert Rice.

The *Apollo* was launched on January 14, 1832, the first three-master Samuel Badger put into the water from his own yard at Kittery Foreside. One of the last contemporary occupants of the site was the Boulter Coal Co., and Samuel Badger's former home is now a condominium complex. The ways for the yard pointed toward the Franklin Shiphouse on the Portsmouth Navy Yard.

The *Apollo*'s first master was the highly respected William W. Thompson, who was with her for three years before commanding another Badger ship, the *Milo*. Captain Thompson intended to take the *Apollo* to New Orleans, sailing out of the Port of Portsmouth on March 19, 1832. However, on her way south, the *Apollo* instead put into Charleston, South Carolina, found a cargo and went to Liverpool. Arriving there on August 8, she sailed for home on September 20, and entered Portsmouth Harbor on November 11. A little less than a year later, the *Apollo*, on August 8, 1833, was back in Portsmouth, bringing in 575 tons of coarse salt and 800 bags of fine salt. She also had two chain cables on her manifest and four casks of "apparatus" for Ferguson & Jewett.

Captain Thompson turned the *Apollo* over to Joseph Grace in 1835. Grace later commanded the bark *Martha*, which sailed from

Drawing of the ship Apollo *when she was serving as store ship on the San Francisco waterfront. The* Apollo *burned in a devastating fire in 1851. Courtesy National Maritime Museum, San Francisco.*

Portsmouth with "Forty-Niners" on board. In July 1836, Captain Grace brought the *Apollo* into Portsmouth with cotton for the Cochecho Mills. The cotton off-loaded into gundalows for the upriver passage. When the ship left on September 6, she scored a first for the Port of Portsmouth: "The ship Apollo was towed down river against wind and current in a handsome manner on Tuesday last by the steamer Tom Thumb. She left her about a mile outside the Whale's Back and returned to her wharf in 30 minutes. This is the first instance noted of a steamer towing a ship down river."[9]

The *Tom Thumb* was lost a year later when she piled up on Boon Island, but what she did with the *Apollo* was well understood by shipping people, and the lesson was quickly learned. No longer would sailing vessels depend on wind and tide to get out of the Port of Portsmouth. In later years most of the big three-masters went down the Piscataqua under tow. Today, tankers and freighters move up and down the river under the guidance of the Portsmouth Navigation Company.

Captain Grace was followed by Samuel Harding, Jr. The latter brought the *Apollo* into port on May 13, 1837, from Cadiz with salt. The vessel was leaking at a rate of between 100 and 200 strokes of the pumps and had been doing so since March 20.

At times the *Apollo* was chartered by various transatlantic packet lines, usually bringing immigrants to the bigger ports like New York. When the Gold Rush started in 1849, the *Apollo* was among the vessels pressed into service for the long journey around Cape Horn. Once she arrived, the *Apollo* stayed on the West Coast. She was serving as a store ship when fire swept the San Francisco waterfront in 1851. The fire started on May 3, and the extent of the destruction was beyond measure. The breeze was blowing offshore, and one of the miracles of the day was that none of the moored merchant ships was destroyed. However, three store ships—the *Niantic*, the *General Harrison*, and the *Apollo*—were lost.[10]

Charlotte

SPECIFICATIONS: *1832. Samuel Badger. Kittery. Billet head, square stern. Burthen, 390 tons. Length, 115 feet; beam, 27 feet; depth, 13 feet. Two decks. Owners, December 24, 1832—Robert Rice, John F. Goddard, and William Parker.*

The *Charlotte* was Samuel Badger's last ship that rated less than 400 tons. William Parker, one of the owners, was her first captain, taking her out of the Port of Portsmouth after her launching on January 14, 1832. She was intended for the transatlantic packet trade, and she often returned to Portsmouth with cargoes of salt for Robert Rice, another owner.

In November 1833, nearly two years after her launching, the *Charlotte* was one of the first vessels to be put on the newly constructed Portsmouth Marine Railway, which was located in the middle section of present-day Prescott Park. The newspaper item didn't offer a reason for the *Charlotte*'s being taken out of the water, but did say "we are pleased to learn that this useful work is completed and gone into operation, having been occupied by the brig *Orleans* and the ship *Charlotte*."[11] It can be surmised that the ship was either being coppered for the first time, or having a new sheath applied. Coppering was intended, of course, to impede marine plant growth and to keep sea worms from doing their destructive best.

The *Charlotte* was in Portsmouth in July 1838, and was sent south for cotton and then was to cross to England. Such was the nature of her career. A ship named *Charlotte*, of her burthen, was listed as sailing in the Packet Line in 1839, under a Capt. N. Gorman.[12] Again, in 1842, a vessel of that name and burthen was chartered in the Packet Line under Capt. Richard Tripe.[13] Through the 1840s, the *Charlotte* continued to work the North Atlantic, but no longer came into the Port of Portsmouth, having been sold to a Boston firm. In October 1841, she ran into a wild storm on Georges Banks, which threw her on her beam ends and stripped away all her sails before she was able to right herself.

When the California Gold Rush began in 1849, the *Charlotte* was one of many vessels that inched their way around Cape Horn to California. In August 1850, the *Journal* listed her as one of the 20 former Portsmouth vessels that were then at San Francisco. There are indications that she was abandoned at sea about September 1, 1850, but details are lacking.[14]

Berwick

SPECIFICATIONS: 1832. William Hanscom. Berwick. Billet head, square stern. Burthen, 472 tons. Length, 128.5 feet; beam, 28 feet; depth, 14 feet. Two decks. Original owners—Timothy Ferguson, Theodore F. Jewett, John Chase, and Thomas Jewett, all of South Berwick; Edward Chandler, of Marblehead, Massachusetts.

One of the proudest vessels ever launched in Old Berwick, the *Berwick* was also one of the most tragic, and it must be noted that only one more three-master would be launched in that once busy upriver port. Some of the deep emotion surrounding the *Berwick* has been preserved in a reminiscence written by John Marr of Rochester, New York, in 1901:

> No event has a more prominent place in my memory than the launch of the Berwick. This ship was built by Captain (William) Hanscom in 1832, at the lower landing in South Berwick, a few rods north of the old House, as seen in Miss [Sarah Orne] Jewett's *Old Town of Berwick*. At the launching of the Berwick I was sprinkled with wine from the bottle broken by Capt. Hanscom in christening the ship. Once I could repeat his eulogy; but my memory retains now but two lines:
>
>> Her timbers were taken from Agmanticus broad back,
>> So firmly joined that Old Ocean can't wrack!

Old Ocean, however, did wrack, for she went down in mid-ocean, in 1833–1834, with all on board. I was then ten years old, and the oft-repeated story of her supposed disaster made a deep impression on my mind.

The Berwick was built by Capt. Theodore Jewett, expressly for his son, — young Capt. Thode, as the townspeople called him. Tim Ferguson may have had a hand in her. I was present when the young Captain said good-bye to his father, and left for Portsmouth to take command of his new ship.

The fate of the Berwick has never been definitely demonstrated. The master of a home-bound ship, reported that in a certain latitude he encountered a gale; about midnight an unusually high wave struck him as he was running free; and when his vessel fell, she struck a ship as it was sailing on an opposite course. The next wave carried him completely over the ill-fated stranger.

The course of the Berwick, so often sailed over by the elder Capt. Theodore, and his knowledge of the usual winds and tides, impressed him with the belief that the Berwick must have been in the latitude described. Time passed without any tidings of his boy; he lost all hope; the lustre faded from his mild blue eyes. I think of him sitting in his favorite slat-backed chair, tilted against the counter of his store, toying with the fob-chain and seals that hung by his side, dreamily awaiting for the coming of the great night that would give him rest forever! God bless my memory of his many kind words and acts to a poor boy![15]

In reality, the aged John Marr's recollection was more than a little faulty, as any one of advanced years can readily understand. The *Berwick* was at sea for nearly 15 years before disaster overtook her, probably early in February 1846. During the decade and a half she had sailed, the *Berwick* saw constant service as a packet and a transatlantic sailer. In her early years, she worked the triangle route of the cotton trade, carrying cotton from southern ports to Liverpool and Le Havre, then back to Portsmouth or Boston, and then south for another cargo of cotton. Edward Chandler was commanding in 1834, and it was on one of his passages that a seaman named Robert Wilson, of Eastport, Maine, fell from the maintop to the deck, dying in a few hours. Parenthetically it should be said that the old-time deck hand had a motto: One hand for the ship, and one hand for himself. Sometimes it didn't work out that well.

Capt. John Chase commanded the *Berwick* for a few years, before she was taken over by Samuel Harding, Jr. Under Harding she sailed in the Merchants' Line out of New York and Boston in the early 1840s. She also had a charter in the New Orleans Packet Line, and in 1845 in the Dispatch Line, under Charles Flanders.[16] On February 3, 1846, a young captain, S. W. Jewett of South Berwick, took the *Berwick* to sea from Boston, bound for Mauritius and Calcutta. A news story reported on May 1, 1847, that she had not been heard from since her departure:

> The only surmises as to her fate are that she may have been in contact with an unknown ship with which a Danish brig was in contact off the Cape of Good Hope in a gale; or that she foundered in a gale which took place Feb. 7, as a vessel which sailed from New York a day or two after the B. left this port [Boston], passed some drift stuff which resembled portions of the cargo of the B.
>
> Her cargo consisted of 300 tons of ice in the lower hold, and naval stores, spars, provisions, shoes, &c. between decks. The Berwick was a good ship of 472 tons, built in 1832 and valued at $18,000. There is insurance in this city [Boston], on one fourth of the vessel for $4,500; on another fourth for $3,500; on her charter out and home, for $14,000, and on part of her cargo, profits, &c. for upwards of $7,000, amounting to about $29,000.
>
> One fourth of the vessel was owned by Capt. T. F. Jewett, and another fourth by his brother, both of which were insured in London on the greater part of the cargo for $12,000.
>
> Capt. Jewett was a young man, only about 25 years old, and belonged to Berwick, Me. His first officer, Capt. Seth Tripe, of Portsmouth, was 48 years old; his second officer, Mr. Edward Fox of Boston, was 44. The rest of the crew were Charles Roberts, steward, of New York, colored, aged 37; Seymour Minkius, cook, Georgetown (supposed D.C.), colored, 24; Jonathan Hallet, seaman and carpenter, of Elizabeth City, 33; John Chadwick of Roxbury, 20; William R. Knight, 25; and Wm. Reattenburg, 22, both of New York; Ruel B. Bogue, Saybrook, 22; James Farland and John Muggs, foreigners; Charles H. Bigelow of Malden, 19; Franklin H. Hussey, of Portland, 21; Augustus Nason, of South Berwick, 21, and Robert W. Thompson of Charleston, 19, seamen.[17]

If it served no other purpose, the disaster that overcame the *Berwick* offers a picture of what a 500-ton square-rigger carried in the way of personnel: 11 seamen, a cook and a steward, and 3 officers. The youth of the master isn't surprising: the seafaring trade demanded young men at the top, and it was no disadvantage to come from a ship-owning family. Nor is it surprising that Capt. Seth M. Tripe was sailing as first officer. Tripe was listed in the 1840 *Portsmouth City Directory* as living on Islington Street, at the corner of Ann (Union) Street. Quite probably, Tripe didn't have a ship to command, so he took the first-officer berth to support his family.

Harriet & Jessie

SPECIFICATIONS: 1832. George Raynes. Billet head, square stern. Burthen, 453 tons. Length, 112 feet; beam, 28.6 feet; depth, 14 feet. Owners—Charles Edmonston, S. W. McKown, and James Williamson, all of Charleston.

Early on, a news item established what was expected of the *Harriet & Jessie*. She was launched on September 12, 1832, and was "intended for the Liverpool, Charleston trade. The model and workmanship of the vessel is highly creditable to the builder."[18] In November 1832, people with bills against the *Harriet & Jessie* were urged by Samuel E. Coues to present their statements either to him or Ichabod Goodwin. The *Harriet & Jessie* left the Port of Portsmouth, under Capt. Samuel W. McKown, later in November.

From the very onset of her career, the *Harriet & Jessie* demonstrated a toughness that took her through more than 60 years of rough treatment at sea. In her first years, she came into Portsmouth frequently with cotton for the upriver mills dominated by Edward F. Sise. The 1,526 bales she brought in were off-loaded and sent to the factory by gundalow.[19] A year later, the *Harriet & Jessie* was sold in Boston for $4,200.[20] She was already 25 years old and had sailed profitable voyages for her various owners, and still was able to work. Around 1861 she was sold to shipping interests in Bombay, India, being renamed the *Shah Allum*. As late as 1897, 65 years after her launching, she was still in the registry of ships.[21]

India

SPECIFICATIONS: 1833. Samuel Badger. Billet head, square stern. Burthen, 433 tons. Length, 122 feet; beam, 28 feet; depth, 14 feet. Two decks. Original owners—Samuel Pray, James Neal, Ichabod Goodwin, and Samuel E. Coues.

The *India* was still another of those vessels that Samuel Badger built so well, even though they resembled floating bathtubs. But why not? Badger was finding a ready market for his vessels. Despite the listing given of the first owners, the *Portsmouth Journal* said the *India* was owned in Boston, and she left the Port of Portsmouth under a Captain Cook. It's quite likely that Pray, Neal, Goodwin, and Coues were a syndicate, with an intent to finance the construction of the ship and then sell her.

The fact that little news concerning the *India* appeared in the local newspapers seems to substantiate Boston ownership. There was a news item in the *Journal* on August 19, 1837, in which a Captain Snow of the ship *India* reported an extensive fire in Calcutta just before he sailed for home. Five hundred buildings were destroyed, causing a million rupees in damage. He also reported that the American Ice Company had started a new building there, an indication that the ice trade was prospering. Customs records indicate that the *India* was sold by her Boston owner, John T. Coolidge, to Silmer of Fredericksshield, Norway, and renamed the *Ida*.[22] The Norwegians sold her during the American Civil War to a firm in Sydney, Australia, and she was listed in 1890 as afloat, but a hulk.[23]

Pontiff

SPECIFICATIONS: 1833. George Raynes. Billet head, square stern. Burthen, 495 tons. Length, 129 feet; beam, 29 feet; depth, 14.5 feet. Two decks. Original owners—Henry Kneeland et al., of New York; and Henry Hall et al., of Boston.

When she was launched on April 6, 1833, the *Pontiff* was the largest vessel yet built by George Raynes, and to her also goes the distinction of being the first ship Raynes constructed in the old Boyd-Meserve yard on the North Mill Pond. With William Neal offering financial support, Raynes laid the keel of the *Pontiff*. The *Journal* reported on April 13: "On Saturday last, the large and elegant ship Pontiff was launched from the shipyard of Messrs. Neal & Raynes in the presence of a large and gratified collection of Ladies and Gentlemen." Residents of Portsmouth and the other Piscataqua Valley towns have always delighted in launchings, perhaps from the sheer pleasure derived in seeing a newly created vessel take on a life of its own, once it hits the water. The *Journal* added that the *Pontiff* "in size, materials, and workmanship, is in the first class of ships built in this place." The launching occasioned a poem published in the *Journal*. The author is unknown:

The Launch.

As maiden by the altar calmly stands,
Nor knows in all her sweet simplicity,
That thousands gaze upon her cheek; nor feels
That she has gathered them—so seemed to me,
The Ship. And when she waved her banners out,
Methought 'twas slowly done, in mournfulness,
To bid farewell, to her loved resting place.
And as the lady moves—with majesty,
And beauteous grace divine—yet slowly,
As by maiden modesty withheld—so moved
The Ship, in dignity to meet the embrace
of her betrothed.
                              The waters parted—
And the sparkling waves, exultant, came to wreath
A coronal for her; and then upon the shore
Leaped up and clapp'd their hands in gladsomeness.
And from the gazing multitude uprose
A mingled shout of triumph and delight.
And yet for many a time before they'd seen
The graceful ship to her own element
Glide in. And it seems well the multitudes
To meet with common thought, and raise the shout
Unanimous, e'en in a simple cause. Methinks
It swells the heart, and stronger binds the cords
Of sympathy. O would they oft'ner met,
To send the glad shout upwards to the throne
Of the eternal One, who made the heavens, and earth,
And all that is therein—the might yocean
In whose depths the loftiest ships go down
With all their hapless crews.
                              Thus was her bridal.
And when her white wings grow, God speed her well
Where'er she goes amid the stormy waves,
And bring her to her native home again.

Even before the launching, the *Pontiff* had been sold to Boston and New York investors at a price of $35,000. The *Journal* published an item from the *New Hampshire Gazette* on February 22, in which it was reported: "This is the second large ship these gentlemen have built within a year, and is by no mean inferior to the first [the Harriet & Jessie] — the model and finish of which elicited so many ecomiums at Charleston, S.C.... They certainly deserve the patronage of the mercantile community."

Despite all the favorable omens attending her construction and launching, the *Pontiff*'s life was short. She left Portsmouth under Capt. William Hathaway on May 16, heading for New Orleans to load cotton for New York. However, as was often the case, she put into Mobile and there picked up a cargo. Returning to New York, she unloaded and went to New Orleans, where she took on 1,820 bales of cotton for Le Havre, France. After clearing from New Orleans, the *Pontiff* was wrecked on Rum Cay in the Bahamas late in December. The *Pontiff* was a total loss, but 1,500 bales of cotton were salvaged and taken to Nassau, where the insurors promptly chartered a vessel to take the cargo to Le Havre. Various New York offices had insurance policies on her in the amount of $165,000.[24]

Rockingham

SPECIFICATIONS: 1833. George Raynes. Billet head, square stern. Burthen, 513 tons. Length, 132 feet; beam, 28 feet; depth, 14.5 feet. Two decks. Original owners—Thomas W. Penhallow, William Simes, Jr., James Kennard, and Stephen Simes, all of Portsmouth.

The *Rockingham* was the largest commercial vessel launched in the Port of Portsmouth in 40 years and the first ever to exceed 500 tons. Way back in 1793, Eliphalet Ladd had built the *Archelaus* at Exeter. She was rated at 498 tons.[25] Today, a motorist crossing the Exeter River on Route 101 might look downstream and wonder how a vessel that size was manuevered out into Great Bay.

The *Rockingham* was launched on September 14 at "high noon," and it was reported that "she is pronounced by good judges to be, in point of model and workmanship, a first rate vessel, and will vie with any ever built in New England. Mr. Raynes, the builder, has already earned, by his ingenuity and correct taste, a high reputation."[26]

Like so many of the three-masters built in the Port of Portsmouth in the 1830s, the *Rockingham* was destined for the triangular cotton trade. Her first master, James Kennard, later distinguished himself by becoming the president of the original Portsmouth Marine Society. Reestablished in the 1970s, the Portsmouth Marine Society has published more than a dozen books dealing with Piscataqua marine history.

During her working years, if the *Rockingham* didn't come into Portsmouth with salt, she went into Boston or New York, and then back to the cotton ports. For example, she arrived in Portsmouth on September 27, 1835, 31 days from Liverpool, bringing salt to her owners—Jones, Penhallow, and Simes. The *Rockingham* reported that she had left three Portsmouth-built ships at Liverpool: *Pactolus*, *Milo*, and *Charlotte*. Captain Kennard turned over command to William L. Dwight, another Portsmouth shipmaster. Captain Dwight made his home for many years at 314 Middle Street, a building once occupied by Dr. George Patten. The change in masters didn't alter the pattern of the *Rockingham*'s days. In September 1837, Edward F. Sise & Co. advertised they had "just received, per ship Rockingham, from Liverpool, a complete assortment of CROCKERY and CHINA WARE, which they offer for sale at Boston prices."27 The last phrase is indicative that the custom of Portsmuthians going to Boston to do their shopping is more than 150 years old.

The *Rockingham* continued in that general pattern of operation through the 1840s. In 1846 she collided with a Spanish brig while en route to New Orleans. The brig was so badly damaged that the *Rockingham* took off her crew and brought the men into New Orleans. However, the *Rockingham*'s luck ran out late in 1849. She had been at Palermo, Sicily, under Pearce W. Penhallow, and was headed for home when she went ashore at Tarifa, Spain, east of Gibraltar. The *Journal* said on November 10 that she had struck on Pear Rock. "H.M. steamer *Janus* proceeded to her assistance, but returned to Gibraltar, having been unable to get her off. The *Rockingham* was owned by Messers Jones & Son, Thos. W. Penhallow, Stephen H. Simes and Capt. Penhallow. She was 513 tons burthen, 15 years old, and insured at the American and Lexington offices for about $18,000. Her cargo was insured at the Astor office for $5,000."

Pactolus

SPECIFICATIONS: 1833. William Hanscom. Berwick. Billet head, square stern. Burthen, 493 tons. Length, 135 feet; beam, 28 feet; depth, 14 feet. Two decks. Original owners—Daniel Wise, Jr. and George Wise, of Kennebunk; Timothy Ferguson and T. F. Jewett, of South Berwick.

The *Pactolus* was, of course, already at sea when the *Rockingham* and the *Pontiff* went into the waters. Why the *Pactolus* was named for a river in what was then called Asia Minor is beyond learning now. The river was noted for the gold-laden vessels that traveled on it en route to the coffers of the legendary Midas. She was the last three-master launched in Berwick, and few vessels of any consequence followed her.

The *Pactolus* sailed from the Port of Portsmouth early in 1834, arriving at the Bar in New Orleans on February 25. On May 31, the *Journal* reported that the *Pactolus*, while en route to Liverpool, had put into Newport, Rhode Island, with loss of rudder, but no other damage. She was carrying 2,354 bales of cotton under the deck, the "largest cargo except one ever taken from the port [New Orleans]." After speedy repairs, she continued on her way. The *Pactolus* came into Portsmouth in October 1835 with salt for Ferguson and Jewett in South Berwick and iron for John Stavers and Richard Jenness in Portsmouth. The next year she went into New York with more than a thousand tons of pig iron. Again, in 1837, she brought 483 tons of salt for Ferguson & Jewett. She kept on making such voyages for the next 15 years, a highly profitable vessel for her owners. In 1850, sailing under Capt. L. M. Moses, she went aground on Romer Shoal near New York while en route from New Orleans.[28] In November she was sold; the newspaper account had it that she "now hails from Venicia."[29] Her ultimate fate isn't known, but a shipping note in the *Journal* on December 4, 1852, reported the arrival of the *Pactolus* at Honolulu, from San Francisco, while sailing to Sydney, New South Wales.

Ruthelia

SPECIFICATIONS: 1833. Joseph Graves. Badger's Island, Kittery. Billet head, square stern. Burthen, 436 tons. Length, 125 feet; beam, 27 feet; depth, 14 feet. Two decks. Original owner—Charles Cushing, of Portsmouth.

Charles Cushing, the owner of the *Ruthelia*, was prominent in Portsmouth in the 1830s, but he shouldn't be confused with the Charles Cushing who lived in the old Benning Wentworth place at Little Harbor. Joseph Graves is credited with construction of the *Ruthelia*, and the work was apparently done in the old Badger yard on Badger's Island. That much is established by a news item in the *Journal* on November 30, 1833, which said it was built in "Mr. Cushing's yard." A later item said: "This elegant vessel, which is now ready to depart on her first voyage was built under the direction of Mr. Joseph Graves for Charles Cushing. She is said by good judges to be of first rate workmanship, and inferior in no respect to the 101 previously built on the same island by the late William Badger."[30]

The *Ruthelia* went immediately into the triangular cotton trade under Capt. John Chase, returning to Portsmouth in 1835 with salt. Cushing sold the *Ruthelia* in Boston in 1836, but unfortunately she was destroyed by fire in 1838.[31]

Solon

SPECIFICATIONS: 1834. Samuel Badger. Billet head, square stern. Burthen, 540 tons. Length, 135 feet; beam, 29.5 feet; depth, 14.75 feet. Two decks. Original owners—Samuel Pray, Samuel Badger, and William Jones, Jr.

Captain Samuel Pray of Portsmouth was a large-scale investor in shipping; at one time or another he held interest in nearly 30 different vessels. The *Journal* let the superlatives flow in its announcement of the launching of the *Solon*, the latest of Captain Pray's investments:

> Launch. — This day at three o'clock P.M. will be launched from the shipyard of Capt. Samuel Badger a fine ship of about 540 tons, — No pains have been spared in workmanship, materials and fastenings, to render her one of the finest Ships of her class built on the Piscataqua River. — It is said her model combines three great essentials in the art of Ship building — fast sailing, great Burthen, with a light draft of water: These qualities rarely accomplished with great judgment and experience. — She is owned by one of our enterprising Merchants, Capt. Samuel Pray, and destined for the European trade.[32]

The *Solon*'s maiden passage was to Charleston, under Capt. William Lambert, and it took 15 days. By June 24, she had been loaded with 1,900 bales of cotton, weighing 618,607 pounds and valued at $101,151.89.[33] Arithmetic indicates that the bales weighed a bit over 325 pounds each, and they were valued at $53 apiece, or roughly $.16 a pound. Lambert brought the *Solon* back to New York in September, and some time during the fall Captain Pray sold her. A Captain Allen went to New Orleans with her in January 1835, and returned to Boston with his cargo of cotton.

In May the *Solon* sailed for Calcutta, making the passage in 99 days. The only incident on the trip was the loss of a young seaman. Albert Hunt of Charlestown, Massachusetts, fell while climbing the rigging to close reef the fore topsail while the ship was off the Cape of Good Hope. She was making 12 knots at the time, with a heavy sea running, so no assistance could be given the unlucky Hunt.[34] When the *Solon* returned from India she brought a large cargo, part of which was a large elephant. In the 1840s, the *Solon* was often on charter to various New York and Philadelphia packet lines, under different masters. Exactly what happened to the *Solon* isn't known. However, the *Journal*, on August 16, 1873, told an odd little story—a testament to a virtue known as integrity:

— Thirty-five or forty years ago, the ship Solon, of Portsmouth, brought a cargo from Liverpool into New York, and a firm in the latter city found themselves unable to pay their freight charges in full, so a portion of the amount was received, the balance charged to profit and loss, the account closed, and nothing more thought of the matter, which was but a small one, and the loss to the owners hardly thought of, then or afterwards. Those owners are now all dead, but their descendants still live here, and that New York firm is yet doing business; and recently, a merchant of this city, and son of one of the Solon's owners, being in New York on business connected with ships, the old firm referred to surprised him by drawing a check for the full amount of that freight deficit, more than a generation ago, with compound interest up to this time, amounting in all to about thirty-six hundred dollars. This sum, distributed among the heirs of the original owners of the old ship, comes in good time, as several of them are women of small incomes; and the incident is of interest, as showing not only a strict sense of mercantile honor, but also the utmost exactness in the mode of doing business. How many firms can show records of transactions after a lapse of thirty years? The recent stories of a Western merchant sending $6000 here to settle an old account, have grown out of the above true relation. —

Milo

SPECIFICATIONS: 1834. Samuel Badger. Kittery Foreside. Billet head, square stern. Burthen, 439 tons. Length, 124.65 feet; beam, 27.8 feet; depth, 13.9 feet. Two decks. Original owners—John Haven, Robert Rice, and William W. Thompson.

One of the owners must have been a classics' scholar to have named a ship for a Greek athlete. Milo was a runner who was said to have carried a four-year-old heifer through the stadium at Olympia, and then eaten the whole animal afterward—presumably barbecued.[35]

It's probably that the *Solon* was still on the ways when the keel of the *Milo* was laid in Samuel Badger's busy Kittery Foreside yard. Little time was lost after her launching, and she sailed for New Orleans under Capt. William W. Thompson. She sailed on January 29, 1835, loaded with cotton, and went to Liverpool.[36] She went straight back to New Orleans for more cotton to feed the hungry mills on the Mersey River. The *Milo* returned to Portsmouth on August 22, 1837, bringing in 472 tons of coarse salt and 500 sacks of fine salt for Robert

Rice and John Haven.[37] She also carried 42 crates and 2 hogsheads of crockery for E. F. Sise & Co.; 8 packages of iron wire; 25 barrels of Venetian red (paint) and 150 bundles of sheet iron for Richard Jenness. For the next few years, her voyages were along that order.

However, after coming into the Port of Portsmouth late in 1839, the *Milo* had problems when she headed down south. She experienced a whirlwind on January 22, 1840, a bit north of the Bahamas, which tossed her on her beam ends, "carried away the main yard, main and top mizzen masts, top gallant masts, rigging and sails, but did not injure the hull."[38]

By September 1840, she was back in Portsmouth with 2,000 hogsheads of St. Ubes (Portugal) salt on board, which the owners were eager to sell. Thompson continued as master until 1843, when the *Journal* reported his death:

> At sea, on board ship Milo of Portsmouth, Captain William W. Thompson, of this town, aged 56 years. A few days after sailing from New Orleans he was severely attacked by paralysis, of which he died four days before the ship arrived at Liverpool. Capt. Thompson was highly esteemed by an extensive audience on both sides of the Atlantic.
>
> Urbanity of manner endeared him to his crew and associates, while a well balanced dignity of deportment commanded a proper deference and respect. As a model for seamen and a gentleman in its best sense, he will be affectionately remembered by many an individual who enjoyed his acquaintance.[39]

A Captain Chick succeeded Thompson, and Chick was relieved by Joseph Grace, a man of deep Portsmouth connections. His son, William D. Grace, was a local apothecary, and his granddaughters were leading benefactors of St. John's Lodge of Masons a few years ago. It's probable Captain Chick was James H. Chick, living on Chapel Street. Grace made his home on Gates Street.

Captain Grace commanded the *Milo* until December 18, 1846, when she piled up on treacherous Sable Island, off Nova Scotia. She left Liverpool on November 2 for Boston, "with an assorted cargo and 34 passengers." All her people made it ashore, but the *Milo* went to pieces in three days. "It is said there is insurance on vessel and cargo in the amount of about $35,000."[40] Notice of the *Milo*'s destruction didn't reach Portsmouth until February. In May, the *Journal* reported that the hull and other materials were sold at auction in April, and later on Captain Grace expressed appreciation for the hospitable way in which his passengers and crew were treated by the commissioners of Sable Island.

Portsmouth

SPECIFICATIONS: 1834. George Raynes. Billet head, square stern. Burthen, 520 tons. Length, 131.3 feet; beam, 29.5 feet; depth, 14.75 feet. Two decks. Original owners—George Raynes and William Neal.

George Raynes and his partner, William Neal, not only were building ships together, but the *Portsmouth* was a joint ownership venture. She was the first of two merchant vessels to bear the name. The launching was reported in glowing terms:

> The Ship *Portsmouth* was launched from Raynes' & Neal's Yard, North End, on Monday last [February 17]. — She is a fine vessel, and was built in less than four months.
>
> The Piscataqua River has sent out several new ships within a year, the workmanship of which need not fear comparison and competition.
>
> The Ruthelia now fitting for sea, and nearly ready, — the Pactolus, and excellent ship on her first voyage, — the Pontiff, — the Rockingham, — and last, but not least, the Portsmouth, — vessels which like a man with an open countenance, carry their own recommendation along with them.[41]

William Neal himself took the *Portsmouth* on her first voyage. She was cleared on March 6, but didn't sail for a few days, perhaps because of contrary winds. The news item noted that she was "in every respect a fine ship. She is handsomely finished, and combines strength and beauty in a remarkable degree." Then, parenthetically, it was reported: "The Portsmouth has not yet sailed, and those who may be disposed to visit her this day will meet a welcome reception."[42] She did not sail the next day, and was spoken on March 9 off Cape Cod. However, as was so often the case, on her passage to New Orleans she poked her bow into Savannah, found a cargo, went to Liverpool, and it was reported: "*Large Cargo.* — The ship Portsmouth of Portsmouth, Capt. Neal, cleared at Savannah 10th instant [April] for Liverpool, with a cargo of 2,050 bales of cotton, weighing 673,756 lbs, and valued at $83,546, being the largest cargo ever shipped from that port in a vessel of her tonnage. Her freight amounts to £1,846."[43]

Arithmetic shows that weight of the baled loaded at Savannah was approximately the same as the bales loaded on the *Solon* at New Orleans on her maiden voyage. However, the value per pound was down to $.12-1/2. The freight was assessed in English money, so, using the familiar concept that a pound sterling was then worth $5, the charges came to more than $9,000. In the familiar pattern, the *Portsmouth* returned to New York and then went to Savannah for another load of cotton. She went to sea from Savannah on December 13, 1834, with 1,901 bales of cotton, valued at $110,000 (cotton prices apparently were on the upswing). In 1844, she was in I. B. Gager's New Line, New York to New Orleans, with Charles G. Glover as master.[44]

Captain Neal, after yielding command, left his partnership with Raynes and returned to sea. He died in 1843 while in command of the ship *Tallahassee*, having been swept overboard in a storm on September 4. Exactly what happened to the *Portsmouth* isn't known. George Nelson listed her as "stranded and sold foreign in 1850."[45]

Susanna Cumming

SPECIFICATIONS: 1834. George Raynes. Billet head, square stern. Burthen, 544 tons. Length, 132.25 feet; beam, 30.1 feet; depth, 15.05 feet. Two decks. Original owners—Ichabod Goodwin and Samuel E. Coues, both of Portsmouth; John and George B. Cumming, of Savannah.

The *Susanna Cumming* was the last 500-tonner launched in the Port of Portsmouth in 1834, and one of the great prides of Portsmouth's Palfrey clan is the silver trophy awarded the *Susanna Cumming*'s builder, George Raynes. The latter was the great-grandfather of Kennard Palfrey and his sister, Priscilla McLane, and their brother, the late William Palfrey. The *Susanna Cumming* was launched from Raynes's yard on November 3.

Ichabod Goodwin and Samuel E. Coues were members of Portsmouth's rising mercantile generation. Goodwin went on to become New Hampshire's first governor in the Civil War. Coues was a brilliant eccentric who had many odd notions on scientific matters, and he frequently published papers and gave lectures. George B. Cumming made his home in Savannah, but he was an annual summer visitor to Portsmouth and became an intimate friend of Goodwin's. So close were Cumming's Portsmouth connections that he became a member of the Federal Fire Society in 1842.[46] Cumming was also associated with Goodwin in the ownership of the *Kate Hunter* and the *John Cumming*, the latter named for George Cumming's brother.

The *Susanna Cumming* was launched on November 3 and went to sea under Capt. William Patterson on December 20, headed for Savannah.[47] From there she went to Liverpool, and then back to Portsmouth in September with salt for Goodwin & Coues and hard-

The owners of the Susanna Cumming, built in 1834, were so proud of their new vessel that they presented the builder, George Raynes, with a silver loving cup. The cup is owned by Mrs. William Palfrey, whose husband was a direct descendant of George Raynes.

ware for Richard Jenness. In 1837, Captain Patterson turned the ship over to Charles H. Salter, who later won lasting fame by commanding the clipper *Typhoon* in her maiden passage in 1851, between Portsmouth and Liverpool. The *Susanna Cumming* came to Portsmouth in August bearing salt, and the *Journal* noted that she brought London papers dating to July 1, "one day later than before received. They contain no new intelligence of any importance." The *Susanna Cumming* worked the cotton triangle throughout her career, and she came into Portsmouth on at least three more occasions. In 1844, Thomas B. Clark took command.

She entered Portsmouth's lower harbor in March 1844, but went on to Boston. From Boston she went to Savannah, carrying as passengers the famed Rev. A. P. Peabody, pastor of the South Church, and James F. Shores, Jr., a bookdealer. William H. Parsons, another noted Portsmouth shipmaster, was in command in January 1846, when the *Susanna Cumming* met her end.

LOSS OF THE SUSANNA CUMMING

Ship Susannah-Cumming, Capt. Parsons, from Mobile for Liverpool, ran ashore at Formby-Point [a few miles north of Liverpool] England on the 29th of January, and is a total wreck. 1100 bales of cotton had been saved from her, up to Feb. 4th, much of it in a damaged state. The Susannah-Cumming was built, and half of her owned here by Messrs. Goodwin and Coues. This half was insured in Boston for $12,000. The other half belonged to G. B. Cumming Esq. of Savannah, and was insured in New York. The cargo was probably insured in England. —

The ship was in charge of an experienced pilot — who mistook the light in a gale of wind; so that no blame can be attached to the captain.[48]

Harriet Rockwell

SPECIFICATIONS: 1835. Frederick W. Fernald. Mugridge Yard, Portsmouth's South End. Female bust figurehead, square stern. Burthen, 447 tons. Length, 127.475 feet; beam, 27.7 feet; depth, 13.85 feet. Original owners—Lewis Barnes and Theodore J. Harris, both of Portsmouth.

The construction of the *Harriet Rockwell* marked the first venture of one of the Port of Portsmouth's greatest shipbuilders, Frederick William Fernald; he was young, and he died young, but he left an indelible mark on the pages of shipbuilding history on the Piscataqua River. Fernald was only 24 when he built the *Harriet Rockwell*. Where he served his apprenticeship isn't known, but there is a tradition that one of his mentors was the famed Samuel Pook, chief civilian constructor of the Portsmouth Navy Yard, who lived at 1 Atkinson Street, corner of State. Whoever trained Fernald, the ships he produced were evidence of good schooling.

Fernald built the *Harriet Rockwell* in John Mugridge's yard, in the South End. Located at the foot of Pickering Street, the site is now occupied by the Portsmouth Marine Laboratory building. And there's reason to believe that John Mugridge, an established ship's carpenter, had a hand in the building of the *Harriet Rockwell*. The ship was named for Harriet Rockwell, Fernald's young wife. She died September 29, 1849, at the age of 36.[49]

The *Harriet Rockwell* was launched on September 11, and the *Journal* said, "good judges have pronounced her one of the finest ships

ever launched on the Piscataqua." A visitor to the area of the Mugridge yard wonders how they were able to get a vessel into the water
in that cramped space. Actually, the *Harriet Rockwell* did have a bit of
trouble: not sufficiently snubbed, she ran up on Pierce Island, but suffered no damage.

Lewis Barnes, a successful shipmaster and merchant, bought
the *Harriet Rockwell*, in partnership with Theodore J. Harris. Barnes
was a native of Sweden who migrated to the United States when only
14 years old. Through the span of his long life (79 years), Barnes rose
through hard work and shrewd business dealings to a highly respected
position in Portsmouth. The *Journal* reported his death on July 4,
1856:

> His bright features, silvery locks, animated tones and
> venerable form are to no longer animate and bless his friends.
> Though had he lived until next October, he would have reached
> four-score years, yet there were to his last days a youthful
> freshness and vigor about him.... He was an enlightened and
> excellent merchant. He was a man of strictest integrity and
> honor in all his dealings; led a systematic life; was a man of
> great courteousness of manner and affability of heart; pos-
> sessed great information and intelligence, and was a diligent
> reader of books [member of the Portsmouth Athenaeum].

Barnes put the *Harriet Rockwell* into the profitable transatlantic trade, hauling cotton to Europe and bringing back manufactured goods or salt to Portsmouth or other East Coast ports. Theodore
J. Harris, Barnes's partner, was her first master, and kept the command until his death. He took the ship out of Mobile in December
1838, headed for Liverpool, and died on the passage. The first mate, J.
W. Jewett, succeeded him, but there was more bad news to come in
the early spring:

> After our paper went to press last evening, we received
> the following melancholy intelligence in a letter from the editor
> of The Boston Transcript: "Dear Sir, — I have just read a letter
> from a friend in Liverpool, announcing the melancholy tidings
> of the loss of Capt. Jewett, the second officer and four of the
> crew of the ship Harriet Rockwell.
> "They were lost by the upsetting of the ship's boat,
> while going ashore for a pilot in the North Channel. The ship
> left Liverpool on the 5th of February, and was in safety at last
> advices, at anchor under the charge of the first mate.[50]

For the next few Saturdays, the *Journal* kept its readers posted on the problems of the *Harriet Rockwell*. For example, on April 6 it was reported:

SHIP HARRIET ROCKWELL. — A postscript, inserted in a part of the impression of last week's paper, mentioned the death of Capt. J. W. Jewett, a mate and 4 seamen of the ship Harriet Rockwell, by the upsetting of a boat belonging to that ship. The owner [Lewis Barnes] has since shown us a Protest, from which we learn, that the ship left Liverpool Feb. 5, for Boston: that she lost several of her most important sails. On the 16th, the gale still continuing, she came to anchor at noon, under the lee of Barra-head Lighthouse [Outer Hebrides, Scotland]; and the Captain, J. W. Jewett, the second mate, and four seamen, were drowned by the upsetting of the jolly boat, in which they were going ashore for a pilot. The chief mate, Charles Wattlesworth, then carried the ship into the harbor of Tobermory in the island of Mull, where the Protest is dated on the 23d of February. — No names are given of the men lost, either in the Protest, or the letter accompanying; — but the Protest is attested by two survivors, viz. Thomas Sims and David Kelly.

The commander of the ship when she began her voyage hence, was Capt. T. J. Harris. At his decease, Mr. Jewett, the mate, took his place; and the present commander was not one of the original crew. — The vessel having been absent about three years, it is not likely any of the original crew remained on board.

On May 4, 1839, the *Journal* continued its story:

Ship Harriet Rockwell, of this port, which sailed from Liverpool for Boston and put into Tobermory with loss of master, second mate and four seamen, was ready for sea again, under command of Capt. Mayhew, late of the *Transit*. Of those lost in the Boat with Capt. Jewett, the second mate, named C. W. Calvert, is said to be a native of Hull; Thos. Moore, seaman, is reported to have belonged to Liverpool. The other seamen were Thomas Ball, John Higgens and Wm. Benson.

The next week, the *Journal* reported "the following additional particulars respecting the Harriet Rockwell are from the *Galloway Register*:"

The ship Harriet Rockwell, after getting as far as St. Kilda, was forced to bear up with loss of sails. Having run down Barra Head for shelter, the captain anchored four or five miles from shore and proceeded with his boat towards the Head, to procure a pilot to take the ship to Tobermory. Unfortunately, however, being unacquainted with the coast, he mistook the landing-place, and attempted to land at another spot, the boat being swamped and all on board perished. Some people from the shore, who saw the incident, launched a boat and went off to the ship, and with their assistance the mate weighed anchor, and proceeded to Battersea Bay, where she rode out a heavy gale on the 21st of February.

The following day, she weighed anchor, and, having obtained a pilot, succeeded in getting into Tobermory Bay. New misfortune, however, here awaited the ill-fated vessel. Scarcely had she anchored, when another heavy gale arose, and she drove from her anchors to within a few fathoms of the rocks where she was threatened with instant destruction.

Fortunately, at this moment the Wellington was coming into the Bay and seeing the sign of distress, Capt. Melville immediately dispatched a boat and a party of hands on board and got the vessels upper yards and top masts down, and by great and continuing exertion succeeded in getting her to a safe anchorage. For the services which Captain Melville and the crew of the Wellington rendered to the Harriet Rockwell, they have been awarded £500, the vessel and cargo being worth £18,000.

Despite her misadventures, the *Harriet Rockwell* headed south on April 11, ready to continue plying the North Atlantic. However, in 1841 she was at Buenos Aires, arriving back in New York on December 22, 1841. Under William A. Briard, she went down to Mobile, where she cleared for Liverpool on May 28, 1842. By October the *Harriet Rockwell* was in Charleston. She had gone into the James River on her way to repair storm damage. In 1843, she came into Portsmouth's lower harbor to pick up a new commander, Capt. Samuel Pickett, who made his home on Summer Street. She proceeded on her way to Boston with her cargo of salt.

Eventually, in 1849, the *Harriet Rockwell* was sold to meet the demand of the California trade for anything with sails. There was an advertisement in the *Journal* on June 23, 1849, in which Lewis Barnes offered her for sale "to close a concern." At least, Barnes was putting up a three-fourths interest. His ad specified that she "sails fast, carries a large cargo, new sheathed with metal, January, 1848 — has nearly two suits of sails — standing rigging nearly all renewed within three years, is well found in every respect, and well calculated for India or California expeditions, or would make a good whaling ship." Once sold, the *Harriet Rockwell* went into the California trade and was thus out of Portsmouth observation.

Harbinger

SPECIFICATIONS: 1835. George Raynes. Burthen, 262 tons. Length, 100.9 feet; beam, 23.75 feet. Single deck. Owners—William Neal and George Raynes.

From this great distance in time, it's a little hard to understand why Raynes and Neal built the *Harbinger*. She was a throwback to the ancient days on the upper river. In fact, the *Harbinger* was the smallest three-master constructed in the Port of Portsmouth since the *Trajan*, at Newmarket in 1810. It wasn't that Raynes didn't build small vessels. He did, but no others were rated as ships. For example, Raynes built a brig, the *Helen Mar*, in 1835, 193 tons, single deck. But right after the *Harbinger*, Raynes built the 581-ton *Hindoo*, his largest vessel yet. The most apt explanation for the *Harbinger* is that she was built to order, because she is listed as having been sold in Boston in June 1835, and went into the whaling business. She was condemned at Paita, Peru, in 1853.[51]

Hindoo

SPECIFICATIONS: 1835. George Raynes. Burthen, 581 tons. Length, 135 feet; beam, 30.65 feet; depth, 15.32 feet. Original owners—Raynes and Neal, Ichabod Goodwin, and Samuel Coues, all of Portsmouth.

When the *Hindoo* slid down the ways on September 12, 1835, she was acclaimed as the largest merchantman yet built on the Piscataqua. However, the syndicate that owned the *Hindoo* had to wait two months before disposing of the new beauty, although some of that time may have been taken up in final fitting: "The beautiful new ship Hindoo, launched from the yard of Raynes & Neal in September last, sailed for Boston last Thursday [November 5], where she has been sold, we understand, for $35,000. She is intended for the India trade."[52]

A little more information about the *Hindoo* is available in Carl Cutler's *Queens of the Western Ocean* (1961). In the 1840s, she was chartered in the various packet lines. In 1845, she was in the Third Line, under Capt. Joseph I. Lawrence; 1848, Philadelphia & New

Orleans Line, Capt. Henry S. Brown; 1850, Ashbridge's Line, Capt. James F. Miller.[53] What finally happened to the *Hindoo* has yet to be learned, but she, too, may have gone into the California trade and stayed on the West Coast.

Fortitude

SPECIFICATIONS: 1835. Thomas Lydston. Badger's Island. Billet head, square stern. Burthen, 566 tons. Length, 134.7 feet; beam, 30.4 feet; depth, 15.2 feet. Two decks. Original owner—Charles Cushing.

Few vessels have been more appropriately named than the *Fortitude*. Thomas Lydston was the master carpenter, and her keel was laid in the old Badger yard, where Joseph Graves had built the *Ruthelia* for Charles Cushing two years earlier. She was the only three-masted square-rigger built in Kittery in 1835, since Samuel Badger was devoting his time to the construction of a bark, the *LaGrange*, 266 tons.

From the day of her launching until her end, the *Fortitude* was a workhorse. It isn't known who first took her to sea, but Capt. Daniel Libbey became the most closely identified with the *Fortitude*. Libbey's association with the vessel began in October 1837, when Charles Cushing sent her to Boston to be sold. Libbey and two Portsmouth investors, Samuel Cleaves and Elisha C. Crane, bought her in.[54] Cleaves operated a tallow factory and Crane was a shoe manufacturer. Cleaves and Crane had just lost a ship, the *Emerald*, on Rye beach. The $26,000 they received in insurance on the *Emerald* enabled them to buy the *Fortitude*. Before being auctioned off by Cushing, the *Fortitude* had made a voyage to Calcutta in which her return passage took 104 days. She brought in, according to the *Boston Courier*, a cargo valued at $400,000.[55] The item also gave the master's name as Spaulding.

When Daniel Libbey took command, it became a partnership between man and vessel that lasted 14 years, or until Libbey retired from the sea after 40 years of sailing. The relationship had another unique feature: closely associated with the master was his wife, Hannah, who was actually the *Fortitude*'s navigator. Her obituary in 1888 offers a different picture of life at sea in the mid-1800s than often given:

> Another of the links connecting this once prominent importing port with its traditions of former greatness in that line has just been broken by the death of Mrs. Hannah F. Libbey, widow of Captain Daniel Libbey, at the age of 82. Mrs.

Libbey was a cousin of the late James T. Fields [editor of the *Atlantic Monthly*] and was a lady of rare excellence. She was a sailor of extended experience, having accompanied her husband on 24 voyages across the Atlantic, and was a skillful navigator.

Captain Libbey commanded the ship *Fortitude*...until she was sold in 1851, when he retired from the sea after 40 years service as master, his wife having sailed with him throughout her entire married life up to that time.

The old *Fortitude* was known to Portsmouth seamen all over the world as a home for all Portsmouth men in every port where she might happen to be, they always being sure of a hearty welcome from Captain Libbey and his wife, it making no difference whether they were green hands on their first voyage or master mariners.[56]

The *Fortitude* often came into Portsmouth with merchandise, including salt, which is understandable in view of her local connections. For example, she arrived from Liverpool on September 16, 1844, with 1,841 bars of iron, 180 bundles of hoop iron, 150 bundles of sheet iron, 100 boxes of tin plate, and 10 tons of pig iron, all consigned to John P. Lyman, a major dealer in iron and coal.[57] On another trip, she came into the Port of Portsmouth from Cadiz with 2,000 hogsheads of salt for Horton D. Walker, son-in-law to Samuel Cleaves. The *Fortitude* knew all the cotton ports, and her passages to Europe most often were to Le Havre.

In 1851, the *Fortitude* was "sold out of the district."[58] Captain Libbey had already yielded command to a man named Chase. In 1852, her commander was William A. Lord, and in the 1850s she often went to the St. Lawrence River and loaded lumber for Liverpool. Captain Lord was still in command when the *Fortitude* went ashore at Cape Gracios a Dios, Honduras, in December 1858.[59] She was reported a total wreck. The *Journal* had earlier said: "New York, Dec. 30 — Advices from the Isthmus state that the American ship Fortitude had been wrecked on Cape Gracios a Dios, and the British frigate Caesar, had gone thither from San Juan to render assistance to her captain and crew, as well as relieve a British merchantman reported to have gone ashore in the same place."[60]

Nearly four months later, there was further information on the wreck of the *Fortitude*:

Ship Fortitude, of Portsmouth, N.H. before reported ashore on the Mosquito Coast, at or near Cape Gracios a Dios, was sold at public auction, on the 21st ult. for the sum of six hundred and forty-one dollars. She was put up at twenty dollars, and rose by dollar bids to this unprecedented price. All were astonished, even the purchasers; vessels laying where she does, or in that neighborhood, usually bring from twenty to fifty dollars. She was stripped by the brig Josephus, of Baltimore. — She is bilged, and the owners of the cargo (250 M. feet of Mahogany) have the right to cut her up to get the cargo out of her.[61]

It's impossible to close the story of the *Fortitude* without also closing out the life of the man who commanded her for so long, Daniel Libbey:

> Capt. Daniel Libbey, a veteran shipmaster and one of our best known and most highly respected citizens, died Saturday morning [August 24, 1878] at the age of 77 years. He was born in Dover, but came to this city about 1816, when a mere lad, and has made Portsmouth his home ever since.
>
> In the days of his youth a large proportion of the young men of Portsmouth who wished to rise in the world by their own exertions, aimed to become shipmasters, and he chose the profession of a seaman, following that avocation until compelled by physical infirmities to abandon it.
>
> Portsmouth at that time was noted for the number and worth of the master mariners she contributed to the merchant service, as well as for her superior ships, and Mr. Libbey was not long in rising to the position of successful shipmaster, at different times commanding the brig *New Hampshire* [248 tons built in Dover in 1823], and the ships *Caroline Augusta* [406 tons, built in Kittery in 1826] and the *Fortitude*.
>
> He was genial and kind-hearted, and from the paternal interest he ever evinced for the seamen under his command was known among them as "Father Libbey." The *Fortitude* we believe was the last ship he ever sailed, and in her he made quite a number of yearly voyages between this city and "foreign ports"; and whenever the word was passed around town that Capt. Libbey had got in again a large part of the male population would flock to the wharf to greet the *Fortitude* and her popular commander.
>
> For many years past he has been an invalid; but none the less will he be sadly missed by a circle of friends that included all who knew the genuine worth of the man.[62]

John Cumming

SPECIFICATIONS: 1836. George Raynes. Male bust figurehead, square stern. Burthen, 721 tons. Length, 141.21 feet; beam, 33.64 feet; depth, 16.825 feet. Two decks. Original owners—George B. Cumming and Samuel D. Corbett, both of Savannah; Robert Taylor, of New York.

The *John Cumming* was the first commercial vessel launched in the Port of Portsmouth to exceed 700-tons displacement. In general, as the decade moved nearer the 1840s, a steady increase in the size of ships will be noted. The *John Cumming* slid into the waters of the North Mill Pond on March 23, 1836. Later a news article marked the event in an unusual fashion:

THE SHIP

The launching of a ship, like any incident which takes place only one in the life of a man, is a subject of particular attention. She may afterwards look more majestic with her towering masts, her full rigging and bended canvas, sailing from or returning to port — but the launch is her *birth-day* — it is anticipated with satisfaction by the builder and the merchant — the carpenter and the sailor. It is the *act*, the important *moment* of entering upon that element in which she will do all the good that she is destined to be accomplishing: and in view of the benefits which commerce has conferred on mankind, that good is not inconsiderable. Without this important vehicle, the theories of a Columbus might have died with him — and no more certain knowledge had of each other by the nations of the different hemispheres, than we have of the inhabitants of the moon.

The *John-Cumming*, which was launched from the yard of Messrs. Raynes & Neal, on Saturday last, descended with a grandeur that we never saw surpassed on a like occasion. A large number of spectators were present to witness the scene. She is a fine ship of 700 tons — the largest merchantman ever built on our river.

After the foaming surges made by her entry, (which rose in regular succession to greet and welcome to ocean's bosom one of the noblest of her class,) had subsided, our attention was turned to a file of men with broad-axes on their shoulders, and their countenances brightened with that inward joy and satisfaction which became the important part they took on the occasion. They were CARPENTERS, and although perhaps little thought of by the thousand who had been viewing their noble work, are of first importance to the commercial community.

History informs us that in the year 1690, Peter the Great, Czar of the Russias, visited Holland, and, desirous of informing himself in those arts which would be most beneficial in the advancement of his kingdom, entered a ship-yard, laid aside his royal suite, dressed and lived in the same manner as the common workmen, worked with his own hands upon all the different parts in the construction of a vessel, and afterwards employed himself in the king's dock-yard in England, until he had obtained that scientific knowledge which rendered him a good ship builder. This was indeed giving a dignity to the profession.

On the skill and patient and laborious employment of the Carpenter, the merchant is dependent for his wealth. On the faithfulness of his labours, the safety of valuable cargoes and more valuable lives, continually depend....

Although the Carpenter was the most important and essential on this occasion, yet it will be found that there is scarcely any trade but what has its time of important, — a time when the good of the community depends essentially upon it, — fully proving the mutual dependence of each upon the other, and the real equality which in fact does exist under a happy constitution of government which declares the equality of all citizens.[63]

Not much is known of the early service of the *John Cumming*. She sailed from Portsmouth under Capt. George Thayer of New York and entered the triangular cotton trade. For a few years, she was commanded by Capt. William L. Dwight, and he was apparently relieved by Capt. Alexander Haven, also of Portsmouth, in 1853. While Captain Dwight had the *John Cumming*, she had a charter in 1846 and 1847 in the New Line. Previously, Captain Thayer had carried out a charter in the Georgia Line.[64] At least once, during the captaincy of Dwight, the *John Cumming* came into Portsmouth with salt.

Alexander Haven didn't have command long. In August 1853, with yellow fever running rampant through the southern ports, it was reported that the *John Cumming*, from New Orleans for Bordeaux, France, had been spoken, and that she was leaky and disabled. But, worse than that, Captain Haven, three seamen, and two passengers had died of yellow fever, and the rest of the passengers and crew were ill.[65] Two days later, a letter written by William P. Healey, second mate, to his brother-in-law, attorney W. H. P. Hackett, was published:

SAVANNAH RIVER, Aug. 14, 1853.

It has come to my lot to report myself under circumstances which tend to show how little one knows of what is before him. The J. C. left Orleans Bar on the 23d of July, since which time death has made his ravages among our company. We have lost two seamen, a passenger, and alas, sad to say, that most estimable man, Capt. Haven, is no more. He was taken ill last Sunday morning, the ship at the time being on the south coast of Florida. On Monday, being seriously ill and somewhat delirious, the mate being also confined to the cabin, it placed me under rather dubious circumstances. I took one of the sailors to stand one of the watches, and have since been endeavoring to get to this place for medical assistance, but unfavorable winds have prevented our arrival before this afternoon. In the mean time the Capt. continued to decline, until yesterday morning, when he breathed his last, a little after 4 A.M. Every thing in our power was done for him, but to no purpose. I was by him much of the time during his sickness; he seldom had his right mind after Monday; he made no allusions to home or friends during his illness. This afternoon at 4 o'clock, we anchored in the mouth of the river opposite Tybee Island, where we have since decently buried him within one hundred yards of Tybee lighthouse. We had wished to carry him to Savannah, had his body preserved and sent north, but the warm weather would allow us to keep him no longer. His complaint was the yellow fever. The mate has been recovering, and resumed his duties yesterday.

We perceive by the papers, that the revenue cutter Hamilton, while off Typee, on Sunday evening, fell in with the John Cumming in a leaking condition. And that an officer and six men were promptly supplied from the cutter, and the vessel run into Cockspur Roads, where she now lies at anchor.[66]

When the bad news reached the owners of the *John Cumming*, they promptly dispatched Capt. Ebenezer G. Adams to take over the ship. Adams, who was then 44, made his home at 1 Mark Street, and he had been following the sea since his teens. He often served as master of Ichabod Goodwin's vessels, and it's quite probable that it was Goodwin who recommended him to George Cumming. Two years after taking command of the *John Cumming*, Captain Adams was involved in an incident in the Chincha Islands off Peru that demonstrates the many hazards of a shipmaster's life. The *John Cumming* was in the Chinchas for a load of guano, a fertilizer deposited over thousands of years by sea birds. In February 1855, Captain Adams shot to death a mutinous seaman under circumstances that would, in the eyes of American law, be justifiable. However, the Peruvian authorities saw the shooting in a different light. Captain Adams was arrested and thrown in jail—an unpleasant experience in any South American country. The correspondent for the *New York Times* in Lima, Peru, reported in detail on the affair. The story affords an excellent example of the boldness with which American officials often had to act when far from home and without specific instructions:

LIMA, Peru, Wednesday, July 25th, 1855.

— In my last I made mention of the case of Capt. Adams of the American Ship John Cumming. Since then we have had some stirring times in connection therewith. It appears that some weeks ago Commodore Mervin came in at Callao with the frigate Independence, having been sent for by our Minister, Mr. Clay, to render him the aid of his presence in the settlement of Capt. Adams's difficulty with the Peruvian Government. It will be remembered that Capt. Adams shot and killed one of his mutinous sailors at the Chincha Islands in February last. The evidence is most conclusive that in this he was perfectly justified by American laws — and also that the strictest code of morals must sustain his course on that occasion. On his arrival here the Peruvian Government undertook to arrest him and hold him accountable for murder; whereupon Mr. Clay took the Captain under his protection, in his own house, and absolutely refused to recognize any and all jurisdiction of this Government in this case.

When the Independence came in here to back up the energetic action of our Minister, the Government became frightened and promised to arrange the matter promptly and amicably. Under these circumstances Commodore Mervin went to sea again; and as soon as his back was turned the Government — with treacherous, knavish faithlessness for which the Spanish race is proverbial — renewed all its claims of jurisdiction, and impudently assumed to take the matter out of our Minister's hands.

Mr. Clay, with a decision and energy which reflect the highest honor upon himself and the country he represents, boldly defied Capt. Adams's prosecutors — warned them of the consequences of their course, and presented the arguments to show that their conduct was violative of the law of nations, insulting to our flag, and must inevitably involve them in serious responsibility to the United States — But all this seemed of no effect, until the Independence put in at Callao again a few days ago. Commodore Mervin at once held another consultation with Mr. Clay, the result of which was that the Independence ran very close in shore, (where the John Cumming had been taken by the Peruvian authorities,) sent men on board, raised her anchor, towed her out to her original anchorage, and placed her under the protection of the frigate's guns.

This proceeding rather astounded the Peruvians. Meantime, on Saturday last, a Peruvian court at Callao proceeded to try Capt. Adams for the murder of the seaman. The Captain was not present, the proceedings were all ex-parte, no evidence was sought except such as was deemed acceptable for the purposes of the prosecution, and the accused was sentenced to death. At the same hour and all day on Sunday, Mr. Clay was engaged in earnest negociations with the government in hopes of bringing about an amicable adjustment of this serious affair. As a primary point he notified the government that at every risk and hazard the John Cumming should be sent to sea under the protection of the Independence, and that Capt. Adams should depart in her as commander, subject to nothing but the responsibility to answer in the United States for any charge that might be preferred against him. From this position the government was notified there would be no retreat, and Commodore Mervin proceeded to prepare the Cumming for sea, and his own ship for whatever might be wanted of her.

These very energetic steps frightened the Peruvian authorities. They saw they had gone too far, but could not see how, honorably, to get out of the scrape. They proposed among other things, that the John Cumming should be brought back to her inshore anchorage; that the Independence should move several hundred yards to the seaward, so as not to seem to menace the castle, and that Capt. Adams be not permitted to take command of his vessel. Upon these they finally professed a willingness to let the vessel and the captain go; but our representative promptly refused to listen to any such overtures, until at last it was agreed that the Independence should change her own position about three hundred yards; upon that basis the difficulty was finally arranged, and the John Cumming with Capt. Adams on board sailed for home this morning, accompanied to sea by the Independence, bound for San Francisco.

When it is remembered that Mr. Clay and Commodore Mervin acted in this case without special instructions, it will be seen that they assumed a great responsibility; but there can be no doubt that the whole country will sustain their noble defence of their countrymen and the honor of our flag.[67]

It should never be overlooked that American diplomats and military officers often gambled on what to do in situations not covered in their general instructions. They had no radio or satellite-telephone contact with their departments in Washington, as would be available to them today.

The Peruvians didn't let go of the Adams case. They asked Secretary of State William L. Marcy to have Adams arrested. When the *John Cumming* arrived in Norfolk, Virginia, on March 25, 1856, Captain Adams was placed under arrest, and released on bail in the amount of $5,000. On April 5, the *Journal* reported that the captain had been cleared by U.S. Commissioner John T. Francis and "honorably discharged."

Finally, in 1864, the *John Cumming* was sold in London for £3,500, not a bad price considering the years of wear and tear.[68] The *John Cumming* was but one of the many American merchant ships that changed owners and flags during the reign of terror imposed by the Confederate raider CSS *Alabama* and her sisters during the Civil War.

Captain Adams, as tough as the *John Cumming*, lived until he was 89. A scrapbook item, in my possession, said he died at the home of his daughter, Mary Augusta Parsons, on April 28, 1898. Mrs. Parsons was the wife of Dr. John W. Parsons, a noted Portsmouth physician in that day. When Captain Adams died only William L. Dwight was left of the old-time deep-water shipmasters in Portsmouth.

Norman

SPECIFICATIONS: 1836. Samuel Badger. Male bust figurehead, square stern. Burthen, 508 tons. Length, 135.6 feet; beam, 28.55 feet; depth, 14.275 feet. Original owners—Theodore Chase, Christopher S. Toppan, and Enoch Wood.

Chronologically, the *Norman* was the second ship launched in the Port of Portsmouth in 1836. She went down the ways on March 22, and it was noted that "the ship reflect high honor on the skill and workmanship of her builder."[69] She was taken out of Portsmouth by Capt. Enoch Wood a month later. Heading for New Orleans, the *Norman* ran into trouble on the notorious Carysfort Reef, off the southeast coast of Florida, on May 3. Wreckers helped her off, and she was taken into Key West, "where salvage to the amount of $4,250 was awarded by arbitration. Her situation on the reef was critical, having lost an anchor."[70] Within a few days, however, she was ready to sail, and she arrived in New Orleans on May 22.

Not much is known about her career. As early as 1837, under Captain Wood, she was chartered in the Packet Line, out of Boston. In 1845, Alfred Kindrick had her, also in the Packet Line. Prior to that she had been chartered in the Dispatch Line under Robert Spavin. Her ultimate fate isn't known.

Alliance

SPECIFICATIONS: 1836. Samuel Badger. Billet head, square stern. Burthen, 524 tons. Length, 131.35 feet; beam, 29.6 feet; depth, 14.8 feet. Two decks. Original owners—John Rice, John B. Haley, and Samuel Badger.

Samuel Badger, cautious businessman that he was, wasn't yet joining in the mad rush toward bigger and bigger three-masters. The *Alliance* was only the third of his ships to exceed 500 tons, the others being the *Norman* and *Solon*. John B. Haley, who made his home on Auburn Street, now Richards Avenue, was her first master, and he held command until at least 1839. George Nelson said she was sold in New York in 1842.[71] However, information provided by Miss Jane S. Tucker of Wiscasset, a Tucker descendant, indicates that R. H. Tucker & Co. bought the *Alliance* late in 1841.

Captain Haley advertised her for New Orleans in February 1837, asking for freight and/or passengers.[72] From New Orleans, she went to Liverpool and then back to her home port.

When the Tuckers bought her in 1841, extracts from her logs, as provided by Miss Tucker, show that she stuck very closely to the triangular cotton trade. For instance, Capt. Richard H. Tucker, Jr. departed New York in her in November 1841, with a cargo of hay for Charleston. He left Charleston in January 1842 for Le Havre, arriving there in March. When she sailed west, she went to Savannah and was off Port Royal Tybee on June 3, 1842. In 1846, the *Alliance* sailed from Charleston to Liverpool, and the log claims the 25-day passage was a record. On the voyage, the *Alliance* was 72 days from Charleston to Charleston, also claimed as a record. Captain Tucker commanded the *Alliance* until the summer of 1847.

Tucker turned the ship over to Capt. W. F. Robinson in July 1847, at New York, and he loaded a cargo of corn and passengers for

Liverpool. On the return she carried immigrants and £402 in freight. The next year, the *Alliance* carried 1,852 bales of cotton, including 95 bales of Sea Island cotton, from Charleston to Liverpool. Returning from Liverpool, she carried railroad iron, salt, hardware, crockery, and passengers. Robinson's voyages in the *Alliance* were similar through 1851, when he turned the command over to Capt. Joseph Tucker, who had Henry Nathan as mate. On his last passage in 1851, Captain Robinson brought railroad iron, slates, and passengers. Trying to get into Charleston, the ship spent four days hung up on Cape Romain Shoal. Joseph Tucker made one voyage, and then Dwight F. Tinkham took over, with John Greenough, mate. On his return from Le Havre in May 1852, Tinkham brought 304 passengers into New York at a rate of 10 Spanish dollars each.

The log indicates that on his last passage in the *Alliance*, Captain Tinkham carried 103 tons of small paving stones, at $3 a ton, plus 1,264 bales of hay at $1.25 each. The Tucker log for the *Alliance* ends on November 11, 1853, with the note that she was sold "to Capt. Tessier and Messrs. Heriot and Wagner of the John Fraser & Co. of Charleston for $18,000, as of commencement of loading for Havre."

And, finally, the *Journal* reported on January 2, 1864, that she had been sold at auction in New York for $8,600.

Lancashire

SPECIFICATIONS: 1836. George Raynes. Female figurehead, square stern. Burthen, 661 tons. Length, 142 feet; beam, 31.9 feet; depth, 15.95 feet. Two decks. Original owners—Robert L. Taylor and Nathaniel W. Merrill, both of New York; Robert Hutchinson, of Savannah.

Named for the county in England where most of the busy cotton mills were located, the *Lancashire* was launched on December 14, 1836, and she cleared from the Port of Portsmouth late in January 1837, under Capt. Nathaniel W. Merrill.[73] Taylor also was a shipmaster, and he joined forces with Merrill to found the successful Taylor & Merrill Line of packets.

Undoubtedly, it was her "foreign ownership" that explains why there's so little information available on the *Lancashire*. But one odd little item about the *Lancashire* was published in 1841: "A CAPTAIN DEPOSED BY HIS CREW. — The ship Lancashire, from Liverpool, arrived below, at Savannah on the 7th inst. [January] in charge of Henry Bradford, first mate, Captain George Bartol Jr. having been, by unanimous consent of passengers and crew, deprived of the command."

The *Journal* apparently copied the item from a Savannah paper, and there the matter was dropped. It can only be speculated that the captain might have become terminally ill or insane. The item appeared on February 6, 1841.

Isaac Newton

SPECIFICATIONS: 1836. George Raynes. Male bust figurehead, square stern. Burthen, 599 tons. Length, 135.5 feet; beam, 31 feet; depth, 15.35 feet. Two decks. Original owners—Ichabod Goodwin, Samuel E. Coues, and William A. Rice.

The *Isaac Newton* was named for the seventeenth-century genius who developed the theory of gravity. William A. Rice, one of the owners, was the first master of the *Isaac Newton*. Registered in the Port of Portsmouth in November 1836, she left home for the triangle trade, returning on June 19, 1837.[74] Captain Rice brought the ship in again in September 1838, and then turned her over to Lyman Spaulding.

Captain Spaulding's first passage with the *Isaac Newton* narrowly escaped disaster. The ship was cleared by Customs on September 12, 1838, and she dropped down the Piscataqua to the lower harbor. There she hove to and anchored to wait out a storm. The winds were so vicious that the ship dragged her anchors and went ashore at New Castle. Luckily, where she grounded was soft muck, and "she got off without any damage."[75] When the storm abated, the *Isaac Newton* continued on her passage to Baltimore, where she arrived on October 3. From there she went to Mobile for cotton. She left Mobile on January 2, 1839, for Liverpool, and while en route fell in with a vessel, the *William Russell*, from St. John, New Brunswick, that had been badly damaged in a gale. The *Isaac Newton* took off the captain and crew. She continued to sail the legs of the cotton trade triangle, coming occasionally into Portsmouth.

Early in 1841 she loaded at New York for Hamburg, Germany. In the cargo were two Norris locomotive engines "worth some $25,000, destined for a railroad in Prussia."[76] Two years later, she ventured into the Mediterranean, sailing from Mobile to Trieste, Italy. There she had to go into quarantine, because one of the crew was down with dysentery. Before the New Year, she was back in Boston. When she left Boston in 1844, it was under charter to the Regular Line, but she returned to Portsmouth with salt for Goodwin & Coues.

William Lambert took command in 1845, and she sailed out of Apalachicola, Florida, for one voyage. She came to Portsmouth with salt in 1846. When she left, Thomas B. Clark, previously master of the *Susanna Cumming*, was in command. In 1848, she arrived in Boston with 220 steerage passengers; 2 had died on the voyage.

Apparently, in May 1852, the *Isaac Newton* was sold because a news item described her as being of Boston, "late of this port."[77] Elisha Whitney was her master, and she cleared out of Boston for Valparaiso, Chile, and a market. Because she had passed from Port of Portsmouth ownership, keeping track of her is difficult, but she did go into the East India and Australian trade. It's recorded that she went into Bombay in distress on April 6, 1861, and "was burned."[78]

Oronoco

SPECIFICATIONS: 1837. David Shiverick. Dover. Billet head, square stern. Burthen, 656 tons. Length, 141.7 feet; beam, 31.9 feet; depth, 15.95 feet. Two decks. Original owners—Robert Rogers, John Riley, and Dan Deshon.

To the *Oronoco* goes the lasting fame of being the last three-masted, square-rigged vessel launched in the upper reaches of the Piscataqua Valley. Robert Whitehouse, in his fine work, *Port of Dover*, devotes a little space to her, but she deserves much more. Further, one would like to know more about David Shiverick, a master carpenter who could create such a large ship on the Cochecho River so long after the trade had moved downstream. In an interview, Whitehouse expressed doubt, with some reason, that the *Oronoco* had to be floated over shallows on barrels. That was the way her last three-masted predecessors, the *Martha* and the *Lydia*, had made it out to sea. Having been built in a yard below the present-day power station on the Cochecho, Whitehouse believes the *Oronoco* would have had enough water to get into the main channel. As Whitehouse emphasized, silting in the streams above Portsmouth has changed everything.

Like most of the other ships of her decade, the *Oronoco* was intended for the lucrative cotton trade. She cleared the Port of Portsmouth on February 13, 1838, under Capt. Robert Rogers, a veteran shipmaster. Rogers began his career at Saco, Maine, moving to South Berwick in the 1830s and eventually becoming a resident of Dover. From the beginning, the *Oronoco* seemed to be booked more towards ports in North Europe, like Cronstadt, Germany. She did take cotton to Le Havre, and in August 1839 the *Oronoco* was in Deal, England, heading for a port on the Baltic to be recoppered. However, it was reported in October 1839:

Ship Oronoco (of Boston) Rogers, got ashore first ult [September 1], at Skager, near Gottenburg [Sweden]. She was from that place, loaded with iron for Boston; crew and passengers saved with great difficulty; Capt. Rogers is very ill. She was a complete wreck on the 8th ult. She was built in Dover in 1837, and was, with her cargo, insured in seven different offices, State St., Boston, for $96,600, viz.: $30,000 on ship, $55,000 on cargo, and $11,600 on freight.[79]

The ailing Captain Rogers apparently never went to sea again, although he did own a boat, the *Franklin*, 23 tons, which was sold in Boston in 1846. Eleven months after the wreck, an advertisement was published offering for sale anchors, sails, chain cables, and shrouds that had been salvaged from the *Oronoco* and brought to Boston. The auction was held of Rowe's Wharf on September 19, 1840.[80]

Henry

SPECIFICATIONS: 1837. George Raynes. Billet head, square stern. Burthen, 434 tons. Length, 122 feet; beam, 28 feet; depth, 14 feet. Two decks. Original owners—Henry Ladd and John E. Salter.

The ship *Henry* was undoubtedly named for her principal owner, Henry Ladd, who was for many years one of Portsmouth's leading merchants. Throughout most of his life, he was closely associated with his brother, Alexander—a partnership that ended with his death on January 29, 1842. Henry Ladd was described as "a gentleman of singular elevation of sentiment, whose unbending integrity as a merchant gave character and dignity to his profession."[81]

The size of the *Henry* seems almost a reversion to the old pattern of similar vessels. Only two other three-masted, square-rigged vessels under 500 tons were built by George Raynes: the *Charles* (1838) and the *Glendoveer* (1841). The ship *Henry* was launched on August 5, 1837, and John E. Salter was her first master. Salter was a veteran mariner, his first command having been the brig *Abelino*, 146 tons, owned by Edmund Roberts, the man who negotiated the treaty the United States made with the kingdom of Siam. Salter had moved up steadily, commanding larger vessels and sharing in the ownership.

The *Henry*'s career was unspectacular: she was a workhorse in the cotton trade. She left the Port of Portsmouth late in November 1837, arriving at Mobile on December 15. However, finding no cargo there, she went to Apalachicola and then, finally, on to New Orleans.

Then she had to go much further up the Mississippi to get a cargo of 1,473 bales for Liverpool, where she arrived on May 22, 1838.[82] For her first three years she traveled principally between the cotton ports and Le Havre or Liverpool. In one instance, she arrived at the Delaware Breakwater, June 5, 1840, 38 days from Liverpool, with merchandise and 170 passengers. Given the size of the *Henry*, it has to be wondered how the passengers ever survived such voyages.

Not until 1841 did Captain Salter and the *Henry* return to Portsmouth. Leaving Penarth Roads, off Wales, on September 1, the ship brought in 600 tons of railroad iron for the Portsmouth, Portland & Saco Railroad. Parenthetically, it can be said that most of the rails used by the early railroads were manufactured in the British Isles. In fact, British-manufactured goods of all kinds, and salt, constituted most of the imports into the Port of Portsmouth for decades—the simple truth being that American industry was still far behind the British.

Before he yielded command of the *Henry*, Captain Salter had a misadventure with the ship that was nearly terminal. She went ashore on Dog Island in Apalachicola Bay, near the East Pass. The *Apalachicola Advertiser* reported on July 7, 1846, that it was expected the ship would be lost. "The ship was valued at $20,000, and insured in Boston on two-thirds of her for $13,000."[83] However, she was saved, and Salter turned her over to James Kennard in 1850. Three years later, she came to her end in the Bimini Islands. During a storm, sailing from Boston for New Orleans, she dragged her anchors and grounded on September 13, 1853. She was carrying a cargo of shoes, fish, domestics, gunny cloth, and other items. The weather was favorable to saving the cargo, and most of the dry portion of it was salvaged by the wreckers in fairly good order. The ship was a total loss.[84] Later it was learned that she had been burned by the wreckers on September 20. The captain and crew arrived safely in Nassau, and salvage was reported at 45 percent, or $12,750. Insurance totaled $13,000.

Some months after the loss of the *Henry*, the *Journal*, on June 3, 1854, published an odd item concerning it. Before quoting the article, it should be explained that the Preston referred to in it was William Rantoul Preston, an apothecary in Portsmouth who also manufactured patent medicines and was a major supplier of medicines for a ship's medicine chest:

> ROMANTIC INTRODUCTION OF A VALUABLE ARTICLE. — In the fall of 1853, the ship Henry, of this port, bound to New-Orleans, was wrecked on one of the Bahamas, near Nassau, New-Providence. — Among the cargo was a gross of Preston's Vegetable Catholicon, in three separate boxes. In collecting the cargo saved, it was found that two of the three boxes were missing,

supposed to have gone for the benefit of the finny tribe. One day, a week or two after the disaster, the captain of the Henry was waited upon by Thomas Brace, a druggist of Nassau, and was told that he had frequent inquiries within a few days for a new medicine, of which he had never before heard, and one applicant intimated that he supposed the Captain might have a supply, and wished if possible to obtain a bottle. It soon appeared that the wreckers had secured and used the contents of the missing boxes, with so good effect, that they were willing to pay any price for a further supply. The remaining case was produced by the Captain and readily sold at a price, which, after paying all the expenses, netted to Mr. Preston six dollars more than the regular wholesale price of the whole amount shipped. We saw a small heap of gold, 72 dollars, paid by the Captain to Mr. P. on his return. Since the disaster, Mr. P. has received three several orders from Mr. Brace for further supplies of his popular medicine, which was by the wreckers thus providentially introduced into New-Providence.

Nicholas Biddle

SPECIFICATIONS: 1837. George Raynes. Male figurehead, square stern. Burthen, 783 tons. Length, 149.9 feet; beam, 33.9 feet; depth, 16.95 feet. Two decks. Original owners—Taylor & Merrill, J. Johnson, and C. A. Hiern, all of New York; and G. B. Cumming, of Savannah.

The New Yorkers who bought the *Nicholas Biddle* were probably insuring themselves financially and politically when they named their new vessel for the president of the United States Bank. From the point of view of her builder, she was the largest he had yet put into the Piscataqua. However, the news account prior to the launching exaggerated a bit as to her size:

LAUNCH. — Will be launched this day, at 2 o'clock, from the ship yard of Messrs. Raynes & Neal, a new ship of 800 tons burthen. We hear from competent judges that this ship is built upon the most approved model; and that in material, style, and workmanship, she is equal to Raynes & Neal's best ships which is equivalent to saying she is equal to any ship built in the country.

It is fortunate for the town, and creditable to these builders, that their skill and fidelity have given a permanency and prosperity to the business of ship building.

This ship is to be called the *Nicholas Biddle*, an appropriate name for none but a good ship. May she bear Mr. Biddle's name, as he has borne himself, safely and gallantly through every storm.

The Nicholas Biddle is owned by Messrs. John Cumming & Son, Savannah; Taylor & Merrill and Capt. Charles A. Hiern, of New York. Captain Hiern is to command her.[85]

Registered on January 12, 1838, the *Nicholas Biddle* left Portsmouth a week later under Capt. C. A. Hiern, headed for Mobile, where she arrived late in February. Loaded with cotton, the *Nicholas Biddle* went to Liverpool. That was to be the general nature of her service. She sailed for the various packet lines from the cotton ports to Europe and back. One of her masters was "stout old S. C. Knight," who was later swept to his death from the quarterdeck of the ship *Ivanhoe*.[86] In 1851 David Caulkins was master. He was relieved by a Captain Gerrish. The *Nicholas Biddle* was in the cotton trade even into the Civil War years. The *Liverpool Herald* reported the arrival of the ship, under a Captain Mulford, on February 8, 1857, from Savannah. On her return passage, she was badly damaged in a storm, spent three days on her beam ends, and had to go into Fayal in the Azores for repairs.

For the *Nicholas Biddle*, the end came—as it did for so many American merchant ships—when she was captured by a Confederate raider. The *Portsmouth Journal*, on September 10, 1864, said that a letter from Pernambuco, dated July 29, reported that the "pirate Florida" claimed to have burned the *Nicholas Biddle* off Brazil, and that the ship had $70,000 on board. Ironically, the commander of the CSS *Florida*, John Maffitt, was a native of Portsmouth, the home of the *Nicholas Biddle*. Maffitt was the son of a Universalist minister, and grew up in North Carolina.

Thomas Perkins

SPECIFICATIONS: 1837. Frederick W. Fernald. Mugridge yard, Portsmouth. Burthen, 600 tons. Length, 157 feet; beam, 31 feet. Two decks. Original owners—Pingree & Johnson, Salem, Massachusetts.

It will probably never be known for certain who designed the *Thomas Perkins*. However, it's more than likely that Samuel Pook had a hand in it, because, with all due respect to the brilliancy of Frederick W. Fernald, it doesn't seem possible that he was yet ready to produce radically designed ships. And the Journal made it clear that the *Thomas Perkins* was different:

> A fine large ship was launched on Tuesday [May 23] from the yard of Mr. John Mugridge near the South Mill Bridge. She is probably the longest merchant ship ever built on the river, being 157 feet in length, but very narrow (only 31 feet) and calculated for fast sailing. — Burthen about 600 tons. The ship is very well built and is highly creditable to the master carpenter, Mr. Frederick W. Fernald.

Again, it's only speculation, but it's possible that Sam Pook was experimenting with a radical design, one that would become commonplace in the next decade. And it just isn't realistic to think that a Salem firm would seek out an untried ship carpenter to build a radical vessel unless someone with the prestige of a Sam Pook was involved.

The *Journal* apparently was correct in styling the *Thomas Perkins* the longest ship ever built on the river. Not until 1846 did George Raynes build a longer vessel, and Fernald himself didn't build a longer one until 1844. Very little is known about the *Thomas Perkins*. She was named for Thomas H. Perkins, a Boston entrepreneur and philanthropist:

> He was a large benefactor to many objects of public interest. He was the projector of the Quincy Railway, which was completed in 1827, and was the first railway enterprise in the United States. He was one of the most active, zealous, and efficient promoters of the Bunker Hill Monument. The Institution for the Blind was one of the cherished objects of the benevolent sympathies of the deceased. Many years ago he presented his mansion house in Pearl street, estimated to be worth $40,000, for the use of the Asylum. His munificence induced the organization to assume the corporate name of "The Perkins Institution, and Massachusetts Asylum for the Blind."
>
> He made the largest donation to the Mercantile Library Association which that useful institution has ever received from a single individual.[87]

Ultimately, the *Thomas Perkins* was sold to go under the Union Jack, and she was renamed *Aprosince*.[88] She was the last ship built on the Portsmouth side of the river by Fernald. He moved his operation to the old Badger yard on Badger's Island.

New Hampshire

SPECIFICATIONS: 1837. Frederick W. Fernald. Badger's Island. Billet head, square stern. Burthen, 595 tons. Length, 138.4 feet; beam, 30.65 feet; depth, 15.3 feet. Original owners—Samuel Hale, Ichabod Rollins, William Shackford, and James Kennard.

John Mugridge, the often-overlooked master carpenter who worked closely with Frederick W. Fernald, was credited in the newspapers as being the builder of the *New Hampshire*. Although the Portsmouth Customs Records show Fernald as the builder, but Mugridge undoubtedly had a share in the work.

Before being sold in New York in 1842, the first *New Hampshire* had established herself as a dependable transatlantic packet. Today's jet aircraft are periodically examined after a given number of landings and takeoffs, and seagoing vessels such as the *New Hampshire* had equivalent inspections. For example, in November 1846 she limped into New York from Liverpool, and the newspapers said:

> Ship New Hampshire, of Portsmouth, at New York, from Liverpool, reports, Oct. 5…lost main topsail and yard, foretopmast stay sail, and main sail, stove bulwarks, lost part of deck load from the stern, one boat, and spare spars in a NNW gale. On the 15th in a NE gale, with a heavy sea, lost main topmast and top gallant mast, fore topmast yard, main spencer, spanker, jib and badly damaged an entire new suit of sails. On 24th every spar was fished, and aloft again, and the sails mended and set. The fore topmast was found to be sprung.[89]

She had to be thoroughly checked in New York, but, like a jet down to one engine, she had made it to port.

She cleared out for Antwerp on January 3, 1847, and was back in New York in April. In January 1851, the *New Hampshire* arrived in Liverpool, having thrown over part of her deck cargo. Finally, on April 11, 1857, the *Journal* reported:

> DISASTER. — Ship New Hampshire, of and for New York, from Glasgow, before reported ashore on Long Island, went on in a heavy snow storm at 2 A. M., 7th inst., high up on the outer bar, opposite South Oyster Bay, about a quarter of a mile from shore. The crew landed in their boats. She went head on, has seven feet water in the hold, and if the weather should be favorable, may be got off after discharging: but she is 20 years old and is thought to be bogged. She was built at Portsmouth,

N.H., in 1837, is 505 tons, and is valued at about $15,000. She is owned by Zerega & Co., and there is no insurance on vessel money. Her cargo is 450 tons pig iron, 400 pkgs. rags, soda ash, bleaching powders, &c. supposed to be insured.

Huron

SPECIFICATIONS: 1837. Samuel Badger. Male figurehead, square stern. Burthen, 514 tons. Length, 132.95 feet; beam, 29.1 feet; depth, 14.55 feet. Two decks. Original owners—Henry P. Salter, John H. and George C. Boardman, and Jonathan M. Tredick, all of Portsmouth.

Capt. George C. Boardman was the *Huron*'s first master, taking her to New Orleans, where she arrived on December 1, after a passage of 22 days. During her stay in New Orleans, she was coppered; why that hadn't been done during construction isn't known. When the coppering was completed, she took on cargo and headed for New York. Reaching there, she unloaded and took on cargo for Hampton Roads, with New Orleans her intended port. It was a classic demonstration of the triangular cotton trade. Once again she was chartered for Liverpool, arriving there prior to September 26, 1838. She was back in New York on Sunday, December 6, coming from Liverpool with 111 passengers. She also brought smallpox with her, and four of the unfortunates in steerage died, with three on the sick list.

Captain Boardman took the *Huron* south to New Orleans to load more cotton for Liverpool. On her run to new Orleans, she went into Havana, Cuba, reaching there on October 3, 38 days out. While at Havana, Captain Boardman died, probably from yellow fever. Along with the master, a young seaman, Lewis Barnabee, 17, also died. Young Barnabee was the son of Willis Barnabee, proprietor of the Franklin House on Congress Street in Portsmouth. The mate, William Paine, took command and sailed the ship to New Orleans; he continued as master until his own death in 1844:

> In New-Orleans, 21st ult. Capt. WM. PAINE, master of ship Huron, of this town. Capt. Paine was a native of the Orkney Islands. Having early left his home, he was obliged friendless and unaided, to be the author of his own fortunes— accidentally thrown in the way of the late Capt. Boardman, he secured as he afterwards merited the confidence of that gentleman. Prompt and decisive in business he commended himself to the notice of the merchant. Simple and unaffected in his manners he prepossessed all with whom he held intercourse. Hav-

ing become a naturalized citizen, it was his intention to have
made this place his home. Though known to but few among us,
yet with that few he had won for himself a high and enviable
reputation. The death of a valuable young man is a loss to any
community, and we hesitate not to say, that for strict integrity
and judicious self government, combined with a manly, independent yet unostentatious character, Capt. Paine had few
equals, and no superiors. One who is under many obligations
for his disinterested self-sacrificing kindness, in administering
to a sick and dying friend, has the melancholy satisfaction, of
paying this simple tribute of respect, to a gentleman of unblem-
ished moral character, and of great private worth. — *Com.*[90]

John A. Payne succeeded William Paine as master. Under him,
the *Huron* was in the Taylor & Merrill Line. Nathaniel G. Weeks
became master at the time of the Mexican War. She was chartered as
a troop transport, taking men to Vera Cruz in 1847. In recognition of
his service, Captain Weeks was presented with a speaking trumpet by
the officers of the 5th U.S. Infantry Regiment, who were his passengers on one trip, "as a testimonial of their regard for him as a skillful
Navigator and courteous Gentleman."[91] The trumpet was displayed in
the store of John W. Abbott in Market Square. It was made by Ball,
Tompkins & Berry of New York and valued at $150.

In 1848, the *Huron* was sold in Boston, but no details were
reported. The *Liverpool Telegraph* noted on July 25, 1850, that the
Huron, under a Captain Lowry, had arrived in port in 42 days from
New Orleans, and was heading for St. Petersburg, Russia. She was in
Scotland in 1851, but further information is lacking.

Pontiac

*SPECIFICATIONS: 1838. Samuel Badger. Burthen, 538 tons. Length,
136.3 feet; beam, 29.35 feet; depth, 14.675 feet. Two decks. Original
owners—John Haven, Robert Rice, Jonathan Tredick, and William
Parker.*

Samuel Badger seemed to be continuing a trend toward using
Indian names in naming the *Pontiac* for an Ottawa chief, but perhaps
it was the choice of the owners. Unfortunately, the Customs Records
don't mention any kind of a figurehead for the ship, but surely it must
have had the well-carved bust of a warrior. The launching of the *Pontiac* did prompt the *Journal*, on September 15, 1838, to publish a real

chamber-of-commerce puff piece on Port of Portsmouth shipbuilding, and it's worthy of quotation because it clearly shows the momentum in the Piscataqua shipyards:

SHIP BUILDING

This business has been carried on to considerable extent the present year. A Boston paper mentions that six vessels of from 500 to 600 tons are on the stocks at Medford, and the Newburyport Herald remarks that there are six ships building on the Merrimack, just above that town. In Portsmouth harbor four are now building and two have been recently launched. The *Pontiac*, a beautiful ship of 550 tons, belonging to Messrs. John Haven, Robert Rice and Jonathan Tredick, was launched from the yard of Capt. Samuel Badger a few weeks since. On Saturday last the fine ship *Charles*, of about 470 tons, belonging to Messrs. Samuel Sheafe, Charles Coffin and Horatio Coffin, was launched from the yard of Mr. George Raynes.

It is a common thing to compliment a new ship, — but as an evidence that the praises which have hitherto been bestowed upon the ships built in our harbor were merited, we have recently had some cases in point. In July last the Ship *Rockingham*, Captain Dwight, with a full cargo, sailed from Liverpool in company with a New York light packet, and brought the latest dates [of newspapers]. A fine ship this! Where was the Rockingham built? At George Raynes's ship yard.

Soon after, ship *Norman* is honored through the country as the bearer of the latest news into Boston. What place can claim the honor of building so fine a ship? The Piscataqua bore her on her natal day, and Mr. Badger was her builder.

Last week a Portsmouth ship arrived at our wharves, — and two days after the New-York Journal of Commerce announces the latest news from England by the ship *Susanna Cumming*, Capt. Salter, at Portsmouth, N.H. No small compliment in these days of packet ship and steam packets! What yard has the honor producing this good sailer? — She was built by Raynes.

On Monday last the Ship *Isaac Newton*, Captain Rice, came up our harbor, one day later than any other arrival from Liverpool. Who built the *Isaac Newton*? may be the inquiry of the curious. The answer is only an echo of the former one — George Raynes.

The first master of the *Pontiac* was William Parker, one of the owners, who had first walked a quarterdeck as commander in 1829 on the ship *Lydia*. At the time of his death on April 12, 1889, the *Chronicle* said:

> Capt. William Parker, one of Portsmouth's oldest shipmasters, died on Friday, April 12th, at the residence of his son-in-law, Col. William H. Sise. Capt. Parker was born in this city on the 28th of March, 1804, and consequently entered upon the 86th year of his age at the time of his decease.
>
> At the early age of 19, he was appointed to the command of the ship *Lydia* of this port; and from that time until 1865, a period of 42 years, he was constantly in command, in all parts of the world, having in his charge many of the best ships ever built on the Piscataqua, among them being, besides the *Lydia*, the *Pontiac*, *Arabella*, *Flying Eagle*, *Emily Farnum* and *Santee*.

The *Chronicle* didn't bother to do simple arithmetic in claiming Parker was 19 when he commanded the *Lydia*. The records show him master of the *Lydia* in 1829, when he was 25.[92] Before taking out the *Pontiac*, he had also been captain of the *Charlotte*. He sailed the *Pontiac* from Portsmouth on November 9, 1838, arriving in New Orleans on the twenty-eighth. The *Pontiac* went into the service so well followed by some of her sisters from the Port of Portsmouth: the cotton trade. On that first voyage, she went from New Orleans to Le Havre, then to St. Ubes, where she loaded salt and came home. Several times she came into Portsmouth with salt. In October 1842, Jonathan Tredick, one of the owners, was advertising salt that was being landed at Portsmouth Pier from the *Pontiac*. Portsmouth Pier was a straight-out extension of State Street into the river. Now part of Prescott Park, in its last working years the pier was used by C. E. Walker & Co. for a coal pocket.

In December 1846, under Capt. George W. Tucker of Portsmouth, the *Pontiac* became page 1 news in newspapers along the East Coast:

DISTRESSED EMIGRANTS

> Two vessels arrived at this port [New York] yesterday, having on board [between them] 312 passengers, 34 of whom were dead, and 41 in such miserable plight as to be sent to the city hospital, where they now lie wavering between life and death. One of these vessels was the Ligonia, from Bremen, whence she sailed on the 1st of September, having been out 110 days; the other was the Pontiac, from Liverpool, whence she sailed October 20th, having been out 63 days. The captain of

the Pontiac is G. W. Tucker, who called at the Alms House and mentioned the following particulars: "The number of deaths on board his ship was 19; the entire navigation devolved upon himself and six sailors, his first and second mates having both been taken sick; the former was a raving maniac during the whole passage; he had crossed the ocean a number of times, and had never experienced such a severe and protracted storm before; and his last loaf of bread was distributed among the passengers some three days before he made the port, and he says that the sufferings of all on board were melancholy in the extreme." — *N. Y. Express.*[93]

Under ordinary circumstances, Captain Tucker's statements would have ended the matter. Travel across the Atlantic in sailing days was a hazardous venture, and the 1840s were seeing the great wave of Irish immigration brought about by famine. The horrible conditions endured by many of the immigrants have often been described, and were simply too terrible to be completely believed. Captain Tucker wrote to Portsmouth about the situation, in which he contended "that the story appearing in the New-York papers respecting the crew and passengers on board his ship, was very incorrect; that instead of being in a starving condition he had plenty of food on board when he arrived, but had been on allowance for a few days only as a matter of precaution. The number of deaths on board his ship was 18. He thinks that the story told of suffering in the Pontiac was intended for another vessel."[94] However, *Pontiac* case became a cause célèbre in the New York papers, and Captain Tucker twice stood trial in the matter, being cleared each time. On March 20, 1847, the *Journal* published the following:

CASE OF CAPT. TUCKER. — The following letter from our correspondent at New-York, who is in no way connected with Capt. Tucker, dated March 10, intended for insertion last week, was not received in season. We give it, although we believe the character of Capt. Tucker stands too high to suffer by such accusations as irresponsible men have brought against him.

The case of Capt. Tucker of the ship Pontiac was brought before the U. S. District Court March 5th, on a charge made by a stranger in the country, a cabin passenger on board the ship on her last passage to this port. — The influence of the press, that mighty but ill-disciplined teacher of men, spread wide and far the most terrible tales of cruelty and wrong, while this young man lay in imminent peril of death, tossing in the wild delirium of the ship fever, from which so many of his passengers, and both his officers were also suffering. When he recovered, he sought the trial of the 5th and was discharged — but as this was not a direct refutation, such as many might require, at his request it was again brought before the Court, when not only was the charge proved a mere shadow, but the noblest evidence of most generous and devoted conduct to the sick and afflicted, was rendered by those who had buried husband and friend in the ocean — by men just risen from that scourge which had afflicted them, and trembling in the garments of poverty, from very weakness — by the mate, who nobly testified that in his experience of sixteen years he had never seen a man so ready to sacrifice time, and rest, to the comfort of passengers. — By all this testimony, I will not say he was exonerated, or as court language has it, honorably *acquitted*, — it was *more*, — he was shown and *proved* to have been, under most trying circumstances, one of whom the whole family of man may be glad — and we thus express our hope, that for the better understanding of those who may have been unfavorably impressed during the currency of those false reports, that the Journal, as well other papers of his native town, will give the statement of the trial as it will appear in the papers of the city.

That misadventure was, of course, before the 1849 Gold Rush and the tremendous expansion of traffic to the West Coast. While no concrete evidence has been found, it's obvious that the *Pontiac* went into that trade, and that she also went to the East Indies. In fact, she cleared at Boston, under a Captain Treadwell, in October 1850, for Madras and Calcutta, arriving at Madras on March 2, 1851. The *Pontiac* continued in the trade until March 27, 1854, when she went ashore on the Gingerbread Ground and was reported a total loss.[95] However, there is a strong hint that she in fact survived that misadventure, because the *Rockingham Messenger*, a Portsmouth newspaper, reported on July 26, 1854, that the *Pontiac*, under the Chinese flag, had come into San Francisco on June 15 and had been seized by the authorities.

Columbia

SPECIFICATIONS: 1838. Frederick W. Fernald and Charles Raynes. Badger's Island, Kittery. Figurehead, square stern. Burthen, 600 tons. Length, 140.15 feet; beam, 30.6 feet; depth, 15.3 feet. Two decks. Original owners—Samuel Hale and Ichabod Rollins.

The *Columbia* was the first ship built by the partnership of Charles Raynes and Frederick W. Fernald. Before they dissolved the firm, they launched four more ships. Raynes was a rather eccentric brother of George Raynes, and toward the end of his career occupied himself making models of his brother's vessels.

The launching of the *Columbia* merited a brief notice. "On Thursday last [November 1] a ship of 610 tons, a fine model and workmanship, was launched from Badger's Island. She is owned by Hale & Rollins. On the day before the launching, there was a heavy fall of snow, good enough for sleighing, if the ground had been frozen."[96]

Thomas B. Clark, a veteran shipmaster who had often commanded Samuel Hale's ships, was the first captain of the *Columbia*. She headed out of Portsmouth for New Orleans, where she arrived in 25 days, after making a stop in Mobile. From New Orleans, the *Columbia* went to Liverpool, putting in briefly at Cork, Ireland. She completed the cotton triangle by going into Philadelphia in 51 days from Liverpool. On one of her passages in 1840, she was in a collision with the British bark *Ritchie*. The bark had to put back to Greenock, Scotland, but the *Columbia*, with all sails set, kept on her course. The *Ritchie* estimated that the *Columbia* was doing about nine knots.[97]

In 1843, John B. Haley became master, apparently buying out Samuel Hale's interest, as shown by the vessel being reregistered to Haley and Ichabod Rollins.[98] Captain Haley had one serious mishap with the *Columbia*, when she ran aground near Memory Rock in the Bahamas (off Jupiter Inlet, Florida). She was carrying 2,000 bales of cotton from New Orleans to Le Havre. Twenty wrecking vessels helped lighten her load so she could be taken into Nassau for repairs. Five hundred damaged bales were sold, and the salvage on the ship and cargo was set at $17,000.[99] A week later, the *Journal* reported that it had been discovered at Nassau that the *Columbia*'s keel had been ground up, so that major repairs were necessary. Once she had been repaired, the *Columbia* was sold in Boston. On July 2, 1849, she cleared Boston for Manila.[100] The ultimate fate of the *Columbia* isn't clear. A ship of that name was still afloat in the 1880s, but Columbia, with its patriotic connotations, was a favorite name for vessels.

Arethusa

SPECIFICATIONS: 1838. Jacob Remick. Kittery. Billet head, square stern. Burthen, 522 tons. Length, 131.8 feet; beam, 29.5 feet; depth, 14.75 feet. Two decks. Original owners—Richard Jenness, William Jones, William P. Jones, and John D. Simes.

Jacob Remick, who once had a yard near the western end of the Portsmouth Bridge, apparently built the *Arethusa* on speculation. Remick began his shipbuilding career in Portsmouth, and his first vessel was the brig *Arno*, 229 tons. That was in 1821. Later in that decade, Remick had young George Raynes working in his yard, and in 1828 Remick moved to Kittery. He was credited with building two small schooners, and the *Arethusa* was his final vessel.

To dispose of the *Arethusa*, Remick engaged the services of Thomas A. Adams, an auctioneer and commission merchant with quarters on Market Street; his home was on Middle Street. Adams advertised the *Arethusa* as being "built of white oak, heavy copper fastenings, a good model, and in every respect a first rate ship."[101] The emphasis on "copper fastenings" was intended, of course, to assure a prospective purchaser that the fastenings wouldn't corrode and rot out, as would iron spikes. The next week, the *Journal* said: "The new ship advertised in our last to be sold at auction on the 13th inst., was sold for $31,405. The purchasers are Messrs. John S. Jenness, Boston; Richard Jenness, William Jones & Son and John D. Simes, all of Portsmouth. Registered tonnage 522 and 58/95ths tons. She is to be called the Arethusa."

The name Arethusa was fitting, in that the original, in Greek mythology, was a wood nymph, with whom the river god Alpheus fell in love. His pursuit was in vain, because one of the goddesses turned Arethusa into a fountain. Edward Kennard, who made his home at the corner of Islington and Ann (Union) streets, was the *Arethusa*'s first and only master. She left the Port of Portsmouth on February 19, 1839, heading for New Orleans for a load of cotton. It took her 20 days to reach New Orleans, after a stop at Mobile. She had to wait for a cargo, but was finally cleared for Liverpool of July 13. In October, she was chartered as a packet ship to bring immigrants to New York, and sailed on October 21. In Portsmouth the next news of her came on December 21:

> Ship Arethusa, Kennard, of this port, 49 days from Liverpool for New-York, with 150 passengers and a cargo of crates, salt and iron, was wrecked on Tuesday morning, 10th,

near Patchogue, L. I. The captain and part of the crew attempted to land in the large boat, which swamped. One passenger was drowned — the rest of the passengers and crew saved. Part of the cargo will probably be saved. — The vessel will probably be lost. The A. is a new ship of 525 tons, valued at 35,000 dollars — belonging to Messrs. W. Jones & Son, J. D. Simes, and R. & J. S. Jenness.

She was insured at several offices in Boston $32,000 on the vessel and $22,000 on cargo (rail road iron). A portion of the cargo was insured in New York.

Two more lighters with goods from ship Arethusa, ashore at Pachogue, are at New-York 18th. A letter from the agents of underwriters dated night of 14th, states that 60 crates and 1 hod earthenware, 3 cases dry goods and 2 bales wool had been got out. They add: "At 10 P. M. the wind light from SE, the wind increasing: the ship not bilged, but full of water, which came in the cabin windows, the sea having stove dead lights. She lays with her head on, and could we be favored with mild weather, I doubt not but the ship may be saved. The ship's stern lays in about 12 feet of water, but she is considerably embedded in the sand."

Charles

SPECIFICATIONS: 1838. George Raynes. Billet head, square stern. Burthen, 486 tons. Length, 127.95 feet; beam, 28.9 feet; depth, 14.45 feet. Two decks. Original owners—Charles Coffin, Samuel Sheafe, and Horatio Coffin.

It's a fair guess that the ship *Charles* was named for one of the principal owners, Charles Coffin. Thomas Sheafe Coffin, son of Charles and brother to Horatio, was the first master of the *Charles*. With all the Coffins involved, it can be said, as a pun, that the *Charles* was all in one coffin. The obituary of Thomas Sheafe Coffin offers background on the vessel and the men who owned her:

Capt. Thomas Sheafe Coffin, who died at his residence at Little Harbor this week, was the son of Charles Coffin, a former ship owner in Portsmouth. The senior Coffin, in connection with the late Daniel Sheafe, and Horatio Coffin [the latter a brother of Thomas Sheafe Coffin] had built for them 40 years ago, by the late George Raynes, the ship Charles of 486 tons, which was commanded by Capt. Thomas Sheafe Coffin, and was always, while owned at this port, a trim, favored ship. Capt. Coffin retired from the sea many years ago. He was married to Miss Anne Cushing.[102]

Captain Coffin commanded the *Charles* for three years, sailing her around the legs of the cotton triangle. In September 1840, the owners advertised the cargo the *Charles* for sale: "Coarse LIVERPOOL SALT; bags of fine ditto."[103] The owners also advertised for a hundred tons of "pressed hay" as cargo for the *Charles*. "Pressed hay" was in a category with what moderns call baled hay, and it was often the only cargo available for ships clearing out of Portsmouth. It was such a popular export that the New Hampshire General Court in 1836 passed an act "to prevent fraud in the packing, pressing and vending of Hay." The act specified that "all pressed Hay which shall be offered for sale in this *State* or shall be shipped for exportation...shall be branded in some conspicuous place, upon each and every crate or bundle thereof, with the first letter of the christian name or names, and the whole surname of the person or persons, packing and screwing or otherwise pressing said hay, with the name of the town and State where said hay shall be pressed." The second paragraph of the act set up penalties for failure to obey the law.[104]

Again in 1841, the *Charles* brought into Portsmouth a cargo of salt. She went to Boston from her home port, looking for a cargo. She picked up a passenger, Moses Knight of Windham, New Hampshire, who succumbed to yellow fever while on the passage to New Orleans. The *Charles* came to Portsmouth in 1842, in ballast, from Hamburg, Germany.[105] Robert Henderson, Jr. relieved Captain Coffin and took the ship to New Orleans. Henderson was a Portsmouth shipmaster, whose father was a grocer on Congress Street. Under Henderson, the *Charles* made her first venture into the East Indian trade, clearing Boston on November 13, 1843, for Calcutta. She arrived there on May 7, 1844, taking more than half a year on the passage. The *Charles* sailed for Boston on July 28, and was in port on November 30, a run of 124 days.[106] She once again went into the cotton trade, going to Mobile and from there to Le Havre, then on to Cadiz for salt. She came into the Port of Portsmouth for the last time on August 18, 1845, 31 days from Cadiz. After her arrival, the *Charles* was sold to Boston interests, and Capt. Thomas A. Harris took her to Boston. On November 10 she sailed for the Sandwich Islands (Hawaii).[107] In April 1846, it was reported that, while on the trip, a passenger had died from consumption.[108]

Because of the existence of several other vessels named *Charles*, tracing the subsequent career of the Portsmouth-built *Charles* is almost impossible. However, it is known that she was wrecked in 1853 in the Straits of Malacca while en route from Singapore to Batavia. A Captain Andrew was master, and she was owned by Charles B. Fessenden. The vessel was insured for her estimated value, $13,000, and $15,000 on her cargo.[109]

Isaac Allerton

SPECIFICATIONS: 1838. George Raynes. Billet head, square stern. Burthen, 590 tons. Length, 137.2 feet; beam, 30.85 feet; depth, 15.425. Two decks. Original owner—Henry F. Jackson, of Plymouth, Massachusetts.

Not much is known about the career of the *Isaac Allerton*. She was owned away from Portsmouth, and her first master was Thomas Torrey. Raynes apparently had built the *Isaac Allerton* on speculation—perhaps in order to keep his work force together—and had to put her up for auction. She was sold quickly on the day advertised, January 16, 1839. Auctioneer Thomas A. Adams was Raynes's agent in the sale. Captain Torrey took the *Isaac Allerton* to New Orleans, the first passage in a long and successful career. Torrey commanded her in two different packet charters between Liverpool and New York. Later, in 1852, under Capt. Sherburne Sears, she again had a packet charter.[110]

It is unknown who the master was when she was wrecked:

> Ship Isaac Allerton, from New York for New Orleans, was driven ashore, night of 28th, upon Washerwoman Shoal, bilged, driven over, and sank in four fathoms water. But a part of the cargo has been saved. The goods in the lower hold have not been touched, and the loss to the underwriters must be very great. The ship is supposed to have had a cargo valued at $350,000. The sales of cargo will probably reach $75,000. The Isaac Allerton was built at Portsmouth, N.H., in 1838; 594 tons, and valued at $15,000; fully insured in New York. Her cargo was also insured in New York.[111]

And that, one would think, would have been the last heard from the good ship *Isaac Allerton*, but such is not the case. A year or two ago a group of pleasure divers, working around Washerwoman Shoal, located the wreck of the *Isaac Allerton*. One of the divers, Ray Maloney of Key West, Florida, came to Portsmouth to learn more about the wrecked ship. In correspondence with me, early in 1989, Maloney reported that the capstan had been recovered.

Ray Maloney of Key West, Florida, is shown holding a piece of gear taken from the recently discovered wreck of the Portsmouth-built ship Isaac Allerton. *She went aground on Washerwoman Shoal, above Key West, and Maloney and some fellow divers are now exploring the heavily silted hull. Courtesy of Ray Maloney.*

In his letter of February 4, Maloney said, in part: "We have recovered much of the ship's hardware and tackle and will send you photos when they are preserved. There is a great deal of the hull of the ship still preserved in the mud and we promised Ken [Palfrey of 495 Middle Road, Portsmouth] an underwater video as soon as the water was clear enough to film.... We still have a lot of diving to do."

In a letter on March 17, Maloney included a listing of more than 150 items recovered so far from the *Isaac Allerton*. These include bits and pieces of the ship's fittings and furniture. It was Maloney's hope his diving team would be able to uncover much of the ship's hull.

Mary Kingsland

SPECIFICATIONS: 1839. George Raynes. Female figurehead, square stern. Burthen, 796 tons. Length, 152.05 feet; beam, 33.9 feet; depth, 16.95 feet. Two decks. Original owners—Daniel and A. C. Kingsland, of New York.

The *Mary Kingsland* was by far the largest vessel yet ventured by George Raynes, and she was built to order for the prosperous New York firm of the Kingsland brothers. The *Journal* noted on October 19, 1839, prior to the launching, "she is to be inferior in workmanship to none of the splendid New York packets." Even in those days, in Portsmouth and other such towns, there was a sense of inferiority to urban centers like Boston, Philadelphia, and New York. It exists today in other ways, but when the *Mary Kingsland* was on the eve of departing Portsmouth, the following was published:

> This splendid packet, built by Mr. George Raynes, for Messrs. D. and A. Kingsland, of the city of New-York, is now nearly completed and will sail for New-York in a few days. She is commanded by Capt. Robert McCerran, and we understand is intended for Johnson & Lowden's line of New-York and New-Orleans packets. — No expense has been spared by the owners, who have had an immediate supervision of the building of this magnificent vessel.
>
> We spent an hour on board a day or two since, and sustained by the opinion of experienced nautical men, we take great pleasure in saying that we think she will compare in point of durability and elegance with any Packet ship belonging to the port of New-York. Her dimensions are 157-1/2 feet long, 34 wide, and 22 deep, and measures 850 tons. — Her cabins, nearly 60 feet in length, contain 17 State rooms. The finish of the cabins is the most splendid we ever saw — the celebrated barge of Cleopatra could not have gone far before it. They are six feet two inches high, clear of the beams; the doors of the state rooms are faced with rose and satin wood; the oval blinds in the doors and between the doors with satin wood, set in holly; the pillars between the doorways of satin and rose wood, resting on marble plinths, and surmounted with gilt capitals. Between the pillars and doors, the space is filled with zebra wood. The cornice is composed of imitation ebony, mahogany and gilt. — The whole presenting a most beautiful contrast of colours, and polished almost to mirror brightness. The curtains of the state-rooms are to be white satin.

Were the Fair of the New-York Institute now open, there is no article we should feel prouder of exhibiting from Portsmouth as a specimen of finished workmanship, than the Packet Mary Kingsland.[112]

The Kingslands put the *Mary Kingsland* into the cotton trade, and she spent the first five years of her life sailing around the triangle. She began her service under a charter in the Third Line. In 1840, she was chartered by the Orleans Line, under a Captain Weare, and in 1841 Captain Weare had her under charter to Fosdick & Charlock of Mobile. On October 29, 1844, the *Mary Kingsland* was destroyed by fire:

THE SHIP MARY KINGSLAND BURNT. — An alarm of fire was given yesterday morning at about 5 o'clock which proceeded, as was soon discovered, from the fine ship Mary Kingsland, Capt. Wear, of New York. She was lying at the foot of Esplanade street, taking in Cotton for Liverpool. She had already on board over 1700 bales when the fire broke out in the hold. Every exertion was made to extinguish the flames, but in vain. The vessel was immediately towed across the river and moored to the levee at McDonoughville. Thousands lined the fronts of the wharves on this side of the river and the levee on the other side watching the slow destruction of the noble ship and her rich freight.

Several of the city fire engineers were pumping water

into the ship for several hours, but owing to the buoyant nature of her cargo, it was impossible to submerge the ship.

The Mary Kingsland was of 797 tons burthen, custom house measurement and belonged three-fourths to the Messrs. Kingsland, of New York, and the remaining fourth to Captain Wear, who purchased his interest since she has been lying at our wharves. The New York owners are supposed to be insured, but Capt. Wear's interest is entirely unprotected.

Of the cargo, about 700 bales of cotton are supposed to be insured in Liverpool, on open policies. The balance is not covered. The rigging and cabin furniture of the ship were saved, and some hopes were entertained that when the vessel should sink, two tiers of cotton might be saved in a damaged state. But upon the whole, the loss can hardly fall short of $150,000. — *N. O. Pic., Oct. 20th.*

The Mary Kingsland was built at the yard of Mr. George Raynes, in Portsmouth, and was a first rate ship. She was insured at New York, on vessel and freight, for $50,000.[113]

Damaged as badly as the *Mary Kingsland* was, it should be safely assumed that her course had been run. However, that wasn't true. A letter to the editor of the *Portsmouth Chronicle*, January 31, 1878, told what happened to her after the fire and the role she played in the Civil War. The writer strongly contended that the *Mary Kingsland* had been an unlucky ship:

AN UNLUCKY SHIP.

Mr. Editor: A recent notice in your paper of the death of the ex-rebel Commodore Hollins, recalls to mind the career and end of one of the "unlucky ships" built on the Piscataqua — the Mary Kingsland. This ship was built by the late George Raynes, in 1839; she was of a fine model, and registered about 800 tons — a large ship for those days. After she was launched, her loading up and fitting out were carried on together, and one day a bale of pressed hay fell out of the slings when high in air, and struck a man named Pike, who was at work on the main-hatch coamings. The man was taken to Mr. Raynes' house and everything possible done for him, but he soon died; a post mortem examination was held, and the physician who made it came near losing his life from blood-poisoning, having been infected through an abrasion of the skin on his hand. It was quite a job to get a crew for the ship when she was ready for sea, the local mariners declining to go in her, shaking their heads and asserting that she would always be an "unlucky ship," having caused

a man's death before she ever dipped her keel in blue water.
But she went to sea, took her cargo of pressed hay, apples and
potatoes to a southern port, and went into the cotton trade. Ill
luck followed her, for after making many successful trips she at
last took fire while lying, cotton-loaded, at New Orleans, and
was burned to the water's edge; the hulk was sold, fitted with
powerful engines and made into a tow-boat, and ran for years
between the Gulf and New Orleans. On the breaking out of the
rebellion she was seized by the rebels, and Hollins (who had
deserted from the Union navy to join the confederacy) altered
her machinery to suit her new career, fitted her with a powerful
ram, and built a convex iron shell all over her, so that she
looked not unlike a mammoth turtle; Hollins called her the
Manassas, but her popular name was "Hollins' turtle." It was
the old Mary Kingsland, transferred into this wonderful "turtle," that caused such a panic among the Union men-of-war
blockading the Passes of the Mississippi early in the war, when
they slipped their cables and put to sea like a flock of gulls on
her appearance — but iron-clad warfare was then a new thing.
This one exploit was about all the famous ram ever accomplished; she never managed to get up another scare, and finally
came to grief and total destruction when Farragut's fleet fought
its way past the forts of New Orleans.

In Flag-Officer Farragut's report to the Secretary of the
Navy of the fight with the forts and the rebel fleet, on the night
of March 23–24, 1862, he tells how his ship, the Hartford, was
crowded ashore by attempting to avoid a fire-raft that was
pushed by the Manassas, and which the ram did succeed in
forcing against the Hartford, setting her "on fire half-way up to
her tops." After the Union fleet had passed the forts and
destroyed eleven of the rebel vessels, the Manassas still kept
up the fight, and Farragut ordered the Mississippi, one of the
big old side-wheelers, to run her down. The Mississippi went at
her at full speed, but when within fifty yards of her the ram
dodged and ran ashore; but though she could escape the huge
steamer she could not dodge her missiles, and two broadsides
of nine-inch solid shot at close range riddled her like a sieve.
She surrendered, and a boat's crew and engineer went on
board her; but the prize crew was recalled, the prize set on fire,
given another broadside and sent down river, a wreck. When
she got down abreast of Commander Porter's mortar boats she
was shot at again by two steamers and some of the mortar vessels; but Porter soon found she was on fire and sinking, "her

pipes twisted and riddled with shot, and her hull well cut up." Porter "tried to save her as a curiosity, by getting a hawser around her and securing her to the bank, but just after doing so she faintly exploded. Her only gun went off, and emitting flames through her bow port, like some huge animal, she gave a plunge and disappeared under the water." And thus the formidable ram Manassas, once the peaceful merchant ship Mary Kingsland, finished her career.

TOPMAUL.

Athens

SPECIFICATIONS: 1839. George Raynes. Billet head, square stern. Burthen, 574 tons. Length, 136.4 feet; beam, 30.4 feet; depth, 15.2 feet. Two decks. Original owners—Edward F. Sise, Mark W. Peirce, J. D. Simes, and Charles H. Chase, all of Portsmouth; Joshua W. Peirce, of Greenland. The same owners were listed in the 1860 City Directory.

George Raynes produced many bigger and faster ships than the *Athens*, but few of them, if any, gave their owners better service. The *Journal* was brief but laudatory at the time of her launching on September 23: "A fine ship of about 600 tons was launched Wednesday from the yard of George Raynes. She is owned by Edward F. Sise, J. D. Simes, the master, Captain John Chase and others. She is intended for the freighting business for which trade she is equal in all respects to any ship heretofore built at the yard."

Unlike many Port of Portsmouth–built ships, the *Athens* was owned by Portsmouth businessmen for a quarter century. John Chase, her first master, stayed in command for years. She was another excellent example of a vessel prospering in the triangular cotton trade. Chase took her to New Orleans on December 13, 1839, a Friday; but, in the case of the *Athens*, that was far from an ill omen. Occasionally, after crossing to Europe, the *Athens* came into Portsmouth. On one entrance, Sise advertised her as having 2,000 hogsheads of salt on board, and that she also brought in 50 tons of cannel coal. (Cannel coal is a bituminous coal, high in gas content but low in heat.)

Chase left the *Athens* in 1851, being succeeded by a man named Chick, possibly James H. Chick, who commanded the *Epaminondas* in 1845. But that made no difference in the quietly efficient way the *Athens* went about her business. Apparently she was a "lucky ship," seldom suffering even the petty problems, like going aground, that plagued her fellows. The *Athens* did get caught in a hurricane in 1848,

losing her sails while heading to Boston from New Orleans.[114] In 1856, she carried 2,015 bales of cotton, which weighed 1,032,204 pounds, from Mobile to Le Havre. The cotton, at 516 tons, almost equaled the *Athens'* displacement of 574 tons. The cargo was valued at $90,527.

Even the outbreak of the Civil War didn't disturb her routine at first. She was at Falmouth, England, on August 28, 1861, having come from the East Indies, via the Cape of Good Hope, St. Helena and Ascension islands.[115] In 1863, she had to go into Fayal, leaking, and had to discharge her cargo while in quarantine.[116] An item in the *Portsmouth Chronicle* on August 1, 1863, gave her captain's name as Shields and said that repairs had been started. The next year, she suffered the fate of so many American merchantmen: she was sold to British interests, driven from American ownership by Confederate raiders. The *Athens* fetched £2,100 when auctioned in London.[117] She had served the Portsmouth syndicate well for 25 years. With the change in ownership, the *Athens* disappeared from Port of Portsmouth shipping news. However, 21 years later, the *Athens* was again a Portsmouth news item:

> There are several good marine paintings to be seen at the office of E. F. Sise & Co., of famous Portsmouth ships of former times. Among them is a picture of the good and successful little ship Athens, built by George Raynes for E. F. Sise and brothers. She at length went under the English flag at Hull, and at last accounts had been refitted with wire rigging and was actively employed.[118]

Robert Parker

SPECIFICATIONS: 1839. Fernald & Raynes. Kittery. Male bust figurehead, square stern. Burthen, 599 tons. Length, 139.65 feet; beam, 30.65 feet; depth, 15.325 feet. Two decks. Original owners— William and William A. Rice.

The *Robert Parker* was the second ship Frederick W. Fernald and Charles Raynes built in collaboration. It was launched on Tuesday morning, September 3. Capt. William L. Dwight was master when she sailed on November 26 for New Orleans. On her passage, she dropped into Charleston to check on the availability of cargo, and found one. From Charleston, the *Robert Parker* went to Le Havre. Dwight continued in command of the *Robert Parker* until 1845, when he was relieved by Capt. Isaac D. Parsons, a Portsmouth shipmaster living on Deer Street. While under Parsons, the ship was chartered by the Commercial Line in 1845. Parsons relinquished the *Robert Parker* to Capt. Thomas N. Weeks, and he commanded her for several years.

Captain Parsons resumed command of the *Robert Parker* in 1850, sailing from Philadelphia for St. John, New Brunswick, on July 15, 1850. She loaded lumber there for Liverpool. When the *Robert Parker* arrived at Bristol, England, on September 21, Captain Parsons had been dead 24 days. The captain had been active in the mercantile world of Portsmouth for many years. His commands dated back to the 1820s. The largest vessel he commanded was the *Kate Hunter*.

In 1852, Capt. James P. Trefethen of Portsmouth became master, and while he had the command he indulged in the pursuit of a monstrous fish. The story was retold in the *Journal* on October 15, 1880:

> The following item of what was news a great many years ago, is copied from a discolored slip of paper cut from the Mobile (Ala.) *Register* of August, 1854: "To thousands of our citizens, the enormous size and occasionally large number of 'Devil Fish' seen at or about the mouth of our bay, are quite familiar, and one of the largest became yesterday the prey of an indomitable sea-hunter, Captain Trefethen, of the ship Robert Parker, of Portsmouth, N. H. While on board or alongside the Col. Clay, near the fleet, the captain espied some three or four of these monsters of the deep, and hastening to get his harpoon, proceeded in chase of the largest. With the practiced aim of a whaler, he drove the harpoon through him, and the wounded leviathan leaped high in the air before he darted off

with the captain and his clinker-built gig — rushing through the water at an awful speed. After a chase of some ten miles the harpoon drew out, but the wounded brute marked his place in the water by his blood, and even returned upon his trail; but the captain, having spliced his weapon, again drove it securely into the huge beast, who, far from being exhausted, carried his boat away again with even accelerated speed. After a long and exciting chase the captain returned with his prize, which is reported to measure sixteen feet from fin to fin — across — and nearly forty feet in length."

By 1852 Capt. Ebenezer Gilman Adams was master of the *Robert Parker*. Captain Adams had just previously commanded the *John Cumming*. Adams had the *Robert Parker* at Mobile and narrowly escaped disaster on the last of August:

The Mobile Register of the 2d just says: "In the heavy gale of Saturday night the ship Robert Parker lost two anchors and drifted foul of the ship Screamer, carrying away her jibboom, fore topgallant mast, starboard bulwarks, &c, and both ships were seriously injured. So heavy proved the gale outside on the night of Thursday, that the sea was breaking in ten fathoms water, and it is the opinion of the pilots and others best experienced in such matters, that from Key West all along the Gulf Coast we shall hear of most frightful disasters. The damage to the Robert Parker and Screamer is estimated at $12,000.[119]

After getting the damage repaired, Captain Adams found a full cargo of cotton and left Mobile in early April for Le Havre. It was an ill-fated passage. On April 9, 1857, the *Journal* reported:

SHIP ROBERT PARKER BURNT AT SEA. — Capt. Crocker, of ship Swordfish at New-York, reports having seen at sea, in lat. 33, lon, 71, a cotton laden ship on fire, masts gone, and burnt to the depth of one tier of cotton below the deck. She is supposed to have been the Robert Parker, of this city, commanded by Capt. Gilman Adams, which left Mobile April 3d for Havre. No news is received of the crew who had abandoned her before she was discovered by Capt. Crocker. The Robert Parker was built in Portsmouth, in 1839, by Messrs. Raynes & Fernald, and registered 600 tons.

Nearly a month later, the city of Portsmouth learned the story of the loss of the *Robert Parker*:

BURNING OF THE ROBERT PARKER

SAFETY OF CAPT. E. G. ADAMS AND CREW. — By the last arrival from England, letters have been received from Capt. Eben. G. Adams, of ship Robert Parker, which vessel was struck at sea by lightning and burnt in a few hours. The crew were all taken on board the English ship Bannockburn, and arrived at Liverpool on the 20th of May, all well.

We have seen a letter from Capt. Adams, giving an account of the disaster.

The ship Robert Parker sailed from Mobile on the 8th of April. On the 22d, in lat. 33 44, lon. 71 07 west, wind blowing hard S. W. with hard squalls, about 4 o'clock in the morning, when the men were on yard furling main top-sail, the main top mast was struck by lightning, knocking 2d Mate off top-sail yard into the top. The lightning, following the top-sail sheets down, struck the bit, splitting it down to the deck. Six or eight deck planks were broke and ripped up, the lightning setting fire to the cotton between decks. In a few moments smoke was discovered coming up the fore scuttle, and cabin soon filled with smoke and gas. As soon as it was discovered that the ship was on fire, everything that could be done to smother it was done; caulked up every place that smoke was seen coming up, filled the decks with water. — At 7 A. M. found the decks very hot, the pitch boiling out of seams, and a number of planks rising up. Found it impossible to save the ship. Set the hands to clear the long boat, and hoist it out with a small quantity of water and provisions. At 10 A. M. the fire had burnt through outside in the waist. About this time a ship was discovered to the westward; made a signal. The ship bore up and run down, and hove to close to the R. Parker. It proved to be the British ship Bannockburn, Capt. Bruce, of Greenock, from New Orleans, bound to Liverpool, who kindly lay by until we could save a small quantity of provisions and part of a cask of water. Sent the long boat with a part of the crew, clothes, stores, &c. on board the Bannockburn. The long boat returned as soon as possible, and secured a few barrels of bread and what stores could be had. All hands left the R. Parker and went on board the Bannockburn. — At this time the fire had burnt through both sides of the ship and decks, from main to fore-mast. In 30 minutes after the last boat left, all three masts went over the side.[120]

Franconia

SPECIFICATIONS: 1839. Samuel Badger. Kittery. Billet head, square stern. Burthen, 560 tons. Length, 137 feet; beam, 29.9 feet; depth, 14.95 feet. Two decks. Original owners—William Jones, William P. Jones, Richard Jenness, and J. D. Simes, all of Portsmouth; John S. Jenness, of Boston.

The *Franconia* was the largest ship yet built by Samuel Badger, a cautious, meticulous man who kept close account of all that was spent on the ships he built. Because of Badger's record-keeping, precise details on the cost of the *Franconia* are available. The original records are in the Portsmouth Athenaeum, along with those for some other ships. The *Franconia* is a study in the economic aspects of shipbuilding. Before listing the items from Badger's accounts, it should be emphasized that the figures can't be translated into the terms of today's inflated prices. Perhaps a multiplicand of ten, or even larger, might be appropriate.

The total cost of building the *Franconia* was $26,168.49. Badger received from the purchasers $25,500, suffering a loss of $668.49. The items of expense he listed are: Gerrish & Son, $1,000 for copper; Goodwin & Coues, copper, $1,429.35; William Martin, masts, $700; Thomas Martin, joiner work, $1,066.30; John P. Lyman, iron, $876.38; John Knowlton, iron work, $533.97; Brown and Joy, cabinet work, $243.45; John Smith, painting, $769.96; Hosea Ilsley, gold leaf, $24.12; Laban S. Beecher, carving, $136.50; John D. Simes, bell, &c., $36.70; Andrew W. Bell, Jr., $40; I. D. Goodrich, trucking, 73 cents; Daniel D. & Abraham Q. Wendell, $18.75; 400 tons, white oak timber, $4,000; 20,688 feet of white oak plank, $1,597.40; white oak knees, $55.38; 26,331 feet of deck plank, $680.09; Robert Rice, 10 hogsheads of salt, $27.50; 3,771-1/4 days of labor, $5,174.66; 322 days of board for blacksmith, $120.75; George Raynes's bill, $15.06; 13 tons, 36-1/4 feet, hard pine timber, $123.80; James Raitt, turning knee shapes, $100; 1,111 feet, deck plank, $120.75; interest (supposed), $600; H. Rollins, wharfing bill, $67.60; James Raitt, iron and coal, $606.56; James Raitt, coal, $72. These items total $20,633.28 and are dated as of the end of December, so other bills came in later that aren't in the journal. It was also Badger's custom to charge $2 a day for his own work as master carpenter.

Even the most cursory of studies emphasizes the importance of shipbuilding in the Port of Portsmouth in the first six decades of the nineteenth century. All of the persons and firms listed in Badger's journal were people who were themselves employers, and the labor items represent income for many families on both sides of the Piscataqua

River. It's fair to speculate that vessels of a similar size cost about the same in any of the three major yards, and the flow of money, especially from the outside, led to a general prosperity in the Port of Portsmouth. In other words, when the wood chips were flying in the shipyards the economic tide was full spate; when business was down, times were grim for builders, suppliers, merchants, and the labor force.

As for the *Franconia*, she sailed to Savannah on February 21, 1840, under Thomas Jones, who lived on Water (Marcy) Street at the Hancock Street corner. The records indicate Captain Jones commanded the *Franconia* all the time she was owned in Portsmouth. Jones brought her home in September 1841, with 1,001 moys of salt for John D. Simes. (A moy was a variable measure used in the salt trade.)

After unloading the salt, the *Franconia* went to New Orleans, returning in December with cotton for the mills on the upper Piscataqua. Two years later, William Jones & Son advertised 2,000 hogsheads of Liverpool salt, plus 1,000 bags "of stone salt of a new and improved brand."[121]

In 1846 the *Franconia* was sold in Baltimore. She had come into Portsmouth in September 1845, reported for orders, and then sailed to Baltimore with her cargo of Liverpool salt. The *Liverpool Telegraph* noted that she cleared for Liverpool on July 3. Three years later, she was reported as having arrived in Mobile from Newport, Wales, with railroad iron for the Charleston & Chattanooga Railroad. The iron was landed at Mobile and then shipped to Montgomery, from whence it was distributed. Because of the change in ownership, her subsequent career is obscure.

A painting showing the harbor at Mobile, Alabama, in 1842. The forest of masts emphasizes the importance of Mobile in the triangular cotton trade, in which so many Port of Portsmouth vessels were engaged before the Civil War. Courtesy of the Library of Congress.

III The 1840s

THE SHIPBUILDING BOOM OF THE 1830s continued unabated in the 1840s, as shipyards all along the East Coast tried to keep up with the insatiable demand for bigger and faster square-riggers. The three major Port of Portsmouth shipyards even got into the clipper frenzy, but that came mostly in the next decade. George Raynes is generally considered the grand master of Piscataqua shipbuilders, and he did produce the most vessels. For example, the Raynes yard, between 1840 and 1860, "produced thirty-two three-masted ships, ranging from 496 tons (the GLENDOVEER) to 1727 tons (the WEBSTER).[1] The figure includes ten clippers that were described in *Clippers of the Port of Portsmouth* (Ray Brighton, 1985). Close behind George Raynes was Frederick W. Fernald, who was entrenched on Badger's Island. As indicated earlier, Fernald at first worked alone, then became a partner with Charles Raynes, a brother to George. That partnership broke up in 1844, and Fernald was associated for the rest of his life with William Pettigrew. In Kittery Foreside, Samuel Badger's yard was ever busy, although Badger always seemed to be trailing behind the others in the constant clamor for speed and size.

In the first year of the 1840s, the Port of Portsmouth yards built 4 three-masted square-riggers, and by the close of the decade, 30 more had been added to the American merchant fleet. However, during the decade a highly significant change took place: ships were being built on the Piscataqua in large part for owners in Boston and New York. For generations, Port of Portsmouth builders catered to local trade, so to speak, and some ships were still being built for enterprising Portsmouth merchants, but the demand from the outside was ever increasing. One of the first in the new decade was the ship *Goodwin*, and her ownership was in the local tradition.

Goodwin

SPECIFICATIONS: 1840. Raynes & Fernald. Billet head, square stern. Burthen, 595 tons. Length, 140.6 feet; beam, 30.4 feet; depth, 15.2 feet. Two decks. Original owners—Ichabod Goodwin, Samuel E. Coues, William A. Rice, John Davis, all of Portsmouth; and G. B. Cumming, of Savannah.

The *Portsmouth Journal* reported on September 12 that the *Goodwin* would be launched that day at 1:00 P.M. The next week it said:

> On Saturday last, a fine ship, of about 600 tons — was launched from the Ship Yard of Messrs. Raynes & Fernald. Great credit is due to the builders for their untiring attention in completing and preparing this noble craft for her destined element, into which she glided in a style rarely equalled if ever surpassed. It is said great pains have been bestowed in the selection of her materials and workmanship, and that her model combines qualities seldom attained in the art of ship-building, — those of fast sailing, great burthen, with a light draft of water. She is owned by G. B. Cumming, Goodwin & Coues, and Wm A. Rice, and is intended for the freighting business.—*Gaz.*[2]

It's a little bit surprising that the *Goodwin*'s figurehead was a billet rather than a bust of the man for whom she was named, Ichabod Goodwin. But Goodwin, like several successful Portsmouth men, was a native of the Berwicks and, while prospering in Portsmouth, might have been a bit diffident about such a move. After all, he hadn't yet become governor and wouldn't for another two decades.

The *Goodwin* was taken to sea by Capt. John S. Davis, who made his home of South Street in Portsmouth. He held the command for seven years. Early in the *Goodwin*'s career, 1841, Captain Davis was presented with a silver pitcher that was inscribed: "A small token of friendship, presented to Capt. JOHN DAVIS, by the Rt. Rev. JOHN ENGLAND, Bishop of Charleston, for kind and assiduous attention to himself and his companions during a protracted voyage from Liverpool in the Ship Goodwin." The dateline was Philadelphia, Nov. 12, 1841. It was several years before the existence of that tribute became known in Portsmouth, and then only because of another gracious act at a later date. With Bishop England on that arduous passage were a priest, a lady superior, and nine Sisters of Charity. The whole was seriously ill while at sea, and Captain Davis devoted great care to them. Bishop England died less than a year later.[3]

The *Goodwin* came into the Port of Portsmouth on September 12, 1843, with salt for Goodwin & Coues. Davis reported that he had spoken the Portsmouth-built *Harriet & Jessie* on August 22. Passengers on the *Goodwin* were the Rev. J. Blanchard of Cincinnati; A. A. Phelps of Boston; J. D. Trevor, Philadelphia; Capt. William Glidden and family of Newcastle, Maine.[4] In March 1846, the *Goodwin* sailed from Liverpool for Boston; the *Journal*, on January 2, 1847, happened on that passage:

GRATITUDE HANDSOMELY EXPRESSED.

Capt. John Davis, in the ship Goodwin of Portsmouth, on the first of April 1846, in lat. 43 26, lon. 57, fell in with a boat belonging to brig Juno, of and from Greenock, for St. Johns, N. B. wrecked among the ice March 8, lat. 45 30, lon. 47 30, and took from her Capt. John Gibbs, master, Adam Curran, mate, Peter Brown, 2d mate, Alexander Burke and John Graffey, seamen; the survivors of the Juno's crew of 12 persons. The others perished in the boat. Those taken on board the Goodwin were frozen, and in an exhausted state, having been 24 days exposed in a small boat, and for a length of time without water, and with but a small supply of provisions. John Graffey died in an hour after he was taken on board the ship. The Goodwin arrived in Boston on the 8th of April, and although but one of the individuals had sufficient strength to get on board the ship without aid, yet they all survived, with the above exception. — Mrs. Davis was on board the ship at the time.

After a correspondence of inquiry of the owners of the Goodwin of where Capt. Davis might be found, Messrs. J. Hunter & Co. of Greenock, have forwarded to the care of I. Goodwin, Esq. an elegant silver Salver, which has been presented to the lady of Capt. Davis, (he being now absent,) bearing a grateful inscription, surrounded by a handsomely engraved view of a wreck with English colors, and the American ship approaching to her aid — a sketch of Neptune, and other appropriate devices. The following is a copy of the inscription:

"Presented by JAMES HUNTER & Co. of Greenock, owners of the Brig Juno, wrecked in the ice in the spring of 1846, to Capt. JOHN DAVIS, of the American ship Goodwin, and LADY, as a mark of esteem for their kindness to Capt.

Gibbs and the survivors of the crew of the Juno, after being picked up at sea."

This elegant piece of plate, about a twelfth of an inch thick, is in the form of a dish or waiter, 12 inches wide, and 15 inches long, slightly elevated on pedals.

The *Journal*'s reporter then learned about the tribute that had been paid Captain Davis by Bishop England, and he quoted a few words from the note that had accompanied the salver from Hunter & Co.: "The value of the Salver is nothing — but it will serve as a token of esteem for the humanity displayed on that occasion.[5]

Captain Davis, of course, had good reason for being absent from home when the salver arrived: he had cleared Boston for Calcutta on May 13, 1846.[6] The *Goodwin* was at Madras by September 20, and arrived at Calcutta on October 17.[7] She was back in Boston on June 8, 1847, and cleared for Bombay a few weeks later under a Captain Kennard, either James or Edward. When the *Goodwin* returned to Boston, she went back into the cotton trade, and sailed from Liverpool for Boston on June 27, 1849, arriving on August 10. She landed 227 steerage passengers, having lost 6 others to cholera. In February 1851, the *Goodwin* was at Singapore, loading for London, under Capt. N. J. Weeks. Previously, the *Goodwin* had sailed from San Francisco to Liverpool in 51 days, "having sailed 8884 miles in that time—averaging 7-1/4 miles per hour for the entire passage."[8]

She headed for Calcutta from London on March 29, 1854, and later than year was abandoned near the Kedgeree, a total loss.[9]

Albania

SPECIFICATIONS: 1840. Samuel Badger. Billet head, square stern. Burthen, 548 tons. Length, 135.3 feet; beam, 29.8 feet; depth, 14.9 feet. Two decks. Original owners—Samuel Sheafe and Horatio Coffin, of Portsmouth.

The *Albania* was another Badger-built ship for which there's documentation as to her construction costs. Materials and labor came to $23,620.35. Most of the items were similar to those cited for the *Franconia*. However, Badger personally fared a little better with the *Albania*. He sold her to Sheafe and Coffin for $24,500, giving him a profit of $879.65, plus "an error" of $54.50, for a total of $934.15. The *Albania* was launched on September 10, "and is intended for freighting." Capt. Ambrose Crowell took the ship to New Orleans, a passage of 25 days.[10]

Crowell was master for several years, working the cotton triangle. In 1844, the *Albania* came into Portsmouth from Liverpool with salt for Sheafe & Coffin. Shortly after her arrival, the owners advertised her cargo: 2,500 hogsheads of Liverpool salt and 600 bags of fine salt, "factory filled in Worthington's brand."[11] In October she loaded for a passage to New Orleans. A longshoreman, John Stockman, 40, living on Islington Street, "was struck by a barrel of potatoes being hoisted up the ship's side, and he was knocked down the hatchway, a distance of 10 or 12 feet, which caused his death."[12] The *Albania* arrived in New Orleans with her cargo intact on November 10.

At one point, the *Albania*, under Crowell, had a charter in the Crescent City Line, a packet service to new Orleans. Exactly when she was sold and to whom isn't clear. A news item said that the *Albania*, "late of this port," cleared at Boston for New Orleans on April 7, 1853. Edwin F. Littlefield was master.[13] And there are indications that she was in the East Indian trade. But what finally happened to her has yet to be learned.

John Taylor

SPECIFICATIONS: 1840. George Raynes. Male bust figurehead, square stern. burthen, 747 tons. Length, 154.4 feet; beam, 32.45 feet; depth, 16.225 feet. Two decks. Original owners—Taylor & Merrill, John Johnson, Andrew Foster, and John Mallett, all of New York.

It isn't clear whom the *John Taylor* honored; perhaps it was some relative of Robert L. Taylor of Taylor & Merrill. The *John Taylor* was launched August 31. "She is the largest merchant ship ever built at this port, being of 850 tons. She is owned by Messrs. Taylor & Merrill of New York, and is to be commanded by Capt. John Mallett, and is intended for the freighting business. For beauty and strength, competent judges say she will compare with any other ship."[14]

The reader will notice the discrepancy between the tonnage taken from the Customs Records and the 850 tons published by the *Journal*. The standards of measurement often varied, and so the displacement figures given in the Customs Records will be used as the official ones.

The *John Taylor* cleared out of Portsmouth on November 17, 1840, "new, of and for New York," under John Mallett. When next mentioned in the *Journal*, on November 20, 1841, she was in bad trouble:

LOSS OF THE SHIP JOHN TAYLOR. — Advices from Havana to the 30th ult., mention the shipwreck of the ship John Taylor, of New York. — This ship left Liverpool on the 5th of September, with a cargo of salt, and some valuable goods, and one hundred and seventy-five steerage passengers, and several cabin passengers. In a violent gale on the night of the 18th of October, after losing her sails and masts, she was driven ashore on the south coast of Cuba, and Punta del Holandes, between Cape Corientes and Cape Antonio. One of the passengers only was lost — a steerage passenger, a native of Sheffield. At the last accounts, the crew were all ashore. But the country had been recently visited by dreadful inundations, which had swept away the houses, cattle, provisions, &c., and the people were suffering from want. It was therefore feared that these shipwrecked persons among whom were men, women and children, would be subjected to much distress. The roads, too, were almost impassable, and the communication between the south coast and Havana was uncertain and unsafe. Consul Trist has addressed a circular to the British and American citizens at Havana, appealing to their humanity for means to render assistance to these unfortunate people. He says:

"The steerage passengers, doubtless, are British emigrants to the United States; countrymen, therefore, both of Britons and American, and having claims both upon their brethren by the land of their birth, and their brethren by the land of their adoption. — They are, in all probability, destitute of every thing; of the means of present subsistence, and of getting away from the spot on which they have been cast. — The crew will come under my charge; and the cabin passengers are perhaps able to command means so soon as they shall reach this place. But it is otherwise with the steerage passengers: they, or the far greater part of them, cannot but be absolutely dependent upon charity."

The ship and cargo were valued at $70,000, and insured in New-York. —*Mer. Jour.*

Kalamazoo

SPECIFICATIONS: 1840. George Raynes. Indian figurehead, square stern. Burthen, 798 tons. Length, 152.4 feet; beam, 33.85 feet; depth, 16.925 feet. Two decks. Original owners—the Kingslands.

The *Portsmouth Journal* described the *Kalamazoo*, in its brief item on the launching, as being over 800 tons. That was on September 26, 1840. It also said that it was the "size and model of the *Mary Kingsland*."[15] When she sailed, under Robert McCerran, on November 10, she was rated at 799 tons and headed for New Orleans. Before the *Kalamazoo* reached New Orleans, she had been spoken of the Hole in the Wall (Abaco Island), with her main mast badly sprung.

The *Kalamazoo* served her time in the cotton trade, but in 1852 she was "sold foreign." Bought for $26,550 by Schmidt and Balchen of New York, she was sent to Savannah to load for Liverpool.[16] The *Liverpool Telegraph* had reported her arrival there in 1850, and as being in the Waterloo Dock.

The *Kalamazoo* was sold to British investors in 1864, in the midst of the Confederate raider panic, and renamed the *Gorilla*. She was burned into a hulk in 1883.[17]

Glendoveer

SPECIFICATIONS: 1841. George Raynes. Billet head, square stern. Burthen, 495 tons. Length, 130.8 feet; beam, 31 feet; depth, 15.5 feet. Two decks. Original owners—Ichabod Goodwin and Samuel Coues.

The launching of the *Glendoveer* on March 23, 1841, was hailed by the *Journal* as a triumph for temperance, a cause ardently supported by the paper's editor, Charles W. Brewster, also known as "The Rambler" for his historical essays:

> COLD WATER LAUNCH. — A splendid Ship of about 500 tons, belonging to Ichabod Goodwin and Samuel E. Coues, was launched from the Yard of George Raynes on Tuesday last. This fine Ship is the first that has broken an iceberg, long resting in this vicinity, which has been the destruction on the ocean of hundreds of vessels, thousands of lives, and millions of property. — There were no appendages of ardent spirits at the launching, in any shape. We are confident she will be a temperance ship so long as she remains in the hands of her present owners, — a recommendation of great weight in any port.[18]

The source of the name for the *Glendoveer* isn't clear, and the newspapers varied in their spelling of it. It might be a corruption of the name of Owen Glendower, the great Welsh hero. The *Glendoveer*, after her sober launching, sailed on April 14 under William H. Parsons, another of Portsmouth's distinguished shipmasters.[19] She head-

ed for New Orleans, but found a cargo at Apalachicola, and went to
Liverpool. She recrossed the Atlantic to New York, probably with
immigrants, and then went down to New Orleans—the triangle trade.
And such was the nature of her work for the next five years, until it
was reported:

LOSS OF THE GLENDOVEER.

PORT MADOC, July 2nd. — We were visited yesterday
morning with one of the most violent gales from the S. W. that
has been experienced in this neighborhood for a long time.
Early in the morning it was almost calm, but about eight
o'clock it began to rain, and the wind freshened until about
nine, when it became a complete gale. Much excitement and
anxiety were manifested at the Port in consequence of the
large American ship *Glendoveer*, Capt. Parson, which was
advertised to leave this place for New-York, on the 20th inst.
being at anchor outside. We are sorry to say that this fine vessel is ashore dismasted, and not likely ever to be fit for repair.
It appears that when the gale increased, the ship drifted, and
about ten o'c. A. M. her masts were cut away, in the hope that
she could be saved. This had not the desired effect; and the
ship came further in shore as the tide advanced, continually
thumping at each rise of the waves. She has docked herself, on
her beam-ends, high on the beach, under Morfa-bychan. The
crew, consisting of fifteen persons, were fortunately landed in
safety in the pilot-boat.

The *Glendoveer* is a fine ship, of 518 tons, (English
admeasurement) and is four years old. She belongs to
Portsmouth, New-Hampshire, U. S. and lately arrived at Liverpool from Savannah with a cargo of cotton.

Most of the vessel's spars, &c. have been saved, but the
vessel is likely to become a total wreck.[20]

That wreck at Portmadoc, Wales, should have been the end of
the *Glendoveer*'s story, but it wasn't. Whatever was left of her was sold
by the underwriters to a German firm, which repaired her and sent
her back to sea as the *Consul*. Then, in a news item datelined Bremen, Germany, December 15, 1846, it was said: "The Consul, Rade, of
and for Bremen, from Trinidad de Cuba, was stranded and totally
wrecked on the Jordinillos, about three days after leaving port. Part of
the cargo has been saved."[21]

Venice

SPECIFICATIONS: 1841. George Raynes. Billet head, square stern. Burthen, 616 tons. Length, 140.5 feet; beam, 31 feet; depth, 15.5 feet. Two decks. Original owners—Mark W. Peirce, Edward F. Sise, John D. Simes, and Jacob W. Thompson.

Throughout the year 1841, the Raynes shipyard was in a well-organized confusion. Having launched the *Glendoveer* in March, the yard was busy constructing not only the *Venice* but also finishing a bark, the *Olafwyk*, 313 tons, for a Massachusetts firm. Then, on September 6, the *Venice* was launched.[22] With the *Venice* in the water, the bridge over to Noble's Island was opened up, and a fairly large square-rigger, the *John Jay*, was brought in. Special ways had been erected, and the *John Jay* underwent extensive repairs. Although not built in the Port of Portsmouth, the *John Jay* was owned by local businessmen. Years later, in a reminiscent account, it was said, "when she was again put in the water, she was probably as sound and strong as when first launched."[23] That was written nearly 40 years after the overhaul. The *John Jay* was then at Port Townsend, Washington Territory, awaiting orders.

The *Venice* sailed for New Orleans on November 13 under Capt. Jacob W. Thompson, already a veteran mariner at the age of 39. Thompson took the *Venice* into Mobile on his way, and there found her first cargo of cotton, which was taken to Le Havre. Early in August 1842, the *Venice* completed her first triangle, arriving in Portsmouth with 2,5000 hogsheads of salt for Edward F. Sise. The *Venice* was back in Portsmouth the next year, after a stop in Boston to put off passengers. On October 21, 1843, Sise was again advertising the arrival of salt. When she sailed again, Charles H. Salter was her master. Salter would later gain renown as the captain of the clipper *Typhoon*, which went from the Port of Portsmouth to England in 13 days in 1851.[24] The change in command didn't change the service the *Venice* was in. On January 11, 1847, she met trouble:

Ship Venice, Salter, arr. at Boston 22d inst. from Liverpool 11th January with 170 passengers. She had a very rough passage. While lying to in a severe gale under a close reefed maintopsail and mizen staysail, had her topsail blown away, which caused her to fall off, when a tremendous sea broke over the quarter, which swept away a boat, broke down the top of the house aft, filled the cabin with water, and washed away the wheel house and two men in it, who perished. The same sea broke the Captain's chronometer, all the compasses, and the main rail aft. When the sea entered the cabin it washed a baby out of its mother's arms into one of the bed cabins, where it was nearly drowned before it could be rescued.[25]

Six months later, the *Venice* took a detachment of 208 recruits for the 2nd Infantry Regiment to Vera Cruz, Mexico, where "Mr. Polk's War" was going on. The men were commanded by Capt. S. P. Heintzenan and a Lieutenant Hayes and a Lieutenant Pratt. Robert Trail Spencer was the surgeon.[26] After disembarking the troops, the *Venice* went to New Orleans and loaded cotton for Le Havre. The *Venice* was in Portsmouth in October 1849, with salt for E. F. Sise & Co. She left home for Mobile, and loaded for Le Havre. On the passage to France, the *Venice* went ashore on Vaca Key, in Florida Bay, but she was able to get off with her 3,000 bales of cotton without the help of the wreckers, which saved her owners and the underwriters a bit of money.[27]

A news item in the *New York Herald* told another story of the *Venice*, in 1853, when she fell in with a Spanish bark, the *Maria*, which had on board the crew of an English vessel that had sprung a leak en route from Callao to Liverpool. The crew and officers, 42 in number, barely had time to get into the boats. The captain of the *Venice* furnished the Spanish vessel with provisions and took ten of the Englishmen aboard, bringing them into Valparaiso. The *Venice* had been off Cape Horn for 30 days, "during which time she did not make 100 miles on her course. At one point the gale filled the cabins with water."[28]

In May 1855, the *Venice* brought an elephant into Philadelphia, which prompted a newspaper item:

AN ELEPHANT'S COMPANION IN TROUBLE.

A Malay named Solomon Debman, who was brought over in ship Venice, to tend upon an elephant, was sent to the Almshouse as soon as the elephant was landed. Being discharged from that institution, he went into the streets in his half naked native costume, and was arrested and taken before Alderman Clement on the charge of indecent exposure. Instead of measures being taken to furnish the poor fellow with clothes, he was sent to prison to answer to the charge of misdemeanor. — *Pennsylvanian*.[29]

The *Venice* met her end in 1859, while sailing under a Captain Whitman:

The ship Venice, Whitman, from Liverpool for New York, which put in at Fayal October 17th, leaky, had completed her repairs and reloaded about half her cargo (coals) when she caught fire on the 18th. She was towed cleared of the shipping, and endeavors were made to beach her, but, owing to the strong tide, she was carried clear of the Points, when the tow boats left her, and she has not been seen since, and is therefore supposed to be totally destroyed. The vessel was a fine white oak ship, of 617 tons, built here by the late George Raynes, and owned by Messrs. E. F. Sise, J. W. Peirce and John D. Simes.[30]

Arabella

SPECIFICATIONS: 1841. Raynes & Fernald. Female bust figurehead, square stern. Burthen, 696 tons. Length, 147.6 feet; beam, 32.1 feet; depth, 14.9 feet. Two decks. Original owners—Robert Rice, John Haven, and Jonathan M. Tredick.

The *Arabella* was the largest ship yet built by Raynes & Fernald. Across the river, George Raynes had already launched two larger merchantmen, the *John Taylor* and the *Kalamazoo*, but this was the first by his brother, Charles, and his partner Fernald to near the 700 mark.

Robert Rice, who lived at Islington and Parker streets, named the vessel for his daughter, Arabella, and she, years later, perpetuated Robert Rice's name by providing in her will for the Rice Memorial Library in Kittery, which was dedicated in 1889. Another Rice, Samuel, was the first master of the *Arabella*, and he headed her toward New Orleans. However, he dropped into Savannah, found a cargo, and hauled it to Le Havre. From there the *Arabella* went to St. Ubes for salt, completing her first triangle in September 1842. The salt she brought in was "of a superior quality in coarse and white."[31]

Samuel Rice found at least one transatlantic charter for her. That was in 1847, when she brought immigrants to Philadelphia for the New Line, Samuel Pleasants, agent. Passage from Liverpool was 45 guineas, a guinea being 21 shillings. At that, the passengers had to provide their own food.[32]

William Parker relieved Samuel Rice early in 1847. Parker was another of Portsmouth's great shipmasters, making his home on Islington Street, about opposite the Farragut apartments. Parker, previously mentioned in connection with the *Pontiac*, apparently at this time made only one voyage in the *Arabella*, and then Captain Rice resumed command. Rice, in 1848, took the *Arabella* to Vera Cruz with 283 tons of hay for the U.S. Army's horses.[33] That service done, Parker again became master, and in December 1849 it was reported:

Ship Arabella, Capt. Parker, arrived in our harbor on Sunday afternoon last, from Cadiz, with a cargo of 1050 tons of salt, the largest cargo ever taken on board at that place. After passing the Narrows she struck on Table Rock, near the Beacon, and the tide ebbing, all attempts to remove her were unavailing. Assistance was immediately sent from town to lighten her, and men from the navy-yard with an anchor and hawser. A considerable quantity of salt was thrown into the river, before lighters could be obtained, and after about a thousand hhds. were taken out, on Tuesday evening she floated, and took her position at the wharf. She bears no evidence of having been in the least injured by the disaster. The Arabella is a superior ship, built by Messrs. Raynes & Fernald, and is owned by Messrs. R. Rice, J. M. Tredick, and estate of J. Haven.[34]

Captain Parker's professional pride undoubtedly suffered injury, but he still had a working ship, and going aground was all part of the business.

Under various masters, the *Arabella* continued to earn profits for her owners until 1857, when her loss was reported: "News was received here last week of the loss of the ship Arabella, of this port. She is said to have been struck by lightning April 14th, and consumed by fire at sea. The crew were taken to Bermuda, where they arrived the 19th. The Arabella, of 696 tons burthen, was built by Raynes & Fernald in 1841, and was owned by J. M. Tredick and the heirs of John Haven, of this city."[35]

Alabama

SPECIFICATIONS: 1841. Samuel Badger. Billet head, square stern. Burthen, 697 tons. Length, 152.5 feet; beam, 31.5 feet; depth, 15.75 feet. Two decks. Original owners—Theodore Chase, of Boston; Enoch Wood, of Boxford, Massachusetts; Tyler Bigelow, of Watertown, Massachusetts; and Christopher S. Toppan, of Portsmouth.

Once again, Samuel Badger's itemized expense book for a ship is in the archives of the Portsmouth Athenaeum. As a glance at her displacement shows, the *Alabama* was big—bigger than any other vessel Badger had put together. And she was another loser for him. He paid out a total of $26,959.71, and received $25,504.44.

It has to be made clear that this *Alabama* is in no way to be confused with the notorious Confederate raider, CSS *Alabama*, nor should she be confused with the U.S. Navy's warship of that name, built at the Portsmouth Navy Yard. The warship underwent a name change to USS *New Hampshire* when the Civil War began. Samuel Badger's *Alabama* sailed from Portsmouth on November 16, prompting the comment:

> SHIP ALABAMA. — This splendid ship of 697 tons built at the yard of Mr. Samuel Badger and owned by Messrs. Theodore Chase, of Boston, Christopher Toppan of this town, Tyler Bigelow of Watertown and Enoch Wood of Boxford, the captain, sailed on Tuesday last for New Orleans. We might have let her pass without more notice than many other of our good ships which do honor to our port, and carry their card with them — but as this fine vessel passed down our river, her stern displayed "*Alabama, of Boston.*" Therefore be it known in every port in this habitable world which the Alabama may visit, that she was reared on the Piscataqua, and that her strength and beauty are all derived from the skill of our artisans."[36]

The *Alabama* worked in the cotton and packet business for several years, and she was en route from Liverpool to Boston on the night of November 24, 1847, when she went up on Cohassett Rock, "backed off and immediately sank." The crew made it to safety with nothing but the clothes on their backs.[37] Later the following story appeared:

> Speaking of the wreck of ship Alabama, the Boston Transcript says; "It is rather singular that not a vestige of the wreck or cargo of this unfortunate ship has yet been recovered in the neighborhood of Cohasset, the scene of the disaster. But we learn that an oil-painting of the ship Capitol which was on board the Alabama, has been picked upon on the back side of Cape Cod at Truro Beach, which leads us to infer that the cabin materials which came ashore near Chatham (as reported in the papers of the 6th inst.) were a part of the ill-fated Alabama, and by the action of wind and current have been set in the circuitous source, some sixty miles from the place where the sunken wreck now lies, off Minot's Ledge.[38]

Clara

SPECIFICATIONS: 1842. Samuel Badger. Female figurehead, square stern. Burthen, 525 tons. Length, 135.4 feet; beam, 29.1 feet; depth, 15.75 feet. Two decks. Original owners—William and William P. Jones, Thomas and John P. Penhallow, and Henry P. Salter, all of Portsmouth.

The *Clara* was unusual in that she was the only three-master launched on the Piscataqua in 1842. A general slump hit the shipbuilding industry, and it was reported in May that "the low rate of freights nearly put a stop to ship building. Last year very few of the freighting ships paid their way, and this year they are doing worse." The article, taken from the *Newburyport Herald*, contended that the country wasn't producing enough goods to load the many ships available.[39] And business didn't improve all that much until 1844. George Raynes's yard was virtually shut down in 1842 and 1843. The *Venice* was his last until he built the *Finland* in 1844. Badger built the *Martha* in 1843. Raynes & Fernald built the *Arabella*, and they did produce the schooner *Richmond*, 198 tons, in 1843. With a new partner, William Pettigrew, Fernald resumed building ships in 1845, as will be recounted later. By 1847, the frenzied building of ships was under way again. The New Hampshire *Gazette* reported:

> a special call to the ship carpenters, ascribing the present demand for vessels, and the consequent prosperity of that enterprising class of oar mechanics, to the *measures* of the present administration; and of course urges them to come out and vote for those who will support James K. Polk.
> Now the demand for shipping is caused by two things, with the occurrence of which I never for once supposed that Mr. Polk had anything to do, viz: the *famine* in Ireland, and the extremely *bad weather* on the ocean. Does the Gazette suppose that our intelligent mechanics can be cheated into the belief that Mr. Polk produced either of these two great calamities? Mr. Polk has done mischief enough without these being ascribed to him.[40]

The *Clara* was launched on August 4, and, as usual, it was said that "for beauty of model and goodness of workmanship, she is not surpassed by any vessel built on the Piscataqua."[41] The *Clara* was advertised in September as "now loading for New Orleans, and will sail October 1st."[42] John P. Penhallow was master, and the *Clara* sailed almost as advertised on October 4, taking 15 days to get to New

Orleans. She quickly found a cargo and headed for Liverpool.[43] From that port, she went to Cadiz, and returned to Portsmouth on October 3, 1843, a year after her departure. William Jones ran an ad, "SALT AFLOAT," proclaiming 2,000 hogsheads of "Cadiz salt of superior quality" were available on the *Clara*.[44] Except for one or two voyages, Capt. John P. Penhallow was master, and he was in command when she met her end, and he his, in 1848.

WRECK OF SHIP CLARA, OF PORTSMOUTH, WITH LOSS OF THE CAPTAIN. — Ship Clara, of Portsmouth, Capt. John Penhallow, from Cadiz, Oct 1st. went ashore on Truro Beach, two miles South of Cape Cod Light, on Monday, at 9 A. M. Capt. Penhallow was lost overboard a few minutes previous to her striking. The remainder of the crew were saved. The ship remains tight, high upon the beach, with mizen-mast gone. At the last advices she remained tight, and it was thought she would be got off. The cargo would probably be thrown overboard, as it would cost more than it was worth to get it to market. The Clara was a good, staunch vessel, a large carrier, built in 1842 by Samuel Badger, Esq.; and was owned by Messrs. Wm. Jones, & Son, Henry P. Salter, T. W. Penhallow and the master. She was insured, (vessel and cargo) for about $35,000.[45]

A week later it was reported:

At the last accounts from ship Clara, of Portsmouth, ashore on Truro beach, her bows were dry at low water, the sand having washed up several feet, while her stern was nearly afloat. About 200 hhds. salt had been taken out and carried to Provincetown, three fourths of it being given to the salvers. It being difficult to save more, a large number of men were employed in throwing it overboard, in the expectation of getting the ship off.[46]

And two weeks later:

SHIP CLARA — We understand there has been several unsuccessful attempts to get off the ship Clara on Truro Beach. We learn the water runs in and out of her as the tide flows and ebbs — has been very badly hogged — one of her beams broken and otherwise badly damaged.[47]

Martha

SPECIFICATIONS: 1843. Samuel Badger. Billet head, square stern. Burthen, 533 tons. Length, 135.6 feet. Two decks. Original owners— Abraham Rich, of Boston; and Samuel Snow, of Bath, Maine.

The ship *Martha* was launched on November 29, 1843. "For beauty of model, workmanship, excellence of materials and capacity, she is not surpassed by any ship ever built on the Piscataqua."[48] (After a while, the reader begins to wonder if the *Journal* kept sentiments like the foregoing permanently in type.)

However, the *Martha* turned a bit of a profit for her builder. Another of Samuel Badger's meticulous journals is in the Portsmouth Athenaeum. Badger figured his total cost at $21,113.98, and he sold the *Martha* for $23,000, a profit of $1,886.02, and no Internal Revenue Service to share it with. Another welcome discovery in Badger's bookkeeping is the reason why ship's measurements were kept in feet and inches. That measurement was required in the builder's certificate. When he filed the certificate for the *Martha*, Badger listed her length as 135.6 feet, and that's what George Nelson found when he searched the Portsmouth Customs Records a half century or more ago.

The ship *Martha* sailed from Portsmouth under Capt. Samuel Snow, and didn't return. And that has led to confusion between her and the bark *Martha*, built by Samuel Badger in 1845. It's the bark *Martha* that will forever hold a place in Port of Portsmouth legend and history. The 205-ton bark carried Portsmouth's Forty-Niners to the West Coast. The bark took 205 days, but she did get to San Francisco.

Epaminondas

SPECIFICATIONS: 1844. Samuel Badger. Billet head, square stern. Burthen, 548 tons. Length, 143 feet; beam, 28.8 feet; depth, 18.35 feet. Two decks. Original owners—William Lambert and Charles Hill, of Boston; G. Abbott, of Beverly, Massachusetts.

Someone must have been a real classical scholar to give a vessel built in Kittery, Maine, the name Epaminondas. The original bearer of it was a Greek general from Thebes, who was killed in 362 B.C. after winning the Battle of Mantinea. The ship was launched on September 17, and the *Journal* gave its usual salute to the skill of the builder.

Shipbuilding was again on the march in the Port of Portsmouth. Three three-master square-riggers were launched during 1844, one by each of the three major builders. Samuel Badger kept his usual journal on the *Epaminondas*, and the entries show that he dealt with most of the same people he had on his other ships. Badger's total cost for the *Epaminondas* was $21,346.36. Lambert and Hill paid $23,350 for her, a profit to Badger of $2,003.64. He paid himself $400 for his labor as master carpenter. The ledger indicates that Badger was financed in his project by William Jones & Son of Portsmouth, because he paid that firm $441.55 in interest. How much the Joneses lent him wasn't entered.

William Lambert was a veteran shipmaster. He took the ship to sea, headed for New Orleans. On the next voyage of the *Epaminondas*, a Captain Chick was in command, but Lambert returned and stayed with the ship several years.

In 1854, the *Epaminondas* was sold to Alfred Ladd for $24,000. That wasn't a bad deal for her original owners, who used her for ten years and then sold her for $650 more than they paid. In all probability the heavy demand for shipping in the late 1850s accounted for the price paid. After the sale, the *Epaminondas* took on a cargo for Valparaiso, Chile, and Callao, Peru. She was reported lost at sea in November 1857, having been abandoned.[49]

Empire

SPECIFICATIONS: 1844. Raynes & Fernald. Female figurehead, square stern. Burthen, 1,049 tons. Length, 170 feet; beam, 36.7 feet; depth, 18.35 feet. Two decks. Original owners—the Kingslands, of New York.

Before the *Empire* ever slid down her ways, the *Portsmouth Journal* in August described the ship as "the largest merchantman ever built on the Piscataqua. She is constructed for Messrs. D. and A. Kingsland of New York, and was built under the superintendence of Capt. J. T. Russell who is part owner." As scheduled, the *Empire* was launched on August 14, and a bit of unscheduled drama attended the affair:

> NOBLE ACT. — On Wednesday last, at the moment the Ship Empire was launching, Charles Stuart, a lad about eight years old, fell through a hole in Mr. Long's pile wharf at the north end, where the water is of great depth. Mr. William Martin, blockmaker, immediately descended to the wharf fender, and discovering the boy's situation, without stopping even to

divest himself of his coat, at the peril of his own life plunged under the wharf and succeeded in rescuing the boy just at the moment he was sinking the third time. Such an act of philanthropy, though it has a richer reward in itself, than fame can bestow, is nevertheless deserving of some lasting momento of approbation from the friends of humanity.[50]

The pride that the residents of the Port of Portsmouth, on both sides of the Piscataqua River, took in the ship *Empire* knew no bounds. Her very size made her a symbol of industrial and community achievement. How the public felt was well expressed in a letter to the editor:

> *Mr. Brewster:* — I have just come from a visit to the magnificent ship EMPIRE, which has recently been launched from the ship-yard of Fernald & Raynes, and is now getting up her rigging and sails at the Pier wharf. By the courtesy of her polite commander and part owner, Capt. Russel, I was permitted to visit every part of the ship.
>
> My admiration of this splendid specimen of naval architecture is only succeeded by my surprise, that a ship like this, which for her beauty of model, strength and excellence of workmanship in every part of her hull, spars and rigging, and in rich and beautiful finish of cabins, furniture and accommodations, I do not believe is surpassed in any port of this or any other country; — that such a ship as this should be built, rigged and ready to sail from our harbor, without a word of description or eulogy in our public prints, or a line in praise of the faithful and ingenious mechanics who have combined to produce so honorable a specimen of the state of the mechanic arts among us.
>
> Had such a ship as this been built and fitted in some of our large seaports, we should have seen the most glowing descriptions of her: and the names, not only of the masterworkmen who modeled and built her, but of the various mechanics who have contributed in their various departments to her completion, would have had honorable mention. I hope this may still be done here — at least that a correct description of this beautiful ship may be presented in your columns. I wish I was enough acquainted with the subject to prepare one myself, for I understand she will soon sail from our port to return no more, having been built for the house of Messrs. Kingsland & Jones, in New-York, where she is to be put on their splendid line of New-York and New-Orleans packets.
>
> I am no friend to vain boasting, yet when our good town is so much underrated by some of our sister seaports, and so

neglected and oppressed by our own would-be statesmen, who would gladly see every spark of enterprise smothered by their legislative fooleries, — it behoves us to speak out upon our own undeniable merits and exertions. It is true, our Portsmouth ships have for years been carrying evidence of the skill of our mechanics, the science of our ship-masters, and the mercantile sagacity of our merchants to every quarter of the globe; — but of late the cheerful ringing of the axe and the hammer have nearly ceased in our ship-yards, and if our domestic energies are in any measure paralized, we should hail with especial welcome the expenditure of foreign capital among us. — Here has a superb ship of over 1000 tons burthen been built and rigged — over $60,000 been distributed in our town and neighborhood, and employment given to numerous mechanics and laborers in so quiet and noiseless a manner that probably one half of our own citizens will be surprised at the statement! I sincerely wish we could see many sorts of manufactories flourishing among us; but for healthfulness of body and mind, as well as profit to the operative, — beauty in the fabric, and I hope good returns upon the capital, I most heartily and above all wish prosperity to the SHIP MANUFACTORIES of Portsmouth.   A.[51]

Capt. Joseph T. Russell took the *Empire* to sea on September 19 at noon:

The ship went down the river in gallant style, and after entering the outer harbor in fair sea room, she spent three hours in a trial of her working, staying &c. The pilot, Mr. [William] Goodwin, informs us that Capt. Russell was pleased with her in every respect, a good sailer and easily managed. Built by Raynes & Fernald — cabin finished by [Thomas] Martin & [Hampti] Kenney — painted by John Smith — rigged by Charles Harrat, and the cordage from the factory of J. [Jeremiah] Johnson, all of this town. We are not ashamed to present her at New-York as a specimen of the skill of our mechanics.[52]

The *Empire* went immediately into the business for which she had been built: packet runs on the North Atlantic. In 1844 she was in the Third Line. The next year the Kermit Line chartered her. In August 1846, on one of her charters, the *Empire* ran into trouble:

DISASTER AT SEA.
The ship Empire, Russell, sailed from New-York for Liverpool 22d day of July. On the 26th, lat. 41, lon, 46, at 1 A. M. was struck by a sudden squall of wind which lasted only fifteen

seconds, and carried away the foremost and head of her main-mast, sails, rigging, and everything attached — sprung the mizzenmast, carried away the mizzen-topmast, sprung the bowsprit, and carried away the jib-boom. There were at the time four men on the main topsail-yard, who were lost. The Empire was boarded on the 5th inst. off Gay Head, by the pilot boat Wm. J. Romer, by which D. & A. Kingsland (her owners) received a letter from Capt. Russell, stating the above, and also that he was making the best of his way back to New-York. She remained perfectly tight, and no fears were entertained for her safety. — *Boston Post*[53]

Having escaped from that difficulty, the *Empire* continued working. The United States had gone to war with Mexico in 1846, and shipping was in heavy demand for moving both troops and supplies. On October 12, 1847, the *Empire* sailed from New York for Vera Cruz, carrying 15 officers and 372 enlisted men—members of Companies L and M of the First Artillery and Companies L and M of the Third Artillery. Contingent commander was a Captain Van Ness. While trying to clear Abaco Island and the Hole in the Wall on October 17, the *Empire* was wrecked. Yet, with all those men on board, only the helmsman was lost. The sole victim died from injuries suffered when the *Empire* went aground; the wheel whipped around and crushed him. All the personnel on board, including the injured helmsman, made it to the reef, but he died after getting ashore. Troops and ship's crew sat on the reef for ten days before rescue. The *Empire* was valued at $55,000 and insured for that amount in New York.[54]

Finland

SPECIFICATIONS: *1844. George Raynes. Billet head, square stern. Burthen, 549 tons. Length, 134 feet; beam, 30 feet; depth 15 feet. Two decks. Original owner—Hiram N. Peck, of New York.*

The *Finland* was the first ship built by George Raynes since 1841, when he launched the *Venice*, and she was the only one Raynes put in the water in 1844.

NEW SHIP. — The Ship FINLAND, 550 tons burthen, built by Mr. George Raynes, and sold to H. N. Peck, Esq. of New-York, sailed from this port on Tuesday, 5th Oct. for New-York. Her dimensions are — 134 feet long on deck, 30 feet breadth above the wale, 31 widest place, 14 1-2 hold, and 7 1-2 between decks. She is built of Piscataqua white oak. She draws 11 feet 4 inches water, with 300 tons weight in her when she left port; and by the report of the pilot no boat could mind her helm better. She was perfectly stiff, and had the appearance of being a very fast sailer. She does credit to her builder.[55]

The *Finland* went into New York under a Captain Symes, quite probably for orders and to let her owner have a look at her. From New York she went south, and mention of her in Portsmouth shipping news was infrequent. However, she did go into Apalachicola often. The *Liverpool Telegraph* noted on March 22, 1850, that the *Finland*, "in hauling out of Pier No. 3 yesterday, went adrift, coming in contact with the ship *Margarita*, and the *Emblem*, knocking them both off their anchors." None of the ships suffered serious damage. Apparently, in 1849 she was examined for the underwriters and given a favorable report. However, in 1851 her master refused to open her for inspection, and so she wasn't rated.[56]

In 1861, with the Civil War in full flame, the *Finland* was blockaded by a Union fleet at Apalachicola. On September 17, 1861, the *Journal* tersely reported: "Ship Finland, before reported set on fire at Apalachicola, by the U. S. blockading squadron, was built at Portsmouth, in 1843. She is of 549 tons register, rated 2 —, and was recently owned in New York by J. & N. Smith & Co. It is presumed she had been transferred to the British flag."

Seeking more details on the destruction of the *Finland*, I was given generous assistance by William E. Greer, treasurer of the Apalachicola Area Historical Society. It came in a letter, dated November 9, 1984:

> To the best of my knowledge, the only documented account of FINLAND which is available locally is in "Naval Operations on the Apalachicola and Chattahoochee Rivers, 1861–65," by Dr. Maxine Turner, Georgia Institute of Technology, Atlanta, 30332. This was reported from her articles in "Alabama Historical Quarterly XXXVI, Fall and Winter, 1974–75."

The following was extracted from pp. 12 and 13 of Dr. Turner's article:

> On the night of August 26 [1861], five boats from the CUYLER and MONTGOMERY were sent on a reconnaissance mission toward a large ship anchored in Apalachicola Bay. The Union force discovered the FINLAND and the schooner NEW

PLAN, and were able to capture the two vessels without opposition. Since the NEW PLAN's papers were in order, it was released after the crew had taken the oath of allegiance to the United States.

The FINLAND, however, was thought a lawful prize and the Union seamen began efforts to remove it from the bay. They found the sails and spars housed and spent all night bending sails and sending spars aloft. At dawn they began, against unfavorable winds and tides, to attempt towing their prize to the Union blockading station at East Pass. Nightfall found the FINLAND grounded on St. Vincent's Bar, four miles from the Union anchorage, and forty men were left behind to free the ship.

Efforts to tow the FINLAND from the bar lasted all night. At dawn a steamer with a large schooner in tow appeared heading into Apalachicola and steered directly toward the Union prize. Unable the free the FINLAND from the bar and unable to call upon the CUYLER or MONTGOMERY for defense, the seamen had to fire the FINLAND and take to their boats. So precarious was the position of the Union seamen that they were routed by nine men from the Apalachicola Guards who came on the scene in a schooner towed by a steamer. That detachment boarded the burning FINLAND and recovered the life boats and a few useful articles that could be salvaged."

Thomas Wright

SPECIFICATIONS: 1845. George Raynes. Billet head, square stern. Burthen, 623 tons. Length, 144.15 feet; beam, 30.7 feet; depth, 15.35 feet. Two decks. Original owner—William P. Gardner, of Providence, Rhode Island.

The *Thomas Wright* was another of the increasing number of vessels being built for shipping interests outside the Port of Portsmouth. She was launched on October 8 and cleared out in November. Although the *Thomas Wright* was owned in another port, a detailed news story about her was published on November 15. The article's value lies in the wealth of detail it provides about the construction of a ship like the *Thomas Wright*:

This fine ship, which is now ready to sail for Mobile, is a specimen of good workmanship, and should not pass from her birth place upon the wide waters without a comment.

She was designed and built by Mr. George Raynes, and sold on the stocks to Capt. Wm. R. Gardner, of Providence, who takes command. Her tonnage is 623 65-95ths. The following are the principal dimensions of her hull. Length on deck, 144 feet 2 inches; — breadth 30 feet 8 inches, (swell 6 inches each side;) depth of hold 14 feet 6 inches; between decks 7 feet 9 inches.

Keel sided 14 inches, moulded at fore end 20 inches, and after end 16 inches; false keel 5 inches thick; stern sided 14 inches; apron sided 20 inches; stern post 14 inches, moulded at bottom 26 inches, at transom 14 inches; main transom 16 inches square; the stern rakes 3 inches to one foot; the keel from after part of stern post to point of stem, straight rabit 133 feet 6 inches; extreme length of keel 137 feet, to front of gripe 139 feet. The frame is of entire white oak, all of which was cut in New-Hampshire. Her keelson is 16 inches square, of New-Hampshire white oak, bolted down through the floor-timbers and keel with 1 1-8 inches copper and riveted under the keel.

We are informed that there are 2650 bolts driven and in sight between the two decks. She has 8 stout and substantial breast-hooks in her bows; those under lower deck are heavily bolted with 1 1-8 and 1 inch copper bolts.

The cabin and sailor's house are on deck. They are both capacious, the latter commodious — warm for a cold climate, and airy for the warm. The cabin is elegantly finished, as the visitor at first supposes, with zebra, rose, ebony, maple, mahogany, &c., but is surprised to learn that the whole work is of pine, prepared by — and painted and polished by — (we were about the say Levi Moses and John Smith, but recollecting the trouble we once got into by telling only a part of the workmen on Ship Empire, we will only say) good workmen. One of the patent windlasses from Mr. Haselton's foundry, is a strong and handsome article. A large company paid their respects on the occasion, "She is a fine ship."[57]

Because the *Thomas Wright* was owned away from the Port of Portsmouth, details of her career aren't available.

Mary Pleasants

SPECIFICATIONS: 1845. Samuel Badger. Female figurehead, square stern. Burthen, 680 tons. Length, 150 feet; beam, 31.4 feet; depth, 15.7 feet. Two decks. Original owner—Hiram N. Peck, of New York.

Hiram N. Peck was pleased enough with the *Finland* to come back to the Piscataqua for another vessel—this one a little larger. Samuel Badger's ledgers for the *Mary Pleasants* are also in the Portsmouth Athenaeum. The cost items are similar to those for the *Franconia*, the total being $25,118.76. The *Mary Pleasants* was sold for $26,000, leaving Badger a profit of $881.24.

Capt. John Wootton cleared the *Mary Pleasants* out of the Port of Portsmouth on October 17, heading for New Orleans.[58] She arrived there on November 8 to begin service in the cotton trade. Back and forth she went across the Atlantic. In 1846, she was in the New Line on a charter, along with Portsmouth ships like the *Robert Parker* and the *Portsmouth*. Samuel Pleasants of Philadelphia chartered her in 1848, when she was commanded by J. Q. Bowne. Undoubtedly it was the Pleasants family that provided the name for the ship, but the link to the owner, Hiram Peck, isn't clear. Anthony M. Michaels took her over in 1850, when the price of a cabin fare was 15 guineas.[59] On one of her passages to Liverpool, the *Mary Pleasants* made the run in 18 days, really respectable time for a ship of her tonnage and model. In 1854, with the Crimean War raging, the ship was chartered to carry supplies from Liverpool to Constantinople.[60]

The *Mary Pleasants* was bought in 1857 by the British firm James Baines & Co. But she had been sold earlier than that in an auction at Liverpool, fetching £11,000. Baines put her to work in the service of the Emigration Commissioners. The discovery of gold in Australia increased the demand for shipping. The English historian, Michael K. Stammers, wrote:

> In fact, Baines & Co. only bought two new ships in 1857, the Maldon which was bought in March and sold in July, and the Mary Pleasants, a somewhat elderly ship built at Portsmouth, new Hampshire, in 1845 of some 809 tons [British ship measurements differed from the American], and a slow sailer to boot. She sailed to New South Wales in 105 days for the Emigration Commissioners in 1857 and made a worse passage of 116 days the next year.[61]

The *Mary Pleasants* was lost at Akyab, Turkey, in July 1862.

Judah Touro

SPECIFICATIONS: 1845. Frederick W. Fernald and William Petti-grew. Male figurehead, square stern. Burthen, 740 tons. Length, 152 feet; beam, 32.6 feet; depth, 16.3 feet. Two decks. Original owners— Daniel Marcy, of Portsmouth; Judah Touro and R. D. Shepherd, of New Orleans.

The life of the man for whom the *Judah Touro* was named is far more intriguing than the career of the vessel. Unfortunately, only a brief sketch is possible within these pages, but an article about him was published in 1936: "The Life and Times of Judah Touro," by David C. Adelman, and published by the Touro Fraternal Association. Following are some highlights in the life of an extraordinary man.

Judah Touro was born on June 16, 1775, in Newport, Rhode Island, the son of an itinerant Hebrew spiritual leader. When he was eight, his father died, and four years later his mother. The youngster grew to manhood in Boston with his mother's family. His first employer was his uncle, and he was sent as supercargo on one of the uncle's ships. The ship escaped capture by French privateers, but young Touro wound up penniless in Havana. He worked his way back to Boston. Then, in 1802, when the uncle refused to let him marry a cousin, Touro went to New Orleans. Only once during his lifetime did he leave the bounds of New Orleans. That one expedition beyond the city limits came in 1815 when he volunteered as an ammunition carrier in the Battle of New Orleans, where he was severely wounded. He was nursed back to health by the family of his friend and business partner, Rezin D. Shepherd. In many ways, he was a man of odd habits. For example, a beloved brother, Abraham, was thrown from a carriage and died from his injuries, so Judah Touro walked wherever he wanted to go for the rest of his life.

Highly successful in his business ventures with Shepherd and the Marcy brothers—Daniel of Portsmouth and Peter of New Orleans—Touro's philanthropy was the talk of his adopted city. He gave liberally, for example, even to the construction of the Bunker Hill Monument in Charlestown, Massachusetts. He practiced his Jewish faith devoutly all his life, but helped the parishes of other faiths.

When he died on January 18, 1854, the city of New Orleans mourned him deeply.[62] The specific bequests in his will amounted to more than $800,000. One of the provisions of his will called for his body to be put on board the ship *Judah Touro* and taken to Newport, his native town, where he had created a cemetery and synagogue. He wanted to lie there "by the side of my mother." However, it was the steamer,

Empire City, that took the remains of Judah Touro to Newport. For the first time in nearly 40 years, Judah Touro left his beloved New Orleans. After his bequests were paid, the executor, R. D. Shepherd, was the beneficiary. The year after Touro's death, the New Orleans City Council voted to erect a $10,000 monument to his memory.

Daniel Marcy's papers, now held by the New Hampshire Historical Society, offer an explanation as to why a syndicate of New Orleans businessmen, Judah Touro and R. D. Shepherd, entrusted the construction of their ships to Daniel Marcy. Born in Portsmouth in 1809, Marcy went to sea as a boy, and, when he was 21, he moved to New Orleans and went to work for Touro and Shepherd, with whom his brother Peter was associated. In 1842, he returned to Portsmouth under an arrangement with the syndicate to supervise the construction of one ship a year. It was agreed that Daniel Marcy would take each new vessel on its maiden passage, a pattern followed until 1852.

The contract to build the *Judah Touro* had come along at the right time for the new partnership of Fernald and Pettigrew. William Pettigrew had been a master workman for George Raynes, but probably, as Stephen Tobey did later on, Pettigrew could see that eventually George Raynes, Jr. would take over the yard, thus limiting his prospects. Why Fernald and Charles Raynes parted company isn't known, but the new team was highly successful from the start. The story of the launching of the *Judah Touro* ran long:

> On Saturday last, two vessels were launched from the yards on our river. The largest was the "Judah Touro" from the yard of Messrs. F. W. Fernald and Wm. Pettigrew, Badger's Island. The description of the launch cannot be better given than by the expression of the Chinaman present on the occasion, as translated by his attendant: "It was exceedingly beautiful." She rode upon the water like a thing of life. We always look upon the ships built here and from the forests of our native State, as children entitled to our regards, and all good citizens feel a parental pride in introducing to the world such oaken progenies as will do credit and honor to the section of the country in which they were constructed.
>
> The "Judah Touro," is of 750 tons burthen, owned by Messrs. Judah Touro & R. D. Shepard of New-Orleans, and Capt. Daniel Marcy of Portsmouth, who is to be her commander. Some idea of her fine model and strength of structure may be formed from the following description, which, although it may be rather too minute for some, will be of interest to those who are acquainted with the construction of ships.

She is 152 feet long, 8 inches dead rise, 32 feet 8 inches beam, 6 inches swell of side, 7 feet 9 inches between decks, and 15 feet lower hold. She has a long flat floor, sharp forward and aft, rake of stem 4 inches to a foot, which gives a most beautiful flaring blow. The keelson is 17 by 18 inches, rider 12 by 13, fastened with 1-1/4 inch copper bolts 5 feet 5 inches long, 2 feet apart, and riveted under the keel. All the other bolts through the ship are driven through from the outside, and rivetted on the inside. She has two bilge keelsons by the side, 8 by 12 inches, then 10 streaks 6 by 5 inches thick 10 inches wide — bolted with 7-8th copper. 8 breast-hooks forward, with a pair of pointers running round with the curve of the bows; 4 hooks aft, in the lower hold; 4 streaks lower deck champs, 12 by 6 inches each; under every lower deck beam, a wooden knee 6-1/2 feet body by 4 feet arm, fastened with 11 9-8th inch bolts. Lower deck water-ways 13 inches square, 2d do. 9 by 10 inches, of white oak, dovetailed to the lower deck beams, and bolted through ship's sides. Wooden knees under every beam between decks, fayed into the thick streaks and fastened with 13 9-8th inch bolts in every knee. Upper deck beams, ledges and carlings of Georgia Pine. The stock (of New-Hampshire white-oak,) and fastenings in the lower hold are of the size and dimensions of a ship of 1000 tons.

She is to be finished on deck with a house aft for a cabin, 33 by 22 feet, in elegant style. There is to be a house forward of main hatch, 34 by 15 feet for the seamen. She is to be steered with Robinson's patent steering apparatus, the first use of it in any of our ships. The easy and regular operation of this newly invented machinery is such as will doubtless soon bring it into general use. The figure-head is probably intended for some semblance of the distinguished merchant of New-Orleans whose name she bears. The visage may not be very accurate, but it is said that in dress and general appearance the carver has been very successful. At any rate it presents a very graceful appearance, and when this noble ship meets the eye of that gentleman, he will be proud to see his statue attached to so noble a vessel.[63]

The second vessel referred to the the *Journal* article was the brig *Matilda*, built by Charles Raynes and James Tobey in George Raynes's yard. They sold the vessel to a New Yorker; she was later sold abroad and renamed the *Australian*, and then sold again and named the *Fortuna*, of Oporto.

On July 30, the *Judah Touro*, under Capt. Daniel Marcy, went to New Orleans. Daniel Marcy is deserving of more than a casual reference, and an increasing concept of his stature in the Port of Portsmouth will become evident as the years go by. No other master took out of Portsmouth the number of new vessels that Captain Marcy did:

> On Wednesday at 11 A.M. [August 26] the ship Judah Touro was spoken by the pilot off Portsmouth harbor, for Boston — having left Liverpool the 27th.... It is a year the present week since the Judah-Touro commenced her first voyage. In that time she has made three trips between Boston and New-Orleans, and has four times crossed the Atlantic: having full cargoes every trip. She proves a first-rate ship.[64]

In support of her sailing achievements, a brief, undated item appeared in the *New Orleans Picayune* in which the *Judah Touro* was credited with bringing into New Orleans, from Boston, 3,100 barrels of provisions, 3,000 hides, and "lots of sundries." That cargo was exchanged for 1,903 bales of cotton, and back north to Boston she went.

John Gilman Moses, over the years ahead, proved to be one of Portsmouth's most able shipmasters, and he brought the *Judah Touro* into Portsmouth, from Liverpool, on May 11, 1858, with 900 tons of coarse salt for E. F. Sise Co. The ship didn't linger long in Portsmouth, and when she sailed a captain named Hanscom was on the quarterdeck.

Inevitably the question arises as to what the *Judah Touro* was doing that she couldn't convey Judah Touro's remains to Newport. A glance at her sailing schedule indicates that the *Judah Touro* was already chartered for a passage to Trieste, Italy, when Touro died. A sharp businessman like Judah Touro wouldn't have interfered with a lucrative charter, even in death.

The *Judah Touro* was one of the more reliable workhorses of the Atlantic trade. On November 20, 1861, the *Judah Touro* left Liverpool headed for Portsmouth, but had to put into Boston on January 17. The ship had been ten days on the coast, trying to claw her way in against the northwest winds. On December 10, 1860, she had lost overboard Thomas Harper, a seaman from St. John, New Brunswick. She finally arrived on January 19.

The *Liverpool Chronicle* reported on March 22, 1862, that the *Judah Touro*, Liverpool for Philadelphia, had been badly damaged in a gale, and that part of her cargo had been thrown overboard. The *Judah Touro*'s death notice came in late March of 1862:

Ship Judah Turo, Hanscom, from Liverpool (Jan. 28) for Philadelphia, owned by Capt. J. Gilman Moses of this city, was abandoned at sea Feb. 26. From Feb. 18th to the 24th, she experienced a series of heavy gales, in which she lost her bowsprit, foretopmast and foremast head, main topgallant mast, and all her sails. Her stern frame was shaken, bulwarks stove, and she sprung a leak, which kept all hands continually at the pumps. Captain Hanscom tried to reach Fayal, but the ship leaked so badly, and the men were so exhausted by continual pumping and exposure, that he was compelled to abandon her. — On the 26th, all hands, including seven passengers were rescued by the ship Byzantium, and arrived at New York 21st inst.[65]

America

SPECIFICATIONS: 1846. Charles Raynes and James Tobey. Female figurehead, square stern. Burthen, 1,137 tons. Length, 170.3 feet; beam, 38.3 feet; depth, 19.15 feet. Two decks. Original owners—the Kingslands, of New York.

The production of the *America* was an unusual enterprise in at least two ways. The partnership of Charles Raynes and James Tobey was new and almost untried. They had built only a brig previously. Second, they had to use the shipyard of George Raynes—but then brother George was in a hiatus and didn't build a ship until late in 1846. The launching story said:

LAUNCH OF THE AMERICA. — On Tuesday, at one o'clock, in the presence of thousands of spectators, this noble ship slid from her ways into the element in which she is destined to move. She is the largest merchantman ever on the Piscataqua, being of 1200 tons burthen: and (with the exception of the ship Rappahannock) is calculated to be a more capacious carrier than any ship now plying from any port in the United States. She was built by Messrs. Raynes & Tobey, for Messrs. D. & A. Kingsland, & Co. of New-York, and Capt. Samuel Weare, by whom she is to be commanded. She is destined for the New-York and Liverpool packet business.[66]

After so many years of casual reference to the shipbuilding industry in the Piscataqua Basin, the *Portsmouth Journal* was taking a much keener interest in it, as evidenced by the following:

The ship America, *built by Charles Raynes and James Tobey. Courtesy Mystic Seaport Museum.*

PACKET SHIP AMERICA.

We have been on board this noble ship to admire her massive strength, elegant proportions and beautiful finish. She will do great credit to her builders and superintendant; — and it is to be hoped, be a successful and profitable ship. The following is a brief but accurate description of her dimensions.

Length of keel 165 feet; length between perpendiculars 172 feet 4 inches; length on deck over all 182 feet; extreme breadth of beam 39 feet 3 inches. She has a full poop deck 7 feet high in the clear, extending to the forward side of the mainmast; and has a spacious topgallant forecastle to correspond with the poop deck. She has 15,421 lbs. of copper and 65,181 lbs. of iron bolts and spikes in the hull of the ship. She was built by Messrs. Raynes and Tobey, under the superintendence of Capt. Sam'l Weare who will command her. She is intended to run as a packet between New York and Liverpool.[67]

Once again, on September 29, the *Journal* sang the praises of the ship *America*:

> In a few days this noble ship of 1200 tons, under Capt. Weare, will leave our harbor for New-York; — and it is no small gratification that we are enabled to present such a card of good workmanship from the shipbuilders of Portsmouth, to the great commercial emporium, and to the world. The goddess of Liberty is the appropriate figure-head she bears. The cabin is finished in a style of superior elegance, with mahogany, rose, satin and zebra wood, and gilt. The carpets and curtains, will not be added until her arrival at New-York.
>
> She has the best accommodations for passengers, and capacity sufficient for from 4000 to 4200 bales of cotton. No merchantman in the country has ever exceeded this.

The *America* cleared on October 3 and sailed a few days later, arriving in New York on the eleventh. No time was lost in fitting out the *America* and loading her for Liverpool. On her way out of New York, the ship went aground on the Southwest Spit, "but was got off after great exertions, apparently without damage and anchored in deep water." She had been chartered by the Empire Line, for whom the Kingslands were agents. While on her maiden passage from Portsmouth, the *America* had fallen in with the packet ship *Roscius*, passed her "with ease" and arrived in New York several hours ahead. The next year Edmund Dunn had her in the Third Line for a charter. J. J. Lawrence became master in 1850. In 1859 she was in the Brigham Line, Capt. J. W. Rowe.[68]

Like so may others in America's great merchant fleet, the *America* was sold to British interests in 1863 to protect her from the ravages of the Confederate raiders. In 1873, while on a passage from Liverpool to St. John, New Brunswick, with railroad iron, the *America* was abandoned on November 26, after being thrown on her beam ends.[69]

Kate Hunter

SPECIFICATIONS: 1846. George Raynes. Billet head, square stern. Burthen, 731 tons. Length, 151.8 feet; beam, 32.4 feet; depth, 16.2 feet. Two decks. Original owners—Ichabod Goodwin and William H. Parsons, of Portsmouth; G. B. Cumming, Savannah.

Perhaps George Raynes had to wait until brother Charles had launched the *America* before he could finish the *Kate Hunter*. Whatever the reason, the *Kate Hunter*'s launching came so late in the year that Nelson described her as an 1846–1847 ship, but she was in water on December 2, and that establishes her year. The launching went off in "beautiful style."[70] It was noted later:

> NEW SHIP KATE-HUNTER. — This fine specimen of naval workmanship, which has cleared last week for Mobile, was built by Mr. George Raynes of this town, for Messrs. I. Goodwin and Wm. H. Parsons of this town, and Geo. B. Cumming of Savannah — to be commanded by Capt. W. H. Parsons. She is 151 feet 8-10ths in length, and 32 feet 4-10th in breadth. — Tonnage 731 28-95ths tons. She is built from a new and improved model — for capacious stowage and fast sailing, — and will not suffer by examination in any clime by the side of the ships of any nation. We feel pride in sending such messengers of the skill of our artisans around the world.[71]

As might be expected, the *Kate Hunter* went immediately into the triangular cotton trade. Capt. William H. Parsons left the Port of Portsmouth on January 17, 1847, arriving in Mobile on February 7. She cleared for Le Havre on March 10, and arrived in France on April 21. She recrossed the Atlantic to New York, coming in on June 18. However, instead of going south for cotton, Taylor & Merrill chartered her for passage to Liverpool, which took her 28 days. But after that assignment, she headed down south for cotton.

One of her crew on her maiden voyage was Albion B. Parsons, a nephew of the captain. Young Parsons shipped on her at the age of 17. He didn't get home for a year, and by that time he had lost all interest in a seafaring life. All his life Albion Parsons suffered from asthma; in 1859 he was a passenger on the *Anna Decatur*, thinking a voyage to Europe might help his health. In 1864, he again tried an ocean cure, taking passage in the *Frank Pierce*, another Piscataqua-built vessel. She foundered at sea in June 1864, as will be told later. The crew was rescued by an English bark and was put ashore in the Falkland Island. They went from the Falklands to London. Albion Parsons reached Portsmouth in January 1865. However, none of his nautical adventures seemed to have done Parsons any harm: he died in 1890, in his sixtieth year.[72]

When the *Kate Hunter* cleared out of Savannah for Liverpool on May 19, 1848, the *Savannah Republican* reported she was carrying a "large and valuable cargo." It included 2,650 bales of Upland Cotton and 364 bales of Sea Island. The total weight in pounds was 1,261,540, of which 121,164 pounds was Sea Island. At the prices of the day, the cargo was worth $95,208.[73]

In September 1853, the *Kate Hunter* took a beating from "very heavy weather on the whole passage" from Liverpool, losing rigging and masts.[74] On one occasion, in 1858, the *Kate Hunter*, sailing from Portsmouth under Capt. William P. Healey of Hampton Falls, had as a passenger Nathaniel K. Raynes, brother of the builder. Two other local passengers were John H. Miller of Portsmouth and Eastman Cutts of Kittery. They went to Mobile.[75] All in all, the *Kate Hunter* was a faithful worker, one in which the Piscataqua shipwrights took pride. She was sold in 1861, and the *Liverpool Telegraph* reported in 1863 that she was at Valparaiso, having put in, leaking, after taking 42 days to come from Callao with guano. By that time she was named the *Charles*.[76]

R. D. Shepherd

SPECIFICATIONS: 1846. Fernald & Pettigrew. Male figurehead, square stern. Burthen, 794 tons. Length, 160 feet; beam, 32.8 feet; depth, 16.4 feet. Two decks. Original owners—Daniel Marcy, of Portsmouth; Rezin D. Shepherd, Judah Touro, and Peter Marcy, all of New Orleans.

While work on the *R. D. Shepherd* was in the preliminary stages, Fernald & Pettigrew produced a 139-ton schooner for Heman Eldredge, Jr. of Chatham, Massachusetts. Members of the Eldredge family eventually migrated to Portsmouth and established the Eldredge Brewing Co., near the famed Frank Jones Brewery. Even as they worked on the *R. D. Shepherd*, Fernald & Pettigrew had on the ways still another schooner, the *Catharine*, 138 tons, also for the Eldredges. However, the *R. D. Shepherd* was the main effort in their building program in 1846. The firm had, of course, built the *Judah Touro*, named for Rezin D. Shepherd's close associate, and it was logical that the next ship should be the *R. D. Shepherd*. Eventually the other two associates, Peter and Daniel Marcy, had ships named for them. Rezin D. Shepherd was a native of Jefferson County, Virginia, born in 1784; he died on his plantation there on November 11, 1865. Like Touro, he had gone to New Orleans as a young man and prospered. While they were both growing in stature as businessmen, Shepherd formed a close bond with Judah Touro. As previously told, Shepherd nursed his friend after the Battle of New Orleans. At the risk of his own life, Shepherd had carried Touro from the battlefield. Touro never forgot. Shepherd's obituary said, in part:

Mr. Shepherd was one of the largest and most enterprising ship-owners in the South; he carried on an enormous business with the North and with Europe, until the death of Mr. Touro who left him his executor and principal legatee, when he retired from public business. The magnificent row of buildings on Canal street, between Royal and Bourbon, is an instance of the munificence of his taste and liberality. That splendid edifice the Touro Alms House, lately consumed by fire, was a noble monument of the charity of these two steadfast friends, whose kindness and beneficence were as comprehensive and unostentatious as their lives were spotless and admirable.

The bulk of Mr. Shepherd's fortune, consisting of real estate valued at $2,000,000, is in this city. His daughter and only child, in whose arms he died, is his sole heir. It will be long before New Orleans will have a more enlightened or excellent citizen, or a more princely benefactor than R. D. Shepherd.[77]

The launching of the *R. D. Shepherd* drew the usual crowd and plaudits, and a news report said:

so slowly, so grandly did she pass into the river that every spectator had the gratification of a long view of graceful movement. She has been built under the direction of Capt. Daniel Marcy, and is said by those who are good judges in such matters to be of the most impressive model and workmanship. The Ship Judah Touro was built under the oversight of the same gentleman, and proves to be a good ship. She promises speed, a steady head and spacious stowage for her cargo.[78]

Captain Marcy took the *R. D. Shepherd* to Boston. She sailed on September 1 and arrived in Boston the next day. From Boston, Marcy sailed her to New Orleans, a passage of 16 days.[79] After her arrival in New Orleans, the owners were so delighted with their new ship that they sent the builders checks for $500 each. "This is the highest compliment a ship-owner can pay to a builder."[80]

Captain Marcy brought the *R. D. Shepherd* north to New York, where he turned the vessel over to Capt. J. J. Nickerson. But no matter who was master, the *R. D. Shepherd* kept on doing the work for which she was built. In August 1849, coming into Boston from Liverpool, a deckhand, Francis Martin of Rotterdam, was swept overboard. She came into Portsmouth on June 27, 1850, with Turk's Island salt for John K. Pickering. When the Civil War started, she once ran the Gulf Blockade into her home port, New Orleans.[81] Although it's not certain what finally happened to her, she may have been destroyed by the Confederates when the Federal fleet swept up the Mississippi.

Matilda

SPECIFICATIONS: 1846. Samuel Badger. Female figurehead, square stern. Burthen, 689 tons. Length, 147.2 feet; beam, 32 feet; depth, 16 feet. Two decks. Original owners—Jeremiah G. Smith et al., of New York.

Surprisingly, Samuel Badger's journal shows very little increase in the cost of building a ship of nearly 700 tons from those in the 500- to 600-ton range. His total cost for the *Matilda* was $25,968.59, and he showed his best profit yet, selling the ship for $28,000.

Capt. Jeremiah G. Smith took the *Matilda* to sea on November 20, "of and for New York."[82] The *Matilda* voyaged in the packet lines, and little effort was made in Portsmouth to keep track of her—after all, she had been "sold foreign"; in those days any registry outside of the Portsmouth district was "foreign." Nelson said she was sold in Melbourne and renamed the *Australian*.[83] Whether or not she became "The Waltzing Matilda," like the Australian army's marching song, is open to question in view of an article in the *Portsmouth Chronicle* on July 26, 1880, which reported that the *Matilda* had been abandoned at sea while en route from the Washington Territory to Callao with lumber. On June 24, the captain, his wife, and half the crew took one boat. The mate took the remaining crew in his boat. They drifted 700 miles before going ashore at Mazatalan, Mexico.

Samoset

SPECIFICATIONS: 1847. Fernald & Pettigrew. Indian figurehead, square stern. Burthen, 562 tons. Length, 136.8 feet; beam, 30 feet; depth, 15 feet. Two decks. Original owners—R. H. Tucker & Sons and Daniel Stone, all of Wiscasset, Maine.

While the *Samoset* was the first ship built in the Port of Portsmouth for the Tucker family of Wiscasset, Maine, she wasn't the first they had owned. As noted previously, in 1842 the Tuckers had acquired the *Alliance*, built by Samuel Badger in 1836. As far as can be determined, the Tuckers didn't buy another from Fernald & Pettigrew, nor did they order any from Samuel Badger. However, in the 1850s they became steady customers of Tobey & Littlefield, and they also bought one ship from George Raynes. The *Samoset*, named for the famed Indian chief who befriended the Pilgrims, was launched on July 19:

LAUNCH. — On Monday last, a fine ship of 560 tons was launched from the yard of Messrs. Fernald & Pettigrew, on Badger's Island in this harbor. Her name is the SAMOSET, in memory of the Indian who welcomed the Pilgrims. She is owned by Messrs. R. H. Tucker & Sons, and Daniel Stone of Wiscasset, Me. and is to be commanded by Capt. Joseph Tucker. She is intended for the Charleston, S. C. trade. — The Samoset is of superior model, having the quality of carrying well, and is undoubtedly of swift sailer. For solidity of construction and beauty of finish she speaks well for the builders. She is built of the best New-Hampshire white-oak, is very heavy copper fastened, and was coppered upon the stocks.[84]

Capt. Joseph Tucker was in command when the *Samoset* left on her maiden passage to Charleston for cotton. With Samuel H. Cobb as mate, the *Samoset* went from Charleston to Le Havre and back in 75 days. Again, extracts from the *Samoset*'s logs have been made available by Miss Jane Tucker of Wiscasset. On her second passage across, the *Samoset* carried 1,974 bales of cotton, including 105 of Sea Island. She returned to New York with 210 passengers, "including 11 infants," plus 600 tons of freight, such as railroad iron. Leaving Savannah July 22, 1848, a runaway slave was found on board. It's not hard to guess what happened to that poor devil when handed over to the shore authorities. That was a slow passage because of a hurricane.

The *Samoset* arrived in Liverpool in January 1850, and Captain Tucker reported to his father, back home in Wiscasset: "This will inform you of the safe arrival of Ship Samoset into Albert Dock, yesterday [January 7] after a passage of 21 days and some hours from Pilot to Pilot. A short time after I took my Pilot, the Danube came down and when she rounded too I made her out and set by flags. While they were flying the Alliance made her appearance round Skerries and set his flags, also the Peter Marcy, so we had a fleet of Master Fernald's ships." Captain Tucker was, of course, wrong about the *Alliance*—she was built by Samuel Badger. But, anyway, the four vessels were all from the Kittery side of the Piscataqua. On his return to the United States, in August 1850, Captain Tucker brought in nine birds and three dogs for a friend who had loaded his out-going cargo; there was other freight as well, like railroad iron.

That year Chief Mate Cobb left the vessel and was succeeded by James Brown, with a man named Ferry as second mate. In 1851, the *Samoset* went to Havana, where she picked up $2,000 in gold for expenses. What expenses? The log doesn't say, but she did load 3,885 boxes of sugar—1,624,456 pounds for £1,862, plus primage. The *Oxford*

English Dictionary (*OED*) defines primage as a percentage paid the captain and crew by the shipper. The *Samoset* returned from Bristol, England, with 800 tons of railroad iron, plus 11 passengers at £5 each.

George W. Chapman had relieved Joseph Tucker for that passage, and he continued as master. In 1852, the *Samoset* hauled 2,001 bales, of which 151 were Sea Island. Mrs. Chapman was on the ship during a later 1852 voyage. In April 1854, Chapman yielded command to John K. Greenough. Hungry for glory and money as they were, the masters occasionally took relief. Captain Greenough sailed the *Samoset* to Havana. The log indicates that during this time the *Samoset* had five different mates, but in Havana she loaded 3,910 boxes of sugar at £3.05ñ—"1,675,662 pounds, loaded to 18 + feet." She came back from Liverpool to Baltimore with salt, soda ash, iron, and a few passengers. Miss Tucker's abstracts show that voyage after voyage was much the same. John K. Greenough brought the *Samoset* to Boston in February 1856, and turned the vessel over to William S. Frost, with W. J. Clark as mate. Captain Frost later commanded the Portsmouth-built clipper *Express* with something less than distinction when she was captured by the CSS *Alabama*.[85] Captain Frost continued in command for several years. In 1859, Capt. Wilson McNear took command at Boston. Little changed during his time on the quarterdeck—the *Samoset* carried the usual large cargoes. However, it's interesting to note that in 1862 a vessel like the *Samoset* would come from Liverpool to New York in ballast. The Civil War was making a difference. By that time, the *Samoset* was eager for any kind of cargo, hauling 887 tons of coal to St. Thomas in the Virgin Islands.

Capt. Daniel M. McCobb became master in 1863, but he, too, was clutching for cargoes. The *Samoset* hauled coal, guano, teak, and whatever else came her way. Times were tough, but she did escape the Confederate raiders. The Tucker company log indicates she was sold in San Francisco in 1868. After that she was cut down to a bark. Which brings her story to 1885:

OLD PORTSMOUTH-BUILT SHIPS.

A letter received in this city, not long since from Mr. C. W. Walker, formerly of Portsmouth but now engaged in the lumber business in Washington territory, makes mention of some of the Portsmouth-built ships of long ago which are still doing good service on the Pacific coast. One of these is the ship (now barque) Samoset, 633 tons register, built on Badger's island in 1847 by Fernald & Pettigrew; and another is the ship Dashing Wave, 1054 tons, built on the same blocks in 1853. The Dashing Wave is slightly hogged, but is about as fast a sailer as ever, and is noted for her quick passages; both the vessels named are owned by a sawmill company at Tacoma, Washington territory, and bid fair for many years of good service yet, provided the rocks do not get in their way. The ship Sagamore, 1341 tons, built in 1856 by Mr. Charles W. Stimson for Wm. P. Jones & Co., on the same blocks as the Dashing Wave and Samoset, is still a fine looking ship, her lines being apparently as true as the day she was launched; she was the last vessel built on Badger's island, and is owned in Port Gamble, W. T., and employed wholly in the transportation of lumber from Port Gamble to San Francisco. Another ship, the Eagle Speed, built on Badger's island and by Mr. Stimson the same year as the Sagamore, and for the same owners, was launched just before the last-named vessel; she was lost on a coral reef in the China sea when three years old, and her dismantled hull was seen standing there by a Portsmouth shipmaster two years afterward.[86]

Columbus

SPECIFICATIONS: 1847. Fernald & Pettigrew. Male figurehead, square stern. Burthen, 1,307 tons. Length, 178.5 feet; beam, 40.1 feet; depth, 20.05 feet. Three decks. Original owners—the Kingslands.

While the pace of shipbuilding in the Port of Portsmouth was accelerating, it was a long way from the zenith attained in the 1850s, which the late Gertrude Pickett so aptly labeled *Portsmouth's Heyday in Shipbuilding*, in a book of that name published in 1979. But, at that, seven three-masted square-riggers, plus three barks and two schooners, were launched in 1847. The enthusiasm expressed by the *Journal* was overwhelming as it told about the *Columbus*, the largest merchantman yet built on the river. In fact, the *Columbus* was the first three-decker built since the *Archelaus* at Exeter in 1792. The *Columbus* was launched on September 25:

> THE LAUNCH OF THE COLUMBUS, a three decker, built at Badger's Island by Messrs. Fernald and Pettigrew, will take place THIS DAY, Saturday, at about 12 o'clock M. She is the largest merchant ship ever built in New-England, being of about 1500 tons burthen, and is owned by the firm of Messrs. D. & A. Kingsland, & Co. of New-York city. She was built under the superintendence of Capt. Samuel Weare, and is intended for a packet ship, to run between New-York and Liverpool, and will be commanded by Capt. Robert McCerrin.

The Columbus is built on the same spot where the ship-of-the-line America was built in the Revolution. The Columbus is within one hundred tons of the size of that 74 gun ship, whose launching attracted thousands of visitors from neighboring towns.[87]

As often happens to well-meant advance notices of events, the time given was wrong. The *Columbus* was actually launched a half hour before the announced time, "which disappointed many, ourselves among them, from beholding the grand sight. The hour we published was received from the builders, and likewise by inquiry from Capt. [Samuel] Weare. Owing to the unforeseen strong east wind, which affected the tide, it was found necessary to launch earlier."[88]

Having survived its erroneous launching report, the *Journal* let itself go about the ship in a later article:

NEW PACKET SHIP COLUMBUS.

This splendid ship, a magnificent specimen of the skill and ability of our mechanics, is now ready for sea. She is the largest merchant ship ever built in the United States; her extreme length being 185 feet 6 inches; breadth 40 feet 6 inches, depth 30 feet 3 inches, and we are told she will exceed 1800 tons carpenter's measurement. The whole height of the main-mast from heel to truck is 200 feet; from the end of the flying-job-boom to the end of the spanker boom is 283 feet 6 inches.

Viewed externally the Columbus presents a noble appearance; her gigantic proportions and beautiful model at once astonishing and delighting the beholder. Her figure-head is a full length statue of the famous discoverer whose name she bears, and her stern is ornamented with a bust of Columbus, supported on each hand by a full length figure of one of the natives who greeted him on his arrival in the new world, the whole surmounted by an American eagle spreading thirteen feet, and bearing in its talons the olive branch of peace.

The astonishment felt on viewing her from the wharf is in no degree lessened on going on board — the extent of her upper deck, her spacious cabins, the vastness of her steerage of "between decks," and the wonderful capacity of her hold, all serve to fill the spectator with wonder, while the excellence of the workmanship and beauty of finish cannot fail to command his admiration.

She has three regular decks fore and aft. Between the upper and middle decks are a saloon, main cabin, and second and third class cabins, beside the necessary accommodations for the crew, cook, steward, &c. The saloon and main cabin are fitted up in most exquisite style. The panel work of the doors and sections are of branch and myrtle mahogany, rose and zebra wood, relieved by pilasters of white and gilt. At the aft end of this cabin, between it and the saloon, is a beautiful transparency, on stained glass, representing Columbus and his followers nearing the shore in their boat, the gallant adventurer himself standing in the bow, with the standard in his had ready to plant on this great continent. At the opposite end is a large mirror, extending nearly across the cabin. Opening from this cabin are the state rooms, much larger than are often seen on shipboard, being nine feet square, each containing two berths, and fitted with every convenience.

She is intended for a New-York and Liverpool packet ship, was built for Messrs. D. & A. Kingsland by Fernald & Pettigrew, from a model of their own, and is to be commanded by Capt. Robert McCerran. She is the fifth ship the Messrs. Kingsland have had built on our river — the best possible evidence of their good opinion of the ability of our mechanics.

The building of this ship was contracted for by her enterprising builders in January last, since which time they have purchased the timber, made her model, and got her ready for sea, besides building the Samoset, a ship of 563 tons, and the schooner Fashion, of 200 tons. They are now engaged in laying the keel of a new ship of 900 tons for Messrs. R. D. Shepard and Daniel Marcy. Such enterprise richly deserves success, and we heartily wish them the rich reward to which they are justly entitled. — *Messenger*.

The rigging of the Columbus is made from the best of Kentucky hemp, by J. Johnson, Esq. of this town.

The experienced Naval Constructor, located at Charlestown, after examining the Columbus expressed the opinion that she would make a good frigate with but slight alterations.[89]

The Journal couldn't be content with that bit of bragging about the *Columbus*. On November 27, 1847, it had more to say:

NEW YORK PACKET SHIPS.

The four largest belonging to New-York, and we think the largest American merchantmen afloat, are the *New World*, the *Constitution*, the *Columbus*, and the *Ocean-Monarch*. It was stated in the account of the Columbus, published in our paper a fortnight since, that she was the largest. In point of carrying capacity this statement is correct, but in the rate of government tonnage the Columbus stands number three. The following is the tonnage of each vessel as recorded on the cus-tom-house books.

New World, built at East Boston, 1404 tons; Constitu-tion, built at New-York, 1322 tons; Columbus, built at Ports-mouth, 1307 tons; the Ocean-Monarch, built at East Boston, 1301 tons. By carpenter's measurement, the Columbus is about 1800 tons. The New-World is eight feet longer than the Columbus, and eighteen inches wider, but is not so deep by 2 feet 3 inches — which makes the capacity of the Columbus fully equal to the New World, and superior to the other two.

We feel a little pride in not only sending some of the best vessels from Portsmouth, but also in providing some of the best captains. Capt. EBEN. KNIGHT, of the New World, was a mechanic of Portsmouth, and made his first voyage before the mast in the ship John-Hale, from this port, nineteen years ago. He now enjoys the highest honors of his profession.

The *Columbus* wasn't primarily destined for the cotton trade. The Kingslands wanted a large ship for service as a packet in the lucrative Liverpool–New York immigrant service. Under Capt. Robert McCerran, the owners leased the *Columbus* to the Empire Line. In 1848, Captain McCerran became entangled in litigation over the man-ner in which he had handled a passenger. Nathaniel A. Smith, an emigrant from Liverpool, was in steerage and died at sea. The com-missioner in New York cleared McCerran of all blame in the death. Testimony showed that Smith had been an uncooperative passenger; urged to clean up his berth, he refused. McCerran then ordered him to do so, and he again refused and was put in irons. The man was hob-bled when killed by the falling of the main topsail boom.[90]

Before the passage that led to Smith's death had even started, an unusual incident took place on the *Columbus*. The story was told by the *Liverpool Mail* and reported by the *Portsmouth Journal*, and it demonstrated the frantic efforts made by some to get to America:

SINGULAR DEATH. — The Liverpool Mail contains the fol-lowing strange account of the death of a woman who attempted to cheat a shipmaster out of the price of a passage to this coun-try, by smuggling herself on board in a box: —

On Wednesday, the ship Columbus was moved out into the river, with the view of getting her ready for proceeding to America. In the course of the day, some of the passengers fan-cied they heard a noise issuing from a box between decks, and on opening it a female was discovered inside. She was immediately taken out, but expired almost instantaneously. It is supposed that she either secreted herself, or was secreted by some one else in the box, in order to escape payment of the passage money out. A man named Thomas Devine, who acts as a shipper of passengers, has been charged with causing the death of the girl by stowing her away. The inquest was held yesterday, before Mr. Stathem, the deputy-coroner, when our reporter at once recognized the prisoner Devine as a fellow who, a few months ago, was brought up before Mr. Rushton, upon the charge of having defrauded a bouncing young lady of a sum of money, by proposing to pack her up alive in a four-and-sixpenny deal box, and stow her away on board an American ship, and thus cheat the shipowners of the proper price for a live passenger. — It appeared at the inquest yesterday, that the young woman who was the subject of the present inquiry, had been acting as nurse to the prisoner's wife, and she had been stowed away on board the Columbus. The key of the box was sent on board, and it appeared that she was once seen out of the box; but, upon the box being subsequently opened, she was found just alive, but died immediately afterwards from suffocation.[91]

The *Columbus* served her owners well until January 6, 1852, when she was wrecked on the rocks at the entrance to Waterford Harbor, Ireland, and went to pieces. "Four passengers, two ladies and two steerage passengers, with eight of the crew, were drowned. The remainder, 20 in number, including the master, first and second mates, were saved. The C. had been towed to sea from New Orleans, Dec. 8th. She had on board 3881 bales of cotton and 2197 sacks of corn."[92]

William Penn

SPECIFICATIONS: 1847. Samuel Badger. Male figurehead, square stern. Burthen, 800 tons. Length, 151.5 feet; beam, 34.3 feet; depth, 17.15 feet. Two decks. Original owners—Anthony Michael, J. C. Hitchcock, and A. R. McHenry, all of Philadelphia.

The *William Penn* was the first ship of 800 tons built by Samuel Badger. As the yard was carrying out the first stages of the *William Penn*'s construction, some attention was directed toward a bark, the *Alice Tarlton*, 309 tons, contracted for by James and Thomas Tarlton and others. The *Alice Tarlton* was active for years, finally being sold in Surinam in 1871.[93] But it was the *William Penn* that attracted news attention:

NEW PACKET SHIP "WILLIAM PENN."

Since the first of the present year, there have been completed and commenced at the four ship-yards in the immediate vicinity, vessels whose united tonnage will exceed 5200 tons.

There was launched from the ship-yard of Mr. Samuel Badger, at Kittery Foreside, on Saturday last, a noble new ship called the "William Penn." Mr. Badger is well known and justly celebrated as a superior ship-builder, as the numerous vessels which he has constructed — remarkable for the same strength, speed, and beauty of model which characterize those of his fellow ship-builders here generally — will fully warrant us in saying the "William Penn" bids fair to prove one of his finest specimens. She is upwards of 800 tons burden, and has been built for Messrs. Richardson, Watson & Co.'s new line of packets, to run between Philadelphia and Liverpool. Her length on deck is 153 feet 6 inches, breadth 34 feet, depth 22. She is built of our well known New-Hampshire pasture white oak, not excelled by any oak in the world, and some of which has lain in dock for two years. Her style of finish is said to be superior to any thing heretofore known on the Piscataqua, and we venture to say that it will equal, if not surpass that of any other ship ever built in the Union. She is extra copper fastened throughout. Her figure-head is a full length representation of "William Penn in treaty with the Indians."

The "William Penn" is to be commanded by Capt. Anthony Michael, of Philadelphia, who has superintended her construction, and during his stay in our town made *everybody* his friend. — *Gazette*[94]

With the owners of the *William Penn* based in Philadelphia, it was only logical that their ship should bear the name of the founder of the "City of Brotherly Love." Anthony Michael was in command when the *William Penn* sailed late in October. A report on her first passage was published:

This new ship, which recently sailed from this port for Charleston, arrived there in six days. A letter received from the first officer states that they had a rough passage, and experienced a heavy gale of wind off Cape Hatteras, in which the vessel behaved admirably. During a perfect hurricane of seven hours, she hove to under close-reefed main top sails. Mr. Malony adds: "She sails very fast — we get twelve knots out of her — she carries sail to great advantage, and is very stiff. Taking the ship William Penn all through, she is the best and easiest working ship Capt. Michael or myself have ever been on board of. She works like a top, and out sailed everything we saw on the passage."[95]

The *William Penn* was chartered in the Black Diamond Line in 1847. Based in Philadelphia, Richardson, Watson & Co. were the agents. They employed her in the cotton trade and in bringing immigrants from Europe. The *Liverpool Telegraph* reported in March 1850 that the *William Penn*, with Captain Michael still in command, left Liverpool for Philadelphia and ran into heavy weather all the way across, causing "the vessel to resemble a block of ice." All hands had to shovel snow and sleet in order to work the ship. Michael was relieved by Capt. T. P. Folger in 1852. In October, 1854, the *William Penn* was wrecked off the Mull of Gallaway, after colliding with the ship *Brother Jonathan*, built in Portsmouth by Tobey & Littlefield in 1853.

Mortimer Livingston

SPECIFICATIONS: 1847. George Raynes. Male figurehead, square stern. Burthen, 748 tons. Length, 155 feet; beam, 32.4 feet; depth, 16.2 feet. Two decks. Original owners—E. W. Barstow et al., of New York.

The *Mortimer Livingston* was named for a prominent New York shipowner and merchant. Livingston founded the Union Line in 1854, but he stopped investing in sailing vessels in 1857 in order to promote steamers. Chronologically, the *Mortimer Livingston* probably should have been the first vessel mentioned in the 1847 crop of Portsmouth vessels. Her launching on April 19 at 2:00 P.M. put her in the forefront. The launching prompted the *Journal* to publish a detailed report on ship construction then going on along the Piscataqua:

> On Monday last another noble ship, the MORTIMER-LIVINGSTON, of 750 tons burthen, was launched from the yard of Mr. George Raynes. She was built under the direction of Capt. G. W. Barstow, of New-York, to whom, with other gentlemen in New-York, she belongs. We shall probably give a more particular description of this beautiful vessel before she leaves Portsmouth.
>
> There is now building at the yard of Samuel Badger, Esq. a ship of 800 tons, under the direction of Capt. Anthony Michaels of Philadelphia, to be connected with a new line of packets between Philadelphia and Liverpool. She is to bear the name of Pennsylvania, and the image of the founder of that state is to be the appropriate figure head, and the state arms

on the stern. She will be launched about the first of August —
and the keel of a 1000 ton ship will be laid immediately after
for the same line.

We saw a few days since an elegant model, prepared by
Mr. Badger, which has been forwarded to Belfast, Ireland, by
which a ship is to be built to run in the Belfast line of packets
from New-York.

Messrs. Fernald & Pettigrew are building a ship of 1400
tons, (the largest merchantman ever built on our river) for
Messrs. D. & A. Kingsland of New York.

Two ships, of 700 tons each, are to be built at Mr.
Raynes' Yard.

Schr. Fashion, of 198 tons, was launched from the yard
of Messrs. Fernald & Pettigrew a few weeks since. She is built
for a line of packets between Boston and New-York, to be commanded by Capt. N. Kelley of Hyanis. The cabin and state-
rooms are elegantly fitted up with almost every accommodation
of the large packet ships. The lovers of good taste in New-York
and Boston will do well to take a look at her, and say whether
they can improve the *Fashion.*

At least one error and an omission take some of the value out
of the *Journal*'s article. The vessel at Samuel Badger's yard, as related above, was the *William Penn*, not the *Pennsylvania*. But that's an
understandable mistake; the same syndicate did have a thousand-ton
ship *Pennsylvania* built elsewhere, and Captain Michael did command her. The omission lies in not mentioning the construction upriver of the *Elizabeth Hamilton* at Hanscom's yard in Eliot, now the
Greenacre property.

Edwin A. Barstow, one of the owners, was in command when
the *Mortimer Livingston* sailed from Portsmouth. She went into the
packet service on the North Atlantic. Few details about her are available, but she was wrecked at Carson's Inlet, New Jersey, January 25,
1863.[96]

Centurion

SPECIFICATIONS: *1847. George Raynes. Billet head, square stern.
Burthen, 744 tons. Length, 152.7 feet; beam, 32.6 feet; depth, 16.3 feet.
Two decks. Original owners—J. D. Taylor and D. W. and R. M.
Oliphant, all of New York.*

An experienced mariner's eye would quickly detect the difference between the *Centurion* and the *Mortimer Livingston*, which had preceded her down the ways, but the two ships were also very similar. The *Centurion* was launched "in beautiful style on Wednesday of last week [September 30], from the yard of George Raynes in the presence of a large number of spectators. She is about 750 tons burthen and is worthy of her enterprising builder, which is praise enough to bestow on any vessel."[97] The *Centurion* left Portsmouth on November 6 under Capt. David Gillespie, who had supervised her construction. She arrived in New York on the ninth.

By 1849, Moses D. Ricker of Portsmouth, who lived on Chapel Street at the corner of Sheafe Street, was master of the *Centurion*, and she was chartered in the Red Z Line. A. Zerega & Co. were the agents. The Zeregas and Rickers were connected by marriage. Edward Coombs had her in 1851 in the Union Line, out of New York. David Caulkins was master in 1859, and on one passage the *Centurion* rescued the crew of the British ship *Dromahair*, on January 9, 1859.[98]

While Ricker was master of the *Centurion*, she had to return to New York, in July 1848, after running into a severe gale in the Atlantic while en route to Liverpool. Her upper rigging was stripped away, "and a few minutes after was struck by a furious whirlwind which hove her on her beam ends; cut away the main top-mast backstays, when the mast went over the side, breaking off the mainmast below the cap, the ship lying on the lee side in the water to the hatches. After clearing away broken spars, she righted, keeping a rank heel to port; sounded the pump — five and a half feet of water in the ship, all hands and passengers at the pumps. Gale abated and they bore up for New York."[99]

Eventually, like so many other American ships, the *Centurion* was "sold foreign" to R. W. Cameron in Melbourne, Australia.[100]

Siam

SPECIFICATIONS: 1847. George Raynes. Billet head, square stern. Burthen, 726 tons. Length, 151 feet; beam, 34.2 feet; depth, 16.2 feet. Two decks. Original owners—Henry L. Williams and Tucker DeLand, of Salem, Massachusetts.

Slightly smaller than her two immediate predecessors, the *Siam* was the third square-rigger launched by George Raynes in 1847. From the beginning, the *Siam* was destined for the East Indian trade. She was launched on November 22, but it was several weeks before she was fitted out and cleared by Customs officials. Often there was a delay between final clearance and actual sailing time, sailing vessels being entirely dependent on wind and tides. The delay led to a news item:

> SHIP SIAM. — This elegant ship has cleared at the Custom-House, but as she will not probably sail until the first of next week, an opportunity is afforded for those who wish to visit her this day. She is intended for the India trade, and is the finest ship Salem has ever employed in that business. In accommodations in every part of the ship, and in the elegance of finish, she will compare with any vessel afloat. She was built by Mr. George Raynes, under the superintendence of Capt. Jacob W. Thompson; is owned by Messrs. Tucker Deland and Henry Williams of Salem; and is commanded by Capt. Charles Mansfield. She proceeds to New-Orleans, thence to England and India. Success to her.[101]

Shipping news items in the Portsmouth newspapers indicate that the *Siam* did sail in the East Indian trade; certainly her name isn't to be found among ships working as transatlantic packets. Her first master was Capt. Charles Mansfield, and he did take her to New Orleans, where she loaded cotton for Liverpool. From the latter port she went to the East Indies. In the mid-1850s she was under a Captain Williams, and in 1853 she was at the Cape of Good Hope, en route from Manila to New York for replacement of masts lost in a storm.[102] A news story reported her sold in New York in 1861 for $19,000 in cash.[103] Nelson didn't give a source, but listed her as sailing out of Sydney, Australia, in 1866, working as a whaler.[104] By 1872, she was reported as hailing from London, and had previously been sold in Hamburg, Germany, to go under "the North German flag."[105]

Finally, on March 8, 1873, the *Journal* said the *Siam*, "built at this port in 1847, on her way from Portland, Oregon, to Queenstown, with wheat was abandoned at sea on January 15, 1873." The crew was saved by the ship *Forest King* of Boston, and taken to Valparaiso."[106]

Elizabeth Hamilton

SPECIFICATIONS: 1847. William Hanscom. Eliot. Female figurehead, square stern. Burthen, 742 tons. Length, 151.5 feet; beam, 32.7 feet; depth, 16.35 feet. Two decks. Original owners—William and William P. Jones, of Portsmouth.

Undoubtedly, the Port of Portsmouth produced many more glamorous vessels than the doughty *Elizabeth Hamilton*, but none excelled William Hanscom's ship in integrity. And she met her end only by a criminal act. Hanscom's yard was on the banks of the Piscataqua on land that is now the grounds of Green Acre, the Baha'i community in Eliot, Maine, which was established through the largesse of Sarah J. Farmer.

William Hanscom, who had worked in nearly every upriver shipyard during his career, settled down in the family shipyard to build the *Elizabeth Hamilton*. Nearly 20 years before, Hanscom had cut a ship in two in that yard, and then lengthened it. But the *Elizabeth Hamilton* was the first he built on the site. The Hanscoms would build five more vessels in the yard before it closed forever. These included two clippers, the famed *Nightingale* and the *Josephine*, a freighting ship, the *Judge Shaw*, and two barks. When these were finished, so were the Hanscoms as civilian shipbuilders. No other upriver yard again figured in major shipbuilding on the Piscataqua. By "upriver" is meant above the Portsmouth Bridge.

Before the launch of the *Elizabeth Hamilton*, it was said:

> LAUNCH. — The "Elizabeth Hamilton," a splendid ship of 750 tons, will be launched from the yard of Mr. William L. Hanscom, at Eliot, on Thursday next (if fair weather) at three o'clock P. M. She is owned by Messrs. William Jones & Son of this town, to be commanded by Capt. Thomas Jones, who has superintended her construction. This fine specimen of naval workmanship, built from a new and improved model for capacious stowage and fast sailing, reflects great credit upon the skill of her builder, inasmuch as the materials, both timber and fastening, used, have been extra to any ship ever built on this river, and which, combined with the beauty of finish, cannot surpassed. — *Com.*[107]

For reasons not specified, the launching was put off until October 28, but it went "off in fine style."[108] Under Capt. Thomas Jones, the *Elizabeth Hamilton* sailed for New Orleans the day after Christmas. On her passage, she poked into Pensacola looking for a cargo, but had to go on to Mobile, where she loaded cotton for Le Havre. Captain Jones stayed with the *Elizabeth Hamilton* until 1856, when he became master of another family-owned ship, the *Kate Prince*. By that time, the *Elizabeth Hamilton* had been sold to New York parties under private terms.[109] She stayed in the transatlantic service for several more years. In 1860, under Capt. R. Harding, the *Elizabeth Hamilton* had a charter in the Z Line. Then she sailed around Cape

Horn to San Francisco and was sold in Newberg, Oregon, for $20,000. She began hauling lumber to the Mare Island Navy Yard in California. However, the next year she was back on the East Coast, putting into Bermuda, while heading back toward San Francisco. At first scheduled to be broken up, she was repaired and kept working until 1879, when it was reported:

> The ship Elizabeth Hamilton, Capt. Hempstead, bound from Philadelphia for Trieste with a cargo of 257,582 gallons of refined petroleum, valued at $21,250, was abandoned at sea on the 12th of February, in latitude thirty-four north, longitude sixteen west; the crew were taken off by the steamer Lykens, from Marseilles, and landed at Delaware Breakwater. The Elizabeth Hamilton was built at Eliot in 1847 by Mr. Hanscom, for William Jones and William P. Jones of this city; at the time of her loss she was owned in New York. She was of 854 tons register.[110]

Over the course of the next few years, it became known that the *Elizabeth Hamilton* didn't come to a natural end. Several years of bitter court infighting finally showed that the ship had been betrayed by her own people:

> The old ship Elizabeth Hamilton, built on the Piscataqua, and fired at sea and abandoned a few years ago, has been the subject of a legal controversy for many years, which was brought to a close in the supreme court at New York last week after a trial that lasted nine days before Justice Van Voorst and a jury. The mate of the vessel, which was leaking at the time she was abandoned, was convicted on a charge of destroying her in order to prevent an examination being made prior to her owners' demanding payment of the insurance. In August, 1873, the ship was purchased for $19,000 from Edwin Atkins by James Bigler, of Newburg. In January, 1875, Mr. Bigler sued Mr. Atkins for $30,000 damages, alleging that the Elizabeth Hamilton was in a leaky condition at the time of the purchase, and that this fact had been concealed. Justice Donohue dismissed the complaint in 1883. It was carried to the general term and a new trial ordered. The defendant sought to prove that the vessel was sound at the time of the sale, calling fourteen witnesses to establish this, but a verdict of $13,000 was rendered for the plaintiff.
>
> The Elizabeth Hamilton was built in 1847 by the late William L. Hanscom, afterward a naval constructor, at his yard

in Eliot, opposite the Rollins farm in Newington, for Messrs. William Jones & Son. She was of 742 tons measurement, and considered of excellent model, being a fast sailer and good carrier, and was for many years commanded by the late Capt. Thomas Jones.[111]

Peter Marcy

SPECIFICATIONS: 1848. Fernald & Pettigrew. Male figurehead, square stern. Burthen, 820 tons. Length, 163 feet; beam, 33 feet; depth, 16.5 feet. Two decks. Original owners—Daniel Marcy, of Portsmouth; Peter Marcy, Judah Touro, and R. D. Shepherd, of New Orleans.

The Peter Marcy for whom the sailing ship *Peter Marcy* was named was a native of Portsmouth, born August 21, 1806. In his early manhood, Peter Marcy left Portsmouth to become a shipbuilder, owner, and merchant in New Orleans, although he made many visits to his home town. Marcy built the first dry dock in New Orleans, and later he was a partner in the firm of Bailey, Salter & Marcy, specialists in dry docks. With his brother, Daniel Marcy, he was a partner in the construction of several successful merchant vessels. He was also associated in shipping enterprises with Judah Touro and R. D. Shepherd. It was noted at the time of his death, January 10, 1886, that "like many others he suffered greatly from the effects of the [Civil War] and was well nigh ruined, but when the peace was restored he set to work with indefatigable energy and perseverance to retrieve his losses and was successful."[112] Peter Marcy died in his home outside his adopted city.

The sailing ship *Peter Marcy* slipped into the water on July 15, launched from the yard "of those enterprising builders, Fernald & Pettigrew...to the gratification of a large number of spectators."[113] When the *Peter Marcy* sailed on August 29, the *Rockingham Messenger* noted:

> This superb ship went down our river on Tuesday morning with a light and favorable breeze, and was cheered as she left the wharf by a crowd of admiring spectators. She was built by Messrs. Fernald & Pettigrew, for Messrs. Touro, Shepherd and Marcy, and is intended for the freighting business. She is about 900 tons measurement, and it is calculated will carry 3000 bales of cotton. Her length on deck is 164 feet, breadth of beam 34 feet 9 in., and depth of hold 23 feet. Her cabin is most beautifully painted in fresco, on pine, in imitation of birch, rose

SALT TO ARRIVE.

3000 HHDS. Trapani SALT, per ship
Peter Marcy;
3000 hhds. St. Ubes SALT, per ship Charlemagne.
Inquire of   **F. W. ROGERS,**
May 26.   No. 2 Congress st. Portsmouth.

and zebra wood, and all bearing a polish equal to any of the
fancy woods which it was intended to resemble. The companion
way or outer cabin is an excellent piece of graining, in imitation of oak and maple, from the brush of Edward Smith. Her
blacksmith work was under the direction of John Knowlton;
the joiner work by Thomas Martin, the painting by Smith &
Swasey, the caulking by Leach & Walton; the spars and blocks
were made by Martin & Fernald; her cordage was from the
manufactory of Jeremiah Johnson, her sails from the loft of
Richard Boardman, and she was rigged by Charles Harrat. She
is to be commanded by Capt. Daniel Marcy.

Captain Marcy first put into Boston, and one of the seamen on
that leg said that the *Peter Marcy* "worked like a pleasure boat and
sailed admirably."[114] More and more of the ships built in the Port of
Portsmouth were heading first to Boston, New York, or Philadelphia
to recruit hands and pick up southbound cargoes. The New Hampshire hinterland had little to offer, other than hay, apples, or potatoes.
Sometimes a load of ice might be taken. Toward the middle decades of
the nineteenth century, ice became increasingly in demand. John
Tudor of Boston pioneered in the ice business, and huge ice houses on
the ponds near Boston were used for storage. Tradition had it that the
first cargo of ice taken to New Orleans in the 1830s produced "general
commotion and consternation, and the ship was ordered to the middle

of the Mississippi, where she discharged her cargo into the river."[115] In 1864, ice was fetching $60 to $100 a ton, and a number of consumers "combined to furnish their own supplies.... After paying salaries and all expenses, and allowing two-third for waste, their ice will cost them $36 per ton. The lowest it ever sold there [New Orleans] was $5 per ton on shipboard, in 1842."[116] But what a sight it must have been to see all those blocks of ice from that first shipment floating down the Mississippi to the Gulf of Mexico.

Whether or not the *Peter Marcy* loaded ice at Boston isn't known, but Captain Marcy booked her into the Packet Line for the run to New Orleans. Arriving there, she was chartered in the New Line, and Marcy took the ship to Liverpool. After the *Peter Marcy*'s return to the United States, Marcy turned her over to Capt. A. Sampson.[117] Under Captain Sampson, the *Peter Marcy*, in 1850, made a passage "from New Orleans to Liverpool in 26 days, which is the shortest passage ever between the two ports. Built by Fernald and Pettigrew, it is evidence that for beauty as well as speed our ships are No. 1."[118]

On at least one occasion, the *Peter Marcy* put into the Port of Portsmouth, and Frederick W. Rogers, a merchant on Congress Street, advertised 3,000 hogsheads of Trapani salt.[119] Shortly after that, under Captain Hickey, the *Peter Marcy* was in the East Indian trade. On her first home passage from India, a seaman named John Frank was brought back in irons. Frank had assaulted Bernard Thompson, the mate, with a knife, so he was held for hearing in the United States. On arrival in Boston, Frank was turned over to the U. S. marshal.

Just prior to the outbreak of the Civil War, the *Peter Marcy* was in Glasgow, having come from New Orleans. She arrived back in her home port a few days before the guns roared at Ft. Sumter. She left New Orleans on April 30, 1861, for Cowes, England, where she arrived on June 17, and then went on to London. From London, she went to St. Stephen, New Brunswick, to haul lumber. Supposedly, she made one successful run through the Union blockade on the Gulf of Mexico, late in 1861. What finally happened to her isn't known. She could have been trapped in the Mississippi after her inward run of the blockade and destroyed in the subsequent river fighting.

Hibernia

SPECIFICATIONS: 1848. Samuel Badger. Billet head, square stern. Burthen, 877 tons. Length, 163 feet; beam, 34.3 feet; depth, 17.1 feet. Two decks. Original owners—Samuel Badger; Charles H. Salter; and Richardson, Watson & Co., of Philadelphia.

The *Rockingham Messenger*, on July 20, 1848, reported that "the *Baron Bareaux*, a splendid ship of about 950 tons was launched in fine style on Tuesday [July 18]. She is owned by Capt. Charles Salter of this town [Portsmouth] and Messrs. McHenry of New York and Richardson of Philadelphia. She is to be a packet between Philadelphia and some port in Great Britain." Greatly embarrassed, the *Messenger* had to admit the next week that it had made several mistakes in its launching story: "our informant said he could not recollect her name, but it was an Irish one, and we, therefore, concluded that given by the *Gazette* (*Baron Bareaux*) was correct." Probably they were all confusing the name of Brian Boru, the great Irish hero. "The *Journal* said she is the *Hibernia*, and has been built for Messrs. Richardson, Watson & Co. for a Philadelphia–Liverpool packet."[120] Perhaps to make amends, a *Messenger* reporter visited the *Hibernia*, and his glowing description was reprinted by the *Journal*:

> This new packet ship of about 900 tons, which left our harbor on Wednesday last for Alexandria, is a specimen of finished workmanship, as well as of the most beautiful model. She was built by Sam'l Badger, Esq., and is intended for Richardson, Watson & Co.'s line of Philadelphia and Liverpool packets, to be commanded by Capt. Charles H. Salter, who, as well as Mr. Badger, are part owners. We visited her before her departure with an intention of giving some description — but the Messenger has done it so well that we will extract from its account.
>
> The model of the Hibernia is beautiful; her lines are gracefully rounded, and although she is upwards of 900 tons burthen, and her capacity for carrying freight is correspondingly great, she look as snug and graceful as a yacht, and her size is lost sight of by the spectator in contemplating her fair proportions. Her length on deck is 165 feet, and her breadth of beam 35 feet. Her cabin is beautifully finished — the sides consist of panel work of mahogany, rose and zebra wood, the handiwork of Mr. Alfred T. Joy, relieved by white and gilt pilasters done by Mr. Smith. A black walnut table, capable of being extended the whole length of the cabin, occupies the centre, on each side of which is a settee — of the same material; an elegant black walnut sofa forward, and two lounges at the after end, one on each side of the mirror, complete the furniture of the cabin. Adjoining the cabin are nine neat and commodious state rooms. The companion way is handsome and spacious, and being above all, and furnished with windows and standing room, affords a

grand opportunity for passengers to witness the fury of the storm without being subjected to its pitiless peltings.

Forward of the mizzen-mast and abaft the main hatch is a fine cabin on deck for second class passengers, painted in an unique and pretty style, and containing six state rooms, each containing two berths. Forward of this cabin, under the same roof and lighted by a vertical window, is the main entrance to the steerage, on each side of which entrance are the rooms appropriated to the mates. — This entrance and the front of the cabin, as well as the companion, is beautifully grained in imitation of oak and maple, by Mr. Edward Smith. — Abaft the windlass and forward of the main hatch, is a spacious house on deck, in which is a room having an entrance to the steerage, and where a stove is to be placed by which the passengers between decks may do their cooking; the room appropriated to the use of the cook in which is placed a monster stove and cooking utensils to match; — two apartments containing six berths each, and another devoted to the accommodation of chickens, pigs, &c. Forward of the foremast are the quarters for the men, — commodious and convenient. Between decks she has 90 berths, in the smallest of which might repose "three in a bed," while some of them are capacious enough take in a whole family. It is well lighted and ventilated.

Take her all in all, she is a splendid specimen of the workmanship of our artizans, and we commend her to the attention of all within whose observance she may come.

Before the *Hibernia* left the Port of Portsmouth, six local people had a small misadventure with her. Two males and four females were in a sailboat, maneuvering for a close look at the *Hibernia*. The male sports weren't very skilled in the handling of their small craft: they ran the sailboat under the *Hibernia*'s bow, which forced their little craft under, "and she instantly filled with water. Her occupants were relieved of their disagreeable position, fortunately without injury, but considerably frightened and very wet."[121]

Built for packet work, it isn't surprising that the *Hibernia* was chartered immediately in Richardson's Line. Later she went to the Black Star Line. That charter was followed by one in the Blue Ball Line, under Daniel W. Maloney. On a packet charter from New York to Liverpool, in the fall of 1852, the *Hibernia* nearly met with disaster. Some of the terror of the situation can be realized from a news account:

The Packet ship Hibernia, which left New York on Friday, Sept. 24, for Liverpool returned to port on Monday, having narrowly escaped foundering at sea, under singular circumstances. — The particulars are thus stated in the New York papers:

"At 8 o'clock on Saturday morning she weighed anchor from Sandy Hook, discharged the pilot at 9, and with a fair wind proceeded to sea. By midnight the wind blew stiffly, with rather a heavy sea; started the pump and found all dry. At 2 A.M. the officer on duty observed that the vessel did not answer her helm readily, added to which she lay over more than usual, with a strange, uneasy motion; so much so that he very prudently aroused the captain and all hands. At this crucial juncture the pumps showed 5 feet of water and on an even keel they gave 14 feet in the hold, with every appearance of the vessel going down by the stern. To avoid a rush, the passengers were not only kept in ignorance of the danger, but no one under any pretence was admitted on deck, although anticipating the fearful struggled for life, all the boats and life preservers were in readiness, besides a number of loose spars with ropes rove into them.

At 3 A.M. the wind increased, huge waves broke over the bulwarks, washing away every thing that was loose about the deck, but not one of the crew disobeyed orders or ceased toiling at the pumps or lightening the ship by staying the water casks and casting overboard all the heavy articles. At this time escape seemed impossible, while the fearful cry, "four feet more water," sounded like the death knell of the devoted mariners. Since the discovery of the danger, the course had been right before the wind for Long Island beach, but as all were deliberating on the impossibility of making it, and the propriety of deserting the sinking vessel, day began to gleam, revealing a large hole underneath the mizzen chains caused by the fracture of an air valve, which fully accounted for the rapid rising of the water. This was with great difficulty stopped sufficiently to reach this port. The passengers were then admitted to the deck, and rendered what assistance they could. The return trip was accomplished by noon on Monday. Had the night held dark one short hour longer, it is probably that no one would have been left to tell the terrors of that fearful Saturday night."

There were seventy passengers on board the Hibernia.[122]

The *Hibernia* went to pieces in 1854 after being wrecked on Indian Island near Philadelphia.[123]

Danube

SPECIFICATIONS: 1848. Fernald & Pettigrew. Billet head, square stern. Burthen, 749 tons. Length, 150.5 feet; beam, 33 feet; depth, 16.5 feet. Two decks. Original owners—Edward F. Sise, Joshua W. Peirce, John Chase, and J. D. Simes.

The *Danube* was on the stocks next to the *Peter Marcy*, but behind it in construction progress by a little more than a month. She was launched on August 27 in a traditional ceremony that was "generally acknowledged to have been the most pleasing exhibition of the kind presented this season. She threw spray in gallant style as she went down to her natural element for the first time, and, as her anchors checker her progress, she sat the water like a swan."[124] John Chase, formerly master of the ship *Athens*, was in command when she sailed for Pensacola in late October. However, it appears that she had to go on to Mobile to find a cargo. The *Danube*'s first transatlantic trip was to Liverpool, where she unloaded before going around to London. Her passage from London to New York took 30 days. In packet ship style, she made a quick turnaround and went back to London, returning to New York at the end of August.

In the course of the next few years, the *Danube* made many passages across the Atlantic. Occasionally, she was diverted to southern ports for cotton, and on a return from Le Havre in 1851, she reached New York "in the very short passage of 17 days."[125] The next year she made a passage to Trieste, Italy, and went ashore during the run. However, she made it off without damage and proceeded on her way. In November 1852, the *Danube* cleared New York for San Francisco, arriving there in May. A mild uproar ensued when her cargo was unloaded. A San Francisco newspaper reported that some of the packages brought by the *Danube* were wet. However, the *Portsmouth Chronicle* insisted, on May 30, 1853, that the item was incorrect, "as letters from the ship speak of her cargo coming out in excellent condition. It is to be remarked that this is the first report of the *Danube* on this voyage published in any paper in this city." From San Francisco, the *Danube* dropped down the Pacific coast to the Chincha Islands, there to load guano. She was back in New York in February.

While on a passage to Trieste in 1854, the *Danube* picked up the crew of the ship *Devonshire*, which had been wrecked on the Italian coast, and brought them home. Besides the *Devonshire*'s men, the *Danube* brought home, manacled, a seaman who had stabbed the master and mate of the bark *Prompt*. Under a Captain Coster, the *Danube* went into the East Indian trade, making a packet run from

New York to London, thence to Calcutta. On passage from Calcutta to London, the *Danube* went into St. Helena, where Napoleon was so long exiled, for water, "having supplied the ship *Rose Ellis* of London who were without any, theirs having been spoiled by salt water."[126] She arrived in London on September 14. From London, she went to Mobile and loaded for Le Havre. Her westward passage was to New York. When she cleared New York on June 6, 1857, for Lisbon, her passengers included Joseph Simes and William F. Chase, both of Portsmouth, but neither of whom were listed in the 1857 City Directory. The *Danube* went to Cadiz from London and loaded salt for her Portsmouth owners. After her first visit to her home port in several years, the *Danube* sailed to Mobile. She hauled 2,300 bales of cotton, weighing 1,215,998 pounds (607 tons) and valued at $141,691.95. She carried cotton east and passengers west, right up to the Civil War. In 1861, it was reported:

> The ship Danube, owned by Messrs. E. F. Sise, J. W. Peirce, P. P. Lyman, and John Chase of this city, was seized May 24 by a detachment of Gulf City Guards. It was understood that Captain Coster had a permit to pass in and out of the Bay. The Guards searched the vessel, but found nothing on board except one eight-pound cannon, though it had been understood she had a quantity of arms and some ammunition. They took possession of the cannon, and brought it to Mobile and placed it in Armory Hall. The Danube was from Liverpool in ballast.[127]

A later marine item reports the *Danube* as being at Mobile, loading for New York. Where she spent the Civil War years isn't clear. Word of her ultimate fate in 1866 came in a terse paragraph:

> By the cable, we have a Liverpool dispatch of the 8th, which says that the ship Danube, from Bristol for the United States, has been burned at sea. Her passengers and crew were saved and brought to Liverpool by the ship Compear, from Mobile. The Danube was built at this port in 1848 by Messrs. Fernald & Pettigrew, for E. F. Sise and others, and rated at 743 tons.[128]

Jersey

SPECIFICATIONS: 1848. George Raynes. Billet head, square stern. Burthen, 849 tons. Length, 160 feet; beam, 34 feet; depth, 17 feet. Two decks. Original owners—Henry L. Williams, Tucker Deland, et al., of Salem.

Launched the day after Christmas, the *Jersey* was a belated gift to her owners, as well as being the last of the four square-rigged ships put in the water in 1848. The news item on the launching was eulogistic, as usual: "She will compare with any other specimens of substantial and good workmanship which have given a reputation to Portsmouth, the world over."[129] Before the *Jersey* left the Port of Portsmouth, a detailed description of her was published:

She is 850 tons register, length on deck 160 feet, extreme breadth 35 feet, depth 22 ft. 6 in. of which 7 ft. 9 in. is in her between decks. She has a handsomely set billet-head with straight rails, and a most beautifully carved and finished stern. There is 6 ft. 3 in. solid timber from her keelson to the bottom of her shoe, all of which is bolted through with 1 1-4 in. copper and riveted.

Her whole frame, we are told, is of the best of New-Hampshire pasture white oak, cut near the Piscataqua river, and thoroughly seasoned. She has five hooks and pointers under how lower deck aft, three of which run up and lock to three separate deck beams; she has also six hooks and pointers forward: the pointers running up and fastening to three separate beams the same as aft; they are all bolted through and riveted securely to the frame. Thick work at floor heads is 8 in. thick, of white oak, lapping the joints of timbers and 24 in. wide, fitted as perfectly as joiner work, having four fastenings in each plank and timber. All the joints of her timbers are securely bolted; a 12 in. stringer covers the joints of the half top timbers and futtocks — two bolts in each timber well riveted. The clamps under her lower deck are 7 in.; a full set of beautiful, very stout, perfectly finished white oak knees under her lower deck, with 14 bolts in each, all through and riveted. Waterways are 16 in. square. The lower deck beams sided 14 to 18 in. moulded 14 in. the streaks over the waterways 9 in. and square bolted. She has very spacious between decks, beautifully and strongly finished, her breast hook between decks is 30 ft. 6 in. long, and is fastened by 67 bolts coming through from her frame and riveted on the inside of 1 1-4 in.; she has two heavy transom knees 20 ft. long, with 60 bolts all riveted. She has a full poop 50 ft. long with every thing conveniently arranged upon it. Her cabin is both convenient and elegant in finish and furniture — equal to any first-class Liverpool packet. Her deck arrangements are excellent, giving her much more room than ships of this class usually have. A large house for passengers, and cook's department between the fore and mainmast, and her forward and after hatches are covered with houses for the convenience and protection of passengers between decks, agreeable to the new passenger law. A large top gallant forecastle finishes forward: it is carefully arranged for the accommodation of a large crew.. Her rigging is of superior quality, manufactured from the best of American hemp, by the Plymouth Cordage Company, and her sails are of cotton duck. Altogether, she is, we think, as fine a ship as our talented mechanics have ever sent away. Her lines are most perfect and beautiful, and indicate the most perfect combination of sailing, steering and carrying qualities of any model we have yet seen.

The painting of the cabin, by Mr. Smith, is so deceptive as to require a very scrutinizing observation to be convinced that it is not really veneered throughout with zebra, satin, and other fancy woods. Mr. A. T. Joy has furnished it in a style to correspond with the other work. The mirrors and stained glass windows are equal to any display in the most brilliant parlors.

She was built for Messrs. Tucker Deland, Henry Williams, and others of Salem, by our townsman, George Raynes. She makes the fortieth vessel constructed by him, and fully sustains the high reputation which this gentleman has so fairly won in his profession. It may not be amiss to add that he now has on the stocks his forty-first and forty-second vessels, one of 700 the other of 900 tons, which are not yet disposed of.[130]

Commanded by John Day of Salem, the *Jersey* cleared early in March 1849 for New Orleans, arriving on April 5. A news item said: "We note in the marine report for this week that this fine ship, belonging to Salem, recently built at the yard of Mr. George Raynes, in this city, made the trip from New York to New Orleans in the short space of 10 days, notwithstanding rough weather. She beat the steamship New Orleans by two days.[131]

Owned away from Portsmouth, not much track was kept of the *Jersey*. She finally was wrecked in November 1856, 30 miles south of Cape Henry. She was en route from the Chincha Islands to Baltimore. One man was lost, another badly frostbitten.[132]

Empire State

SPECIFICATIONS: 1849. Fernald & Pettigrew. Female figurehead, square stern. Burthen, 1,324 tons. Length, 180 feet; beam, 40 feet; depth, 20 feet. Three decks. Original owners—the Kingslands.

The *Portsmouth Journal* proudly acclaimed that the *Empire State* was the largest packet ship in the world when she was launched on March 9, "in fine style."[133] The *Empire State* was also the first of the 1849 crop of big merchantmen launched in the Port of Portsmouth. Five others would follow, as the demand for big, fast vessels continued to grow due to the outbreak of "Gold Fever" and the towering wave of immigration from Europe. In its prelaunch account, on March 3, the *Journal* described the *Empire State* as being of 1,640 tons, "carpenter's measure." During the construction, Capt. Joseph G. Russell, a part owner, supervised the work, and he later became her first master. Russell had been the commander of the ill-fated ship *Empire*, built five years before by Fernald & Pettigrew. After the *Empire State* sailed, the *Journal* treated its readers to a detailed description of her:

> The noble specimen of naval architecture, the Packet Ship EMPIRE STATE, built by Messrs. Fernald & Pettigrew, sailed from our harbor on Thursday last. — She went down the river in handsome style, and amid the cheers of numerous spectators she wended her way to the broad ocean, which in all its vast extent bears not its superior — either in size, or in beauty and strength of finish. She has sailed for New Orleans, under the command of Capt. Russell, thence taking freight for Liverpool, where she will take her place in Messrs. Kingsland & Co.'s line of New-York and Liverpool packets.
>
> We went on board a few days since for the purpose of giving some description of the Empire State, but finding a good account at hand well done by the Messenger, we adopt it.
>
> The Empire State is 190 feet in length, and of 1640 tons burthen, carpenter's measurement. Her capacity, we are assured, is greater than that of the Constellation, launched in New-York last month, although the registered tonnage of the latter is the greater. The Empire State being two feet deeper than the Constellation gives her about 200 tons more actual capacity than that ship, notwithstanding the latter is several feet longer.
>
> Viewed from the wharf, the Empire State presents a noble appearance, her masts towering some two hundred feet

☞ *Removed to Nos 1 & 9 Pier Wharf,*

Deering & Yeaton

RIGGERS,

PORTSMOUTH ,N. H.

A. K. P. DEERING, } *Nos. 1 & 9 PIER WHARF.*
JOHN A. YEATON. }

☞ Blocks and Falls to let at reasonable rates

above her gigantic hull; and the beholder is at a loss which most to admire — the vastness of her proportions or their perfect symmetry. Her bow is worthy of all admiration, being unusually bold and graceful. The head rails being carried out with the shear of the mouldings, makes an unbroken line of the white streak, and gives a remarkably easy appearance to the bow, which is ornamented with a female figure bearing in her hand a sprig of laurel — a representation of victory. Her run is clean and beautiful, and her stern is in keeping with the other portions of the hull, being ornamented with the seal of the state of New York, and surmounted with a large carved and gilded American eagle.

Her spacious spar or upper deck appears uncommonly clear, the cook and boat house, companion ways and skylights being so well arranged as to present no obstruction to the labors of the crew in working the ship, and affording the man at the wheel a complete view of all their operations. A half poop extends forward from the stern some twenty feet, and just forward of this is the steering wheel. A miniature rudder, or "tell tale," lighted at night by a lamp below, protrudes above the projecting deck just alluded to, unerringly pointing out to the steersman at all times the position of the rudder.

In proceeding to the cabin we pass through a beautiful

saloon, splendidly furnished, containing the staterooms of the captain and surgeon, and other conveniences, and lighted from the stern by six stained glass windows. The main cabin, like the saloon, is magnificently furnished and finished. A beautiful and substantial mahogany table, 23 feet in length, and capable of six feet extension, occupies the centre, on each side of which are ranged settees of the same material, covered with crimson plush cushions. At either end of the cabin is a rich rosewood sofa, the cushions covered with purple velvet; over that at the forward end is a grand mirror, and over the other, separating this cabin from the saloon, is a colored glass transparency, representing the American eagle sustained by Liberty and Justice, accompanied by the highly appropriate motto — "Excellence." At the sides of the cabin, from which they are [—?— —?—] most beautiful mahogany, zebra and rosewood panel work, relieved by white and gilt pilasters, and surmounted with a polished white ceiling, having two tasteful strings of gilt beading, are seven staterooms, 9 by 10 feet, each containing two berths and a lounge, and furnished with washstands, drawers, and everything requisite for the comfort and convenience of passengers. The pantry, which is spacious and convenient, connects with the forward part of the cabin.

Forward of the cabin, and arrived at by the entrance to the pantry, a space across the ship of eight feet is divided into rooms from the accommodation of the officers — on one side a mess room for the three mates and boatswain, and on the other apartments for the sail maker and carpenter.

Forward of this is an apartment fitted with berths to accommodate forty second class cabin passengers; and still farther forward, and having a separate entrance, is what is termed the "upper between decks," very spacious and exceedingly well ventilated, where berths will doubtless be greedily seized upon by the "aristocracy" of the steerage. And forward of this are two rooms for the accommodation of the sailors, of which she will carry thirty before the mast. The three bulkheads dividing the three apartments, are of extraordinary strength, being strengthened by diagonal braces let into the deck beams and a heavy perpendicular timber fastened to the deck by two heavy iron bolts running completely through it, thus forming a partition like the truss work of a bridge, and all covered by a sheathing of inch boards. This, it is confidently believed, will prevent any surging of the ship in violent weather.

On the lower deck, in the capacious steerage, which is

clear fore and aft, the visitor is afforded a full view of the form of the hull, and of the strength and superiority of her construction; and a momentary examination is sufficient to convince any one that it would be difficult to put iron and wood together more securely.[134]

Apparently there hadn't been any demand for the *Empire State*'s services in New York to carry passengers to Liverpool, so she went to Mobile, arriving there on May 8 and clearing for Liverpool on May 24. She came back to New York with passengers and then returned to Liverpool carrying passengers. On that passage, the *Empire State* lost part of her rigging in a squall on October 23, 1849.[135] She continued to carry passengers between New York and Liverpool for the next few years. Captain Russell still had her when she rescued 60 crew members and passengers from the ship *Eudocia*, of St. John, New Brunswick.[136] In 1862, there was a report in Portsmouth that a one-eighth share in the *Empire State* had been auctioned off at $1,000.[137] In 1864, a news item reported the *Empire State* as being at Cardiff, Wales, where she had been examined by the underwriters, a statement that hints strongly that she had been in difficulty. It was decided to dock her and discharge part of her cargo.[138] In October, it was reported that the *Empire State* had been sold in London for £5,000.[139] This was probably when the Bombay and Bengal SS Co. came into possession of the *Empire State*. She was renamed the *Bombay*.[140]

Mary Hale

SPECIFICATIONS: 1849. Samuel Badger. Female figurehead, square stern. Burthen, 648 tons. Length, 148.3 feet; beam, 30.8 feet; depth, 15.4 feet. Two decks. Original owners—Ichabod Rollins, Samuel Sheafe, Horatio Coffin, all of Portsmouth.

While Fernald & Pettigrew were busy on Badger's Island getting out their big ship, the *Empire State*, and the *Granite State*, a 198-ton schooner, Samuel Badger was making the chips fly with the construction of a bark, the *Oriental*, 467 tons, and the ship *Mary Hale*. It's noteworthy that the *Oriental* was larger than many of the ships Badger had built in his early years. The *Oriental*, incidentally, was condemned in Rio de Janeiro in 1851. The *Mary Hale* was launched amid the traditional fanfare on August 18. Her master was Capt. Charles H. Rollins, another of the veteran Portsmouth shipmasters. He had, at one time, commanded the ships *Columbia* and *King*

Philip. His maritime life was mostly spent sailing the cotton triangle, but he also was in the East Indian trade. When the Civil War broke out, Captain Rollins retired from the sea and settled on Pleasant Street in Portsmouth. He became active in banking. He also served as secretary and treasurer of the Portsmouth Athenaeum. He commanded the *Mary Hale* throughout her short life.

And the *Mary Hale* had more than her share of misadventures. On her maiden passage, Rollins took her to New Orleans, where she loaded for Liverpool. In her first two voyages, she went into New York, but her returns were directed to Baltimore. In 1851, she occasioned much concern: She was 102 days crossing from Liverpool to Baltimore, where she arrived on April 25. Fighting contrary winds, she was 60 days out when she ran out of food, so Captain Rollins put in at Fayal, in the Azores. After getting fresh supplies, the *Mary Hale* couldn't get out of the harbor at Fayal, being windbound. However, her 38 passengers were all in good health, although perhaps a bit annoyed at the length of the passage.

For the next three or four years, she was a sort of shuttle service between Baltimore and Liverpool. Then she went back to hauling cotton. On June 22, 1855, she cleared at New Orleans and was towed to sea three days later. On July 25, the *Mary Hale* piled up on Alligator Reef, a few miles off the Florida Keys. The wreckers came and lightened her by 400 bales, and she was taken to Key West, where the cargo was reshipped, although she had to delay departure until the salvage claims were settled. An Admiralty Court decreed salvage "at $7,500, and her expenses were $1,015 more; being 10 per cent to the salvors. Two shares amounting to $140 were withheld, the holders having tampered with the crew, and influenced them to refuse to assist in getting the ship afloat."[141] The rest of that voyage was equally inauspicious for the *Mary Hale*. After finally getting to Liverpool, she began loading for New Orleans. When nearly ready for sea, on October 4, she was struck by lightning while tied up at Victoria Dock. No one in the crew was hurt, but her top gallant mast was shattered. Getting to New Orleans, she once again loaded cotton, this time for Trieste. She was towed to sea on December 4, and again became news:

LOSS OF SHIP MARY HALE.

Extract of a letter from Capt. Rollins of the ship Mary Hale.

On the 5th inst. (Jan'y) at 10 P. M. the ship struck on Key Sal in a gale of wind from the north, ship under three close reefed topsails and reefed foresail — immediately commenced thumping heavily — in five minutes the rudder was torn off and the stern frame parfly torn out. At daylight the water was as high inside as out, and thinking the ship would soon go to pieces, concluded to endeavor to make a landing on the Island. Got a small cask of water into the long boat with some provisions, and with the crew in the other boats left the ship, wind then N. E. blowing hard. Succeeded in landing through the surf on the south side of the Island. — Next day, 7th, more moderate, got some more provisions and water from the ship.

On the 8th hauled the long boat on the beach and put her in order. Fitted her with mast and sail, and on the 9th dispatched the mate with five men for Key West, in search of assistance. He reached Key West at 2 A. M. on the 11th. On the 12th a schooner from there hove in sight, to our great joy. Commenced loading her immediately. Have loaded this vessel with 900 bales cotton, and most of the ship's materials. I have been at the Island from the 5th to the 24th. When I left, all the cotton on board was under water, and the ship nearly broken in two. All hands safe.[142]

Later it was learned that she had gone on Dog Rocks, north of Cay Sal. The wreckers saved 908 bales of cotton, and all but 180 were dry. The total number of bales was 1383. It is thought the entire cargo would be sold. "The sale of materials from the ship amounted to $2,638.28."[143] The good cotton was loaded on the bark *John Colby*; the U.S. marshal sold the other bales at an average of $25 each.

James Browne

SPECIFICATIONS: 1849. George Raynes. Male figurehead, square stern. Burthen, 996 tons. Length, 170 feet; beam, 35.7 feet; depth, 17.85 feet. Two decks. Original owners—Arthur Child, W. T. Glidden, and W. H. Wilson, of Boston; George Raynes, of Portsmouth.

While his fellow shipbuilders across the Piscataqua River were turning out new vessels, George Raynes was no less industrious in his efforts. The *James Browne* was his first in 1849. She was launched on August 23, the same afternoon the *John Haven* went into the water off Badger's Island. The news accounts glowed with praise; when the *James Browne* sailed in September, she was described as "a sample of the product of the Raynes yard, of which the builder may not be ashamed."[144] (In truth, the continuing praise heaped on every departing vessel became rather fulsome, but how can you blame the *Journal* for touting these ships?) Although intended for the packet trade, the *James Browne* headed for New Orleans. As passengers, she took with her Charles B. Blunt, his wife and four children; S. Marcy, wife, child, and niece; and Nathaniel Raynes, brother of the builder.

Under Capt. Arthur Child, the *James Browne* sailed for several years, working as a packet. Her main service was in the Philadelphia Line. Child commanded her until 1857, when William Crabtree became master. Like so many vessels flying the Stars and Stripes, the *James Browne* was sold in 1863 and renamed the *Rockhampton*.[145]

The new owner was James Baines & Co., a firm that dominated the trade between Australia and England for some years. Truthfully, the *James Browne* wasn't one of the Baines Company's more fortunate purchases. When bought, she was the oldest vessel the firm had ever acquired. Michael Stammers wrote that her career in the BlackBall Line was marred by two slow passages and many deaths among her passengers:

> On the first occasion, she arrived in Keppel Bay 116 days out of Liverpool on October 12th, 1863, with 436 men, women and children. There had been 29 deaths on the voyage and her accommodation had been condemned as being unsanitary and ill-ventilated, while there were accusations of acts of immorality between the female passengers and the crew.... She was not advertised again for the company until June 5th, 1865.... She certainly sailed again for Queensland in January 1866, for she was advertised to sail on the 5th but actually left on the 24th. Her passage outwards was slow and tragic, for she had to put in at the Cape of Good Hope because she had sickness aboard, and she was 127 days out when she dropped her anchor in Moreton Bay.
>
> Twenty-eight people had died on that passage, including the surgeon, and many were still ill with fever. The remaining 455 passengers were landed at Dunwich, on Stradbroke Island [off the Queensland coast, near Moreton Bay] to recover, but while they were there another 23 died....
>
> Messrs. J. & G. Harris and Bright Brothers, the firm's agents at Brisbane, had spent a lot of money on food and services while the ship lay in quarantine but, by the latter months of 1866, Baines & Co. were in no position to repay them. The ship was already mortgaged to London merchants so she was arrested by the Vice-Admiralty Court for debt and sold on March 20th, 1867, to meet her creditors' claims. She was bought by Captain T. Francis of Brisbane for only £1750, and he put her into the guano trade, after which all track of her seems to have been lost.[146]

John Haven

SPECIFICATIONS: 1849. Fernald & Pettigrew. Male figurehead, square stern. Burthen, 1,038 tons. Length, 171.85 feet; beam, 36.5 feet; depth, 18.125 feet. Two decks. Original owners—Robert Rice, Jonathan M. Tredick, George W. and Alfred Haven, all of Portsmouth.

Residents of Portsmouth and the neighboring towns who enjoyed going to launchings had a busy day when the *John Haven* slid down the ways. First, the *James Browne* had gone into the water at the Raynes yard, and then came the *John Haven* from Badger's Island. The ship honored the memory of one of the Port of Portsmouth's leading merchants in the first half of the nineteenth century. John Haven's early training was a practical one for a merchant of that day: he clerked for Joshua Wentworth, then went to sea as a supercargo, and finally became a master. He died on October 23, 1845, in his eightieth year.[147] With two members of his family among the owners, the name was appropriate. Before the *John Haven* sailed, a detailed description was related:

SHIP JOHN HAVEN

On Tuesday last we visited this noble ship, then lying at Pier wharf, and nearly fitted for sea. Although our yards have produced larger ships for merchants of the great cities, the John Haven is the largest that has ever been owned in Portsmouth. She is 172 feet in length, 36 1-4 feet wide, 23 1-4 feet deep, has 10 inches dead rise, at half floor, and measures 1038 10-95th tons. She is of excellent model, combining all the qualities of a large carrier, fast sailer and easy steering. She has a perfect shear, and although a full ship has very easy lines, with a beautiful bow, and her counter and stern are light, airy and finely turned. Her frame, we are told, is large and square, composed entirely of New Hampshire white oak cut in the vicinity of Portsmouth last winter.

Her between-decks is very spacious, showing much strength and extra fastening, and having great height, 8 feet. Being ventilated with 5 patent lights on each side and four stern windows, it is most admirably adapted for emigrant steerage passengers for which there is ample room for 350.

On deck, her arrangements are a house 36 feet long, with a half poop round it connecting with the side. This house is divided into forward and after cabins: the latter finished elegantly with polished mahogany, zebra, and rose woods, with pilasters and capitals of polished white and gold. The forward cabin is handsomely painted in maple and oak. The cabins are carpeted and furnished with black walnut furniture. The after cabin is furnished as a drawing-room and the forward cabin as a dining-room.

She has a house on deck forward, 36 feet long by 15 feet wide, two-thirds of which, the forward end, is set apart for the use of the crew. This gives them a most excellent and comfortable cabin and speaks much in praise of the owners in thus providing such comfortable quarters for the ship's company.

She is fitted with Allen's newly invented patent steering apparatus, which has great power and speed and is very compact. Her substantial windlass is from the foundry of Mr. I. Haselton, in this town, of his approved model which is getting into general use.

For her head, she has a fine bust of the late Mr. Haven, whose name she bears.

The stern ornaments are well executed, with several emblems are a portrait and a well turned vine, stars, &c.

She was joinered outboard by Willard Brown; and her inboard joinery and cabins by Thomas Martin; her after cabin was veneered and polished by S. M. Dockum; the iron work on hull by John Knowlton; and on the spars and blocks by John Dame; the brass work and fixtures by Samuel Gerrish & Son; her spars and blocks made by Mr. Thomas Odiorne; the rigging, from best Russia hemp, made by Jeremiah Johnson; and filled and rigged by Mr. Harratt; the painting and graining, gilding, &c. by Smith and Swasey; the cabin furniture by J. C. Colcord; her suit of sails by C. Walker: all mechanics of Portsmouth.

She was modeled and built by those enterprising builders, Messrs. Fernald and Pettigrew of this place, and reflects great credit on them as ship builders, as well as on all who performed the work in the various departments.

The John Haven, from the time her keel was laid, was built under the superintendence of Capt. Jacob W. Thompson, well known as one of our first shipmasters, and who for several years past has been employed in superintending the building of ships — the J. H. being the fifth or sixth ship built and fitted under his inspection. She is owned by Messrs. J. M. Tredick, Robert Rice and George W. Haven of this place, and is to be commanded by Capt. Samuel Harding, late of ship Pactolus. She sailed for Mobile on Thursday.[148]

Capt. Samuel Harding, yet another of the highly respected group of master mariners who hailed from the Port of Portsmouth, was first master of the *John Haven*. He was born in Bath, Maine, March 11, 1806, and went to sea at the age of 13. His first command was the brig *Iris*, 245 tons, built by William Badger in 1823 and owned by the same Robert Rice who had an interest in the *John Haven*. He was only 22 when he took over her quarterdeck, so Harding and Rice had a relationship dating more than 20 years. After the *Iris*, he commanded other Port of Portsmouth–built ships, such as the *Apollo* and the *Berwick*, along with the Boston ships, *Robert Harding* and *Criterion*. He retired from the sea in 1862 and went to work for Bureau Veritas (the French version of Lloyd's). In the 1870s, he was pilot commissioner for the New York and Sandy Hook pilots. He died in Poland Springs, Maine, July 23, 1891.[149]

Harding was with the *John Haven* only a year before turning her over to Capt. John B. Haley, whose career as a master had started in the year 1822 on the ship *Lycurgus*. Captain Harding's maiden voyage in the *John Haven* was around the cotton triangle—Mobile, Liverpool, and Boston. Haley took the ship to Cadiz for salt and returned to Boston on July 25, 1850. Having had a brief rest, Harding resumed command, and went back around the triangle. On another voyage, the *John Haven* went into Newport, Wales, and brought a cargo of railroad iron to New York. Rails were a common cargo in the days when American railroads were casting their iron tentacles everywhere.

Moses D. Ricker became master in 1852. On his first voyage, Ricker sailed the *John Haven* around the cotton triangle, and on the westward passage the ship was nearly destroyed by a hurricane. Finally, in 1854, the *John Haven* was sent around Cape Horn to San Francisco. From that port, the ship went to Calcutta—an increasingly common pattern—and returned to Boston by way of the Cape of Good Hope, a round-the-world voyage. Again, under a Captain Sherburne, the *John Haven* went to Calcutta, returning to Boston on March 9, 1856. Under various masters, she continued in that trade. Capt. Edwin E. Salter, of the Portsmouth Salters, cleared Boston for Apalachicola in January 1858, with Mrs. Charles D. Salter as a passenger. In 1861 it was reported:

> CAPT. EDWIN SALTER. — Our last paper contained a notice of the death of Capt. Edwin Salter of the ship John Haven, and son of the late Henry P. Salter of this city. Capt. Salter died of fever, on the passage from Manila to New York, on the 29th of November, at the age of 26 years. He was a young man of more than ordinary ability, and had already taken a high stand in his profession, having received a thor-

ough mercantile education before going to sea. To a judgment unusually matured, strict morality and integrity, and a quick perception, he added devotedness to his business, and gave eminent promise of usefulness and success. He had won for himself the affection and respect of numerous friends at home and abroad, by an amiable and thoughtful disposition; and his death will be sincerely regretted by all who knew his noble qualities. The deepest sympathy will be felt for those who have been thus early bereaved of a most loving and dutiful son and brother.[150]

If nothing else, sadly, the item demonstrates how young the men were who commanded large vessels out of the Port of Portsmouth. For the great discretionary powers they held, both disciplinary and financial, the role those young mariners played was stellar.

In 1863, with the Civil War raging, the *John Haven* was sold in London for £4,800 cash; a short article noted that the *John Haven* had been owned by Jonathan M. Tredick of Portsmouth.[151] With that, the *John Haven* seems to have disappeared from local annals, but Portsmouth-built vessels weren't that easily forgotten. In 1879, a report on the *John Haven* stirred a new controversy:

> In the shipping-disaster columns of the press we find a statement going the rounds to the effect that the ship Faderneslandet, Nielson master, of 1085 tons register, which sailed from Pensacola Nov. 13th for Greenock, Scotland, and was abandoned at sea, "was built at Portsmouth, N. H., in 1848, and hailed from Christiansand." There was but one ship built on the Piscataqua at or about the date mentioned of which we can find any record, that would nearly answer the description of the ship above named, and that was the "John Haven," of 1035 tons register, built by Fernald & Pettigrew in 1848 and launched and registered in 1849, and originally owned by J. M. Tredick and three others. The John Haven, after making a number of successful voyages, was sold to go under the British flag, and thereafter for several years hailed from London, as the "King of the Seas." The vessel of course must have been again sold and had her name and flag once more changed, before she became the "Faderneslandet," of Christiansand, Norway, — that is, if the latter and the "John Haven" were identical.[152]

Journalism being the competitive industry that it is, the *Chronicle* immediately attacked the statement of the *Portsmouth Times* that the *John Haven* was the only ship built in the Port of Portsmouth in 1848. Its version still leaves one guessing:

The *Times* is in error stating that the ship John Haven "was the only ship built at this port in 1848," for ship-building was brisk at that time. The John Haven was the only ship built here in '48 or '49 that nearly answers to the description of the abandoned Norwegian ship Faderneslandet; she was registered in 1849. The Empire State, also registered in 1849 and built by the same contractors, would answer as to size, but is known to have been totally lost. Besides these two vessels, the ships James Browne and North Atlantic, built by George Raynes, and the Mary Hale, built by Samuel Badger, were all registered in 1849. The ships Danube, Hibernia, Jersey and Peter Marcy, all registered in 1848, were none of them nearly so large as the Faderneslandet.

North Atlantic

SPECIFICATIONS: 1849. George Raynes. Billet head, square stern. Burthen, 799 tons. Length, 158.5 feet; beam, 33.1 feet; depth, 16.55 feet. Two decks. Original owners—Jacob Norton, H. Cook, J. H. Boardman, and T. Coffin, Jr., all of Newburyport; A. H. White, of Boston.

Among the purists in the scholarship of clipper ship construction, there might be an argument forthcoming to the effect that the *North Atlantic* was really George Raynes's first venture in that field. Certainly some of the *North Atlantic*'s specifications hint at clipper style. In a strict, length-versus-breadth ratio, the *North Atlantic* was a leaner vessel than the *William E. Roman*, Raynes's first acknowledged clipper. The *North Atlantic* had a ratio of 4.78 length to beam, compared to the *Roman*'s 4.58. Yet, although no one labeled it a clipper, the *Thomas Perkins*, built by Frederick Fernald in 1837, was trimmer than either the *North Atlantic* or the *Roman*, which was built in 1850. Whatever the merits of the debate, it was obvious that George Raynes was tending toward fast, sleek craft. At the time of the *North Atlantic*'s launching, it was reported: "The North Atlantic is a ship second to none of the ships built by Mr. Raynes. She has a full coop inclosing the mainmast, and her finish and deck arrangements are the same as the James Browne, built by him, which sailed last week."[153]

Before the *North Atlantic* cleared the Port of Portsmouth, a clear description of her appeared in public print:

Among the great variety of attractions to draw visitors to our wharves the present week, not the least to us was a visit to this beautiful ship, which will probably sail to-day for New Orleans.

This vessel has not been surpassed in beauty of finish and strength of material by any predecessor from the Yard of her experienced builder, George Raynes, Esq.

Her accommodations for passengers are excellent. — She has a full poop deck, 90 feet long, which extends before the mainmast, and is about 7 1-2 feet high amid ships. In this poop she has two cabins. The after on is 25 feet long by 12 wide, and contains 7 state-rooms, each room 7 feet by 6 1-2 square. The state-rooms have each 2 berths, a deck and a side-light and are furnished in the best style to secure the comfort of passengers. — The cabin is wainscotted with rose, satin and zebra woods, and has enameled cornices enclosed between burnished mouldings. No expense has been spared to make the cabin as perfect as any part of the ship. Before the after cabin, is its pantry, a spacious apartment with a skylight over it; and it is tastefully fitted with receptacles for the necessaries and luxuries of life. On the starboard side there is a passage 50 feet long, leading out of the after cabin to the main deck. In the wing of this passage there are seven state-rooms, two water closets, and other apartments.

The second cabin is 36 feet by 12 and contains 6 large state-rooms. Before it, on the larboard side, there is a store-room 9 by 6 feet 2 inches. Like the first cabin, the arrangements of the second are excellent; nothing is wanting that is necessary for the comfort of its occupants. The entrance to it is protected by the projection of the deck above.

Abaft the foremast is a house, 35 by 13 feet, which contains an apartment aft fitted with berths, suitable for the forward officers or passengers. Before it is the galley and several other useful divisions.

She has a topgallant forecastle 20 feet long amidships, in the wings of which, aft, there are four water closets. The interior of the forecastle is fitted for the accommodation of the crew. All the hatchways leading to the between decks are protected from the rain and sea by substantial houses. Her after cabin, independent of its communication with the main deck, has a staircase aft on the larboard side, which leads to the poop. It is enough to say, without entering into further details, that her accommodations for passengers are not surpassed by those of any packet ship of her size.[154]

After the *North Atlantic* cleared out of Portsmouth and arrived in New Orleans, there appeared another report:

> The New Orleans Picayune of the 24th [January] speaks in terms of the highest praise of the new and splendid ship North-Atlantic which was launched last Fall from the yard of George Raynes, Esq. in this city, and is now in that port preparing for a trip to Boston, as "presenting many and superior inducements to passengers and freighters," and says, "The entire arrangements and construction of the North-Atlantic do infinite credit to her builders" — a well-merited compliment to one of our best Piscataqua ships.[155]

The *North Atlantic* worked primarily as a North Atlantic packet, later going into the East Indian and Australian trade. In June 1863 she was sold in New York for $35,000.[156] Under a Captain Briard, she cleared out of Boston on June 28, 1863, for Calcutta. Six months later, by way of Madras, she arrived in Calcutta. To the *North Atlantic* goes the dubious distinction of being perhaps the only American merchantman sunk by the guns of the Royal Artillery. The news report said:

> Calcutta advices of Feb. 22 state that at 2 o'clock A.M. 21st, a fire broke out on board the ship North Atlantic, owned by Wm. F. Parrott, Esq., of Boston, lying at the Police Ghat moorings (as before reported). She was laden with jute and saltpetre. How the fire originated has not been discovered; but it appears a fire broke out in the galley the previous day; and a supposition is entertained that it was not extinguished, and worked its way into the hold.
>
> With such a highly inflammable cargo, the difficulty of saving the ship with every available means would of course have been great, but in the absence of any means whatever the thing was impossible. The officers and crew soon abandoned the ship to her fate, within a short time after the discovery of the fire she was in flames from stem to stern. To prevent the ship blowing up by the ignition of the saltpetre on board, a battery of Royal Artillery was brought on the wharf, and several shots were fired into her hull in order to scuttle her, which was finally successful. It is expected, however, that the ship is for the most part destroyed.[157]

Another news item on April 30 confirmed the destruction of the *North Atlantic*, along with her cargo, which consisted of 210 tons of saltpeter, 5,491 bales of jute, 42 bales of hemp, and 60 bales of gunny bags. According to the story the cause of the fire hadn't been determined, but there were grounds to suspect arson. One report had it, with no source given, that members of the crew were arrested and jailed. What was left of the *North Atlantic*—anchors, rigging, etc.— fetched 8,900 rupees.

Western World

SPECIFICATIONS: 1849. Fernald & Pettigrew. Male figurehead, square stern. Burthen, 1,334 tons. Length, 183 feet; beam, 40.25 feet; depth, 20.125 feet. Three decks. Original owners—the Kingslands.

The *Western World*, launched on November 27, was the next to the last Port of Portsmouth ship built in the decade of the 1840s. The launching story was typical:

PACKET SHIP WESTERN WORLD.

The above noble ship was launched from the Yard of Messrs. Fernald & Pettigrew, in Portsmouth harbor, on Tuesday last, the 27th ult. a few minutes before 9 o'clock. She is owned by Messrs. D. & A. Kingsland & Co. of New-York, and is intended for the Empire Line of New-York & Liverpool Packets, and is to be commanded by Capt. Charles Cheeven, late of ship Severn. She is 195 feet in length over all, 41 feet beam, 31 feet deep, has three regular decks, and is 1903 tons carpenter's measurement, or 1400 custom-house measurement. She is the largest merchant ship ever built on the river, being some ten feet longer than the Empire-State launched by the same builders in March last — since which time they have launched the beautiful schooner Granite-State of 200 tons, the ship John-Haven of 1000 tons, and this mammoth ship.[158]

The *Journal* praised her further on January 19, 1850:

The Western World is intended to take a place in Kingsland & Co.'s line of N.Y. and Liverpool packets. The Messenger says very truly of her — "As she lies at the wharf, nearly ready for sea, she presents a magnificent appearance — her gigantic hull and towering masts causing ordinary sized ships in the vicinity to appear insignificant in comparison; and the beauty of her model is no less worthy of admiration than her immense dimensions. Stepping on board, the spectator cannot but be surprised at the ingenuity and skill displayed in converting the heavy and hardy trees of the forests into such shape and beauty; and his wonder at her vast proportions while standing on the wharf is increased as from the quarter deck he looks forward to her bow. The manner in which the heavy oak timbers in this ship are braced and secured surpass any idea we ever had of strength of construction. Her saloon or after cabin is finished in good style — the panel work doing much credit to Mr. Dockum. Forward of this is a second class cabin, mostly grained, and still further forward numerous private rooms for the accommodation of passengers, the officers of the ship, &c.

The *Western World* went into the packet service for which she had been designed and built. She plowed the North Atlantic, west to east, east to west, for more than three years before coming to grief. News of disaster came in October 1853: "SHIP WESTERN WORLD. — The ship Western World, Capt. Moses from Liverpool, went ashore at Squam Inlet, on Friday night [October 24]. Her passengers, 600 in number, were all landed safely, and the ship was making no water, and would probably be got off."[159]

That optimistic speculation proved premature, as a later news report showed:

SHIP WESTERN WORLD. — The packet ship Western World, Capt. Moses, ashore on Squam Beach, will be a total loss. She was built here, by Messrs. Fernald & Pettigrew, in 1850, 1354 tons, is owned by Messrs. D. & A. Kingsland & Sutton, of New York, and is valued at $80,000; on which there is insurance to the amount of $70,000, in four offices in New York. Her cargo, which is very valuable, is insured in whole or in part. On the 23d, 4 P. M., the tide ebbed and flowed in the ship, and all her cargo was wet. It consisted of 200 tons dry goods, 400 do iron, 800 sacks salt, 150 crates, &c. She was much hogged, and it was feared the steam pumps would not be able to free her. The steam tug Achilles, which returned to New York on Monday morning, reported that the ship had bilged, and had ten feet of water in the hold. She has, ever since built, till now, been run successfully between Liverpool and New York. How the accident happened we are at present unable to say, but probably the entire matter will be laid before the public in a few days.

The vessel lies six miles north of where the Cornelius Grinnell was cast on shore about three years ago. The morning she ran on shore the moon shone with great brilliancy, and the wind, which was blowing from the south east, was a fair one for vessels going into the port where the Western World was bound. It was wonderful, considering the circumstances, that no lives were lost, which was owing, in a great measure, to the coolness of the officers on board, and to the delightful state of the weather, while if it had been bad or the wind blowing fresh from the east or northeast, the loss of life would have been awful, and a repetition of the fatal and heart-rending ship-wreck of the Robert Minturn would have taken place.[160]

The next week, another news report made it evident that the *Western World* had made her last passage:

> Accounts from the wreck of the ship Western World, at Squam, are to the 25th inst. when she was broken in two amid-ships. The hull forward of the main mast appeared firm, while the after part is all loose. People are engaged in saving the baggage, anchors, rigging, &c. The cargo is floating about in the ship, and little of it can be got at until she goes to pieces, which will be during the next easterly blow.[161]

Albert Gallatin

SPECIFICATIONS: 1849. Samuel Badger. Billet head, square stern. Burthen, 849 tons. Length, 160.1 feet; beam, 34 feet; depth, 17 feet. Two decks. Original owners—John E. Salter, William and William P. Jones, Christopher Toppan, and John H. Boardman, all of Portsmouth.

Following the *Western World* into the water the next day, the *Albert Gallatin* was the last ship launched in the 1840s. As much as any one ship could, the *Albert Gallatin* typified the workhorse charac-ter of Badger-built vessels. Because the ownership was based in Portsmouth, the *Albert Gallatin* occasionally returned to her home port; she was one of the last of the Piscataqua-built ships to do so. On December 1, after her launching, it was reported:

SHIP ALBERT-GALLATIN.

> This splendid ship of 900 tons was launched from the yard of Samuel Badger, Esq. on Wednesday morning at half past 3 o'clock. She is intended for the carrying trade, and is very capacious, as well as handsome and substantial. She is owned by Messrs. Wm. Jones & Son, C. S. Toppan, J. H. Boardman, and Capt. J. E. Salter. The latter gentleman will be her commander.

The Boston Daily Advertiser states that a ship bearing the same name hails from New-York, and suggests the propriety of another name for the Portsmouth ship. Our ship, we think, has the priority in the name. Mr. Gallatin died on the 16th of August last. The Portsmouth Journal of August 18th announced the name of Albert-Gallatin as given to this ship. It is ardently hoped she will sustain as good reputation in the commercial world, as he whose name she claims bore in the financial department of government — and escape in its pleasant voyages those shoals, quicksands and tempests through which the well-trimmed course of Mr. Gallatin has borne him to his desired haven.

The *Journal*'s point on the confusion over the two ships is well taken. Their comings and goings are difficult to track accurately. At one point, I was pursuing assiduously the wrong ship, and I may still be wrong. Anyway, as long as John E. Salter was master, the career of the Portsmouth-built *Albert Gallatin* was easy to trace. Salter had her for several years, bringing the *Albert Gallatin* into Portsmouth Harbor in October 1854 with 7,550 bags of salt, weighing 600 tons.

She was probably the *Albert Gallatin* that was sued in the U.S. District Court, Boston, for back wages by a seaman named Joshua Burton. The defense contended that Burton had forfeited his wages because he "was dirty, disobedient and negligent; that he brought liquor on board the ship at New Orleans, which the captain threw overboard."[162] It was also the contention of the defense that Burton had obtained "false keys" to the captain's locker and stole liquor; that he brought improper persons on board the ship; and that he had been paid £4 in Liverpool and so was due only $17. The case was taken under advisement.

In March 1864 it was reported that the *Albert Gallatin*, like so many other American vessels of the period, had been sold in Liverpool for £4,800.[163] Confirmation of this is found in the *American Neptune* (January 1943), which states that the *Albert Gallatin* was renamed the *Crusader*, and that she was lost on the Goodwin Sands on February 11, 1877, while on a passage from Quebec to South Shields, England, with lumber. But, just to leave the whole matter in a state of Gallatinized confusion, the following item appeared in the *Journal* on December 4, 1875:

> — Capt. Groves of Portsmouth ship Albert Gallatin, before reported abandoned, states that he left Antwerp for Callao on the 28th of April in ballast, there being thirty souls on board. The voyage was prosperous until off Cape Horn,

where, on the 2d of Aug. the rudder was carried away. From
that time until the 15th was spent in ineffectual endeavors to
rig a steering apparatus; and on the evening of that day, as the
ship was within a short distance of the rocky shore of Ildefen-
so, upon which she was drifting, she was abandoned, all hands
taking to two boats. In one was Captain Groves, his wife and
two children, the second mate and four seamen. The other boat
carried the first mate and twenty seamen, and she was not
seen by the captain after leaving the ship. August 16 they
effected a landing on Hermit Island, where they remained
until the 22d; then two days in the boat looking anxiously for a
sail, and four days on another island, suffering meantime
severely from cold and wet. The allowance of food per diem was
one and a half crackers to each person, and two pounds of salt
beef divided among nine; water was obtained from melted
snow gathered on the rocks. Eighteen days after abandoning
the ship the boat was picked up by the ship Syren, at Honolulu. Capt. Groves and his family and the rescued seamen
speak in the highest terms of the kind and generous treatment
received by them from Capt. Newell, his officers and crew.

IV The 1850s

WITH THE LAUNCHING OF THE *ALBERT GALLATIN* in the late fall of 1849, the new decade of the 1850s began, a period that saw shipbuilding reach a frenzied "heyday" that has never been equalled or surpassed.[1] In that span of time, 59 three-masted, square-rigged vessels were built and launched, with a combined displacement of 82,201 tons. Total tonnage—adding in schooners, barks, and brigs—built in the Port of Portsmouth in the ten years was 85,695. Not only were the three established yards going strong, but new ones came into being, the major one being the Tobey & Littlefield operation on Noble's Island. They all worked to satisfy the insatiable demand for big, fast, strong ships, not only to move people and goods across the Atlantic but also to meet the needs of the newly created Pacific Coast trade. The Gold Rush of 1849 changed the United States forever, and the pace of development in California, thanks to accelerated shipping, was such that the state was admitted to the Union in 1850.

The Pacific development created an urgency for the fastest possible method of transporting goods; there was money to be made in California, and not necessarily in the gold fields, and that gave birth to the Clipper Era. As chronicled in *Clippers of the Port of Portsmouth* (Ray Brighton, 1985), 28 of those fast-sailing vessels were built between 1850 and 1859 on the Piscataqua River. While the clippers were the glamor girls of the sea in the 1850s, East Coast builders, from Maine to Florida, were producing many of the more solid working vessels that endured as cargo carriers until well into the steamship era. The clippers will get only incidental attention in the course of this work, with the emphasis centered on their slower, plain-

159

er sisters. There were only three of these in the first year of the new decade: the *Constantine*, the *Germania*, and the *George Raynes*. Master builder Raynes built two of these, plus the first clippers fabricated in the Port of Portsmouth: the *William E. Roman* and the *Sea Serpent*. Raynes apparently put the Constantine together either between the two clippers or along with them.

Constantine

SPECIFICATIONS: 1850. George Raynes. Billet head, square stern. Burthen, 1,161 tons. Length, 186 feet; beam, 36.6 feet; depth, 18.3 feet. Two decks. Original owners—Grinnell & Minturn, et al., of New York.

The *Constantine* was built for the transatlantic packet service, and she started out in the Swallowtail Line, under Capt. Richard L. Bunting. Richard Duryea became master in 1853, and Samuel Macoduck had her during 1855–1857. The Swallowtail Line was enlarged in 1851 to have eight regularly scheduled packets sailing from Liverpool on the sixth and the twenty-first of each month.[2] The career of the *Constantine* is somewhat obscure, but she was a tough vessel, as evidence by the fact that years after her launching she was still in service. A news item in October 1880 reported her as being sold in New York for $14,500. She had been repaired in 1876, and the report said that her New Hampshire "Pasture oak" frame was one of the heaviest ever put in a ship by George Raynes.[3]

She had the occasional troubles that were ever the lot of sailing vessels. In 1854, she survived a hurricane that lasted 56 hours, stripping away most of her rigging and much of her deck gear. The clipper *Red Gauntlet* and the *Constantine* struggled through the storm within hailing distance; both made it to port.[4] In 1862, she was dismasted off Liverpool, and two steamers took her in tow. She did go aground, but the steamers finally arrived in port with her.[5]

The news items are somewhat confusing, but apparently the *Constantine* was lost in 1882. She had sailed from New York for London on November 14, 1881, under Capt. William E. Culdrey of New York. The *Constantine* was carrying 7,800 barrels of refined petroleum. (The Oil Age had arrived.) The captain's wife and two children were also on board.[6] Fears for the safety of the *Constantine* were voiced in January 1882. Captain Culdrey was then a part owner, and his partner in the ship, John Zittlesen of New York, had no news of her. Her cargo was valued at $35,000, and the ship at $36,000. On March 1 it was reported the ship had been abandoned. The next day

This is one of few existing photos of the old Raynes Shipyard on the North Mill Pond, and shows one vessel still on the ways. Patch Collection, Strawbery Banke, Inc.

the abandonment story had been confirmed, with the added information that the crew had landed at Falmouth, England, after leaving the ship of February 14. "It's probable the *Constantine* will never be heard from again."[7]

Germania

SPECIFICATIONS: 1850. Fernald & Pettigrew. Billet head, square stern. Burthen, 996 tons. Length, 170.8 feet; beam, 35.6 feet; depth, 17.8 feet. Two decks. Original owner—William Whitlock, Jr., of New York.

Fernald & Pettigrew had put the finishing touches to the *Western World* when the *Germania* gave them a late-summer launching. A news item reported that the firm was ready to launch the *Germania* on September 7, and the readers were assured that the *Germania* "is built on an improved model of the best New Hampshire white oak; and for size and quality of fastenings, elegance of finish, &c., the builders are confident that she will compare with any ship built in New England."[8]

When Capt. Daniel Marcy took the *Germania* to sea, she had already been lauded in print: "The Germania and the Constantine, two beautiful ships, samples of the work of mechanics of Portsmouth and vicinity, sailed down the river for New York. The former on Sunday evening, the latter on Monday. They have been wind-bound for several days. During that time, they were visited and admired by great numbers of our citizens."[9] A few days later, Portsmouth was to hear more applause for the *Germania*:

> SHIP GERMANIA. — This beautiful ship, on her late trip from this port to New York, proved fully equal to the commendations of her admirers, and her performance came quite up to their expectations. She outsailed every craft she fell in with during the trip, including the fast-sailing packet ship Gallia, of the same line to which she is attached — beating up the Long Island coast with studding sails set when other craft were compelled to reef and lay to. Her unsurpassed builders, Messrs. Fernald & Pettigrew, have won new honors in her construction, and are alone entitled to the credit for her superior appearance and sailing qualities, she being built after their own model, and every way fitted according to their views of expediency. Her purchasers, on receiving her, declared themselves more than satisfied — they were delighted with her. — *Messenger*.[10]

One of the most dramatic moments in the career of the *Germania* came in February 1856; the story was told in the journal of her young first officer, Charles H. Townshend, of New Haven, Connecticut. The passages in Townshend's diary are a grim recital of the perils faced in sailing days. At that time, the *Germania* was commanded by Capt. D. H. Wood:

> February 29th fine breeze from the NNW, ship under reefed sails, standing to northward. It had been blowing hard the night before and a tremendous sea was heaving up from the NW. At meridian I was relieved by the second mate after dinner. I went to my room to write the log book up. About 2 P.M. the 2nd mate came and said he was forward with some men rebending the outer jib, and thought he saw a boat ahead with a signal of distress flying. I took my glass, went on deck and went into the weather fore rigging, and made out a ship's boat with a man sitting in it, and to all appearance frozen stiff. I ordered the other watch to be called up, the lee quarter boat to be cleared away, ready to be lowered, main sail to be hauled up, and went and called Captain Wood, who was asleep having

been up the greater part of the night before. He came on deck. We got ready to lower the boat and stood toward him until when about a mile from him the wind veered to the NNW, and as we could not fetch him on the other tack we hauled the main topsail to the mast — lowered the starboard quarter boat, and four men and myself went to his relief. After leaving the ship we could not get sight of the boat, the seas being so high, but was directed on our course by Captain Wood standing on the veranda deck pointing with his telescope towards the object of our search. When we were midway between the ship and the boat and in the trough of the seas the skysail truck of the *Germania* was out of sight, and another thing which was not agreeable, the intense cold. Every drop of spray which touched the boat seemed to turn to ice. I think I never suffered so much with cold.

From the time we first saw the boat until we were within three rods of her the man in her did not move, and I made up my mind that he was dead, but it proved to the contrary. Previous to our reaching the boat I had an opportunity to judge for myself the condition that I would find her frozen crew as every toll of the sea added horror to the scene. There sat a man in the stern with his pea jacket buttoned tight to his chin and on his head was his southwester slouched over his eyes, with both legs in water up to his knees, bare footed and frozen white. In the bow was an oar lashed to the stem blade up, and to that a stick about four feet long, with the back of a shirt lashed to it, and a spring stay running from the top of the oar blade to the boat's stern, on which hung two shirts a red and a white one. He had raised them that morning hoping some passing ship might be attracted and rescue him from the jaws of death.

In the bow lay a man with his hat off, eyes wide open staring you in the face, and from the expression of his countenance showed he must have died a dreadful death. In the stern lay another still and cold in death, and about midship lay two women with their long hair washing from side to side with every roll of the boat, eyes and mouths wide open, firmly clasped in each others arms so firm that it was with difficulty that they were separated.

Upon the stern lay the ship log book, compass, chief officer's quadrant and epitomie, and floating around in the water was a number of belaying pins, bottles, blankets, shawls and wearing apparel of both sexes, also a coil of rope, a bolt of canvas, twine, etc. In the bottom a hammer, knife, ship's bell, binnacle, lamp and many other things showing discouragement and suffering.

When we had approached within four rods of the boat, I called to him, he looked up and showed his care worn face and crawled on his knees to the bow of the boat. I called to him, telling him that I could not board him bow on, but to give me a rope so that we could tow the boat. He caught hold of the boat rope or painter and tried to clear it. It being foul in the middle of the boat (the women that lay in the midship of the boat lay on it). He gave it a feeble jerk and made the following expression which was the first words I heard him utter — "God damn the rope, I can't clear it, for Christ sake let me get into that boat." By the time he had finished what he had to say our boats came together, he sprang head first into the boat (striking his head) and said, "O damn the boat let her go she is good for nothing."

As soon as he got into the boat he commenced to tell me his name which was Thomas W. Nye of Fairhaven, Mass. He said he belonged to the ship *John Rutledge*, which was lost in the ice on the evening of the 19th of February. Five boats left the ship and about forty or fifty passengers went down with the ship, the mate and carpenter being among the number. Said the dead bodies in the boat (there being four) were Mrs. Atkinson, the first mate's wife, a woman passenger and two men, one of them a passenger and the other a sailor. Said there were 13 in the boat when she left the ship, and all had starved to death excepting himself. Eight he had buried with his own hands and the others he had not the strength to do so. It was a horrid sight all laying with their mouths and eyes open, frozen stiff. He had no boots on. He said when they froze they pained him so much he cut them off and put them in one of the passengers coats. Said he expected to lose the use of them. After he had been in the boat ten minutes a stupor came over him and he became insensible. Got to the ship about 5 P.M. Passed a rope about Nye and took him aboard and put him in one of the cabin staterooms. Captain and Mrs. Wood commenced staying with him and with the greatest difficulty brought him to. The dead were consigned to the deep. Hoisted boat on board and filled away, stood on the starboard tack until 6 P.M. when we hove to, set lights in the rigging and kept a good lookout in case any of the boats should be near we might render them assistance.

Morning came. Sent men aloft at daylight but saw nothing, filled away. Set all sail with a fresh breeze from the NE.[11]

It turned out that Thomas W. Nye was the sole survivor of the *John Rutledge*'s collision with an iceberg. Cutler added that the captain and 24 from the crew, along with 160 passengers, crowded into boats, "leaving the first mate and about one-third of the steerage to go down with the ship." After months spent in recovery, Thomas Nye showed up in New York one day and signed on as a crew member with the *Germania*.

Nelson recorded that the *Germania* was sold in San Francisco in 1877. Perhaps it was her new owners who stripped off her upper deck, changing her rig to that of a bark: that is, square-rigged on the fore and main masts, fore- and after-rigged on the mizzen mast. After the sale in San Francisco, the *Germania* disappeared, and was quite likely used as a lumber hauler on the West Coast.

George Raynes

SPECIFICATIONS: 1850. George Raynes. Billet head, square stern. Burthen, 999 tons. Length, 176 feet; beam, 35 feet; depth, 17.5 feet. Two decks, Original owners—Glidden & Williams, of Boston; and George Raynes.

If George Raynes was showing a bit of conceit by naming this vessel in his own honor, at least he was modest enough not to use a bust of himself for a figurehead. The *George Raynes* was launched on October 16, 1850, preceding the clipper *Sea Serpent* by three weeks. Capt. Pearce W. Penhallow took the *George Raynes* to sea on December 8, and she was at the Bar in New Orleans 15 days later. Her arrival provoked comment:

SHIP GEORGE RAYNES AT NEW-ORLEANS.
The Daily Orleanian of Jan. 11th contains a column from the editor, giving a description of his visit and an account of the "novel improvements and magnificent accommodations of the new ship George-Raynes, Capt. Penhallow," of and from Portsmouth. We do not give the detail of the description, for many of our readers are personally acquainted with the ship. The editor says:
The cabin, the entrance to which is protected by a house on deck, is as splendid and commodious as the parlors of many of the upper tendom. The carpeting, furniture, seats, sofas and chair of state, on which latter an emperor might be seated, but which a republican graces — for Capt. Penhallow throws a

Lithograph of New Orleans which was one of the busiest ports in the world before the Civil War. Ships built on the Piscataqua were frequent visitors to this great cotton port. Courtesy Library of Congress.

halo over all — are of American manufacture. As we gazed around and on each side, examined the cabin, the state-rooms, the ameliorations made on ancient plans, and the novelties introduced, we took the liberty of referring to our old friend the wharfinger, and involuntarily expressed a desire that he might never be a passenger in the George-Raynes! not from any ill feeling to him, but for the benefit and advantage of Capt. Penhallow; as, with a hogshead of the *weed* on board, and Capt. B. in less than a month; he would destroy all the finery in the cabin — remove the polish, and discolor, with tobacco juice, pannelling, carpeting, wainscotting, *et al.*

As a passenger vessel, we think the George-Raynes has no superior: the second and third cabins are comfortable, convenient and commodious: while for another and a more numerous class the lower deck is admirably adapted. Between decks, and adjoining the cook's galley, is an apartment set apart for the culinary purposes of the steerage passengers, where, unexposed to the elements, and as comfortably situated as in their own kitchens, they can prepare their meals. Never, at any time before, have we seen accommodations for the middle and lower class of passengers on a like scale of convenience and perfection.[12]

The *George Raynes* was loaded and cleared for Liverpool, where she arrived on April 2, 1851. She was chartered by the Train Line, Boston-based packet operators, and sailed from Liverpool on May 7 with a load of immigrants. Arriving in Boston on June 12, the ship was ordered to Magagudavic, New Brunswick, for lumber, and her accomplishments, to date, drew praise:

PORTSMOUTH SHIPS.

The ship George Raynes left Boston on Saturday, 6th inst. and arrived at Magagudavic, N. B. in forty hours — and Mr. Raynes received notice in Portsmouth, by the way of Boston, of her arrival in 48 hours from the time she left Boston. Her first passage from Portsmouth to New Orleans was made in 15 days; from thence to Liverpool in 32 days, with 3552 bales of cotton, weighing 1,576,722 lbs.; from Liverpool to Boston in 30 days, and her last trip as above stated. Capt. Penhallow, our townsman, deserves credit, as well as the good qualities of the ship, for her performance. — We understand the ship is highly spoken of as a freighting ship, at all the ports which she has visited. She is 1100 tons.[13]

With a cargo of lumber, the *George Raynes* sailed for Liverpool from St. Stephen, New Brunswick, on August 10, arriving on September 10. Again she was chartered as a packet, this time for Philadelphia. From the Quaker City, she went to New Orleans, loaded cotton, and sailed to Liverpool. On July 15, 1852, the *George Raynes* came into Boston with merchandise and 300 passengers. A three-day storm had damaged her rigging and made life miserable for the steerage passengers.

After spending three months in Boston, Glidden & Williams sent the *George Raynes* to San Francisco. She sailed on the twelfth of October and arrived at her destination on February 18, 1853, apparently a passage of 129 days. Her time was nowhere near that of the best clipper passages, yet is was only days longer than the run of the *Sea Serpent* on her maiden voyage in 1851—although is has to be said that the *Sea Serpent* lost at least 8 days undergoing repairs in Valparaiso.[14] From San Francisco, the *George Raynes* went south to the Chincha Islands to load guano for Hampton Roads, Virginia. Her rate for hauling guano was $22 a ton to either the United Kingdom or the United States. During the stay of the *George Raynes* in San Francisco, the *San Francisco Herald* printed a laudatory notice on February 28:

> A CARD. — The undersigned, a Committee on behalf of the Passengers in the ship GEORGE RAYNES, from Boston to San Francisco, desire to avail themselves of an opportunity to express, in a public manner, to Capt. P. W. PENHALLOW, their gratitude for his uniform courtesy and kind consideration, as evinced towards them throughout the voyage; as also their high appreciation of his ability and character as an accomplished navigator and gentleman. — And the undersigned, in the same behalf, while tendering their heartfelt thanks, would also express their best wishes for his continued health and prosperity.
> [Signed]   FRANCIS W. BIGELOW
>   Chairman, Mass.
>   DANIEL SCOTT, Maine.
> Feb. 20.   ALBERT F. SAWYER, Mass.[15]

When the *George Raynes* came into New York, after dropping her cargo in Hampton Roads, a Captain Batchelder relieved Penhallow, and the ship cleared out for Valparaiso on March 23, 1854. From the latter port she went to the Chincha Islands, and was at Norfolk, Virginia, in early February of 1855. Her next voyage was to Europe, and she was in and out of several ports looking for cargo before putting in at Queenstown, Ireland, where she was ordered to Trapani, Italy, to load salt for Boston. The *George Raynes* went out to Australia in 1858, arriving in Sydney, New South Wales, July 16. From there, she sailed to Calcutta and Singapore. Once home again, in 1859, she went to Valparaiso, then to the Chinchas. In 1863, on a passage from the Chinchas to England, she was repaired in Valparaiso. The repairs cost $5,000, and she sailed on August 24.[16] The shipping notices strongly indicate that the *George Raynes* spent most of her time on the guano run in her last years, either to the United States, England, or Germany. She was on such a voyage when she met her end:

> DESTRUCTION OF AMERICAN SHIP AT VALPARAISO. — Three American ships have been burnt at Valparaiso. Says Capt. Batchelder of the ship George Raynes, one of the vessels destroyed, that the fire broke out in the night, and at 1.30 A. M. had made so little headway that he was in hopes to save the ship with the aid of the crew, who were actively employed to that purpose, but the fire suddenly spread to such an extent as to entirely baffle all attempt to extinguish it, and in forty-five

minutes the vessel was enveloped in a sheet of flame, and in a short time was burned down to the water's edge.

A survey was held and the remains of the vessel were sold for $2000, and the cargo for $45.

The George Raynes was a good vessel of 993 tons, rates A 1-1/2, was built at Portsmouth, N. H. in 1850, and was owned in Boston by Messrs. Glidden & Williams and others. She was valued at $50,000 and insured for $48,000.

The other vessels burnt were George V, 949 tons, on the 16th of Feb. owned in Boston; and the Flora McDonald, of Baltimore, 841 tons.[17]

Levi Woodbury

SPECIFICATIONS: 1851. Fernald & Pettigrew. Billet head, square stern. Burthen, 1,200 tons. Length, 186 feet; beam, 38 feet; depth, 29 feet. Three decks. Original owners—Daniel and Peter Marcy, James N. Tarlton, J. J. Nickerson, and Fernald & Pettigrew.

Few New Hampshire men have ever equaled or surpassed the national prominence achieved by Levi Woodbury. A native of Francestown, Woodbury played key roles in both the state and nation before his untimely death on September 5, 1851, seven weeks after the launching of the ship bearing his name. Levi Woodbury served as governor, U.S. senator, secretary of the U.S. Treasury, federal judge, and was being prominently mentioned for the Democratic nomination to the presidency in 1852. A New Hampshire Democrat did win the presidency in that year, but it was Franklin Pierce, not Levi Woodbury. The latter made his home in Portsmouth, in a three-decker, federal-type mansion that was razed some years ago to make way for the Woodbury Manor housing project for the elderly. The news story about the launching doesn't indicate that Levi Woodbury was present, but if he was in the city, he was probably there; everyone went to launchings in those days, and there can be no doubt that he appreciated the honor paid him by his fellow Democrats, the Marcy brothers:

On Tuesday last, from the ship-yard of Messrs. Fernald & Petigrew, was graceful and majestic. She was rigged on the stocks, and apparently almost ready, like a young patridge from the shell, to go forth into the wide world, the moment she touched the water. "Three cheers" from the yard, and "three cheers" from the wharves, were heartily responded to by

Ship Levi Woodbury *was built in 1851 by Fernald and Pettigrew. She was named for* Levi Woodbury *of Portsmouth, who was the leading national political figure of the day. Woodbury died a few weeks after the vessel was launched.*

"three cheers" from the large company who were willing to run the chance of a short run under the flying banners of the "Levi Woodbury." She rounded to in good style, and displayed a handsome model, and good finish. She is a three-decked ship, 186 feet in length, 38 feet beam, 29 feet deep, and measures about 1200 tons. She is intended for a freighting ship, and will carry a very large cargo. Her stern is ornamented with an excellent bust of the distinguished gentleman whose name she bears, supported on each hand by the goddesses of Liberty and Justice, and surmounted with a splendid gilt eagle. She is owned by Messrs. Daniel and Peter Marcy, Fernald & Petigrew, James N. Tarlton and Capt. Nickerson, who is to command her, and will hail from New Orleans. She will leave here next week for Boston.[18]

Although her assigned master, Joseph J. Nickerson, was present, it was Capt. Daniel Marcy who sailed the *Levi Woodbury* to New Orleans, where Nickerson took command. The *Levi Woodbury* was towed to sea from New Orleans on October 19, heading for Liverpool. Her westward passage was to Boston, leaving Liverpool on January 13, 1852, arriving on March 9 "with a large cargo of merchandise and 90 steerage passengers."[19] She had had a long, rough passage. Her next voyage was roundtrip between Boston and New Orleans. Capt. Joseph Grace was her next commander. Captain Grace had a long career at sea and lived to nearly 88. Taking the ship to Liverpool, Grace returned to Boston, making the trip in 35 days. Captain Nickerson resumed command and, in 1854 had the ship at Goteborg, Sweden, where she loaded 1,000 tons of pig iron at eight dollars a ton, for Boston, plus 400 passengers.[20] Throughout her service, she worked the cotton ports and places like Liverpool and Le Havre. Various masters had the *Levi Woodbury*, among them Capt. Samuel Young of York. Captain Young, a frequent Portsmouth visitor, was injured in a freak accident in 1867, when a wagon he was driving caught its wheels in the railing of the Portsmouth Bridge and upset. On one trip, Young had the *Levi Woodbury* at Pugwash, Nova Scotia, when she collided with a schooner. The owners of the schooner sued for damages, but the outcome went unreported.[21]

During the Civil War, the *Levi Woodbury* was sold and renamed the *Southerner*. Running from Quebec to London, the *Southerner* tried to get into St. Pierre on the night of November 24, 1864, struck the rocks on the south end, and immediately bilged.[22]

Globe

SPECIFICATIONS: 1851. Samuel Badger. Billet head, square stern. Burthen, 797 tons. Length, 163 feet; beam, 32.9 feet; depth, 16.25 feet. Two decks. Original owner—Peter Destebecho, of New Orleans.

First word of this ship was contained in a routine launch notice in the Journal on May 31: "a beautiful ship of 800 tons was launched in good style from the yard of Samuel Badger, Esq., in this harbor, on Thursday morning at half past ten o'clock. Her name is the *J. P. Proutz*. She is owned by some gentlemen in New Orleans, and is intended for the freighting business."

Apparently this ship became the *Globe*. Why, how, or when isn't clear. In 1857 the *Globe*, under Capt. George Baker, was in the Pelican Line, sailing out of New Orleans. Her first master was Peter Destebecho, and there her saga ends.

Sabine

SPECIFICATIONS: 1851. Samuel Badger. Billet head, square stern. Burthen, 694 tons. Length, 148 feet; beam, 32 feet; depth, 16 feet. Two decks. Original owners—Robert Rice, Jonathan M. Tredick, George W. Haven, and John B. Haley.

Almost from the beginning, the *Sabine* was destined for the East Indian trade. One of the owners, John B. Haley, was her first master. Then an experienced mariner, 63 years old, Haley took the *Sabine* to New Orleans on October 23, arriving there on November 18. The ship went to Liverpool, then back across to Boston. From Boston, the *Sabine* went to Calcutta on June 4, 1852, with Capt. Henry L. Libbey in command. He, too, was a top-notch shipmaster, later commanding ships such as the Boston-built *Orion* and the *Triumphant*. He also commanded the Portsmouth ship *Kate Prince*. His last vessel was the bark *Furness Abbey*, on which he died at Singapore on January 23, 1880.

Captain Libbey commanded the *Sabine* for some years, with occasional intervals at home. When be brought the *Sabine* back from her first East Indian voyage, the ship arrived in Boston on March 13, 1853. Among her passengers were Joshua W. Peirce, of Portsmouth, and Rev. J. Dulles and family, missionaries. Captain Libbey then sailed the *Sabine* around Cape Horn to San Francisco. The ship's arrival there prompted an item in a San Francisco newspaper:

> CARGOES, RECLAMATION &C. — The late arrival of a number of clippers at this port from the Atlantic states, has called forth attention to the condition of their respective cargoes. Notwithstanding the whole fleet experienced severe and stormy weather off Cape Horn, (which was against them,) it is stated that the Comet, Kaven, Witch of the Wave, North Wind, Hurricane, Mandarin and Trade Wind have all turned out their cargoes, as far as discharged, in excellent condition. This augurs well for the character of the vessels, and is alike creditable to masters as well as to builders.
>
> The ship Sabine, of Portsmouth, which arrived some time back, with a full freight of miscellaneous goods, discharged

her entire cargo in the best possible condition, the whole amount of reclamation not counting up to $100. These things are worthy of more than a passing notice, as it will be recollected that a short time since much complaint was made of the damaged condition in which cargoes arrived from Atlantic ports. — Scarcely a vessel arrived which was not loudly complained against on account of damage done the cargo from various causes, the most conspicuous of which was sweating.[23]

The *Sabine* went to the Chincha Islands for guano, and came into New York on July 31, 1854, with 1,100 tons. After an 1855 passage from Calcutta, Captain Libbey arrived home in time to bury a child who had died at Chelsea, Massachusetts, on October 3.[24] Thomas W. Hendee relieved Libbey, taking the *Sabine* to India. Libbey was given command of the ship *Orion*, but before sailing he had the grim task of burying his first wife, who died in Chelsea on November 24 of tuberculosis.[25] Captain Hendee commanded the *Sabine* until 1860, when he was relieved to take command of a new clipper-style bark. Hendee had once lived in Portsmouth but moved to Lowell, Massachusetts.

An odd little incident took place on the *Sabine* on December 17, 1856, when she was lying at the Fort Hill Dry Dock in Boston. The *Chronicle* said the shipkeeper, Ammi L. Knowlton of Portsmouth, fell through the hole of the mainmast and had to be treated at Massachusetts General Hospital. Knowlton returned home, his injuries less severe than first believed.

New master of the *Sabine* was John T. Cromwell, who sailed her to Liverpool and there loaded for Calcutta. In September 1861, the *Sabine* was chartered at Calcutta to carry rice to Colombo at 12 annas per bag; from Colombo, she was to get £3 per ton.[26] On the passage from Calcutta, the *Sabine* went aground on Garden Beach, New Jersey, but cleared off with the rising tide and proceeded on her passage.[27] Tragedy struck two days before Christmas, 1862: in a wild storm Captain Cromwell was swept overboard while crossing the Bay of Bengal. He was between 25 and 30 years of age. A native of Portsmouth, he was then making his home in South Berwick. Two weeks after the news report, a letter from one of the owners to the captain's brother was published: "I feel very sensibly the loss I have sustained in the death of Captain Cromwell, who has given me entire satisfaction and had proved himself as a smart intelligent shipmaster and gave great promise of becoming eminent in his profession."[28]

One of the Salters brought the *Sabine* back to London from the Bay of Bengal. There she was sold on private terms for £3,900.

Hope Goodwin

SPECIFICATIONS: 1851. Fernald & Pettigrew. Billet head, square stern. Burthen, 1,198 tons. Length, 182.5 feet; beam, 37.7 feet; depth, 18.875 feet. Three decks. Original owners—Ichabod Goodwin and William H. Parsons, of Portsmouth; George B. Cumming, of Savannah.

The *Hope Goodwin*, named for a daughter of Ichabod Goodwin, was the last venture of the 1851 season by Fernald & Pettigrew. They had built and launched the ship *Levi Woodbury*, the bark *Whatcheer*, 334 tons, and their first clipper, the immortal *Typhoon*. The *Hope Goodwin* probably went on the stocks vacated by the *Levi Woodbury*, and she just barely made it as an 1851-launched ship. News accounts were glowing:

THE NEW SHIP.

LAUNCH. — On Wednesday last, between 11 and 12 o'clock in the height of the snow-storm, Messrs. Fernald & Petigrew launched from their yard a handsome three deck ship of 1200 tons, not yet named, owned by Ichabod Goodwin, Esq. of this city. She went as easily and as gracefully into the water as the snow flakes which fell around her. Her frames and planking are of white oak and most thoroughly fastened with iron and copper, and no pains have been spared by the builders to place her high on the long list of their vessels, noted the world over for their great strength, beauty and durability. She is intended for the freighting business, and will be commanded by Capt. Parson, late of the ship Kate Hunter.

The fine ship Levi Woodbury, launched by the above firm the past summer, we learn, is advertised as the packet ship of Jan. 6, in Train's line of Boston and Liverpool packets.[29]

Before the *Hope Goodwin* cleared out, under Capt. William H. Parsons, there was another enthused news report:

HOPE-GOODWIN.

Floating in the breeze from the mast-head, we see from our office window a flag bearing the above euphonious name. This fine three deck Ship was launched a few weeks since from the yard of Messrs. Fernald & Petigrew, and is now lying at the wharf nearly ready for sea. Her model is similar to that of the ship Levi Woodbury, being two feet longer, and six inches broader. Length of her keel is 175 feet; length on deck 188 feet; depth of hold 29 feet 4 inches; breadth of beam 39 feet 3 inches. Her tonnage is about 1200.

The finish of the cabins is in excellent taste — rich, chaste and symmetrical. There is almost every accommodation for passengers, which could be expected at a city hotel. We doubt whether a better ship is afloat on the ocean. We don't know but we may have said the same of some other ships, but we feel certain that what we say will hold good of the Hope Goodwin, — at least until another new vessel appears. As no less credit is due to the makers than to the owners of such specimens of art, we will give their names so far as we have heard them: The painting and gilding by Swasey & Rowell; cabinet and upholstery, and cabin veneering by S. M. Dockum; joinering by T. Martin; ironwork, by J. Knowlton; spars by Martin & Fernald; cordage, by J. Johnson, rigging by C. Harratt.

She is owned by Ichabod Goodwin, Esq. of Portsmouth, George B. Cumming, Esq. of Savannah, and Capt. W. H. Parsons, who commands her. She will probably sail early next week for Mobile. In the meantime those who wish to see a specimen of the best work the builders are capable of producing, would do well to visit the Hope-Goodwin.[30]

The *Journal*'s office was on Ladd Street, and, in those days, Charles W. Brewster, the editor, could easily see the upper masts of ships tied up along the waterfront.

The *Hope Goodwin* went immediately into the cotton trade. In 1853, she was chartered in the New Line, operated by Samuel Pleasants. She came into Philadelphia from Liverpool on March 30, 1854, and cleared for Mobile on April 22. The thirteenth of May found her in Mobile Bay, and the next news of her came on May 17, when it was reported she had been destroyed by fire while at anchor.[31] A follow-up story the next day reported that there was $52,000 in insurance on the ship along with her freight money. Later it was learned the *Hope Goodwin* had been fired by her crew:

> THE HOPE GOODWIN. — The Mobile Register of the 17th inst. says of the fire on board of this vessel:
>
> Some of the crew had proved very hostile and are reported to have stated that they would never go to sea in her again. We learn, also, that a barrel of tar had been brought up from below and secretly placed on deck. About midnight the mate was roused by the alarm of fire, and speedily found that the tar had been again taken below, allowed to run over the second deck, and fired from end to end. Every effort proved unavailing to save the ship, the boats were launched and they saved themselves as best they could. We learn that the crew are now all in irons; and further; that some of them were found on the first alarm with their dunnage packed up and ready for moving. We hear that the hull was partially towed up, although it is said she subsequently grounded on a sand bar. It was to have been only the second voyage of the Hope Goodwin, and would have far more than cleared her to her owners. She had been chartered at a penny per lb. for Liverpool, and 2-1/4 cts. for Havre.[32]

Captain Parsons died in Germany in 1867, at the age of 54. Funeral services were held in New York and interment was there. What happened to his rebellious crew isn't known.

Piscataqua

SPECIFICATIONS: 1852. Fernald & Pettigrew. Billet head, square stern. Burthen, 549 tons. Length, 141.5 feet; beam, 29 feet; depth, 14.5 feet. Two decks. Original owners—Horton D. Walker, George Pendexter, Jonathan Barker, Samuel Adams, Frederick W. Fernald, William Pettigrew, Thomas D. Bailey, John Knowlton, John Harrat, Nathaniel Walker, and Thomas Weeks, all of Portsmouth.

The ship Piscataqua *was built by Fernald & Pettigrew in 1852. She once took a load of ice to Madras which melted on one side, nearly putting the vessel on her beam ends. Courtesy Mystic Seaport.*

The first ship *Piscataqua*, 323 tons, was built in Dover in 1804 by Stephen Paul. John Rindge of Portsmouth was her first owner, but he sold her in a matter of weeks in Philadelphia, and she then disappeared from local annals.[33] That ship is mentioned here only because the second of the name seems a startling throwback to that time. Nearly 50 years later, in an era of big ships, the second *Piscataqua* wasn't even twice the tonnage of the original. However, the syndicate that owned her was composed of shrewd men who, no doubt, had good reason for what they did. The second *Piscataqua* probably was framed on the stocks vacated by the clipper *Typhoon*. The clipper *Red Rover* followed her, and work on the *Frank Pierce* began shortly afterward. The new *Piscataqua* was launched on July 8:

> LAUNCH. — The *Piscataqua*, a noble ship of about 600 tons, was launched in fine style from the yard of Messrs. Fernald & Petigrew on Thursday afternoon at 5 o'clock. She is owned by gentlemen in Portsmouth, and will be commanded by Capt. T. M. Weeks, late of ship Robert Parker.
>
> On the stocks by the side, is the frame of another ship of 1500 tons, to be owned in Portsmouth and New Orleans. The enterprising builders will also immediately set on the ways of

the Piscataqua the frame of a clipper ship of 1100 tons, to be owned in New-York.[34]

The *Portsmouth Chronicle* of August 11, 1852, reported that the *Piscataqua* had been towed down the river the day before by the steamer *C. B. Stevens*. For a few days, while waiting for a favorable wind, the *Piscataqua* was visited by "a large number of persons. Marine architects greatly admire her lines.... The joiner work was done by Thomas Martin; rigging by Charles Harrat; cabin furniture by Samuel M. Dockum." Swasey & Rowell did the painting. It was noted that she was heading east to the St. Lawrence River to load with deals for London. In her westward passage, she had trouble at Newport, Wales, getting on the West Mud. However, she was off on the next tide, and picked up a load of railroad iron. She finally sailed for New Orleans on January 17, 1853.[35] From New Orleans, the *Piscataqua* went to Liverpool and then to Boston. Capt. George P. Wendell took command, clearing Boston for Madras on October 26, and sailing the next day.

The Piscataqua's cargo was ice. And, for the moment, the importance of ice as a southbound cargo should be discussed. Two companies were in the business of cutting and storing and shipping ice in the Port of Portsmouth. Between the 1840s and the mid-1850s ice was mostly sent to Boston by rail, but in 1854 the companies loaded vessels on the Piscataqua and sent them south. One of the companies, Rockingham Ice Co., cut its ice on a pond in Raymond and shipped it by rail to Portsmouth. In February the brand-new clipper *Express* was loaded with 1,050 tons of ice in Portsmouth. The ice was described as "handsome cakes about 17 inches thick, and about two feet square, which costs on board about $2 a ton. It is packed in sawdust, of which about 40 cords are used. The freight will probably be $2 or $3 per ton, — making the cost at New Orleans perhaps about a third of a cent a pound. Several small vessels have been loaded, and arrangements are being made for going into business pretty extensively."[36] Ice was only beginning to be appreciated for domestic consumption, and it was costing the average family about five dollars for six to eight pounds of ice a day from June through September.

However, the main center of the ice business for export was in Boston. Ice cutters in New Hampshire found it simpler to load the ice on trains and send it to big icehouses in the environs of Boston. The experts had it figured out down to the prospects of 40 percent waste per shipload. But what a sight the *Piscataqua* was when she arrived at Madras in 1854:

ARRIVAL OF A BOSTON ICE SHIP AT MADRAS. — The American bark Piscataqua from Boston, has arrived at Madras. She will already have attracted the notice of all whom business or pleasure have drawn to the beach, where she presents the curious appearance of a vessel on her beam ends and about to sink. She left Boston nearly five months ago in good trim, and filled with ice for Madras. — By some strange chance it has nearly all melted away on one side of her hold, shifting the centre of gravity till she floats as she is now to be seen. The length of her voyage is to be accounted for by the difficulty of sailing her in her present trim. The Piscataqua has brought some American missionaries for Madras and for Calcutta. This supply of ice brought by the Piscataqua is well timed. — The stock at the ice houses had got so low that the greatest economy could not make it last at the present rate of demand, for more than ten days or a fortnight. — Madras Examiner, April 21.[37]

The *Piscataqua* cleared out of Madras, after unloading her unbalanced cargo, and went to Calcutta. There she was sold for $65,000.[38] The master, Captain Wendell, came home a passenger on the ship *Lotus*; her crew stayed with her or went along the docks looking for new berths. Such sales, which were frequent occurrences, showed the obviously great discretionary power of a ship's captain. Because there were no instantaneous communications, the captain had to be trusted to sell his vessel—if he could get a price set by the owners.

Captain Wendell was a Portsmouth native, the youngest son of Jacob and Mehetabel Wendell. After working in the East Indian trade for some years, Captain Wendell went into business in New York and then in Quincy, Massachusetts. He died there in 1881.[39]

Samuel Badger

SPECIFICATIONS: 1852. Samuel Badger. Billet head, square stern. Burthen, 848 tons. Length, 170 feet; beam, 32.75 feet; depth, 16.375 feet. Two decks. Original owners—William Jones & Son, Richard Jenness, and James S. Salter.

Perhaps because they had been well pleased in their previous dealings with Samuel Badger, the owners honored the veteran builder with a ship bearing his name. The news item on the launching was laudatory:

LAUNCH. — A very superior and beautifully modelled Ship of about 1000 tons burthen, was launched from the yard of Samuel Badger, Esq. on Thursday. She is owned by Messrs.

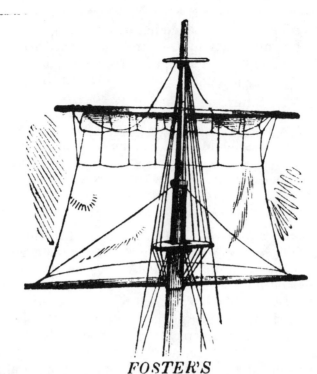

FOSTER'S
Patent Deck-Reefing Gear.

BY the application of this GEAR the topsails of any vessel may be reefed from the deck with remarkable facility, and carry sail much longer than when rigged in any other way. This Gear can be readily applied to any old rig, and at less expense than any other now in use.—The following is an extract from a letter recently received of Capt. Pickering of the ship Ocean Rover of this port, concerning its merits:

"It has given me *perfect satisfaction*, and I have only to regret that it is not applied to all the topsail yards. On the passage to this port, (Charleston, S.C.) I experienced strong gales from the S. W. and had occasion to use it several times and on every occasion it worked finely."

Apply to   **WM. H. FOSTER,** Portsmouth,
Feb. 3.   or **YEATON & HALL,** Portland, Me.

William Jones & Son, Richard Jenness, Esq. and Capt. James Salter, who is to command her. She bears the name of her enterprising and skillful builder, "Samuel Badger." As a fine specimen of naval architecture, combining great capacity with beautiful symmetry and excellent workmanship, she has never been surpassed by the many noble ships heretofore built upon our river.[40]

If the age of 63 given in his obituary in 1895 is correct, Capt. James S. Salter, another sprig of the seagoing family, was only 20 when he took command of the *Samuel Badger*.[41] Another source said he was 22; whatever, shipmasters began early in their profession. Captain Salter later commanded the big packet *City of New York*, succeeding another able Portsmouth master, John Gilman Moses. Salter was the only master the *Samuel Badger* had during her brief life.

The ship left the Port of Portsmouth in June for Bic on the St. Lawrence River, taking ten days in the passage. She loaded lumber. Bic is an obscure little town, east of Rimouski, Quebec, and that was probably where the vessel was loaded. She went to London, and from London to Le Havre. From the latter port, she went back to New Orleans, arriving on December 22, 1852.[42] She went back and forth across the Atlantic as her owners dictated. After one voyage, she came into New York, September 30, 1854, with her sails split, cargo shifted "during heavy weather," and had "considerable sickness among the seamen, four of whom died."[43]

On her next voyage, the *Samuel Badger* was sent to Mobile, loaded cotton and then went to Europe. She poked around European ports looking for cargo, and then went to Trapani. (Again, a clear demonstration of the license given trusted masters to find cargoes where they could, at the best freight rates.) At Trapani the ship was loaded with salt. First news of problems came in the *Portsmouth Chronicle* on November 14, 1854, when it was learned that the *Samuel Badger*, "of and from this port, from Trapani, had sprung a leak." More details were in the November 16 issue:

Ship Samuel Badger, from Trapani, with 1100 tons salt, foundered on the 8th ult. The S. B. left Trapani, Sept. 7, and passed Straits of Gibraltar 21st. On the 8th Oct. in lat. 35 1-2, lon, 31 1-2, during a south-east gale she sprung a leak. On first sounding the pumps two feet of water was found, and the leak continued to gain. Next day the Danish brig Dorothea came along, and the ship then having seven feet of water in her hold, Capt Salter and crew abandoned her, going on board the D. which landed them at Fayal, Oct. 15. The first and second officers arrived at Boston, on Wednesday, as before stated, in the ship James Guthrie. Capt Salter and his seamen were waiting the arrival of the bark Azor from Boston, in which vessel they would take passage home.

James Montgomery

SPECIFICATIONS: 1852. Samuel Badger. Billet head, square stern. Burthen, 893 tons. Length, 174 feet; beam, 33.2 feet; depth, 16.6 feet. Two decks. Original owner—S. C. Thwing, of Boston.

Perhaps it was the liberal spirit that the English poet James Montgomery espoused all of his long life that inspired S. C. Thwing, a pragmatic Boston merchant, to honor him. Montgomery was once jailed in England for his poetical support of the French Revolution, and he was jailed again for a report he wrote on a political riot in Sheffield, England. The authorities considered him a radical, and that drew the admiration of many Americans. One of his most memorable and quotable poetic lines read, "Tomorrow — oh 'twill never come." Montgomery died in 1854. Whether he ever knew anything of the ship named in his honor isn't known.

The ship *James Montgomery* was launched on July 22 and, like the poet for whom she was named, the ship had a long and useful life:

> LAUNCH. — A ship of about 1000 tons burthen, called the "J. Montgomery," was launched in good style from the yard of Capt. Samuel Badger, on Thursday afternoon, 22d. She was built for the freighting business, and is to be commanded by Capt. John Davis, late of the R. D. Shepherd. — She is owned by Messrs. R. D. Shepherd of New-Orleans, S C. Thwing of Boston, and John Davis of this city. — *Messenger*.[44]

Captain Davis cleared the *Montgomery* for New Orleans and went there for cotton for Liverpool.[45] Clearing out of New Orleans on September 30, the ship was in a collision with the ship *Neptunas* off Point Lunas, outside Liverpool, on December 19. The *Neptunas* went down, and the crew was saved by the *Montgomery*.[46] After minor repairs, the *Montgomery* sailed for New Orleans, where she was loaded for Boston, arriving there on April 18. In December 1853, at Philadelphia, Davis was relieved by Capt. John S. D. Dennett, and the ship continued in the cotton trade. Captain Dennett died of yellow fever on October 8, 1855, while on a passage from New Orleans to Le Havre. The news item said several other persons were ill. A later report on Dennett's death said: "We are pained to announce the death of another young man of our city, viz, Capt. John S. D. Dennett, master of the J. Montgomery, who died at sea on October 8th, aged about 27. Captain Dennett was an enterprizing shipmaster and a man of great promise."[47]

With the death of the master, the first mate brought the ship back to New Orleans, where a Captain Bradford took over. In 1857, she was in the East Indian trade under a Captain Hamilton, and came into Boston on November 12. Hamilton continued in command for several years, and the *Montgomery* sailed regular passages between Boston and New Orleans. Along with the *Levi Woodbury*, she was trapped for a time in New Orleans because of low water at the Bar.[48] Later that year she went to Liverpool and ran aground on her way out. After being examined, she was allowed to resume her passage.[49] Captain Hamilton still had her in 1861, and somehow she escaped the blockades. She came into New York and, in March 1862, went up on the rocks in the East River. Her cargo had to be unloaded, and she went into dry dock.[50] The owners diverted her to the East Indian trade during the Civil War, hoping to evade the Confederate raiders. There was a sad note in a news column in 1863: it marked the loss, overboard, "on a passage from Melbourne to Callao of a youngster, Taylor Holt, 17 years, six months, 20 days."[51] Young Holt was the son of the late Rev. Edwin Holt, former pastor of Portsmouth's North Church.

In 1865, the *Montgomery*, still under Captain Hamilton, survived the greatest threat in her long career:

Ship J. Montgomery, Hamilton, arrived at Melbourne March 1st. We copy the following from a Melbourne paper to show what a narrow escape she had from the pirate Shenandoah:

Considerable excitement was manifested yesterday morning in Collins street, and till about noon it was supposed by many that the Shenandoah had made her first capture in Australian waters. The ship James Montgomery, with tobacco, kerosene, and lumber, from Boston — one of the American ships expected for some time past — was reported at five o'clock on the previous evening as being off Cape Otway, with a fair wind for the Heads. It was expected she would reach the entrance of the Bay at daylight, but as nothing was heard of her from Queenscliff at a late hour in the forenoon, the suspicion became strong that she had been pounced upon by the Confederate cruiser. This conjecture was supported by the fact that the owner of the James Montgomery is believed to be so thoroughly Federal in his principles that his ship would sail under the stars and stripes, and no other flag. Shortly before noon, however, anxiety was set at rest by the arrival of the ship, unseen and unmolested by the enemy. It was stated in town yesterday that the Shenandoah is at anchor in a bay on the Tasmanian coast, where she is having a double deck laid down, and being made stronger and more formidable as a fighting ship.[52]

Having escaped destruction, the *Montgomery* continued to voyage for years. Finally, there's a small clue as to her ending in the *American Neptune* (January 1943): the *James Montgomery* was sold to a German firm in 1872 and renamed the *Bremerhaven*. She was abandoned at sea in December 1895.

Orient

SPECIFICATIONS: 1852. George Raynes. Billet head, square stern. Burthen, 1,560 tons. Length, 201 feet; beam, 41 feet; depth, 20.5 feet. Three decks. Original owners—Spofford & Tileston & Co., Capt. Francis M. French, all of New York; and George Raynes.

In a news item on August 16, 1852, the *Chronicle* said,

> George Raynes has a ship ready for launching at his yard — intended for packet or freighter — of Herculean dimensions, — and of finish and fastening the most perfect and solid which timber and metal can form. Mr. Raynes has laid out upon this ship all the science and mechanism, for which, during years of experience, he has been distinguished, and the ship is a castle of strength and solidity which will challenge the admiration of every observer.

Pretty heady praise, but it was deserving. George Raynes was nearing the peak of his years as a shipbuilder. Not only did he excel in quality but also in quantity. During the year prior to the launching of the *Orient*, Raynes had constructed two clippers, the *Wild Pigeon* and the more famed *Witch of the Wave*. In addition, he had built and launched, to order, two almost identical schooners, the *Minna*, 299 tons, and the *Brinda*, 300 tons. The *Minna* is known to have had an alligator figurehead and a round stern. The two vessels were built for people in Boston, who sent them to China to work in the highly lucrative opium trade. Great Britain had fought a war with China a decade earlier, and her victory opened up the Orient to Western trade, one of the by-products of which was opium. The launching of the ship *Orient* was reported:

> LAUNCH OF A LARGE SHIP. — On Wednesday noon a noble ship of 1800 tons was launched from the yard of George Raynes, Esq. in fine style. — Not having been sold, she is yet a

candidate for a name as well as for a market. The high reputation of the builder will not leave her long on upon his hands.
Her extreme length is 201 feet, 1 inch; extreme breadth 41 ft. 8
in.; breadth at plank shear 38 ft. 3 1-2 in.; whole depth 29 ft. 6
in.; length of keel 191 ft. 3 in.[53]

Well, that was praise from the *Chronicle*. On October 16 the
Journal joined the chorus:

> This ship which we announced a few weeks since as
> having been launched from the yard of Geo. Raynes, Esq. and
> awaiting a market and a name, has been disposed of to Messrs.
> Spofford, Tileston & Co. and Capt. F. M. French of New York,
> — Mr. Raynes retaining an interest in her. She has last week
> received the smooth name *Orient*. This term, expressive of the
> east as well as of the place for the rising sun, might a few
> years since have been regarded inappropriate for an American
> vessel, which is built on the sunset side of the Atlantic. But the
> westward course of empire has in fact made our States the Ori-
> ent of the golden region.
>
> The Orient is a noble ship of 1500 tons. Her extreme
> length is 201 feet, 1 inch; extreme breadth 41 ft. 8 in.; breadth
> at plank shear 38 ft. 3 1-2 in.; whole depth 29 ft. 6 in. length of
> keel 181 ft. 3 in. Her model is new, and her arrangements for
> passengers, very extensive and convenient. The arrangements
> for ventillation of the hold, are such as should be generally
> adopted in all large ships. Her deck cabin is finished in a style
> of elegance rarely surpassed — and as a whole she is an honor
> to the builder, and to all those who have aided by the exercise
> of their respective arts. She will sail probably in the course of a
> week, either for New York or for the South, — to be command-
> ed by Capt. French.

The *Orient* went to sea on Friday, October 19, headed for New
York and probable passage to Liverpool The next day, the *Journal*
commented:

> We would commend her to the attention of connoiseurs
> in ship building in New York, having some improvements
> which have not been before met with, which Captain French
> can readily point out. She has accommodation between decks
> for 870 passengers, allowing 14 superficial feet to each. Her
> government tonnage is 1,560 — carpenter's 2,200.
>
> Those not acquainted with shipbuilding are not aware
> of the amount of salt used to preserve the hull. In the Orient

over 400 hhds. of salt were used for the purpose — and will probably have to be renewed at the end of a year.[54]

Ships usually left the Port of Portsmouth under carpenter's measure, and that was the way burthens were entered in the Portsmouth District Customs Records, dating back to 1789. The news story again emphasized the importance of salt in the construction of vessels.

The *Orient* startled New York's shipping industry when she cleared for Liverpool on December 7. It was "the largest cargo which ever for that port.... Her cargo consists of 31,751 bushels wheat, 1970 bales cotton, 2259 barrels flour, 1826 barrels rosin, 165 tierces clover seed, 63 tierces ashes, 13,000 hhds. staves and other packages; besides which she has 70 second class passengers."[55]

Spofford & Tileston had operated the Dramatic Line, which was sold in 1852, and the partners established the Patriotic Line, with the new ship *Orient* and the rebuilt *Henry Clay* as a nucleus for a packet fleet. "The Orient was a three-decker, 201 feet in length and measuring 1560 tons by the existing rule. Under the rule adopted in 1865 she measured 1833 tons."[56] It was also noted that the tide of immigration had ebbed slightly, but there were hopes it would flood again. And, in 1854, the *Orient* did come into New York with 400 steerage passengers out of Liverpool. Her various adventures were well told in an article in *Harper's* (January 1884), reprinted by the *Chronicle* on January 5, 1884:

> Spofford & Tileston's Liverpool line was started about 1852 with the "Orient," the "Henry Clay" (rebuilt from the burned Henry Clay of the Grinnell line,) the "Webster," and the "Calhoun." Captain Truman. The "Orient" and the "Webster" were built in Portsmouth, New Hampshire, by George Raynes, and the former is afloat* to-day, carrying cotton from New Orleans to Liverpool. Her commander in the packet period was Captain George S. Hill, the well known secretary of the Marine Society, who once commanded the "Henry Clay." In 1856, the "Orient" was chartered by the French government to take freight from New York to Havre at the rate of twenty-five cents a bushel of wheat. She carried 80,000 bushels (or 2100 tons) in shippers' bags, and 1000 barrels of flour, but on arriving at Havre, was run aground by the stupidity of a French pilot, and swung directly across the entrance to the harbor, and while some steamboats were trying to tow her off, she brought up on the old wall of a fortification and broke herself in two. Her master had her towed to Liverpool for repairs. On one of his

trips to that city and back, Captain Hill collected $50,000 in freight money; and Captain Joseph J. Lawrence, of the "Webster," of the same line, once "grossed" $60,000.

*The Orient when launched was put down at 1561 tons register; in the treasury list of merchant vessels for the year ending June 30th, 1883, she is down as measuring 1833 tons, the difference being in the methods of measurement employed at the two periods. And her name, in this list, is marked with a "star," which indicates that the vessel referred to has been reported to the treasury department "as lost, wrecked, burned, abandoned, sunk, stranded, foundered, condemned or missing," and that she "will be dropped from the next annual list, unless reported within one year as being in service." Something over a year ago the Orient was dismasted in the Gulf of Mexico, shortly after leaving New Orleans for Liverpool with a cargo of cotton, and was towed back to New Orleans; we have never seen any account of her sailing again, and doubt if she ever makes another voyage.

In 1870 the *Orient* was working in the guano trade. Her freight charge was in gold. In the last year of that decade, the *Orient* was sold for $24,000—not a bad price for a vessel 27 years old. George Raynes's estate still held an interest in her. The beginning of the end came three years later when the *Orient* was wrecked in the Gulf of Mexico. She was abandoned on September 9, 1882, dismasted and waterlogged, floating with her second deck under water, her cargo of lumber keeping her from sinking. She was "towed from the Southwest Pass on the 18th by the pilot boat *Underwriter*, and taken up to New Orleans on the 19th by tug boats. Her bow was badly stove, her upper decks nearly all gone, and her topsides carried away down to the second deck on the starboard side. Had she not been put together, as was customary with ships built on the Piscataqua 30 years ago, and ever since for that matter, the hammering she received from the sea would have made matchwood out of her."[57]

The damage apparently was severe enough to end the *Orient*'s career as a sailing vessel. She was stripped down and turned into a barge—often the fate of rugged Piscataqua ships. On September 21, 1885, the *Chronicle* reported:

GONE AT LAST.

A despatch of Sept. 18th, from Galveston, Texas, gives the following particulars of the loss of the coal barge Orient, with her crew of five men:

While the tug Ranger, towing the barge Orient, from New Orleans with coal, was rounding the bar this morning, the hawser parted. The barge anchored, and the tug came in for a new cable. A heavy sea was on, and the anchor chain parting, the barge was driven aground five miles from the island. When the Ranger returned she was unable to reach the barge, or to rescue her crew of five men. A lifeboat was immediately manned by five experienced seamen, and started for the Orient. When they reached the barge the sea was fast wrecking her. The lifeboat drew close to the barge, when one of the imperilled seamen jumped into the boat and capsized it. All of the seamen who went out in the lifeboat came ashore near the Beach hotel, floating on their life preservers. The man who jumped into the lifeboat is undoubtedly lost, as are his four companions on the barge. Quantities of drift floating ashore indicate that the Orient has gone to pieces. The Ranger has returned. It is impossible for any boat to reach the scene of the wreck in the heavy sea now running.

Such was the tragic end of the old ship Orient, 1834 tons register, which was built in this city in 1852 by the late George Raynes for Spofford, Tileston & Co. of New York, and which was in active and remunerative service up to the latter part of 1881, escaping all the dangers from confederate cruisers during the war. In the fall of 1881 she loaded with cotton at New Orleans for Liverpool, but was totally dismasted two or three days after sailing, by a storm which sent many vessels to the bottom of the gulf or piled them up on its shores; she was towed back to New Orleans, her cargo forwarded by another means of conveyance, and her hull laid up for several years. Some months ago she was made into a barge for the transportation of coal from New Orleans to Galveston.

Frank Pierce

SPECIFICATIONS: 1852. Fernald & Pettigrew. Billet head, square stern. Burthen, 1,143 tons. Length, 185.8 feet; beam, 36.4 feet; depth, 18.2 feet. Three decks. Original owners—Daniel Marcy, Richard Jenness, and Washington Williams.

Other than the *Levi Woodbury*, no Port of Portsmouth–built ship was more deliberately named to honor a living politician than the *Frank Pierce*. Franklin Pierce of New Hampshire was elected presi-

Daniel Marcy and other prominent Democrats had Fernald & Pettigrew build the Frank Pierce in 1852. The vessel was named for the 14th president of the United States. Mariner's Museum, Newport News, Virginia.

dent of the United States three weeks after his namesake vessel was launched. Although it has nothing to do with the craft of shipbuilding, the politics involved are interesting. Daniel Marcy and his fellow Democrats never bought a vessel from George Raynes, who probably was a Whig, although not very active. They preferred to go across the river to Badger's Island to get their vessels built. In no way can that predilection be attributed to superior competency; it was simply a matter of political belief, which, in the mid-nineteenth century, was almost a religion.

The *Chronicle* published a notice on August 16 to the effect that "Fernald & Pettigrew have a new ship, over 1400 tons, built entirely of New Hampshire white oak, the hull three-quarters finished." The vessel was described as a three-decker, owned in Portsmouth and New Orleans. She would be able to carry 4,500 bales of cotton, when properly ballasted. On October 9, the *Chronicle* announced that the ship "now building at the yard of Fernald & Pettigrew, is to be named the Frank Pierce in compliment to the nominee of the Democratic Party."

Briefly, Franklin Pierce, a one-time law student in Portsmouth, was the leader of the New Hampshire troops in the Mexican War in

1846. After more than 30 ballots in the 1852 Democratic Convention, Pierce became the party's reluctant nominee. As always, those were troubled times, and Pierce, after winning election, found himself out of step with northern antislavery thought, mostly because Pierce believed the states had the right to determine their own destiny in such matters, even to the point of seceding from the Union. His whole administration was a disaster, speeding up the confrontation between North and South. By the way, Pierce was also the first president to send troops into Nicaragua.

The ship *Frank Pierce* was launched on October 22, about 5:00 P.M., and the *Journal*, a staunch Whig newspaper, commented:

> If the General can slip into the Presidency as neatly and smoothly as the ship glided into the water, he will have a good time of it. There was a ship launched from the same place, about the time our lamented townsman was talked of for the Presidency, and she was complimented with the name of *Levi Woodbury*. He lived but a short time after the compliment was paid.

Capt. Daniel Marcy headed the *Frank Pierce* toward New Orleans on November 25, taking with him the cheering thought that his friend, Franklin Pierce, had won the presidency. His wife and a Captain Baker of the Marine Corps were with him. The ship took 22 days on the passage, running into rough weather on most of the journey. In a letter, Captain Marcy detailed some of the problems encountered and expressed satisfaction that the *Frank Pierce* had reached the Hole in the Wall, on the southern tip of Abaco Island, in 9 days, "although we had only 24 hours' fair wind, during which time we ran 286 miles, with main royal set. When within three miles of the Isaacs, it fell calm, and we drifted out of the Gulf with a four-knot current. Tried to get on the banks but could not; beat for three days, losing about 40 miles per day. Finding that there was no alternative but to return to the Hole in the Wall again, we did so, thus making two passages for one. After passing the Hole in the Wall for a second time, we were 80 hours to the Bar."[58]

The *Frank Pierce* cleared out of New Orleans on January 27, 1853, with 4,768 bales of cotton, weighing 2,184,887 pounds, or an average of 458 pounds per bale. In addition, she carried 102 tierces of beef.[59] (Tierce, according to the *OED*, was a liquid measure, usually involving a 42-gallon cask.) The *Frank Pierce* returned to Boston in June, and it was reported in the *Journal* on the eleventh:

> PASSENGERS. — The statement that Capt. Marcy landed 710 passengers at Boston is correct: but the story about such a

lot of babies is not true. Capt. M. informs the Journal that through the excellent arrangement of the means of ventilation and the conveniences of the ship, general health prevailed among the large company — not one death nor scarcely any case of sickness occurred. But he lays no claim to any peculiar advantage on this score for bringing into port 11 more passengers than he took from Liverpool, as the papers are reporting. There was no increase on the voyage.

With Pierce in the White House, a Democratic staff was running the Boston Custom House, and the members presented Captain Marcy with an oil portrait of the fourteenth president as an ornament for the main cabin. However, it was Capt. Joseph B. Currier who enjoyed the painting as he took the *Frank Pierce* to St. John, New Brunswick, for lumber, which she delivered to Liverpool. From Liverpool, she went to New Orleans. A news item about this time reported:

> We saw a beautiful oil painting at the residence of Capt. Marcy [then 57 Pleasant Street], representing the ship *Frank Pierce* under full sail, up the Mersey river, at Liverpool; in the distance, the *Levi Woodbury* is seen coming around Bell Rock, and the *Peter Marcy* is just being taken into her dock. It was executed by an artist in Liverpool, and is one of the finest paintings we ever saw. The frame is very handsome and costly, being carved and gilded. It is intended as a gift to the President, and would grace any room in the White House.[60]

The *Frank Pierce* drew news comment in 1855, when she came into Boston in a passage of 30 days from Liverpool, despite heavy weather all the way. Then commanded by Capt. Joseph W. Leach, the *Frank Pierce* was carrying an unusually heavy cargo and was drawing over 20 feet of water when she arrived, "which speaks well for the perseverance and skill of her young captain."[61] From Boston, she went to Savannah and was loaded for Liverpool with 4,207 bales of Upland cotton, weighing 1,872,115 pounds, valued at $176,674.45; Sea Island cotton, 155,656 pounds, valued at $31,820.90, making an aggregate of 4,705 bales, weighing 2,027,771 pounds, with a total value of $208,014.35. "One of the largest, if not the largest, cargoes of cotton ever cleared from this port."[62] It's of note that the Sea Island bales weighed much less than the Upland—312 to 448. Further, the Sea Island variety was worth double the Upland—$.20 to $.09 per pound.

An odd little item about Captain Leach testifies as to the problems of shipmasters during the Civil War. It first appeared in the *American Ballot* and was reprinted by the *Journal* on January 14, 1865:

Capt. Joseph Leach, formerly of the ship Frank Pierce, and subsequently captured as a blockade runner, or for some other impropriety against the laws of Father Abraham, and held as a prisoner by Uncle Sam, has been in town of late, the guest of Hon. Daniel Marcy, member of Congress from this District. Whether our Representative has succeeded in obtaining a pardon and allowing Joseph to sojourn with his brethren we are not informed. — *Ballot*.

Members of the Marcy family frequently traveled on ships in which Daniel and Peter Marcy had interests; this was especially true between Portsmouth or Boston and New Orleans. Despite the distances, the families often visited each other, with the Portsmouth Marcys going south in the winter and members of the New Orleans family coming north in the summer. The outbreak of the Civil War stopped this fraternization, but once the war was over it resumed, until death separated the Marcy brothers. Mrs. Daniel Marcy, her daughter and son, Henry L. Marcy, took such a trip in January 1857.

The *Chronicle*, on August 22, 1861, published a short article on the delights of a brief passage from Portsmouth to Boston on the *Frank Pierce*:

A SEA RIDE TO BOSTON.

BOSTON, Aug. 18, 1861.

Dear Chronicle: — You are familiar with the beauties of the river scenery of the Piscataqua, and are doubtless more than ever sensible to its picturesque attractions since our memorable aquatic festival of Friday. But have you ever sat in the foretop of a noble ship as she glided down to the sea on the moon-lit surface of the full flood tide, propelled by a powerful little tug clinging close to her side, like an ant bearing off a chip many times larger than itself?

The clear tones of the nine o'clock bell of Saturday night were ringing, as the Frank Pierce swung out from the Pier, with cheers from on board and sweet music from the little fleet of boats around us. The panorama of the broad river and its borders, the white buildings of the quiet town, and the stately houses of the Navy Yard, the dark battlements of the earth forts, the shadowy lines of the bridges, the tiny islands dotting the shining expanse of Little Harbor, and, farther off, the silvery windings of Sagamore through the pine woods, — all combined to make the view from our select perch aloft a scene of enchanting loveliness.

In half an hour we passed the lighthouses, standing like

sentinels keeping guard over the diamonds that sparkle on the surface of the sea; while, far away from the shore, the Shoals light flashed its alternate crimson, white and orange. On the deck below we could hear the songs and laughter of the passengers and crew, and the voices of our tall, stout captain, and our short stout ditto, — all of whom we found to gether, when the cool air sent us down among them.

Soon followed a search for sleeping accommodations, (for berths there were none); and none of our number being too fastidious to make a virtue of necessity, soft planks, coils of rope, cabin floors and tables were seen occupied by recumbent mortality. But the spirit of revelry triumphed over that of sleep, and the cabin, to whose tempting retirement the captain had kindly recommended his friends, was soon a pandemonium. A medley of hideous noises, speaking trumpet solos and boot heel choruses, with snatches of melodious discords from Glory Hallelujah and Dixie filled the air, with the exception of a small space occupied by migratory chunks of cheese and ship bread flying at random through the darkness.

Long after midnight, however, a party went on deck to anchor the cat, (our friend says "cat the anchor," but I have no faith in his nautical experience,) — and we sank into peaceful slumber, to be disturbed by the heavy fall of a portly gentleman, around whose limbs unseen hands had wound a rope, which was pulled by some invisible power at the other end; and finally a noisy chorus of

"The morning light is breaking,
The darkness disappears,"

called us on deck to view the glorious sight of sunrise at sea.

Many were the ludicrous and pleasing incidents of the night's voyage, of which vivid recollections will exist in the minds of the passenger who sought repose in a *quiet* state-room, — the sailor who was so long as to be adapted to the uses of a hawser, — the youth who was convinced that on Sunday mornings the sun rises in the west, — and the ill-used by patient "Tappy," who only escaped a half-completed execution at the yard-arm to be posted when off Cape Ann with instructions to watch for the receiving ship at Charlestown Navy Yard, to which duty he faithfully adhered.

In passing up Boston harbor, one cannot help remarking its inferiority in many respects to that of the Piscataqua; and wishing that our city had possessed the proper elements of commercial prosperity, enterprise and liberality.

For the pleasure of this trip the invited guests are indebted to the politeness of the owners.

T. U. B.

In the middle of the Civil War, badly damaged in a storm, the *Frank Pierce* put into Portsmouth for repairs. However, she had to be sent on to Boston because all the shipwrights were working on the Portsmouth Navy Yard. A gang of workmen had been imported from Portland to do the job, but they, too, went on the Navy Yard.[63] (This explains a point that will be touched on in discussion the slowdown in shipbuilding on the Piscataqua in the 1860s.)

Ironically, the *Frank Pierce* successfully eluded the pack of predatory Confederate raiders for more than three years, only to be lost in a storm. She was sailing from New York to Acapulco, Mexico, under Capt. John C. Bush, when she was abandoned. Bush was another of the company of great sea captains who hailed from the Port of Portsmouth. He died in Brooklyn, New York, September 8, 1884, at the age of 70.

When she was lost, the *Frank Pierce* was west of the Falkland Islands, overcome by a winter gale on May 21, 1864. In a letter to her owners, Captain Bush gave the graphic details of abandoning a ship at sea:

LOSS OF SHIP FRANK PIERCE. — Capt. Bush, of ship Frank Pierce, of Portsmouth, before reported abandoned on the

passage from New York to Panama, with a load of coal, reports:
— Sailed from New York March 16th, with a crew of 24 persons — the mate's wife as a passenger. On the 31st, M. Melvin,
seaman, a native of England, fell from the foreroyal yard, on
deck, and died a few days after. May 25th, made Cape St.
Johns, on Staten Island, and on the 27th of May was in lat
55,50 S, lon 63,50 W, by observation, after which the weather
was thick and stormy and no observations. May 29th, the ship
lay to under storm sails, head to the SSE, blowing very heavy,
sea running mountains high, and wind hanging more southerly; at 12 o'clock noon wore ship to westward. At midnight it
was blowing a terrific gale, with a high cross sea, the ship
rolling, lee rail under; found that the cargo was shifting to leeward; endeavored to veer ship, but she would not pay off; set
the jib and reefed the foresail but to no avail.

While thus employed, the ship gave a heavy pitch forward, which as afterwards ascertained, caused a large quantity of the coal to shift from midships forward, at the same time
rolling to leeward, which hove the ship on her beam ends,
washing bulwarks and everything away fore and aft on the lee
side. In this position I saw she was likely to remain, and, not
knowing what moment she might fill and go down, the water
standing up to hatch commons, I ordered the mast to be cut
away, which was accordingly done; but she continued to lay on
her beam-ends.

By this time I found that the rudder head was twisted
off, and that we were drifting at the mercy of wind and sea. I
sent a man down in the pump well, and another down in the
forehold to ascertain what water there was in the wreck. They
reported the water standing over the keelson in the well, and
up to the lower deck beams in the forehold. Nothing was left us
but to pump or sink. The ship lying over so much, the men had
to sit down on deck to work the pumps. Set one gang at work
throwing overboard coal from lee side of upper between decks,
which we continued night and day up to Sunday, June 5, when
we saw a barque about six miles distance from us. Finding the
barque was coming toward us, I concluded to leave the wreck if
possible, five of the men being laid up, and the rest exhausted
and ready to give up.

Commenced getting our two small boats ready, the long
boat being stove by the falling of the mast. We succeeded in
getting one of the small boats afloat, but the other was
swamped and lost. It then being quite dark, and the barque

close by us, got the mate's wife and one boy in the only remaining boat, intending to put all the sick men in the first boat, but, through some misunderstanding, the boat's crew pulled alongside the barque; when the boat returned we were all ready to get in, but unfortunately the boat was stove and sunk, and Peter Boardman, a native of France, was drowned. All that night and next day it was blowing a gale, and nothing could be done but pumping ship to keep her afloat. The barque kept around us all the time. On Tuesday, June 7, the wind moderated; we went to work patching up the holes in the bottom of the long boat with canvas, the only means left us to get off the wreck, and by noon got her safely afloat, and by making two journeys to the barque got all safely on board."

The barque proved to be the Charles Lambert, (of Sunderland E) Capt. Thomas Roberts, bound to Coquimbo, which bore up for Falkland Islands, and landed the shipwrecked crew at Port Stanley June 13. Capt. Bush returns his thanks to Capt. Roberts and first officer, Mr. Benj. Harris, for their kindness while on board the barque.[64]

Judge Shaw

SPECIFICATIONS: 1852. Samuel Hanscom. Eliot. Billet head, square stern. Burthen, 689 tons. Length, 151 feet; beam, 31.5 feet; depth, 15.75 feet. Two decks. Original owners—Seth Cushing, Matthew Cobb, et al., of Boston.

The *Judge Shaw* was the last vessel of any real size built on the upper river. In 1847, William Hanscom had built and launched the *Elizabeth Hanscom* from the family yard, and, in 1851, his younger brother, Samuel, built the famed clipper *Nightingale*, a vessel very probably designed by still another brother, the brilliant Isaiah Hanscom, who became chief constructor for the U.S. Navy before his career ended. The *Nightingale* was followed in February 1852 by the *Josephine*, another clipper. The *Judge Shaw* was built on the same ways, and not only was the last ship built in Eliot, but also the last launched on the Piscataqua in 1852: "LAUNCH. — The Chronicle understands that a fine ship of 650 tons burthen, was launched this week from the yard of Samuel Hanscom, on Eliot neck — clearing our ship yards, and making the tenth ship launched this season, with an aggregate tonnage of about 9000."[65]

Named for Lemuel Shaw, chief justice of Massachusetts, who died March 31, 1861, at the age of 81, the *Judge Shaw* sailed from the Port of Portsmouth on Christmas Day, heading for Boston under Capt. Henry Prior.[66] She apparently followed the familiar track of going to New Orleans and then to Liverpool. There she was loaded for Calcutta, returning late in 1854. Not much is known of her subsequent career. Nelson said she was sold in Hong Kong, but he gave no date.[67]

Adelaide Bell

SPECIFICATIONS: *1853. Samuel Badger. Billet head, square stern. Burthen, 1,091 tons. Length, 181.6 feet; beam, 36 feet; depth, 18 feet. Two decks. Original owners—Edward F. Sise, John Chase, Isaac Bell, Joshua Peirce, and John D. Simes.*

The clipper frenzy was near full spate. Shipyards in the Port of Portsmouth launched only four ships in 1853 that weren't rated as clippers, and there were six of the latter. Even Samuel Badger had succumbed to the craze in 1852, launching his little *Fleetwood*, which, at 663 tons, was the smallest clipper built on the Piscataqua. But the diversity in yards such as Badger's was shown by his construction of a 20-ton schooner as he was building his biggest vessel of the year, the *Adelaide Bell*.

The new ship was launched on July 20 at 11:00 A.M. and towed across the Piscataqua to a wharf in Portsmouth to be rigged and made ready for sea. Towing her across was the famed tug and harbor steamer, *Grace Darling*. The *Adelaide Bell*'s first passage, under Capt. John Chase, was to St. John, New Brunswick, where she loaded lumber for Liverpool. Until 1855, her voyages went around the triangle: into Boston, south to New Orleans, over to Liverpool, and then return. Late in 1854, the Liverpool agents sent her to Calcutta, and her East Indian service won her listing as a vessel in that trade.

In 1864, after four years of evading Confederate cruisers, a brief news item appeared: "DISASTER. — Ship Adelaide Bell, of Portsmouth, Baines, took fire at Chincha Islands, Nov. 29, and was totally destroyed.

"The A. B. was 1091 tons, rate A1, built at Portsmouth, in 1853, where she is owned by E. F. Sise & Co."[68]

Webster

SPECIFICATIONS: 1853. George Raynes. Billet head, oval stern. Burthen, 1,727 tons. Length, 206.8 feet; beam, 42.55 feet; depth, 21.275 feet. Three decks. Original owners—Spofford & Tileston, of New York; George Raynes.

The *Webster* was designed and built for service as a New York–Liverpool packet, and that was what she did almost entirely throughout her 20-year career. Named to honor New Hampshire's famed native son, Daniel Webster, who had died the year before, the ship was the largest ever built by Raynes and one of the largest merchant sailing vessels ever built on the Piscataqua. The *Webster* was launched on July 23, shortly after 1:00 P.M. Such was her tremendous weight that she snapped a 13-inch manila hawser "as though it were a thread" on her way to the water.[69] The *Webster*, commanded by Francis M. French, left the Port of Portsmouth under tow by the tug *Leviathan*, which prompted a commentary:

> REMARKABLE PERFORMANCE OF A STEAM TUG.
> The splendid ship WEBSTER, built by our neighbor George Raynes, Esq. for Messrs. Spofford, Tileston & Co.'s line of New York and Liverpool packets, left this port on Thursday, 8th inst. at noon, in tow of the steam tug LEVIATHAN, and reached New York at 2 o'clock on the morning of Saturday, the 10th — thus accomplishing the distance in 38 hours, which is at the rate of about 10 miles per hour, a speed never before equalled in the annals of towing.
> The Leviathan is probably the most powerful steam tug in this country, and was built by Mr. Eckford Webb, under the auspices of several New York ship owners, expressly for the transportation of large vessels. Her engine was constructed at the Allaire Works, and is a duplicate of one of those in Mr. Vanderbilt's famous steam yacht "North Star." Her power is estimated at about 600 horses.[70]

The *Webster* joined the Raynes-built *Orient* in the Patriotic Line, managed by Spofford & Tileston, and crossed and recrossed the North Atlantic, under various masters, year in, year out, until the faster-moving steamships took away the bulk of the passenger business. In 1861, the *Webster* had a mishap on the Mersey River at Liverpool: her starboard anchor chain snapped, and she was dragged along by the ebbing tide. A tug brought her to, but she fouled the ship *North America*, and tugs had to pull them apart.[71]

Three years later, the *Webster* was the scene of a mutiny while waiting for a cargo at Liverpool. Capt. J. J. Lawrence brought charges against the mutineers, and they were hauled into police court before Magistrate Raffles. The men involved were Frank Lynch, Thomas Connor, Alan McDonald, James Kelly, William Jones, John Hughes, Peter Walsh, Francis Durant, James Kennedy, John Brown, John Williamson, Richard Duran, Edward O'Quinn, Stephen Kennedy, and John Lynch. The cause of the mutiny wasn't mentioned in the news accounts. The sailors had created a disturbance, and the Liverpool police were called. When Police Inspector Carlyle attempted to arrest the ringleaders, a scuffle ensued. Francis Lynch was charged with unlawful wounding after he drew a knife and slashed at Inspector Carlyle's throat. Captain Lawrence drew his pistol to shoot Lynch, but was prevented by Inspector Carlyle. When more police arrived, the men were taken to the Liverpool Bridewell.[72] When they were arraigned in December, all the men were discharged except Francis Lynch, who was sentenced to 18 months.[73] One of the men acquitted, William Jones, was in trouble again a few days later. The *Liverpool Telegraph* reported on December 22 that he was in court for attempting to assault a housekeeper. Jones was fined five pounds, but defaulted and went to jail for two months. The incidents are of value in showing the caliber of the crews that packet masters had to handle on each passage. Liverpool's waterfront, like Portsmouth's old Water Street, wasn't a place for those of delicate, refined tastes.

The *Webster* was eventually sold by Spofford & Tileston in 1872 to go into the guano business. The next year she brought a load of bird phosphate home, stopping in South Carolina. En·route to New York she went ashore on Barnegat Beach, on April 9, 1873, and was a total loss.[74] A week later she had gone to pieces.

Brother Jonathan

SPECIFICATIONS: 1853. Tobey & Littlefield. Noble's Island. Male figurehead, square stern. Burthen, 790 tons. Length, 159 feet; beam, 32.95 feet; depth, 16.475 feet. Two decks. Original owner—Richard H. Tucker, of Wiscasset, Maine.

Construction of the *Brother Jonathan* marked the emergence of a new firm in the Port of Portsmouth's shipbuilding industry, one that would eventually be ranked with the three leaders. Stephen Tobey had been the top-ranking shipwright in the Raynes yard until he struck out on his own, in partnership with Daniel Littlefield.

This chair was taken from the wreck of the Portsmouth-built Brother Jonathan, *wrecked after a collision with another Piscataqua-built ship, the* William Penn. *Collection of Miss Jane S. Tucker.*

Tobey's move undoubtedly was prompted by the elevation of George Raynes, Jr. to partnership, which meant Tobey couldn't go any further in that organization. The *Brother Jonathan* was the second vessel the increasingly influential Tucker family of Wiscasset had bought from a Piscataqua firm. The first was the *Samoset*, built by Fernald & Pettigrew in 1847. Why Richard Tucker shifted his business to Tobey & Littlefield isn't known, but it was an enduring connection. The *Brother Jonathan* was launched on December 3 and was described as being "intended for a Charleston and Liverpool packet."[75]

The *Brother Jonathan*, which sailed from the Port of Portsmouth on January 14, 1854, under Capt. Joseph Tucker, headed for Charleston, where she arrived 10 days later. From Portsmouth, the *Brother Jonathan* took out a cargo of hay, 1,091 bales, which was sold at $1.40 a bale, a total of $1,527.40. She cleared out of Charleston on March 2, carrying 2,043 bales of Upland cotton and 424 bales of Sea Island. In addition, she had 362 barrels of rice, 36 barrels of flour, plus cotton yard and sundries on board. The freight and primage totaled $17,504. Her passage to Le Havre took 28 days. Leaving Le Havre on May 6, she headed for New York with 416 passengers, at $7.75 each, a total of $3,224. The reader should remember that immigrant passengers provided their own food.

Miss Jane Tucker of Wiscasset has provided excerpts from the *Brother Jonathan*'s log on her last voyage. The ship took its passengers from Le Havre into New York. From there, she went to Charleston in ballast. Her officers were Captain Tucker; George Belcher, mate; Calvin R. Fredson, second mate; Noah Broughton, third mate. She loaded 3,328 bales for Liverpool, plus rice, sailing on August 18 and arriving on September 21. She took on a cargo of railroad iron, salt, coal, canon ware, slates, and 150 packages, 28 bales, and 30 casks of merchandise. She also had four steerage and six cabin passengers. One first-class passenger, ill with consumption, paid $70 for the trip.

On October 29, 1854, the *Brother Jonathan* went ashore on Ballyquinton Point, near Portaferry, Northern Ireland. She had been in a collision with the Portsmouth-built ship *William Penn*, badly damaging her running gear. She went on shore, becoming a total wreck, as was the *William Penn*.

Poring through voluminous correspondence files of the Tucker family, Jane Tucker has produced letters concerning the loss of the ship *Brother Jonathan* after its collision with the *William Penn*. The letters establish that the *William Penn* had at some point been sold and gone under the British flag. It wasn't a cheerful Joseph Tucker who wrote home about the loss of the ship:

> Dear Father
>
> With much gratitude to kind Providence in the safety of our lives I have a sad duty in informing you of the loss of our fine ship. I made exertion to get safely out of the Channel [Irish] but the gales, thick weather, and misfortune of a collision with the Eng. ship Wm. Penn came overwhelming on me, not ceasing even now. I cant write, I can only say the ship will be a total loss, thank God we are all saved.

The correspondence between Captain Tucker and his father, and with their English agents, English and Brandon, runs for many pages, faithfully transcribed by Miss Tucker. Suffice it to say, a day after his first report to his father, Richard Hawley Tucker, Captain Tucker had collected his wits enough to make a detailed report. He described what happened in the nautical jargon of the day, coming to the conclusion that no one on the *William Penn* was paying the slightest bit of attention to sailing her. While the ships were tangled, the cook on the *William Penn* went on board the *Brother Jonathan* and stayed. The cook, John Cluney, later swore in a deposition that no one on the *William Penn* seemed to know another vessel was in the vicinity. The collision was his first knowledge of it.

Granite State

SPECIFICATIONS: 1853. Samuel Badger. Billet head, square stern. Burthen, 956 tons. Length, 174.2 feet; beam, 34.4 feet; depth, 17.2 feet. Two decks. Original owners—Horton D. Walker, J. H. Tarlton, William Simes, John French, Samuel Adams, George W. Pendexter, and Samuel Clark, all of Portsmouth; Samuel Badger, John Neal, and John F. Mathes, all of Kittery.

The *Granite State* distinguished herself long before she slid down the ways, and that last was an act she was reluctant to do. After all, it was a bit late in the year to be getting one's bottom wet in the chilly Piscataqua, and the *Granite State* apparently was well aware of the fact. Her launching was scheduled for 4:00 P.M. on December 6, but she didn't hit icy waters until 4:00 A.M. A snowstorm kept her frozen fast to the stocks, and the launching crew had to keep fires going close to her throughout the night. It was probably the smallest number of spectators ever to gather for a launching in the Piscataqua Valley. The *Granite State* was also unusual in being one of the few ships to be fully rigged before launching.

Whether the rigging on the stocks was intended to save money, or just expedite her readiness for sea, isn't clear. But cost, as might be surmised, was ever a factor in ship construction. Early in 1853, the *Journal* published a table showing the cost, per ton, of building a clipper ship in the yards of Boston and New York, as compared to Portsmouth and yards in Maine and New Brunswick. New York and Boston were listed as $62 a ton; Portsmouth, $65; Maine, $50; and New Brunswick, $45. The *Journal* decried the estimate for Portsmouth:

> The price of building ships of the above class [clipper] at Portsmouth is much over-rated. We have made particular inquiry of various builders, and they state the proper sum, as a general average, to be about fifty-five dollars per ton. In some cases they have been built much below that price, — and in no case have they come up to sixty dollars. The New Brunswick vessels are built of softer materials, and their inferiority corresponds with their price.

Of course, the article was discussing clippers, but, basically, the same grade of materials went into the construction of all the American square-riggers. The clippers were much more ornate in their cabin treatment and other details. A vessel like the *Granite State*, probably cost about $50,000. It can't help but be wondered if the *Journal* might not have conveniently overlooked the luxurious, costly clipper *Nightin-gale* when defending the Port of Portsmouth's clipper costs. The *Nightingale*, built in Eliot, reputedly was one of the most expensive ever built. It took a lot of financial finagling to get her to sea.[76]

While Capt. Samuel Billings held command, Edward McNulty, a seaman, brought charges of cruel and abusive treatment against Billings and the second mate. The preliminary hearing was held in Portsmouth before William H. Y. Hackett, the U.S. commissioner in such matters:

ADMIRALTY CASE.

FRIDAY, Sept. 14.

Before W. H. Y. Hackett, Esq., U. S. Commissioner: — Edward McNulty, a seaman belonging to the ship Granite State, complained against Samuel Billings, captain, and Wm. Valentine, 2d mate, for an assault and severe beating. The testimony showed that Valentine, on the 27th August, at sea, cruelly beat and abused McNulty, (who was disabled by a lame hand,) for not going aloft as ordered in the night, by the mate. McNulty ran for refuge or redress to the captain, who instead of relieving him, justified the mate.

The Commissioner discharged the captain, on the ground that he was not fully aware of the seaman's disabilities. But he held the mate to answer at the U. S. Circuit Court, Oct. 2, in $200 bonds. Four witnesses were also bound over in $50 each, and committed.

Towle for the U. S. Hatch and Storer for defence.

Captain Billings sold his interest in the *Granite State* to Capt. Nathaniel G. Weeks of Greenland, who commanded the ship until 1861. On a passage from Calcutta to Boston, Weeks's 18-month-old daughter, Myra, died. Myra and her mother, Elizabeth, had accompanied the captain on the voyage.[78] If a captain's wife was willing, her joining him on his voyages was one of the "perks" of a master mariner's life. Indeed, how else could a shipmaster enjoy a touch of family life? When Captain Weeks gave up the *Granite State*, his first mate, Benjamin F. Jacobs, became master. Jacobs had served under Weeks for five years and four months. Jacobs, who kept the ship until 1867, was still active as a shipmaster when the second *Granite State* was launched more than 20 years later.

The *Journal*, on August 29, 1857, published a letter from Captain Weeks to his owners in Portsmouth concerning a passage to Liverpool from New Orleans. All too clearly, the letter describes the method by which crews were often recruited for ocean voyages:

We are here and all well, after a very smooth passage, fortunately for us, for I have had only *two* sailors on this passage, the other thirteen being landsmen, never at sea before, and do not to this day know a rope in the ship! They were picked up soon after the 4th of July, by the landlords, dressed up in red shirts and put on board. When they came to their senses, they were perfectly astonished to find they were in a fair way to visit Europe; and I was equally astonished to find I had a company of soldiers instead of a crew of sailors. Many of them had just returned from Nicaragua, and it requires pretty constant drilling to make sailors of soldiers.

While under Captain Jacobs, the *Granite State*, heading for Liverpool in 1862, was chased by the Confederate cruiser *Alabama*. In the news report, the *Alabama* was described as the "pirate steamer 290." The numerals were the *Alabama*'s hull number in the Laird's shipyard in England, where she was built. Captain Jacobs took advantage of a heavy gale to escape the raider, after a chase of four hours.[79] Jacobs had the *Granite State* in Calcutta in February 1864, where she loaded 100 to 150 tons of saltpeter, at $25 a ton; plus 800 tons of general merchandise, at $18 a ton; for a freight charge in excess of $15,00 for the passage.

Captain Jacobs relinquished command of the *Granite State* to her former commander in 1867. Jacobs took the new ship *Merrimack*, of which more will be said later. "Capt. Weeks sailed from New York to San Francisco, and thence to Dublin, Ireland, but, on account of ill health, gave up his command to Captain Samuel G. Gardner (Manning street) of this city, his first officer during the voyage."[80]

Nathaniel G. Weeks's career as a merchant officer is typical:

> At the time of his discharge of the cargo at Dublin, Capt. Weeks had been engaged in ships thirty years — 1 year 4 mos. before the mast; 2 years 6 mos. 2d mate; 3 years first officer; and 25 years, 4 mos. 11 days as master of ships Marion, Mary & Susan, Huron, Goodwin, Panther, Annie Sise, Fleetford, and Granite State; thus showing his industry, his perseverance and his devotion to his calling.
>
> During the period of thirty years he had sailed 569,300 miles, had crossed the Atlantic 53 and the Equator 46 times.... Few men had a better record — few shipmasters, for intelligence, industry, capability and integrity have been his equals.

The information about Captain Weeks's career came in a report of a meeting held at the Rockingham House for those who had held interests in the *Granite State*. The ship had gone to Callao to get a permit in 1869, and then to the Chincha Islands for guano. She sailed, but had to put back when she developed a leak. "Her insurance policy was canceled by the underwriters and she was, with her usual good luck sold at but little less than half her first cost."[81] The former proprietors of the *Granite State* sat down for dinner and directed congratulations toward Horton D. Walker, "who has been her agent from the first."

The *Granite State* was renamed the *Providence* in 1870, and sold again in 1874 at Liverpool.[82]

Moultrie

SPECIFICATIONS: 1854. Tobey & Littlefield. Male figurehead, square stern. Burthen, 883 tons. Length, 168 feet; beam, 33.7 feet; depth, 16.85 feet. Two decks. Original owners—R. H. Tucker et al.

One of the first of the 1854 class of ordinary freighters, the *Moultrie* was launched on July 11, the second vessel bought from Tobey & Littlefield by the Tuckers of Wiscasset. For a yard barely a year old, Tobey & Littlefield was moving at a fast pace. The firm had already launched in 1854 the big clipper *Sierra Nevada*, then came the *Moultrie*, which was followed by another freighter, the *Ladoga*, and then a second clipper, the *Ocean Rover*. The *Moultrie*, in all probability, was named for William Moultrie, one of the heroic defenders of Charleston, South Carolina, in the early days of the Revolutionary War. What Moultrie's connection was to the Tuckers, if any, isn't known, but a fort in Charleston Harbor that played a role in the Civil War was named in his honor.

George W. Chapman, who owned an interest in the *Moultrie*, took the ship to Savannah, departing the Port of Portsmouth on October 13, a Friday. The mate was William S. Frost. Again, thanks to Miss Tucker's help with ships' logs, information about the voyages of the *Moultrie* is at hand. She left carrying the usual cargo of hay and apples. The passage to Savannah took 7 days, but she went to Charleston for cargo. She was at Charleston nearly two months before leaving for Liverpool with 3,220 bales of cotton, weighing 1,241,000 pounds. It took her 45 days to reach Liverpool. From there she went to Cardiff, Wales, and loaded with railroad iron, weighing 907.5 tons. The freight paid was £1333.6.0, which included the primage. She went to Charleston with her railroad iron.

She arrived there in mid-April, and left on May 29, carrying 3,500 bales of cotton, copper ore, and rosin. Freight rate was £2,159, including primage. Chapman was still master, Frost was first officer, and John Hayes was second mate. She also had Daniel Stone of Wiscasset, one of the owners, as a passenger. The passage took 24 days. On August 6, she departed Liverpool with 11,359 sacks of salt, at 20s. plus primage. The freight totaled £1,220. That cargo went to Savannah, and the *Moultrie* left Savannah on October 24, 1855, with 2,740 bales of cotton and 5,000 bushels of wheat. Freight was £3,215. She came back from Liverpool with more railroad iron. In May 1856, she left Charleston with 3,070 bales of cotton, including 180 of Sea Island—freight, £1,668, plus primage. From Liverpool, she returned to Charleston in September 1856, with 6,4000 sacks of wheat. She had been badly beaten up in a hurricane. From Charleston, she went to LaPreaux, New Brunswick, for lumber, which she took to Liverpool. She loaded some salt and went to Charleston, but her freight amounted only to £338. The *Moultrie* left Charleston on May 24 for the last time. She was carrying 2,255 bales of cotton, at varying rates, plus 824 bales of Sea Island and 71 casks of rice. Freight totaled $10,788, plus primage. She went to Le Havre, and then to Cardiff for railroad iron, at 28s. a ton, total freight of £1,260.

The *Moultrie* sailed on June 3, 1857, for Charleston. On July 22 she was wrecked on the Charleston Bar, North Breaker.[83]

Chatsworth

SPECIFICATIONS: 1854. Samuel Badger. Billet head, square stern. Burthen, 1,152 tons. Length, 190.6 feet; beam, 36 feet; depth, 18 feet. Two decks. Original owner—Enoch Train & Co.

For some reason not now understood, the *Chatsworth* was given the name of the estate of the dukes of Devonshire, where, in those days, a fountain played water 267 feet in the air. She was the first Port of Portsmouth ship ever contracted for by the famed Enoch Train & Co., operators of transatlantic packets. Daniel Marcy superintended her construction for the company.

SHIP CHATSWORTH. — This splendid ship of 1200 tons burthen, intended for a place in Train & Co.'s line of Boston and Liverpool packets, left here on Wednesday, in tow of a steamer for Boston.

She was built by Capt. Samuel Badger, at Kittery Fore Side, under the direction of Capt. Daniel Marcy, of this city, which is equivalent to saying that she is a superior ship in every particular.

Her cabins are beautifully and tastefully finished and furnished, her between-decks spacious, of good height and well ventilated, and her equipment throughout is complete. She is probably not excelled by any ship ever sailed in that line.[84]

Capt. Josiah Gorham was the *Chatsworth*'s first master, and she immediately became a Boston-Liverpool packet. The Train Line had been established in 1844, but by the time the *Chatsworth* joined the fleet it was going through hard times. Fourteen vessels flew the line's flag, including the clipper *Cathedral*, also built by Samuel Badger. Whether it was an ebb in the tide of immigrants or other economic factors that brought it about, Enoch Train ceased to be active in December 1855, and the line was taken over by Warren & Thayer, which also had several Piscataqua-built vessels.[85] The drop in emigration forced the *Chatsworth* into the guano trade, and it might be well to take a look at the Chincha Islands through the eyes of a Portsmouth shipmaster, in early January of 1854:

We have been at the Islands 18 days, and have on board about 124 tons of Guano. It is brought on board in small boats, each ship waiting its turn. Frequently we have to remain an entire day before obtaining a load. It is much more agreeable getting it in this manner, as we escape the fine Guano, which covers the ship from the mast head to the hull, when they receive it on board from the *Manguera* — a large hose made of canvas, which runs about 120 feet from the top of the rock to the vessel's hold.

The labor on the Island is performed principally by Coolies, who are treated in the most cruel manner by their masters. For the slightest offence they receive one or two dozen lashes. Such cruelty I have never before witnessed. The slaves of the south suffer nothing in comparison with them. Many to escape punishment, throw themselves headlong into the sea from the rocks.

The Islands are completely covered with Guano, in many places to the depth of 100 feet. The body of a negro who died a few years since was recently found petrified. I have several petrified eggs found at a depth of 50 feet from the surface.

There are about 100 vessels loading at the Islands, averaging 16 men each. Religious services are held every Sabbath on board the ship "Beatrice," Capt. Rodgers. She is called the Bethel ship. Capt. Harding of the "Robert Harding," and Capt. Parker of the "Flying Eagle" are here, loading for the United States. The health on board the shipping is very good, but few deaths having occurred. On Christmas day about 40 ship masters were invited to dine on board the ship "Roscoe" of New York. We were favored with the company of several ladies, wives of the Captains, and passed a very agreeable day.[86]

The *Chatsworth*, along with dozens of other Portsmouth-built vessels, were increasingly involved in the guano trade as the packet trade faltered. The *Chatsworth* was regularly engaged in that business when she met her end on the coast of Chile in 1860:

> WRECK. — Ship Chatsworth, Horn, from Callao June 22, in ballast, on the 13th of July was driven ashore on the rocks, 150 miles south of Valparaiso. The sea swept over her, and to ease her, the masts were cut away. James Davis, one of the seamen, took a line ashore, by which a hawser was made fast. By these means all hands were saved; but Davis returned to the ship for his clothes, and while going ashore again was drowned. When Capt. Horn left the scene of the wreck, the ship had gone to pieces. The Chatsworth was built at Portsmouth in 1854, was 1150 tons and rated A1. She is owned in Boston and insured. Loss $58,000.[87]

Governor Langdon

SPECIFICATIONS: 1854. Fernald & Pettigrew. Billet head, square stern. Burthen, 1,095 tons. Length, 183 feet; beam, 35.9 feet; depth, 17.9 feet. Two decks. Original owners—Horton D. Walker, George W. Pendexter, Frederick W. Fernald, William Pettigrew, et al.

The reasons for Portsmouth's intense interest in the ship *Governor Langdon*, although built in Kittery, Maine, are easy to surmise. For one thing, the *Governor Langdon* was named for a man who, although dead for 35 years, had been known to many who were still alive, and he was a hero to most. Also, the ship's ownership was a cross section of the community, with men from several different walks of life participating. Nor can it be overlooked that those who lived in the Port of Portsmouth 135 years ago were enthralled by the big ships that were being produced by the various shipyards. The *Governor Langdon* was launched on August 15 and, once in the water, became the third new vessel tied up to a wharf in the city. A day or two after her launching, it was reported:

> SHIP GOVERNOR LANGDON. — A compliment paid to a name so distinguished in the history of our town, state and

country as that of John Langdon, is one in which others besides the owners of the ship feel an interest. The history of Gov. Langdon is too well known to need a repetition here. He was born in December, 1739, the second son of John and Mary Langdon, at the head of Witch Creek. He was in the counting house of Mr. Daniel Rindge; he went to sea and carried on foreign trade for some years; he was in the first Congress of the United States, and his name ought to have been on the Declaration of Independence, for he was a member of it, and Matthew Thornton was not at that time; he built several vessels of war for the States during the Revolution; he was in the convention to make the Constitution of the United States; then twelve years Senator; was afterwards many years Governor of New-Hampshire, and also held other offices. He died in September, 1819, not quite 80 years old.[88]

However, it's rare when any event, no matter how enjoyable, is held without some controversy, and the launching of the *Governor Langdon* was no exception:

SHIP GOVERNOR LANGDON. — On Tuesday last a large company by invitation visited this noble ship to inspect her accommodations and give her such a clearance as will be satisfactory to all concerned. The unanimous opinion seemed to be that no better ship need be built; no more elegant finish need be made of the fanciful, nor more strength given to the exposed parts of this bird of the ocean. She has apparently no lack of the prominent trait in the character of the patriot whose name she bears — ability to go rapidly before the breeze, and strength to resist the counter currents. On Tuesday, hundreds went to see her, and on Wednesday, says one of the visitors, as if there had not been sight-seeing enough, she actually went to sea herself.

We have received a communication respecting the appearance of wine at the levee on board the Gov. Langdon, reflecting upon the clergymen, ladies and temperance men present, for not rebuking the matter upon the spot. Now there was no lady present at the table when the wine appeared — so they cannot be blamed. — The clergymen had a better sense of the proper place to preach effectually than to have opened a tirade at such a time and place. They, and we believe all temperance men present, did rebuke the matter by declining to partake. Neither of the clergymen would probably have declined attending a wedding even with the knowledge that wine was to be used on the occasion. They would on such occasion do their

whole duty as the friends of temperance by declining to partake. The wine, of which perhaps a pint was drank in all, was
not provided by the owners of the ship for the levee, but was
furnished by the captain for the benefit of a few of his particular friends — and we have little doubt that the person who
makes so much ado about the matter, partook as freely of the
wine as any one present.

    We are no apologists for the use of wine any more than
for other ardent spirits. But we have doubts whether the cause
of temperance is not frequently injured by its friends from inju-
dicious and untimely movements.[89]

News coverage of the *Governor Langdon* was more detailed
than usual, and even went so far as to give a breakdown of the ownership. Horton D. Walker had 3/16; Pendexter, Fernald and Pettigrew,
2/16 each; Knowlton, Bailey, Harrat and Nathaniel K. Walker, 1/16
each; Barker and Adams, 1/32 each; Weeks, 2/16.[90]

Elizabeth Langdon Elwyn, the only child of the late governor,
was in the city on a visit, and was so pleased by the honor to her
father that she presented the ship with a full set of colors.[91] Mrs.
Elwyn died in 1860 at the age of 82.

Before the *Governor Langdon* put to sea under Capt. Thomas
M. Weeks, another incident attracted attention. A black seaman, after
having drawn an advance payment for his services, decided he wanted
no part of the bargain, so he jumped off the ship onto the wharf. Hang-
ers-on around the dock grabbed him and put him back on board. With
that, the *Governor Langdon* dropped out into the current. The sailor
then decided his life was in danger, so he jumped overboard. A river
boat picked him up, and for a second time he was put back on board.
Presumably by the time the ship reached Mobile, her first port of call,
the seaman had settled down.[92] The *Governor Langdon* went back and
forth between Liverpool from Mobile for a year or more. William P.
Stone took over as master in 1856, and in June took a mixed cargo to
Liverpool from New Orleans, including 2,661 bales of cotton, 224
hogsheads of tobacco, 109 barrels of rosin, and 5,600 staves.[93]

Throughout her long career, the *Governor Langdon* sailed the
freight routes of the world. Because of her local ownership, the
Portsmouth newspapers kept fairly good track of the ship's voyages.
Captain Stone continued in command through much of the Civil War.
On a passage from Liverpool in 1861, the *Governor Langdon* had to
put in to Gloucester, Massachusetts, after being badly beaten up in a
gale on the Grand Banks. Why she went into Gloucester and not
Portsmouth wasn't explained; perhaps a northwest wind was howling
across Great Bay and down the Piscataqua Valley. For three days on

that passage she was in a field of icebergs, and observed one chunk of ice 200 feet high and 360 feet wide.[94] In November of that year, her crew mutinied while going down Boston Harbor. The mutineers hoisted a distress flag; the ship was boarded by the harbor police, and the crew was talked into continuing the passage.[95] At the end of that voyage, the *Liverpool Chronicle* reported on January 18, 1862, that the *Governor Langdon* limped into port on the tenth with her decks swept clean and cargo shifted. She was in a collision in 1863 with the British steamship *Kangeroo*, damaging her stern, and she had to put back to discharge cargo and undergo repairs.[96] Later that year, she was sent from Boston to San Francisco and loaded at that port for Liverpool, taking on grain at a rate of £2.16.6 per ton.[97] Still under Capt. Alex G. Davis in 1865, she was chartered by a German house in Calcutta in August to load a cargo of 1,500 tons of seed and 200 tons of measurement goods at $8.50 a ton.

The worth of the *Governor Langdon* was demonstrated at an auction in 1866, when she was 12 years old. One thirty-second interest in her fetched $1,250, which would put her total value at $40,000.[98] At that same auction, 1/54 of the first *Granite State* went for $745, a value for that ship of $40,230. Five years later, a 1/16 share in the *Governor Langdon*, held by the estate of Thomas D. Bailey, went for about a thousand dollars. It was commented:

> The sale of parts of ship Gov. Langdon and brig Sally Brown, both which vessels under excellent management, and are sources of good income to the owners, at auction on Tuesday by Mr. [William] Hackett, and the Bank Stock to be offered at the same time, will afford a chance for investment of funds under safe control and doubtless good profit.[99]

The *Governor Langdon* continued to sail the guano routes, and, at some point, she was converted to a bark. That probably came in 1872, when the final Portsmouth interests in the ship were sold to William H. Kinsman & Co. of Boston on private terms. In 1874 the Kinsman firm sold her in London for £7,500. Using the rough standard of $5 to the pound, the 20-year-old ship fetched $37,500, a strong testimonial to the integrity of her construction.[100]

The only hint that the *Governor Langdon* might have had a brush with any of the Confederate raiders is contained in an item in the *Portsmouth Chronicle*, March 23, 1882, that offered instructions to former owners of the ships *New Hampshire*, *Piscataqua*, *Portsmouth*, and *Governor Langdon*, who were giving powers of attorney to William H. Hackett to represent them before the Alabama Claims Commission.

The *Governor Langdon* was a tough vessel. In 1883, after carrying a load of lumber from Quebec to Liverpool, she struck a pierhead and sank at the dock. Three years later, again on a lumber passage, Quebec to Liverpool, she was badly straining off Anticosti Island, St. Lawrence River, and became waterlogged. She was condemned and sold and renamed the *Atlantis*, of Chatham, New Brunswick. Stranded on June 25, 1888, at Anchor Point, Ste. Barbe, Newfoundland, she was refloated and sold to a Norwegian firm and renamed the *Stanley*. Finally, on September 29, 1893, near Pictou, Nova Scotia, she was stranded and lost. The 16 in her crew were saved.[101]

Ladoga

SPECIFICATIONS: 1854. Mechanics Shipbuilding Co. Noble's Island. Eagle figurehead, square stern. Burthen, 867 tons. Length, 167.4 feet; beam, 33.45 feet; depth, 16.725 feet. Two decks. Original owners— William Ropes & Son, of Boston.

The construction of the *Ladoga* marked the entrance of yet another firm into Port of Portsmouth shipbuilding. Daniel Moulton headed a band of 39 Piscataqua artisans in the formation of a company to take advantage of the steady demand for ships. Little is known about Daniel Moulton; he first appeared in a Portsmouth City Directory in 1851. In December 1853, a news item said:

> A joint stock company, organized here to build ships, have leased part of Noble's Island, near Tobey & Littlefield. Capital, 40 shares at $500, with half to be reserve and half paid down. The stockholders are nearly all mechanics, and most have been employed at some period in the construction of ships.[102]

On April 27, 1854, the *Chronicle* reported:

> Mechanics Shipbuilding Company. — This company is composed of 40 industrious and enterprising mechanics of the various trades and occupations in building ships.
> They have commenced building on Noble's Island and have two new ships under construction; of about 1,100 tons, which is under contract to Ichabod Goodwin, who is always willing to assist the enterprising and industrious. The other ship is of 900 tons, of a good model for a carrying ship and is for sale. We feel assured that this company can and will build as good vessels as any shipbuilders on the river.

The company, or its various members, did launch five square-riggers, two of them clippers—the *Morning Glory* and the *Star of*

Hope. The *Ladoga* was launched on August 26. She was named for a lake in Russia, near Leningrad, which was an appropriate choice because the owners intended her for the Russian trade. A Boston firm bought the *Ladoga*, and it can only be surmised that they trusted a new firm because someone like Ichabod Goodwin put in a good word for the company. As noted above, Goodwin had a vessel on the company's stocks at the time.

The Ladoga's career wasn't closely followed in Portsmouth. However, on January 16, 1875, the *Journal* reported: "Ship Ladoga, 865 tons, built at Portsmouth, N.H. (?) in 1854, now at New York, has been sold for the Pacific trade, at about $20,000. — *Boston Advertiser.*" That's probably when she was renamed the *Rita Norton.* In 1888 she was sold again, to Wincelau & Co., of Lisbon, Portugal, and renamed *Zeimira.* In 1891 she was again sold in Lisbon.[103] That last establishes that the old *Ladoga* was still afloat 37 years after launching. Daniel Moulton and associates built good ships. Moulton's career in Portsmouth was brief, and there is reason to believe that he later lived in Lynn, Massachusetts.

Colorado

SPECIFICATIONS: 1854. Fernald & Pettigrew. Billet head, square stern. Burthen, 1,143 tons. Length, 191 feet; beam, 35.8 feet; depth, 17.9 feet. Two decks. Original owners—Jonathan M. Tredick, Samuel Sheafe, and George W. Haven, all of Portsmouth.

The *Portsmouth Journal* used glowing language to mark the launching of the *Colorado* on November 11, 1854:

> As our paper goes to press at 3 P.M. [Saturday], a noble ship of 1200 tons is being launched from the yard of Fernald & Pettigrew. She has been built under the superintendence of Capt. John B. Haley, and is No. 1 extra. She has an entire seasoned oak frame; most of the planking in her hold and outside are of the same material, and will not suffer in comparison with any vessel in the world, — so say good judges.

On February 17, 1855, the *Journal* said:

> SHIP COLORADO. — This superior ship, built by Messrs. Fernald & Petigrew, and owned by Messrs. J. M. Tredick, S. Sheafe and Geo. Haven, is now ready for sea, and under command by Capt. J. B. Haley, had cleared for N. Orleans. She is

the largest ship now registered at our Custom House, being of 1145 tons burthen. Her model is approaching the clipper, but is not classed as such. She is handsome, and her whole appearance pleasantly fills the eye. Between decks the room is spacious. Instead of the array of water hhds. is an iron tank of 3500 gallons capacity, holding fresh water in much better condition. Her cabins are elegantly furnished and a better ship the ocean has rarely borne.

Captain Haley had only a limited opportunity to enjoy his new command. He took the *Colorado* to Mobile and there found cargo for Le Havre. On the passage to Le Havre, the *Colorado* put in to Portsmouth's lower harbor to land the captain, who had become too ill to continue the trip. The owners scouted around and in a few days they hired Moses G. Ricker as master. After unloading at Le Havre, the *Colorado* went to Liverpool to load for Calcutta. While there, Captain Ricker suffered sunstroke.[104] For the next few years, the *Colorado* voyaged between Calcutta and London. The vessel's long absence prompted Mrs. Ricker to join her husband, with one of their two sons. On one voyage the *Colorado* loaded at Calcutta with 20,000 bags of rice for China. On April 24, 1859, the *Colorado* was in the Indian Ocean:

> By the arrival from Liverpool of steamer North Briton, we have the melancholy intelligence that the ship Colorado, of this port, Capt. Moses Ricker, from Galle, Ceylon, for Tondemonar, was wrecked at Point Ceylon, April 24. Capt. Ricker, his wife and two seamen were lost. Capt. Ricker's age was 46. He was the adopted son of Capt. Andrew Daniels, who was also lost at sea. Mrs. Ricker, of about the same age, was the daughter of Mr. James Clinton, of Newcastle, who was also lost at sea, in the privateer Portsmouth. They have left three children. A son of eight years, who was with them on board the Colorado, was saved.
>
> A letter from the English Consul to the owners received on Thursday, states that the Colorado had been lying at the port two days, preparing to load. A sudden tornado arose, driving the ship on shore which went to pieces in twenty minutes. Mrs. Ricker was knocked overboard by a spar, and Capt. Ricker immediately sprang overboard after her, and perished in his attempts to save her. The son, Clinton, was taken into the family of the American Consul, where he will remain until an opportunity offers to send him home. The sailors lost were a boy and a Lascar. The officers and crew numbered twenty-eight.
>
> Ship Colorado was valued at $60,000, and her freight at

$50,000. There is insurance in Boston as follows: Washington $10,000, National $15,000, Neptune $5,000, Boylston $10,000, Mercantile $10,000, Boston $10,000, American $5000, Alliance $10,000. Total $75,000. The Merchant's office in Providence has $3000 on the Colorado.[105]

In a letter to the owners, the British consul, John Black, said:

> Dear Sir: — It is my painful duty to inform you that the "Colorado," which left this port on the 17th ult. for Tondimonar, Point Pedro, where she arrived on the 22d, was wrecked on the 24th, during a terrific gale which commenced on the evening of the 23d. The Captain, Mrs. Ricker, one boy, and one Lascar were drowned; the second officer, Captain's son, and thirteen seamen were landed here this morning from the Ceylon government steamer Pearl, which fortunately touched at Point Pedro, on the 27th. The chief officer and seven men remain in charge of the wreck until I can procure a vessel to go round, which I hope to do in a few days, to realize what has been saved. The vessel went to pieces within twenty minutes after striking. Mrs. Ricker was struck by a spar and washed overboard; Captain Ricker sprang after her, and in his endeavors to rescue his estimable wife he was drowned. We feel their loss as personal friends, having found them both so truly estimable. Their little boy is in excellent health and spirits; he will be treated as one of my own family until an opportunity offers of sending him home in charge of some American friends. I will provide funds for his passage, and advise you by next mail what has been done with the property saved.[106]

Arkwright

SPECIFICATIONS: 1855. George Raynes & Son. Billet head, square stern. Burthen, 1,243 tons. Length, 198.4 feet; beam, 36.6 feet; depth, 18.8 feet. Two decks. Original owners—Edward F. Sise, John Davis, Isaac Bell, and John D. Parsons, all of Portsmouth.

Seven ships were launched by the various yards in 1855, 3 of them clippers, which was a sharp falling off from the total of 11 built in 1854. Business would pick up a bit again the next year, before a gradual decline set in.

The *Arkwright* has particular significance in the story of Port of Portsmouth ships because she was probably the last with which

George Raynes, Sr. had any connection. Raynes died on April 12, 1855, and so he might have seen the keel laid for the *Arkwright*. The last big ship in which he had an active role was the clipper *Emily Farnum*, but, in 1854, he built and launched a brig, the *Ida Raynes*, in which he took much pride. She was named for his daughter, who later became the grandmother of Kennard Palfrey, Priscilla McLane and the late William Palfrey, all of Portsmouth.

The *Arkwright*'s first visit to New Orleans occasioned a letter to the editor of the *Portsmouth Journal*. The letter was loud in its praise of the *Arkwright*, but, more importantly, it offered commentary on the political and economic situation in New Orleans in the already turbulent days before the outbreak of the Civil War. The letter is dated October 22, 1855:

> By invitation of her gentlemanly commander John Davis, Esq. a party of "the Sons" have just visited the new Ship Arkwright, which arrived on the 18th inst., after a passage of 19 days from your port. We were entertained by that gentleman in the generous and liberal manner for which he has so long been proverbial. The Arkwright is a splendid specimen of the skill of your mechanics. The company examined her from keel to royal truck (tho' we didn't climb quite up to the latter,) and found her fitted and furnished in the most complete and workmanlike manner. Her rig (Howe's patent) was a novelty to many of us, and Capt. D. pronounces it the best plan he ever saw, and "just the thing," as it works to a charm. She has proved herself a fast sailer, having repeatedly run 14 knots an hour; and there is no doubt, when she is in the right trim she will be as fast as any cotton ship afloat. As she laid so long in your port, it is of course needless for me to describe her interior arrangements, and for fear of compromising our friend Kimball, I shall say nothing of her medicine chest; though the compound (*not an intoxicating one*) in which we drank to the "success of the Arkwright and her gallant commander," proved on the occasion anything but a "drug," neither did it taste as though "camphor" formed any portion of it. Take her "all in all" the Arkwright is a noble vessel, and a *little* ahead of anything now in our port, notwithstanding there are 15 other entirely new ships at the levee — and the "Portsmouth Boys" may well be pardoned if they do exhibit a little vanity when they point to a ship like the Arkwright, and a man like John Davis to command her, as representatives of their native city.
>
> Within the last fortnight there have been 121 arrivals from sea, of which 68 are ships of the largest class, and in con-

sequence, freights have declined a little, though they are still favorable to ship owners. Three ships were laid on for Havre on Saturday at 1-1/2 cents per lb. for cotton, — and 3 farthings is offered to Liverpool, though as there are but few ships in port not taken up, the impression is that 7–8d will be offered before the close of the week.

The cotton market has been very quiet for the last few days; the news by the last steamer from Europe has caused a decline, which holders are not prepared to submit to. It still continues to come in freely, though most of our rivers are not yet in boating order. The receipts since Sept. 1st, have been 241,416 bales; exported 119,938 bales; stock on hand and on ship-board not cleared 159,679 bales.

The fever having entirely disappeared, our fellow citizens and strangers are flocking here by thousands, and the city begins to look like itself once more. Business is briskening up perceptibly both in the levee and streets; and the prospect is now most flattering for our having a flourishing season, and that the losses sustained last year by our merchants, will be more than made up by the profits of this.

The political cauldron is fast verging to a boiling-over point: the K. N.'s and the anties are each putting their best foot foremost to see who is the strongest at the coming election. In view of the excitement that is anticipated, and to prevent what might tend to increase that excitement, our mayor has issued a proclamation requesting "all Bar-room and Coffee-house keepers to close their houses on the day of the election (5th November), and requesting that "all citizens and voters indiscriminately will deposit in Boxes specially provided for that purpose the same that otherwise would be expended in convevial and stimulating indulgences, as contributions on their part, towards completing the monument to perpetuate the name of Washington." This is a good move on his part, and if carried out will accomplish a good result in two very practical ways.

In haste,   Yours, &c.   "S. F. K."[107]

The *Arkwright* was chartered in New Orleans for Liverpool, and sailed in late November. Her westward passage from Liverpool was to New York. Captain Davis had her in Train's Line for a year, then she went into the Philadelphia Packet Line under John Robertson. At the end of 1856, the *Arkwright* was briefly converted into a troop carrier, transporting U.S. soldiers to fortifications along the Gulf Coast of Florida. After delivering her troops, the ship went to Mobile, where she was loaded with 3,882 bales of cotton, weighing 1,975,824 pounds and valued at $173,596.

The *Arkwright* had a narrow escape from destruction in February 1862, when she went ashore at Long Beach, New Jersey. Her cargo, 2,000 sacks of salt, was gotten out and she sat high on the beach, the sea not reaching her. Because the hull appeared intact, the salvage plan called for stripping her of masts, etc., and then waiting for the spring tides to get her off. While engaged in the stripping work, a rigger named Cufferty was killed when he fell from the fore-topsail yard.[108] After more than two months on the beach, the *Arkwright* came off "in better order than any ship that has ever touched that treacherous coast, and, as insurance inspectors say, not one ship in a hundred could bear such a strain. This was the last ship built by the late George Raynes, and we, last week, chronicled the sale of the bark *Alexander*, now some 32 years old, which was one of his first."[109]

Both the *Arkwright* and the *Webster* were sold on February 9, 1872, to go into the guano trade, but remained under the American flag.[110] Six months later, the *Arkwright* was sold to the Talbott Co. of New York for $28,000.[111] In 1884, the *Arkwright* was owned in Port Townsend, Washington Territory, and employed as a lumber hauler.[112] Like many other Piscataqua-built ships on the Pacific Coast, the *Arkwright* probably wound up her days as a barge. Steam replaced wind as the propulsion power, but the salt-aged hulls of those old vessels were rugged and could stow a lot of cargo. The clipper *Dashing Wave*, built in 1853 by Fernald & Pettigrew, was working as a barge in 1920 when she was wrecked.

Othello

SPECIFICATIONS: 1855. Tobey & Littlefield. Male figurehead, square stern. Burthen, 883 tons. Length, 169.6 feet; beam 33.5 feet; depth, 16.25 feet. Two decks. Original owner—R. H. Tucker, of Wiscasset.

September was a busy month for the Port of Portsmouth shipyards in 1855. Each of three yards launched ships during the month, with Tobey & Littlefield leading the way on the fifth with the *Othello*. She was the third ship the Tuckers had acquired from Tobey & Littlefield.

Richard H. Tucker, Jr. sailed the *Othello* to Charleston, leaving Portsmouth Harbor on October 15. Ship's officers were James Groves, mate; Benjamin Frost, second mate; Sam Jackson, third mate. Once again, thanks to Jane Tucker's work on the logs of Tucker ships, much detail is known about the *Othello*'s career. Captain Tucker turned the ship over to brother Joseph on arrival in Charleston. The *Othello* left Charleston on December 30, carrying 3,234 bales of Upland cotton; 2,360 bales were at $.01 a pound and the balance at $.01-1/8. She also had on board 53 bales of Sea Island at $.01-1/2 and 42 casks of rice. Total freight money was $14,306, plus primage. She arrived at Le Havre on February 5, 1856, and sailed for Savannah, in ballast, on March 1, arriving on April 15.

Capt. Asa T. Lane was the *Othello*'s next master. He left Savannah on May 14, 1856. His officers were James Groves, mate; Daniel Broughton, second mate; Silas Beals, third mate. She was carrying 2,600 bales of Upland at 5/16 of a penny (English), and 520 Sea Island. Freight money was £1,999, plus primage. From Liverpool, the *Othello* went to Alexandria, a passage of 48 days. She carried 300 tons of coal, salt, and 84 crates, a total of 1,213 tons. Freight money was £1,213. While in Liverpool she had been sheathed. She brought wheat and corn back to Liverpool. Capt. John K. Greenough took command in Liverpool, with Joshua Trevett as mate and Noah Broughton, second mate. The *Othello* left Liverpool in ballast, headed for Callao. After getting the necessary licenses at Callao, the ship went to the Chincha Islands, where 1,378 tons of guano were loaded, at a rate of £4.10, for total freight of £5,816.0. She took 108 days to get to Cowes, England, and was back in Charleston on February 10, 1858. Captain Greenough loaded the vessel for Le Havre, carrying cotton and rice. From Le Havre to New York, she was under a $2,500 charter, and carried 160 tons of stone and light freight, plus 190 passengers.

Such entries continue, year in, year out. Joshua Trevett became master when she departed Liverpool early in 1861, going to Cardiff for 1,302 tons of coat at 34s. a ton. The cargo was for the Pacific Steam Navigation Co. at Callao. From Callao she went to the Chinchas and loaded 1,348 tons of guano at a freight of £4.044. She put into Cork for orders after a passage of 126 days, going from there to Hamburg, Germany. In 1862 she went from Hamburg (Cuxhaven) to Buenos Aires. Oscar Saunders was mate for Captain Trevett. Coal, live cargo, and merchandise had freight money of $8,600, although the coal was on the ship's own account. The logs show a D. W. Tinkham becoming master during the Civil War. The *Othello* was active in the guano route through the Civil War years, which may have barred interference from Confederate raiders because the cargoes were destined for Liverpool. Captain Tinkham still had the *Othello* after the Civil War. In 1868, Captain Tinkham, with Mrs. Tinkham aboard, sailed from Savannah, carrying 1,343,280 pounds of cotton, at 7/16 of an English penny. Freight equaled £2,571.

In 1869 the logs show Capt. S. N. Greenleaf as master, and the *Othello* appears to have been working the Pacific Coast. Eventually, by way of Hamburg, the log shows the *Othello* at Philadelphia and then at Savannah, with the captain's wife and babies on board.

When the *Othello* departed Savannah on April 7, 1872, the captain's family was not on board, but, on October 14, 1872, on departing New York, his family was with him. General cargo was 250 tons at 35s., with the balance at 40s. In December 1872 she went on the rocks after leaving Liverpool. Miss Tucker, in her notes to me, said, "There is some mention, in one of the captain's last letters that parties in Liverpool were going to salvage the ship." That substantiates that the *Othello* was "sold foreign" about 1875, going under the Union Jack. On a passage from Akbar, Turkey, to the United Kingdom with a load of rice, she sprang a leak and was condemned.[113]

Isaac H. Boardman

SPECIFICATIONS: 1855. Fernald & Pettigrew. Billet head, square stern. Burthen, 1,432 tons. Length, 199 feet; beam 39.4 feet; depth, 19.7 feet. Three decks. Original owners—Isaac H. Boardman, Henry Cook, J. B. Morse, A. Blood, and R. Smith, all of Newburyport.

In a way, it was like "carrying coals to New Castle" to have a syndicate of proud Newburyporters come to the Port of Portsmouth to have a ship built. Why they did it isn't known, but potential shipowners, like people today buying automobiles, shopped around for the best deal.

It's doubtful that the talented and famed Frederick William Fernald had much to do with the construction of the *Isaac H. Boardman*, or with the building of the clipper *Noonday*. Fernald died on April 30, 1855, 18 days after the death of the other master builder, George Raynes. The *Noonday* and the *Isaac H. Boardman* were both September launches. Shortly after Fernald's death, the old Badger yard was bought by John Yeaton and others. The two Fernald & Pettigrew ships mentioned above were the last launched by the firm. A notice, as usual, appeared on the launching of the *Isaac H. Boardman*:

THE LAUNCH. — Thousands witnessed the beautiful launch of the ship *Isaac H. Boardman*, from the yard of Mr. Petigrew, on Saturday afternoon last. She is of very graceful model, and is pronounced "the most perfect merchant ship that ever floated. She is a noble monument of the skill and fidelity of the master builder, Mr. Petigrew, and he might rest his fame, as a builder, on this hull alone, in the proud assurance that it has never been surpassed in the past or the present, or can be in the future. It is the full fruition in this department of mechanical skill and excellence." — The ship is owned by Isaac H. Boardman, Esq. for whom she has been named; by Captain Henry Cook, who is to command her; Hon. Albert Currier, Mr. Edward Blood, Messrs. Morse & Brewster and others of Newburyport. She is about 1500 tons, carpenter's measurement, and will carry upwards of 5000 bales of cotton.[114]

Despite the loss of his relatively young partner, the *Isaac H. Boardman*'s launching wasn't the last for William Pettigrew. Later he became associated with Daniel Marcy in the construction of several worthy vessels in Portsmouth—in the same yard where Frederick W. Fernald had begun his career nearly 30 years before.

Capt. Henry Cook, a partner, commanded the *Isaac H. Boardman* when she left the Port of Portsmouth for New Orleans. On her passage, she dropped into Mobile, but went on to New Orleans, arriving on December 12. Instead of heading for Europe, the ship carried cotton north to New York and then returned to Mobile to load for Liverpool. A Captain Brown was the master. From Liverpool she went to Callao, then back to Liverpool. The *Liverpool Chronicle*, on September 17, 1859, reported under an Aden dateline of August 29 that the *Isaac H. Boardman*, "an American ship of 2400 tons, for whose safety fears were at one time entertained, arrived here on the 13th with hardly any water on board. She brings a cargo of coals for the Peninsular & Oriental Company, which a few days ago were reported to be on fire. As this turned out to be true, she has been moved into the harbour and scuttled, and the coals are being landed as expeditiously as possible. It is believed she suffered no damage by the ignition. There are twenty vessels in the harbor and nearly all of them brought out coals for the P&O Co."

The figure of 2,400 tons given in the news item emphasizes the difference between British and American ship measurements. Under the American formula, she was rated at 1,432 tons.

A year later the *Isaac H. Boardman* was at Rangoon, under charter by an English company to load rice for London at £3, but the charter was renegotiated to £3.15.[115] In 1862, probably because of Confederate raiders, the *Isaac H. Boardman* was sold in London for $42,000 and renamed the *Commander-in-Chief*. She later burned at sea.[116]

S. C. Thwing

SPECIFICATIONS: 1855. Samuel Badger. Billet head, square stern. Burthen, 1,340 tons. Length, 195.8 feet; beam 38.4 feet; depth, 19.2 feet. Three decks. Original owners—Daniel and Peter Marcy and Samuel Badger; and S. C. Thwing, of Boston.

News reports on the launching of the *S. C. Thwing* were highly flattering and challenged Bostonians who might see her to find any flaws. After the launching, the ship was brought across the river to Pier Wharf, which is now the upper end of Prescott Park. While she was at the pier, an Englishman named George Rose was killed in a tragic accident. Rose, a sawyer on the Navy Yard, used his own boat to row across to work. In tying her up, he was making sure his boat wouldn't be crushed between the *S. C. Thwing* and the wharf. He slipped and fell, striking his head on a piling. The body was recovered two days later. Only 40, Rose left his widow and five children.

The *S. C. Thwing*, under Capt. Joseph J. Nickerson, cleared the Port of Portsmouth for New Orleans. It was her only voyage under the American flag. Failing to find a cargo in New Orleans, she sailed to Mobile, where she loaded for Goteborg, Sweden. She carried 4,482 bales of cotton, weighing 2,323,830 pounds and valued at $194,421.61. The next news of her was of disaster:

> LOSS OF A PORTSMOUTH SHIP. — The ship S. C. Thwing, recently built in this city by Master Badger, was lost at Lessoe, in the Baltic Sea. She sailed from Mobile, February 27, for Gottenburg, with a cargo of 4482 bales cotton. She was a ship of 1341 tons, and was valued at $80,000. Her freight money amounted to $30,000, which, together with the vessel, was said to be insured in Boston, to the amount of $85,000.
>
> The cargo was on foreign account, and was probably insured in Europe. Capt. Daniel Marcy and Richard Jenness, Esq. of this city, Peter and Samuel Marcy, Esqs. of New Orleans, S. C. Thwing, Esq., of Boston and the Captain, were the owners.[117]

A later report from Goteborg said 1,718 bales of damaged cotton "and seven lots in a loose state, saved from the ship S. C. Thwing were sold yesterday at high rates and will average, it is thought, £7, 15 shillings per bale gross. The 182 bales slightly damaged, but not under salvage, were sold at full prices."[118]

The *S. C. Thwing* was surveyed and condemned. She was sold to the Tecklenberg Co. of Bremen, Germany, and, after repairs, was renamed the *Mobile*. In January 1857, she returned to the United States, under the German flag.[119]

Anna Decatur

SPECIFICATIONS: 1856. Tobey & Littlefield. Noble's Island. Billet head, square stern. Burthen, 1,044 tons. Length, 180.5 feet; beam 35.3 feet; depth, 17.65 feet. Two decks. Original owners—William P. Jones, Albert Jones, Ichabod Goodwin, John H. Boardman, and William H. Parsons.

The *Anna Decatur* was the first of 11 three-masted, square-rigged vessels built on the Piscataqua in 1856—and only 2 of them were clippers. Apparently the clipper fad had run its course, and the shipping firms were turning back to the construction of more stable carriers. In terms of numbers of ships built and launched, 1856 was equaled only by 1854, and the tonnage was slightly larger in the latter year.

The *Anna Decatur* was named for the daughter of John P. Decatur. Anna Decatur later became the wife of the first master of the *Anna Decatur*, William H. Parsons. When the ship was sold in 1877, the new owners kept the baptismal name.[120]

As usual, the workmanship and materials put into the *Anna Decatur* were highly lauded in the press: "Her frame and planking are entirely of white oak; she is heavily fastened throughout."[121] She was launched on March 1 and taken to Charleston for cotton by Captain Parsons. She sailed from Charleston on June 2 carrying 811 bales of Sea Island and 3,114 bales of Upland cotton to Liverpool.[122] From Liverpool she went to Trieste and then to Mobile. In the winter of 1857, she loaded at Le Havre, then traveled back across the Atlantic to New York. From there, she went to St. John to load lumber for Wales. When she came back to Mobile, she was loaded for Liverpool, for 15/16 of an English penny per pound. Back and forth she went, picking up cargoes wherever available. Captain Parsons retained command until 1862. In November 1860, the *Anna Decatur* arrived at Brunswick, Georgia, with 1,100 tons of rails for the Brunswick & Florida Railroad. She then went to Savannah and loaded cotton for Liverpool. Instead of returning to the United States, the *Anna Decatur* went to Calcutta, arriving August 3, 1861, and loaded for London. Under a Captain Alden, she left Calcutta for Colombo. When she arrived in London, Capt. M. F. Pickering took command, but she was idled for a time—the Civil War had slowed the demand for ships. Finally, she was chartered to take a cargo from Sunderland, England, to Singapore. She worked out the Civil War years in the East Indian Trade and apparently didn't return to the United States until after the war. In 1868, under a Captain Barnes, the *Anna Decatur* was at Calcutta, and was loaded with saltpeter at $8 a ton; linseed, $13.50; hides, $13.25; and indigo at $16. She arrived in Boston on July 5, after a passage of 132 days from Calcutta. She made voyages to the Chincha Islands for guano. In 1874, she was in Calcutta loading for Boston, arriving there on August 22. In November 1874, the ship cleared out of Boston for Valparaiso, carrying "the choicest and most valuable cargo of lumber ever shipped from that port. One invoice of 603,000 feet of clear white pine was furnished by Messrs. Skillings and Whitney Brothers, which average in price over fifty dollars per thousand feet. Probably no port on the Atlantic coast could furnish a duplicate cargo from a single stock."[123]

The next year, in October, the *Anna Decatur*'s owners were involved in an odd lawsuit:

> — A law suit concerning a Portsmouth ship has just been decided in the Supreme Judicial Court of Massachusetts, between William C. Fowler and M. F. Pickering. The defendant was part owner of the ship Anna Decatur of this port, and the plaintiff a pilot of the port of Boston. The plaintiff carried a communication from the charterer of the vessel to the ship, directing the ship to proceed to Gloucester instead of to Boston, whither she was bound, upon which the captain acted; and the plaintiff claimed a certain compensation therefor from the owners of the ship, to recover which this suit was brought. The plaintiff relied upon a usage among the pilots of Boston to be paid by the shipowner for delivering such a communication. The defendant, among other things at the trial in the superior court, claimed that the usage, if any were shown, was a local usage, and could not bind defendant unless brought home to the knowledge of the master. The court declined so to rule, and instructed the jury that the usage claimed is a local usage, and that in order to charge the defendants they must be satisfied that either said Pickering or the master had knowledge thereof, and that if they should find that either of them had such knowledge, then it was for the jury to say whether a usage to charge the shipowner is proven, and that if they found such a usage to be proven, they must find for the plaintiff. To these rulings the defendant excepted, and the jury found for the plaintiff. The supreme court has sustained the exceptions on the ground that it is the master's knowledge that is important and not that of

the defendant, also on the ground that the ruling that if the jury should find such a usage to be proven they must find for the plaintiff, was erroneous, because it was still a question of fact whether in view of such a usage if known to the master, a promise to pay for delivering the communication is to be inferred from the conduct of the parties. The counsel for the owners was Frank Goodwin, Esq., son of Ex-Gov. Goodwin.[124]

Under a Captain Proctor, in 1876, the *Anna Decatur* developed a leak while in the Chincha Islands and had to put into Callao for repairs. It was reported that she was "discharging her cargo alongside one of the wharves previous to repairing. It has been found cheaper and more convenient to unload into one of the cellars on the Mole and repair alongside, instead of in the Bay [Independencia], as has been customary heretofore."[125]

Fifteen months later, the *Anna Decatur* was sold in New York for $23,000. A German firm was the new owner, and the amount paid is in itself testimony to the sturdiness and seaworthiness of a vessel more than 20 years old.[126]

Jumna

SPECIFICATIONS: 1856. George Raynes, Jr. Female figurehead, round stern. Burthen, 782 tons. Length, 166.5 feet; beam 31.7 feet; depth, 15.875 feet. Two decks. Original owner—William F. Parrott, of Boston.

The *Jumna* was built under contract for William F. Parrott, according to a news story in August 1855. The report was hailed by the newspaper as being good news for ships' carpenters because it meant a winter's employment.[127]

The *Jumna* was appropriately named, considering the type of service planned for her: East Indian trade. The River Jumna in India is a tributary of the Ganges, the stream sacred to Hindus. Launched on April 24, she was taken to Boston by the tug *R. B. Forbes* on June 11. Capt. John Barnes loaded her for a passage to Calcutta. When she returned to Boston, a Captain Martin took her to the East Indies and Australia. One of the crew became the subject of a temperance lecture in the *Journal* on April 18, 1857. It was reported that a party of 15 sailors, traveling by train to Portland, became intoxicated. The article continued:

Presently, before we had crossed Newburyport Bridge,

the train stopped, and everybody got out to see what was the matter. It appeared that one of the drunken sailors had fallen between two cars in going from one to the other; and part of the train passed over him. One arm was crushed off, and he was much bruised and bloody and remained insensible when the train started on.

His name we learned was James Powers, — a native of Bristol, England; and he had recently arrived in Boston in the ship Jumna from Calcutta. We judged his age to be not far from 35 years.

The sailors were afterwards placed in a car by themselves, and locked in, — regardless of the earnest protestations of one of them. — *Chronicle*.

The *Jumna* was gone from the United States for two years, sailing around the East Indies, Australia, Singapore, and Manila, finally arriving in New York on November 20, 1859.[128] In 1863, with the Civil War flaming, the *Jumna*, like so many other American vessels, was sold to go under the British flag to avoid capture by Confederate raiders. Despite being only seven years old, the Jumna fetched £4,500.

Ella E. Badger

SPECIFICATIONS: 1856. Samuel Badger. Billet head, square stern. Burthen, 1,121 tons. Length, 186 feet; beam 36 feet; depth, 18 feet. Two decks. Original owners—Horton D. Walker, Lewis Tarlton, J. H. Tarlton, William Simes, John F. Mathes, Joseph E. Cox, Samuel Billings, John French, Abraham Brooks, and John Neal.

Launched on May 27, it was some weeks before the *Ella E. Badger* was named. In fact, the delay between launching and registration hints strongly that Samuel Badger had built the vessel on speculation. Badger was finally rewarded when a Port of Portsmouth syndicate bought the ship and named her for the builder's daughter. More than two months after the launching a poem was published:

Ship Ella E. Badger

Let Poets praise the Aquatic tribes,
The Naiads, Dryads, Neptune's brides,
They're all phantoms of the brain,
By a fabled god they all were slain.
But when the ship Ella E. Badger's viewed,
Outside and in, the critic shrewd

In ecstasy is heard to say,
She'll wear her laurels any day.
The veteran builder showed his skill
As Architect, that she might fill
A space upon the Ocean wide,
With beauty, comeliness and pride:
Then from the forest took the best,
And all her stock put to the test
          of workmanship from stem to stern:
Methinks she would please Fanny Fern,
          or any lady in our land
Who has good judgment at command.
But stop, my muse, your wild career,
May this ship float for many a year.
                    "Boiling Rock"[129]

Nearly two months after the poem was published, the *Chronicle* said, on August 2, 1856: "we understand the new ship *Ella E. Badger*, lying at Pray's Wharf, has been disposed of...and is to be commanded by Captain Lewis Tarlton. When Captain Tarlton took the ship out, she was towed down the Piscataqua by the tug *John Taylor*. Once in the open sea, beyond the Whale's Back, the vessel headed for St. John. The master's wife and infant child were on board."[130]

The *Ella E. Badger* loaded lumber in New Brunswick, and went to Liverpool. She was chartered for a passage to Calcutta, sailing on December 8, but had to put back because the captain and crew became exhausted in fighting southwest gales.[131] Eventually, the ship got out and went to Calcutta, where she loaded for Boston. Back in the friendly waters of Massachusetts Bay on October 16, 1857, the ship went to New Orleans, loaded for Liverpool, and then started the Calcutta cycle all over again.

In 1860, Tarlton was relieved by another partner in the *Ella E. Badger*, Capt. Samuel Billings, who took her from London to Melbourne, a passage she made in 89 days. Billings went from Callao and the Chincha Islands, where he loaded guano for Cork, Ireland, at three dollars a ton, but the cargo went to Baltimore instead. Considering the communication systems of those days, the newspapers deserve praise for keeping the passages of vessels as straight as they did. A Captain Healey had her for other voyages to the Indies.

In 1865, the *Ella E. Badger* was sold to British interests because of the Confederate raiders. She was renamed the *Thorndean*, and her home port was Shields, England. On October 1, 1869, she was stranded on Oarun Reef, near Bombay, but was refloated. She was lost in 1880.[132]

James Buchanan

SPECIFICATIONS: 1856. Samuel Badger. Burthen, 1,100 tons. Original owners—Daniel and Peter Marcy, Washington Williams, True M. Ball, and Richard Jenness.

The preliminary fanfare for the launching of the *James Buchanan* noted that the owners were also shareholders in ships like the *Levi Woodbury* and the *Frank Pierce*, "which latter named ship has been one of the most successful in the American fleet."[133] However, as was so often true, there was a slip-up, and the *James Buchanan* didn't go into the water as announced: "The noble ship still sits on the stocks, and we hear will not be launched for several days. So it remains to be seen whether *James Buchanan* will make a successful 'run' or no."[134] As the *Chronicle* supported the candidate of the newly formed Republican Party, John C. Fremont, it was delighted to find an ill omen for the Democratic candidate, James Buchanan. Most of the owners of the *James Buchanan* were ardent Democrats. When the launching did come off, Daniel Marcy had a galaxy of New Hampshire political personages (mostly Democrats) on hand for the event:

LAUNCH OF THE SHIP JAMES BUCHANAN.

— At half-past 8 o'clock, on Saturday, the noble ship James Buchanan glided gracefully from the yard of Samuel Badger, Esq. into the river Piscataqua, amid the cheers of numerous spectators. In behalf of the owners, Capt. Daniel Marcy, the Senator from this district, had extended an invitation to the Senate of New Hampshire, to witness the event, and Messrs. Rowell of No. 4, Herring of No. 5, Hall of No. 6, Hobbs of No. 7, and Burns of No. 12, with ladies, accepted the invitation. In company with other distinguished gentlemen from abroad, including Judge Sargent and Hon. Geo. W. Kittredge; and the Mayor, and many ladies and gentlemen of this city, this large and respectable portion of the Senate were launched on the water with flying colors. All present spoke in terms of admiration of the ship and the handsome manner in which her first performance was executed.

By invitation of the owners, about fifty gentlemen set down to a fine dinner at the Franklin house, on Saturday afternoon, given in honor of the launch of the James Buchanan. The tables were loaded with the delicacies and luxuries of the season, reflecting credit not only upon the generosity of the entertainment, but adding another wreath to the well earned

laurels of Barnabee, the veteran landlord and experienced
caterer. The most social and happy feelings prevailed; the sentiments and speeches were pithy, patriotic and humorous, and
everything passed off handsomely. His Honor Major Jenness,
one of the owners of the ship, presided, and in a few well-cho-
sen remarks, welcomed the guests to the entertainment, as an
offering in behalf of commerce and the commercial interests of
Portsmouth. At the close of the banquet, speeches and sentiments were given by Senators Hall, Burns and Marcy, Hon. G.
W. Kittredge, Hon. Mr. Hoyt of Durham, W. H. Y. Hackett, J.
W. Emery, George S. Barton, Clerk of the Senate, Wm. P.
Jones, Zenas Clement, W. Williams, Dr. Boardman, N. K.
Raynes, A. W. Haven, A. R. Hatch, H. H. Ladd, E. N. Fuller,
G. H. Rundlett, E. F. Sise, Lory Odell, John Knowlton and
others, and the party separated with an expression of the wish
that each of the ships now on the stocks in this city might be
named for a Presidential candidate, and the same company
invited to celebrate the launch in as good style as was that of
the James Buchanan.[135]

As often happened, the poet known under the pseudonym
"Boiling Rock" had a verse for the occasion. It would be fun to know
who "Boiling Rock" was, whether male or female, but the poems are
all that exist:

For the Chronicle.

SHIP JAMES BUCHANAN.

Do you wish for a model, a paragon form,
    A trophy of mechanical art,
That will brave the dire storm, —
    Awaiting her time to depart.
Although built in Maine, "James Buchanan"
        by name,
    A form that now graces our River;
Lies near Strawberry Bank, be sure she's not
        crank —
    Choice name, but I know not the giver.
On the Ides of March, our collars we'll starch,
    And hie to the White House with glee;
For there a true man called James Buchanan
    Will preside o'er the whole of our country,
No sectional feeling, no good laws repealing,
    No bickering between North and South;

Like the fabled fish, he'll season each dish,
Send vagabonds to Salt River feeling:
BOILING ROCK.

Perhaps inspired by "Boiling Rock," the *James Buchanan* finally sailed, going to Boston at the end of a towline from *R. B. Forbes*. Capt. James Burdick, one of the most admired skippers in the American merchant marine, was in command. Burdick was born in 1825 in Stonington, Connecticut, and went to sea early in life. He worked his way up to being first officer of the Portsmouth-built clipper *Express*. From that post he gained command of the *James Buchanan* and later the *Sarah E. Pettigrew*, built by Daniel Marcy and William Pettigrew in 1857. More of Burdick's story will be told in connection with the latter vessel.

Captain Burdick took the *James Buchanan* to New Orleans, where she loaded for Liverpool. She arrived in that port on December 12, and loaded cargo for Mobile. Leaving Liverpool on January 6, 1857, the *James Buchanan* was wrecked on the Irish coast, near Dungarvan. The *Liverpool Chronicle* reported on January 17: "The James Buchanan...went ashore yesterday at Ballymarast, County Waterford, and is lying in a very exposed situation on a bed of rock, with rudder gone and the water flowing in and out of her. The vessel is being stripped."

The ship was valued at $73,000, and there was $60,000 in insurance on her. Her cargo was uninsured salt. When it was determined that rocks had stove in her hull, she was sold for £100. The crew was safe.[136] The item noted that three Badger-built ships had met disaster in a short span of time: the *S. C. Thwing*, the *Samuel Badger*, and the *James Buchanan*.

Kate Prince

SPECIFICATIONS: 1856. Tobey & Littlefield. Billet head, oval stern. Burthen, 995 tons. Length, 178.8 feet; beam 34.6 feet; depth, 17.3 feet. Two decks. Original owners—William Jones & Son, and Martin Parry Jones.

Launched on September 19, the *Kate Prince* went to New Orleans in December under Capt. Thomas Jones, who had once commanded the *Elizabeth Hamilton*. She went to Mobile and loaded with 3,610 bales of cotton for Le Havre. From Le Havre, she went to Cardiff, Wales, and loaded for New York, where she arrived on July 7, 1857.[137] Her next passage was to St. John for lumber, which she hauled to Liverpool. She worked steadily in and out of the cotton ports, or in lumbering, up to the Civil War. When the war started, the cotton trade virtually came to a halt and freighters had to struggle for cargoes. Under Capt. Henry L. Libbey, the *Kate Prince* sailed from Philadelphia for Acapulco, Mexico, but had to put in at Bermuda:

> Ship Kate Prince, Libbey, (owned in this city) from Philadelphia for Acapulco, with a cargo of coal and iron for Pacific Mail Co., anchored in Five Fathom Hole, Bermuda, on the 7th Jan. in distress. The K. P. sailed from Philadelphia on the 30th Dec. On the 1st and 2d of Jan., while lying to in the Gulf Stream in a heavy gale from the N and a high sea from the ENE, had her decks swept, foremast and rudder sprung and shifted cargo, which caused the ship to leak. On the 8th inst., while being towed into port by steamer Phoebe, the hawser parted and the ship went on the rocks, where she remained 24 hours. On the 9th she was floated off and taken into port, and was being lightened for examination on the 14th ult. She will probably leave a portion of her cargo there, and proceed to Boston or New York for repairs.[138]

Her repairs completed, the *Kate Prince* proceeded to Acapulco. On her way out of that port, she was in a collision with the ship *White Falcon*, but suffered little damage. She went south to Callao and then out to the Chincha Islands for guano, which she took to Ireland, arriving at Queenstown (Cobh) on July 25, 1864. From Ireland, the *Kate Prince* went over to Cardiff and took on a load of coal for Bahia, Brazil. On November 12, 1864, she was captured by the Confederate cruiser *Shenandoah* and had to post a $40,000 bond before she could continue on her passage.[139] After unloading in Brazil, she was sent to Calcutta, arriving back in Boston the day after Christmas:

> Ship Kate Prince, (of Portsmouth,) Libbey, Calcutta, July 5, Sand Heads 11th, ar. at Boston 26th. Had a very heavy monsoon down the Bay of Bengal, and was 46 days to the Equator. — Passed Cape of Good Hope Oct. 12, and had a long continuance of westerly gales off that point. Touched at St. Helena Oct. 30, and sailed Oct. 31. Crossed the Equator Nov. 30, in lon 31 W, and had light winds and fine weather until we arrived off South Shoal, Nantucket, since which time have had very cold and stormy weather. — Was signalized off Cape Cod Dec. 19, and has had very heavy and bad weather in the bay. Had sails split and anchored off Marblehead Sunday forenoon, with six men disabled during the severe cold weather. Men from that port came off and assisted in furling the sails free of

charge, to whom Capt. Libby renders his thanks. Passengers from Calcutta — Mrs. E. G. Pritchard, of Newburyport; Mrs. H. Libby, 2 children and a female servant.[140]

From Boston, the *Kate Prince* went south around Cape Horn to San Francisco, taking 175 days on the passage—a very slow time. The shippers were able to load her with 45,000 sacks of wheat for Dublin, Ireland. Under various masters, the *Kate Prince* sailed the trade routes of the world. Under a Captain Hamilton, she was in Cadiz in the spring of 1872, loading salt for Portland, Maine. On the passage, two of her crew went at each other with knives, and one of them was stabbed in two places.[141] Captain Hamilton was still in command in January 1875, when the *Kate Prince*, "owned by Mark H. Wentworth and others of this city," cleared out of Charleston "with a cargo consisting of 85 tons of phosphate rock; 3,793 bales of Upland cotton, weighing 1,700,027 pounds, and 316 bags of Sea Island cotton, weighing 108,949 pounds; total weight of the cotton, 1,808,976 pounds, total value $334,475. This cargo is one of the largest ever shipped from this port, being the equivalent of 4,300 bales of Upland cotton."[142]

Again, in 1876, sailing out of Norfolk, she carried 4,484 bales, weighing 2,137,129 pounds. After more than 20 years of service, the *Kate Prince*, rugged and dependable, was sold in 1876 to a German firm. "No stronger ship was ever built on the Piscataqua."[143] She went for $23,000 and was renamed the *Pauline*. Under her new name, the *Kate Prince* broke up later in the year, when she went ashore near Harlingen, The Netherlands. Her crew was saved.

In the one nasty comment found so far about a Piscataqua-built ship, and really undeserved from the point of loyal service, the item on her end said: "She was a homely old box—one of the few clumsy looking vessels ever built on the Piscataqua."

Henrietta Marcy

SPECIFICATIONS: 1856. Portsmouth Shipbuilding Co. Noble's Island. Female figurehead, round stern. Burthen, 1,098 tons. Length, 168 feet; beam 35.4 feet; depth, 17.7 feet. Two decks. Original owners —Daniel Marcy, True M. Ball, William Martin, William D. Fernald, all of Portsmouth; Joseph J. Nickerson and Peter Marcy, both of New Orleans; S. C. Thwing, of Boston; and J. H. Butler, of Nottingham.

The Portsmouth Shipbuilding Co. essentially was made up of the same artisans who formed the Mechanics Shipbuilding Co., which built the ship *Ladoga* and the clippers *Morning Glory* and *Star of Hope*. Daniel Moulton was the master carpenter and, with his associates, built the vessel that would become the *Henrietta Marcy* on speculation.

A well-laid plan sometimes goes awry, and so it was with Moulton's new ship: a gale delayed the launching 24 hours to September 25.[144] The ship wasn't long without owners. Daniel Marcy headed the syndicate, and the vessel was named in honor of Marcy's first wife, Henrietta Priest Marcy. She was the mother of two of his sons, Henry and Judah Touro Marcy, both of whom became distinguished shipmasters. She was also the mother of a daughter. After Henrietta's death, Marcy married Katherine Tredick, by whom he had a third son, George D. Marcy, who became mayor of Portsmouth.

The Marcy group paid $48,000 for the vessel, and Capt. Joseph J. Nickerson was in command when she left for New Orleans in November.[145] After taking on a load of cotton, the *Henrietta Marcy* came north to Boston, arriving on January 4, 1857. She made a second passage to New Orleans and a return to Boston. Mrs. Daniel Marcy, her son, and stepdaughter came as passengers on that return from New Orleans. Again, the ship went to New Orleans, but loaded for Liverpool, where she arrived on December 7. Nickerson continued in command until 1860, and the ship's voyages were between New Orleans and the European cotton ports.

A Captain Keyser relieved Nickerson. In July 1861, after a final cotton run from New Orleans, the *Henrietta Marcy* loaded some cargo at Liverpool and then went to Cardiff to get the rest of her consignment for a passage to Paita in northern Peru. While on her way, the ship had to put into Rio de Janeiro to repair storm damage. Later she had to go into Valparaiso to repair damage suffered while rounding Cape Horn. Shipping news notes leave unanswered the question of why Capt. Joshua W. Hickey of Portsmouth was sent out to Paita to take command of the *Henrietta Marcy*. He left in the middle of April, going by way of Panama.[146] When the ship was unloaded, Hickey took her to the Chincha Islands to load guano for a market in Antwerp. When she eventually arrived in Boston, June 13, 1863, Hickey was succeeded by a Captain Pike. However, the *Henrietta Marcy* was sold to a British firm later in the year. She was renamed the *St. Albans*, and her home port was St. John. A Danish company bought her in 1872 for £5,000. "When bound from Quebec to London with lumber was abandoned 13 November 1888 dismasted and sinking.... Crew of 28 was shortly afterward picked up and landed at Queenstown, Ireland. Ship's value 70,000 kroner, only half insured."[147]

Eagle Speed

SPECIFICATIONS: 1856. John Yeaton. Badger's Island. Spread eagle figurehead, oval stern. Burthen, 1,113 tons. Length, 190 feet; beam 35.4 feet; depth, 17.4 feet. Two decks. Original owners—William Jones & Son, and Richard Jenness, of Portsmouth; David S. Fuller, of Boston.

The *Eagle Speed* was John Yeaton's first venture in the old Fernald & Pettigrew yard on Badger's Island. Prior to the launching of the *Eagle Speed*:

> The yard the present year passed into the hands of John Yeaton, Esq., and others. Under his immediate superintendence the business is now being carried on. The master builder is Charles W. Stimpson, Esq., who has had long experience in the business.
>
> There are now on the stocks two ships of 1200 or 1300 tons each, of beautiful model, and the most substantial frames and workmanship. A visit to the yard at the present time gives a better opportunity to inspect the strength of ships than when ready for launching. One of these vessels is owned by Wm. Jones & Son and others; and the other is for sale. They will be launched in six or eight weeks. Some movements of the old buildings in the Yard have been made — the contemplated changes will add much to the beauty of the Yard as seen from the wharves.[148]

Also in the prelaunching item, the *Eagle Speed* was described as "a magnificent medium clipper ship." However, the *Eagle Speed* wasn't considered one of the Port of Portsmouth's clippers. A tragedy marred her construction period: a young man, Leonard S. Staples, was struck by a falling plank and died of his injuries.

The launching story concentrated on the eagle figurehead:

> A "FINE BIRD." — The figure head of the splendid new ship "Eagle Speed," just launched from the yard on Badger's Island, is an immense Eagle, considerably larger than life, and, as a whole, very natural in appearance. The bird is just rising, with wings extended about ten feet, and neck ruffled as if in anger or earnestness. He measures about eight feet from beak to tip of tail — and is a very appropriate and showy finish to the prow of the noble vessel.
>
> This fine specimen of carving and gilding is from the

in this city — whom we would recommend to all in want of work in their line.[149]

Capt. Davis S. Fuller was master when the *Eagle Speed* left the Piscataqua forever, heading for the cotton ports. She took on a cargo at Mobile and went to Liverpool. There she was chartered for a passage to Melbourne. In December 1857, she was at Rangoon, loading for Falmouth, England, and eventually winding up in London.[150] Bombay was her next destination, and she loaded there for a passage to Liverpool. Leaving Liverpool on December 2, 1859, the *Eagle Speed* cleared for Boston and met trouble:

> We learn from the marine list that the ship Eagle Speed, Fuller, of this port, bound to Boston, from Liverpool, sailed from the Mersey Dec. 2, having a crew of 30 seamen, chiefly Americans, and the vessel in excellent order. The passage began with very bad weather; on the 5th, she had to put in to Studwell Roads, on the Welsh coast, for shelter, and on the 11th of January, in a heavy gale from the northwest, the rudder twisted and sprang, thus rendering the ship almost perfectly unmanageable. At the same time all her sails were blown away, and to make matters worse, the crew were sick and exhausted with working at the pumps, — the vessel at the time being in a leaky condition. Under these circumstances, Capt. Fuller put about, and bore up for Cork Harbor. The ship was then in lat 44 02 N, and lon 41 10 W, having about one-half of her voyage completed. She sighted Cork Harbor during the terrific gale of the 21st, which was so disastrous to the shipping all around the coast of the United Kingdom. His crew being all sick and his ship in her crippled state, Capt. F. could not get into Cork harbor, and, having carried away his topsail yards in the gale, he bore up for Liverpool, where he arrived after being out 56 days, the ship in a very leaky condition.
> The Eagle Speed is a fine ship of 1384 tons, and is well known in the American trade. Capt. Fuller showed great skill as a navigator in bringing his disabled ship to port through the recent heavy gales with an exhausted crew. The loss by the leakage to either ship or cargo cannot be accurately ascertained until the ship is dischg'd.[151]

The *Eagle Speed* reached Boston in April, and in June she was sent to St. John, taking 36 hours on the passage. From there, she crossed to London with lumber. Once more she was sent to the East Indies. Loaded with rice, the *Eagle Speed* started for England from

Bassein, Burma. She struck on Orestes Shoal, at the mouth of the
Bassein River, on June 17, 1861. The crew was saved, but the ship
was a total loss. A pilot was in command at the time.[152]

Annie Sise

*SPECIFICATIONS: 1856. George Raynes, Jr. Billet head, round
stern. Burthen, 1,030 tons. Length, 183 feet; beam 34.75 feet; depth,
17.325 feet. Two decks. Original owners—Edward F. Sise and John
Chase, of Portsmouth.*

The launching of the *Annie Sise* attracted newspaper attention, as such events were wont to do in the mid-nineteenth century:

LAUNCH. — The splendid ship Annie Sise, of about 1050
tons, was launched from the yard of George Raynes & Son, on
Wednesday last, at 10 o'clock, A. M. She is built entirely of
white oak, heavily copper and iron fastened; 180 feet long on
deck, 36.10 beam, 23.6 deep. She is intended for the general
freighting business; is owned by Isaac Bell, Jr., Lemoyne &
Bell, and John D. Simes, New-York; E. F. Sise, John Davis and
John Chase, Portsmouth; and will be commanded by Capt.
Charles F. Sise.

Messrs. Raynes & Son have now on the stocks another
ship of the same size and dimensions of the above, which is for
sale.[153]

The *Annie Sise* was truly a Sise family affair. She was named
for Ann Sise, the wife of Edward F. Sise and mother of the ship's first
master, Charles Fleetford Sise. She sailed on December 27 for Mobile,
with laudatory words and best wishes following in her wake:

SHIP ANNIE SISE. — This new and elegant ship sailed
from our port on Saturday last, for Mobile under command of
Capt. Charles F. Sise. She was built at the ship yard of George
Raynes & Son, and will well compare with any of the renowned
ships which have been there built. The workmanship will bear
a scrutinizing examination in those parts where strength and
not beauty has usually been sought. Particular care has been
taken for most effectually ventilating the ship, and such
arrangements are made for clearing the pump as will enable
any obstruction to be removed without disturbing the cargo.
The cabin is finished in elegant style — the wheel-house is well
arranged for comfort, as well as safety of the ship. The tonnage

of the Annie Sise is 1030. She is owned by Messrs. E. F. Sise, John Chase, John Davis, Portsmouth; Isaac Bell, jr., Lemoyne & Bell and John D. Simes, New-York. She will take a freight at Mobile for some European Port. Success attend her![154]

Charles F. Sise became one of the most successful of Portsmouth's widely scattered sons in a different field: he was a pioneer and executive in the Canadian telephone business—but that story has been told elsewhere.

In his maiden passage with the *Annie Sise*, the young Captain Sise had a misadventure that threatened his reputation for a short time. The day after the *Annie Sise* left Portsmouth, she was in a collision with the schooner *Rankin*, which was flying a distress signal. On seeing the signal, Captain Sise bore down on the schooner, spoke with her, and learned she was short on supplies. In the maneuvering, the schooner caught under the bow of the *Annie Sise* and was severely damaged. After getting clear, the *Annie Sise* gave the appearance of leaving the *Rankin* to her fate. But when Captain Sise saw the renewed distress signal, he brought his ship about and stood by the schooner until the bark *Maryland* came to the *Rankin*'s aid. Nevertheless, the story did go the rounds of the waterfronts that Captain Sise had plowed into the *Rankin* and then sailed off. The tale was categorically denied by both the master and the mate of the *Rankin*.[155]

When the *Annie Sise* arrived at Mobile, she was loaded with 3,388 bales of cotton, weighing 1,706,508 pounds. Ship and cargo went to Liverpool. After unloading, the ship came back to New York with immigrants. From New York, it was down to Mobile and then to Liverpool. During the next few years that was a familiar pattern for the ship.

Not that things were always peaceful for the *Annie Sise*. While lying at Mobile in 1858, there was a mutiny, caused by the refusal on the part of one or two of the men to do duty. A sailor named Murphy pursued the mate into the cabin with sheath-knife drawn. In self-defense, the mate drew his pistol and put two bullets in Murphy. The mutinous sailors, including Murphy, were subsequently arrested and arraigned before U.S. Commissioner Owen. What happened to them wasn't reported.

A Captain Sullivan relieved Sise late in 1860. In 1862, a Captain Weeks became master, and the *Annie Sise* went to work on the East Indian trade routes.

In 1868, the *Annie Sise* was reported as carrying coal from Australia to Newcastle, England. In a later issue it was explained that "some blundering typesetter" mistook the word "wool" for "coal."[156]

The next-to-the-last master of the *Annie Sise* was Capt. Charles Briard, who made his home in Greenland. Briard took the ship out of New York in January 1871, and died when 21 days out. It was April 8 before news of his death reached Portsmouth. Capt. George Wallace Tucker was hired to go out to Australia and take command of the *Annie Sise*. Tucker had the ship only for a passage from Sydney to San Francisco. A harbor pilot was in control when the *Annie Sise* went ashore on Point Keys in a heavy fog on September 15, "and soon commenced breaking up. The ship was loaded with a cargo of coal from Sydney, Australia, for the Central Pacific Railroad."[157] Tucker returned home in October:

> Capt. Geo. W. Tucker of this city, who left here last spring to take command of the ship Annie Sise at Sydney, Australia, has arrived home by the way of the Pacific Railroad from San Francisco. It will be remembered that the Annie Sise was wrecked on a reef in San Francisco bay while Capt. Tucker was in charge of her, and he states that it was with the greatest difficulty that the crew were enabled to get into the boats, saving none of their effects, the captain coming off bare-headed, with nothing but slippers on his feet. All succeeded in getting away from the ship in safety, and rowed all night, reaching San Francisco early in the morning. The vessel was a helpless wreck the moment she struck. The crew were left penniless in the city, as under the marine laws of that locality they cannot get a dollar of their pay unless something is saved from the wreck. The owners of the vessel have offered to indemnify Capt. Tucker for his losses, as they hold him blameless in the matter.[158]

Sagamore

SPECIFICATIONS: 1856. John Yeaton. Badger's Island. Billet head, round stern. Burthen, 1,163 tons. Length, 190 feet; beam, 35.3 feet; depth, 18.15 feet. Three decks. Original owners—William Jones & Son, Jones & Mendum, and Mark H. Wentworth, all of Portsmouth.

Port of Portsmouth shipwrights built their vessels to last, and for many of the ships it was only the misfortune of contrary winds and a rocky shore that ended their service. No better example of the rugged strength of the Piscataqua vessels can be found than the *Sagamore*. John Yeaton and his master carpenter, Charles Stimpson, built and launched only two ships: the *Eagle Speed* and the *Sagamore*. As noted earlier, the *Eagle Speed* ran into trouble and was destroyed, but the *Sagamore* lasted for years.

The *Sagamore* was launched on November 26, the last of the 1856 crop of nonclipper three-masters. When launched she hadn't yet been named and was up for sale.[159] It was perhaps indicative of the slackening demand for ships that the *Sagamore* was on her builder's hands for a few months, forcing him to publish this ad:

SHIP AT AUCTION.
PEREMPTORY SALE.
On SATURDAY, the 4th day of April at 12 M.
AT PORTSMOUTH, N. H.
Will be sold to the highest bidder,
A SUPERIOR NEW W. O. SHIP, lying at Pray's Wharf, now ready for sea, of the following dimensions, viz.

Length 190 feet, Beam 37 1-2 feet, depth 24 feet. Her materials are of the very first class, and are all seasoned — is extra fastened, both with Copper and Iron, and locust trenails through and through. Salted on the stocks, and has been built without regard to cost.

Parties wishing an *extra* Ship, will find this a rare opportunity of obtaining as good a Ship as can be built. She may be examined at any time on application to

JOHN YEATON

Portsm. March 14, 1857.   H. F. WENDELL, Auct.[160]

The Jones syndicate bid the ship in at the auction, named her the *Sagamore*, and sent her to sea under Capt. Edwin A. Gerrish. However, instead of going south for cotton, she went to the Maritimes for lumber and then to Liverpool. Coming west, she went into New York, and then returned to Liverpool, taking 18 days on the passage—a remarkably fast time. She went from Liverpool to Mobile, and then back to Liverpool on August 13, 1858. At one time, Gerrish had a charter in the Warren & Thayer Line, and later in the Philadelphia Line. Returning to Philadelphia in 1860, Captain Gerrish was relieved by Pearce W. Penhallow, also of Portsmouth, who had formerly commanded the big clipper *Sierra Nevada*. Captain Penhallow sailed the ship to St. John, where she loaded lumber for Liverpool. On her return to North America, a Captain Treadwell had command. She crossed to Liverpool and there loaded for Calcutta. At Calcutta, she was loaded for London at £3.15.9. per ton. Treadwell commanded the *Sagamore* on Asian voyages until 1863, when he was replaced by a Captain Alger. On passage from Calcutta to London, the *Sagamore* put into St. Helena to bury Captain Alger.[161] The ship *Mendoza* reported that on February 7, 1864, she spoke "American ship Sag-amore of Portsmouth.... 114 days from Calcutta for London, reported having left captain at St. Helena, insane, obtained another, and he had poisoned himself with potash — he was alive but speechless. The chief mate, who was in charge, asked for a doctor's assistance, which we were unable to give." The *Sagamore* finally arrived at Deal, Eng-land, on March 14.[162]

Treadwell apparently again assumed command, sailing from Gravesend to Cardiff in April, and loaded railroad iron at 25 shillings per ton, with the ship paying war risk insurance.[163]

By 1867, Capt. McLauren F. Pickering, a resident of Green-land, was in command. In January, coming from Calcutta to Boston, the *Sagamore*'s carpenter, George Brown of Glasgow, died of dysen-tery. All the way from the Cape of Good Hope she met heavy weather, and she shipped a heavy sea while hove to in the teeth of a northwest gale. The wave stove in "the main hatch house, booby hatch, and port bulwarks, and drew the spar bolts from the water ways, and carried away head and head rails." The ship had been five days off Cape Cod before she could limp into port."[164] Later that year, on another pas-sage from Calcutta, she had more misfortunes before arriving in Boston on October 4:

> Ship Sagamore, (of Portsmouth), Pickering, Calcutta May 2, Sand Heads 6th. Was detained off Cape of Good Hope 17 days by heavy westerly gales. June 10, lat. 7:05S, lon. 90E, William White of New York, seaman, died of dysentery. June 29, lat. 26:19S, lon. 49:15E, Isaac Maguire of Germany, fell from the topsail yard and was killed instantly. July 14, off Cape Lagulnas, lat. 35:10S., lon. 20:15 E., in a heavy westerly gale, shipped a sea, stove boats and hatch houses, and washed a seaman overboard, named Antonia Friend of Jamaica. Sept. 1, lat, 13 N., lon. 37:30 N., experienced a hurricane, which came on very suddenly, commencing at NW, with the wind going round by the way of South, blowing hardest when the wind hauled to ENE, with very heavy confused sea; lost sails, shipped heavy seas, stove water casks and main hatch-house and strained rudder-head. It continued to blow for about 12 hours very hard.[165]

Through the next few years, Captain Pickering apparently alternated with a Captain Richardson. Their voyages were usually to India and China. In the mid-1870s a Captain Knapp was master. On a passage from Rio de Janeiro to San Francisco, the *Sagamore* was damaged so badly that she had to put into Callao for repairs. In San

Francisco she was sold; a news items said the price was $17,000, and it was conjectured that she would be converted to a bark for service in the lumber trade.[166] A week later an article about the *Sagamore* was published, giving details of her early days:

> We notice the sale of the ship Sagamore at the port of San Francisco.
>
> The Sagamore was the last of a long catalogue of ships built on Badger's Island and where Master William Badger, after whom the Island was called, built his hundred ships, the last of which was named for him. This island was once owned by Gov. Langdon and bore his name, before it received the name of "Badger's Island." Here the America was built, and Paul Jones often was pulled across the rapid tides of the Piscataqua to inspect her construction. After passing the ownership of several persons, the site of this year was purchased by Messrs. Wm. Jones and Son and others, and the Eagle Speed and Sagamore were built by a company consisting of the late Messrs. Jones & Son, Capt. John E. Salter, and John Yeaton. They employed Chas. W. Stimpson as Master Constructor. The Messrs. Jones contracted for the Eagle Speed, and continued to own and sail her. The Sagamore was rigged at Pray's wharf, and on one fine day in April 1857, was sold at auction to Mark H. Wentworth, Esq. and associates for sixty-five thousand dollars, ready for sea, and left this port for Lepreux to load for Europe under the command of Capt. Edwin A. Gerrish.
>
> Twenty years has shown the last of the Badger's Island ships to have been such as maintained the reputation of the Piscataqua built vessels for strength and speed.[167]

The bark *Sagamore*'s new home port was Port Gamble, Washington Territory. Exactly how long she lasted isn't known, but she was mentioned in 1884 in an item about the former clipper *Dashing Wave* and again in 1885 in a story about the *Samoset*. Probably she, too, ended her days as a barge.

Alice Ball

SPECIFICATIONS: 1857. Tobey & Littlefield. Billet head, square stern. Burthen, 898 tons. Length, 166 feet; beam, 34.25 feet; depth, 17.125 feet. Original owners—Daniel Marcy, Peter Jenness, True M. Ball, Washington Williams, Joshua W. Hickey, and William Pettigrew, all of Portsmouth; and Peter Marcy, of New Orleans.

The slackening of the tide in shipbuilding became evident as 1857 opened. In 1856, 11 three-masters, including two clippers, had been launched. In the course of 1857 only 6 regular freighters were built, and no clippers. Probably the simple economic facts were that there was an overabundance of shipping, coupled with the increasing use of steam-driven vessels.

In March it was erroneously reported in the *Journal* that the new ship at Tobey & Littlefield's, recently purchased by Daniel Marcy, had been named the *Alice Bell*. With True M. Ball among the partners, it soon became obvious that the ship was the *Alice Ball*. Under that name, she left the Port of Portsmouth, commanded by Joshua W. Hickey, who had previously been master of the *Henrietta Marcy*. She went to St. Stephen, New Brunswick, and loaded lumber for the London market. After unloading, she took on a passage to Calcutta, and returned to London. She arrived on the Thames on November 4, 1858, and then she went back to Calcutta. Hickey was still master when the *Alice Ball* arrived in Boston, January 17, 1860.[168] She went to New Orleans and then to Bordeaux, France, then back to New Orleans. Late in 1860 she was in Liverpool, going to New Orleans; she arrived there on May 30, although the Civil War was under way.

Part of the *Alice Ball*'s story shows the desperate measures taken by the Marcy brothers to keep their prosperous shipping business alive. When the *Alice Ball* was spoken on June 23, latitude 40° longitude 32° (north of the Azores), she was flying the Stars and Bars of the Confederate States. Clearing out of Liverpool, she headed for St. Stephen, but, along with another Marcy-owned ship, she was captured by the U.S. Revenue Cutter *Arago* and taken into Eastport, Maine.[169] The exact charges weren't spelled out, but the flaunting of the Confederate flag must have played a role. Further, the political sentiments of the Marcys were well known, and their vessels were obvious objects of suspicion. The cutting off of the cotton trade was ruinous for men like Peter Marcy, and there was no hesitancy in playing the game of supplying papers to protect a vessel against Confederate cruisers, while the regular papers held off capture by the Federal warships. In fact, the CSS *Alabama*, the most notorious of the rebel raiders, burned such a ship, the Portsmouth-built clipper *Express*, which was carrying Confederate documents.[170] Peter Marcy, incidentally, owned a fourth interest in the *Express*. Shortly after being captured, the two ships were released by order of Treasury Secretary Salmon P. Chase, a native of New Hampshire.[171] Daniel Marcy, another major investor in the two vessels, was a rising political leader, which probably helped in winning their release. Marcy was even elected to the U.S. House in 1863, although his pro-Confederacy views were well known. A bit of digression permits the observation that Portsmouth, with large economic interests in ships and shipping, wasn't wildly enthused over the war. There was even a riot against the draft in 1863.

Capt. Ebenezer G. Adams had the *Alice Ball* in 1862, and she seems to have come through the Civil War unscathed. She is credited with at least one successful run through the Federal blockade off the Carolinas.[172] The maritime news notes indicate that she spent much of the war in the East Indian trade, safely away from Confederate raiders.

In 1867, the *Alice Ball* was again in the news when her chief officer, John Stanley, was arraigned before U.S. Commissioner Hallett in Boston on a charge of assault on seaman Thomas Wallace with a belaying pin. Wallace contended he had been beaten on the head. But it was the proverbial dark and stormy night, and no one had clearly seen the belaying pin in the mate's hand. The charge was reduced to beating and wounding, Stanley had to put up $200 bail, and the case faded from view.[173]

The *Alice Ball* had another adventure in the spring of 1868. She was sent to St. Thomas, Virgin Islands, to take on the cargo of the condemned ship *Sarah Newman*. The cargo consisted of arms and ammunition for Valparaiso, Chile, which was in revolt against the Spanish government. The Spaniards had a gunboat stationed outside St. Thomas, which then belonged to Denmark. The warship kept the *Alice Ball* bottled up, and the two played a deadly cat-and-mouse game which went on for several weeks when it was reported:

> The ship Alice Ball, laden with material of war for Valparaiso, has been lying in the port of St. Thomas several weeks, watched by a Spanish gunboat, which had orders to bring her to, on the ground that Spain and Chili were at war, and therefore the Alice Ball was liable to capture. Late advices from St. Thomas report that she had escaped, and that the gunboat had gone in chase of her. If captured it will afford our government an opportunity to interfere, for she is an American ship.[174]

Ultimately the *Alice Ball*, then commanded by a Captain Colson, made it to New York with her deadly cargo. The *Journal*, on September 7, 1872, reported more misadventure on the *Alice Ball*:

> In July, 1869, says *The Shipping Gazette*, Capt. L. G. Means sailed the ship *Alice Ball* (built here in 1857) from New York for Callao. The voyage was pleasant until off Cape Horn, where the ship encountered fields and bergs of ice. The weather was intensely cold, and while drifting in those ice fields 45 days, the passengers and crew experienced the rigor and sever-

ity of sea life. Mrs. Means unraveled her sontag and other worsted garments out of which she knit, herself, 13 pairs of socks for the crew. Most of the time the sea was so rough, that to knit she was obliged to lie down. Besides being frost-bitten, for want of vegetables, the crew were attacked with scurvey, which complicated the suffering and added to the distress. At the end of about two months, the wind changed, and the ship was enabled to proceed.

Exactly how long the Alice Ball stayed afloat isn't certain. Nelson, without giving a source, said she was lost in 1872 off Honolulu.[175]

Rockingham

SPECIFICATIONS: 1857. Portsmouth Shipbuilding Co. Billet head, round stern. Burthen, 976 tons. Length, 180 feet; beam, 34.1 feet; depth, 17.05 feet. Two decks. Original owners—William Jones & Son, and Jones & Mendum.

The third, and largest, full-rigged vessel to bear the name the *Rockingham* was a financial disaster for her builders. Not only that, to her went the dubious honor of being the last ship captured and burned by the CSS *Alabama*. The *Rockingham* was launched on April 18, and it was a proud moment for the artisans who formed the company. "Her frame is entirely of New Hampshire white oak; wales and planking of white oak. She is fitted for the general freighting business and is for sale."[176] But, as indicated in the case of the *Alice Ball*, the shipping industry was coming into slack times around the world, and the *Rockingham* went unsold for nine months. The builders, none of them men of large means, had invested $60,000 in her, and it was now a buyer's market. Finally, it was reported:

> SHIP ROCKINGHAM. — The new ship built by the Union Company of this city, at a cost of $60,000, it is said, was purchased last week by the Messrs. Jones of this city for $33,000. She is to be called Rockingham and will take a cargo of hay and ice to New Orleans, under the command of Captain George Melcher.[177]

The loss was more than the working man's syndicate could stand, and the outlook for more ship construction in general was so gloomy that the *Rockingham* was the last vessel built in that yard. For the buyers, she was a well-constructed bargain, and they put her

Depicted are a chest for a doll's clothes and a doll's chair. The toys were made for Helen "Brownie" Gerrish of Portsmouth when she and her parents were prisoners of war on the Confederate raider Alabama *in 1864. Courtesy of the Virginia Historical Society.*

into the cotton trade. Her first cargo of cotton was delivered in Boston, as was her second. With two passengers, Woodbury Melcher and Joseph Laighton of Portsmouth, the *Rockingham* sailed from Boston to Liverpool early in 1859.[178] She brought freight and immigrants back to Boston and then went to the Maritimes. With the outbreak of war, the *Rockingham* was diverted to the East Indian trade, with Melcher still master. In 1863, Capt. Edwin A. Gerrish, long a highly thought of mariner in the Port of Portsmouth, assumed command of the *Rockingham* at Philadelphia. Gerrish took the ship to Panama and then around Cape Horn to Callao and the Chincha Islands. On

February 24, 1864, the *Rockingham* started on her last passage, heading for England. What happened to the *Rockingham* and her cargo brought up a ticklish legal point. Although the *Rockingham* was flying the Stars and Stripes, the cargo was intended for a neutral nation. The bad news was published in the *Journal* on June 25, 1864:

> The ship Rockingham, from Callao for Queenstown, was burned by the Alabama April 23, in lat. 15 south, lon. 32 west. The Alabama was spoken the following day by a vessel which has arrived at London. The Rockingham was commanded by Capt. Gerrish, and was on the voyage from Callao for England with a cargo of guano, having sailed from the former port on the 24th of February last. This is the second instance among the various captures by the rebel pirates in which a cargo of Peruvian guano has been destroyed. The pirates heretofore have usually bonded vessels having cargoes from the Peruvian guano islands, on the ground that the cargo was owned by foreign parties. It is likely that Jeff. Davis has latterly sent more stringent orders to his sea robbers.

> She was owned by Wm. Jones & Co. of this city; was built in 1858, and was a first-class vessel of 976 tons.

The burning of the *Rockingham* was a story that echoed through the years in the annals of the Port of Portsmouth. Obviously, she figured in the Alabama Claims allocations, and her case was argued on December 21, 1874, with William H. Hackett sitting as commissioner. Attorney James W. Emery of Portsmouth appeared for the owners, and a Boston lawyer represented the United States.[179] How much was paid the owners isn't clear.

In 1883, Hackett wrote an article for the *Granite State Monthly* in which he told of the capture of the *Rockingham*. Hackett's main interest was to tell of the escape of the Piscataqua-built clipper *Emily Farnum* from destruction by the *Alabama*. The *Alabama*'s commander, Capt. Raphael Semmes, needed to get rid of the prisoners he had jamming his decks, and he put the prisoners on the *Emily Farnum*. The *Brilliant*, another ship Semmes had captured, was burned. Hackett contrasted those events with the way the *Rockingham* was treated. The *Rockingham*'s crew was landed by the *Alabama* at Cherbourg, France, and the *Alabama* became trapped in that port by the USS *Kearsarge*, built at the Portsmouth Navy Yard, which had spent months dogging the *Alabama*. Somehow Captain Gerrish of the *Rockingham* got word to Capt. John A. Winslow, commander of the *Kearsarge*, that he wanted to sign on as a volunteer in the expected battle; he was refused, and he had to watch the fight from a cliff overhanging

the English Channel. Naval rules barred him from serving, as a civilian, on the *Kearsarge*. Gerrish, who still had a long, successful maritime career ahead, had to content himself with seeing Semmes and
the *Alabama* sunk by the *Kearsarge*, which forever ended the *Alabama*'s marauding career.

Many years later, another small chapter in the story of the
CSS *Alabama* came to light. Captain Gerrish of the *Rockingham* had
on board his wife and daughter, Helen. Only a little girl, Helen
became a great favorite with the crew of the *Alabama* while she was a
prisoner of war. These hard-bitten men, most of them English nation-
als, months, years away from home and family, were probably easily
captivated by a child's smile and laugh. On May 28, 1932, the story
was told in the *Portsmouth Herald*:

> During the period of captivity on the Confederate ship
> little Helen Gerrish evidently became a great pet with the
> officers and men of the Alabama, who made for her various
> gifts that would be pleasing to a child. Lt. Wilkens made her a
> doll's stool, the carpenter of the Alabama made for her a chest
> of drawers, and Dr. D. H. Llewellyn, the surgeon, presented to
> her a framed picture on which he wrote "Brownie Gerrish last
> prize of this pirate from D. H. Llewellyn, C.S Pirate Alabama,
> May 21, 1864.

Helen Gerrish lived her long life in Portsmouth. It was reported in the article above that Miss Gerrish had given her souvenirs of
the captivity on the CSS *Alabama* to the Virginia Historical Society.

Mary Washington

*SPECIFICATIONS: 1857. George Raynes, Jr. Billet head, round
stern. Burthen, 933 tons. Length, 180.9 feet; beam, 33.2 feet; depth,
16.6 feet. Two decks. Original owners—the Tuckers, of Wiscasset.*

While others were hesitant about buying ships and sending
them to sea, the Tuckers of Wiscasset had two being built in different
yards in the Port of Portsmouth. The first of the Tucker ships into the
water in 1857 was the *Mary Washington*. The second, the *R. H. Tucker*, from the yard of Tobey & Littlefield, was only an hour behind the
Mary Washington. When the latter was launched, it was reported:

> The fine ship on the stocks at the yard of Messrs. George
> Raynes & Son, is named the "Mary Washington." She is of

about 1000 tons burthen, and owned by Messrs. R. H. Tucker, R. H. Tucker jr., P. & W. P. Lennox, and Capt. Geo. W. Chapman, who is to command her. These are all Maine men, we think — belonging to Wiscasset. The Messrs. Tucker are exceedingly enterprising, and evince a high regard for Portsmouth ships. The ship is of course A No. 1, and will not injure the exalted reputation of her builders. The name is patriotic, beautiful and appropriate, and we wonder it has never before been borne abroad by one of our gallant American ships.[180]

Before she left the Port of Portsmouth, the *Mary Washington* provoked a bit of confusion. In a letter to the editor, a reader said: "I see by the papers that one of the ships recently launched is named Mary Washington. Can you inform your readers where the owners of this ship secured the name, or whom she is named for? I have lived some time and I have never heard of Mary Washington. The wife of President Washington was Martha."[181] Editor Brewster explained that the mother of George Washington was named Mary.

Again, thanks to Jane Tucker, much detail about the service of the *Mary Washington* has been made available. The ship sailed from Portsmouth on November 12, under Capt. George W. Chapman. His officers were Ichabod Frisbee, mate, and John Smith, second mate. The cargo was hay. She took 14 days to get to Charleston and there loaded with 3,148 bales of cotton, including 260 bales of Sea Island. The freight was £1,988, plus primage. After her arrival in Liverpool on March 10, 1858, a 39-day passage, she was coppered. After the sheathing work, she left Liverpool on March 29, heading to Charleston carrying salt, 200 crates of metal, and merchandise.

With John Smith promoted to mate, Captain Chapman left Charleston on June 10, bound for Liverpool, carrying 3,254 bales of Upland and 708 bales of Sea Island. The freight money was £2,304, including primage. Her passage took only 22 days, and she left Liverpool July 19 with 140 tons of salt charged to the ship's account and 1,300 sacks of salt. John Benson was second mate. This time she went to St. John for lumber, and returned to Liverpool. She returned to North America and put in at Boston, working as a passenger packet in the Warren & Thayer Line. On entering Boston Harbor she hit a rock, but wasn't seriously damaged.

When the *Mary Washington* went south again, leaving Boston on February 11, 1859, she had a cargo of hay and 100 tons of ice, the whole at a dollar a ton. Charles Ricker was second mate. She was a little over two months in getting a cargo, but departed Charleston on May 1 carrying 2,916 bales of Upland, 575 of Sea Island, and 492 casks of rice. Freight money was £2,124, plus primage. Except for one voyage, Captain Chapman commanded her, working back and forth across the Atlantic. On July 29, 1860, she left St. John with Dwight F. Tinkham as master; David C. Sparks, mate; Andrew Hanson, second mate. Unloading her lumber at Liverpool, the ship took on a general cargo for £1,365 in freight money, which she took to Philadelphia.

Captain Chapman resumed command and left Philadelphia for Charleston on December 11, 1860. In January 1861 the ship was ordered to Key West to pick up the cargo of the wrecked ship *Ocean Star*. The *Mary Washington* sailed from Charleston on the ninth, and on the eleventh she was wrecked on Elbow Reef, Great Abaco Island.

R. H. Tucker

SPECIFICATIONS: 1857. Tobey & Littlefield. Billet head, square stern. Burthen, 898 tons. Length, 168 feet; beam, 34 feet; depth, 17 feet. Two decks. Original owners—the Tuckers, of Wiscasset.

The day the *R. H. Tucker* was launched, the *Portsmouth Chronicle* published a general story about ship construction in the Port of Portsmouth, and spoke of the *R. H. Tucker* and the man for whom she was named in glowing terms:

> The staunch and handsome ship at the yard of Messrs. Tobey & Littlefield, also belongs to an eastern company — Messrs. R. H. Tucker, R. H. Tucker Jr., and D. Stone, — and is to be commanded by Capt. Joseph Tucker. She is a little less than 1000 tons burthen, and is named the "R. H. Tucker," whose bust has a place in the stern moulding. This craft is worthy to be enrolled in the list of Piscataqua Ships — which is honor enough.

Launched about an hour behind the *Mary Washington* on September 30, the *R. H. Tucker* cleared the Port of Portsmouth on November 24 under Capt. Joseph Tucker, with W. J. Clark as mate and B. R. Jackson as second mate. She took with her 213,432 pounds of hay, which had freight of $2,124. Along with the hay, the *R. H. Tucker* carried two of the owner's children, Richard, Jr. and Mary.

On her way to Charleston, the *R. H. Tucker* fell in with the abandoned bark, *Mary C. Porter*, and towed the derelict to Charleston, from some 200 miles off Cape Fear. The bark was waterlogged, but carrying a load of mahogany that netted the Tuckers £300 when sold in Charleston. The ship needed the money, since it took four months to get a cargo. When she finally cleared out, she was carrying

2,862 bales of Upland and 215 bales of Sea Island. The total weight was 1,310,639 pounds and the worth £1,925, plus the primage. While in Liverpool, the *R. H. Tucker* was coppered and took on a load of 1,880 bags of salt. She came into Wiscasset, spent a couple of days, and then went to St. John. From there, the ship took William Lennox, probably a Tucker in-law, and seven steerage passengers to Liverpool. She also hauled deals for a freight of £1,440. Back and forth she went, making money. Finally, in late December 1859, Joseph Tucker turned the ship over to W. J. Clark, his chief officer. Captain Clark took the *R. H. Tucker* out of Charleston on January 16, 1860, with a freighting fee of $14,735, plus primage, but he had to come back in ballast. The *R. H. Tucker* went back and forth for a year, and came back into Charleston on March 17, 1861. Captain Clark then had to face the problems created by secession. He wrote to R. H. Tucker on April 8, and the letter was received in Wiscasset on the thirteenth: "Yours of the 1st has been received and I am grieved to say the ship is still unengaged and not a freight of any kind offering. The people seem in great confusion and in the greatest excitement as they have stopped all supplys this morning from going into Fort Sumter."

Clark struggled to find a crew to bend on sails so he could get out of Charleston. He informed Tucker that he was ready to go, and then on April 17 he had to write:

> Doubtless you will be surprised to find that I am still here as I told you in my last letter I received your dispatch date April 10th and on the 11th had the sails bent intending to obtain crew on Friday and proceed to sea without delay, when to my great astonishment I was awakened at the dawn of day by the fireing of heavy cannon, it being the bombardment of Fort Sumter, which continued to one o'clock Saturday when the fort being all wrapt in flames, when [Maj. Robert] Anderson was compeled to surrender.

Captain Clark gave a lucid account of the confusion and red tape involved when he tried to clear the ship out. Merchants didn't want to ship goods under the American flag. Then Jefferson Davis issued a proclamation to the effect that he would license privateers. On April 24, the *R. H. Tucker* was still at Charleston, but Clark happily reported that he had managed to find a cargo. He wrote again on May 5, expressing perplexity as to why R. H. Tucker had telegraphed to clear for Wiscasset. Clark insisted he had told Tucker of getting a cargo, and he continued to load it. The correspondence is long and involved, but Clark ultimately took the ship out of Charleston for Liverpool. The log shows the freight money as £2,414, plus primage. The

R. H. Tucker didn't get back to Charleston until November 1867.[182] Through the Civil War years, the *R. H. Tucker* worked the East Indian and Pacific trade. Captain Clark kept the ship until 1867, when he was relieved by Capt. R. T. Rundlett, who was in command when the *R. H. Tucker* departed Liverpool on September 6, 1868, for Boston. Two days later the ship was lost on Blackwater Bank, Ireland. Nelson has her lost at Tuscar light, but gives no date.[183]

Sarah E. Pettigrew

SPECIFICATIONS: 1857. Daniel Marcy and William Pettigrew. Old Mugridge Yard, South End. Billet head, square stern. Burthen, 1,192 tons. Length, 192 feet; beam, 36.5 feet; depth, 18.25 feet. Three decks. Original owners—Daniel Marcy, William Pettigrew, Peter Jenness, Washington Williams, True W. Ball, and Albert R. Hatch, all of Portsmouth; S. C. Thwing, of Boston; Peter Marcy and Joseph J. Nickerson, of New Orleans.

The *Sarah E. Pettigrew* was the first venture of a new partnership: Daniel Marcy and William Pettigrew, the former partner of Frederick William Fernald. The two men were well acquainted, yet it seems ironic that they built their first ship in the yard Fernald had abandoned 20 years before. At that time, Fernald thought it was too cramped.

Marcy & Pettigrew had on the stocks a ship honoring Sarah E. Pettigrew.[184] She carried "on the stern moulding a bust of a lady, which will doubtless more resemble the original a score of years hence. The ship is of about 1500 tons, and will hail from New Orleans.... Her builders are experienced men, and no labor expense has been spared to render this one of the best vessels ever launched. Her superior will hardly be found afloat."[185]

Pessimists abounded the day the *Sarah E. Pettigrew* was launched. Old times along the waterfront remembered the problems Frederick W. Fernald had had with two ships he launched there: the *Harriet Rockwell* and the *Thomas Perkins*. The *Sarah E. Pettigrew* was almost 40 feet longer than the *Thomas Perkins*. A news item made note of this in reporting the launching:

> Ships were formerly built there; but it was doubted whether there was enough water there, in the right place, to launch the large ships built at the present time. Mr. Pettigrew's known skill in launching, however, obviated the difficulty; and good ships may be built and launched at the South End, as this very fine one proves.[186]

The construction of the *Sarah E. Pettigrew* wasn't entirely attended by good fortune. Shipbuilding, like other mechanical trades, has its risks. William Rea, a Nova Scotian, was working with a gang raising staging early in the production. One of the poles fell, striking him on the head and knocking him down. He fell on an axe, suffering a severe facial cut. A doctor came immediately, but he died a day or two later, leaving his widow and two small children.[187]

The *Sarah E. Pettigrew*'s first and only master was James H. Burdick. She sailed from the Port of Portsmouth on November 10 for her home port, New Orleans, arriving there on December 2. She loaded for Liverpool and plowed back and forth across the Atlantic until the outbreak of the Civil War. She made one run through the blockade off New Orleans, but then was trapped inside.[188] A contemporary account, tinged with the political bitterness of the times, seems to cast some shadow on the character of Captain Burdick:

> The ship Sarah E. Petigrew, seized a few weeks since, off the bar at New Orleans, and taken to the levee, we are informed by one of the owners, has been condemned by the Southern courts. Capt. Burdick was advised by the pilot not to attempt to enter but to bear away for a Northern port. He is now a lieutenant on board of one of Jeff. Davis's privateers, which may account for his reckless disregard of the timely advice.
>
> The ship was built at Portsmouth in 1857, is 1192 tons burthen, and has been recently coppered and repaired, and originally cost $83,000. The freight money of her former voyage, amounting to $17,000, had been invested in salt, which constituted her cargo. The total loss to the owners therefore, is $100,000. One-quarter of the vessel was owned in New Orleans, and the remainder by D. Marcy, W. Petigrew, A. R. Hatch, T. M. Ball, P. Jenness, and estate of W. W. Williams of this city. — *Chronicle*.[189]

In fairness to Captain Burdick, it has to be said that we should not try to judge in hindsight what men did in the stressful times of the Civil War. It was brother against brother, and the claim that Burdick might have signed on as officer on a Confederate cruiser was plausible. The irony of the situation was pointed out in a newspaper item after the *Sarah E. Pettigrew*'s capture:

> The brothers Marcy, one residing in Portsmouth, and the other in New Orleans, owned jointly four ships. The Southern brother hoisted the secession flag on two, and the old stars and stripes floated over two. The fortunes of war have so

turned that the two secession crafts have been seized by the United States authorities while the Confederates have captured the two belonging to the loyal Northerner.[190]

Many years after the war it became clear that Captain Burdick had been maligned. The *Sarah E Pettigrew* had been captured by the Confederate cruiser *Ivy* and was interned in New Orleans. When the Federal Navy swept up the river, the Confederates burned the ship rather than let the enemy have her.

During one of the voyages under Burdick, the *Sarah E. Pettigrew* drew laudatory remarks from a Philadelphia paper:

> A SPLENDID SHIP WITH A LARGE CARGO. — The fine ship Sarah E. Pettigrew, Capt. Burdick, just arrived at Philadelphia, from Liverpool, is a splendid A 1 ship of 1192 tons register, and about three years old. She has now on board 2715 tons of cargo, but carries, when fully laden, 3000 tons; her capacity being equal to 6100 bales cotton or 25,500 bbls. flour. She now draws 23 feet water, and crossed the bar with all ease, in tow of a steam-tug. — *Philadelphia Paper*.[191]

Captain Burdick died in June 1887, still active as a Bar pilot in New Orleans. An obituary in the *New Orleans Picayune* on June 24 painted a different picture of this former sea captain than that published during the Civil War:

> Living in hospitable seclusion, surrounded with mementoes of their calling and with the comforts and refinements that can be procured, with the front door always open, particularly to their comrades of earlier times, are the retired sea captains who, after a stormy life of battling the waves, settle down to simple and comfortable lives on shore.
>
> Such was the latter part of the life of one of the best known and most popular men that ever trod the deck, a man who allowed his love for the sea to keep him "on deck" until he fell victim to the treacheries of the sea.

The obituary explained that after the war Burdick went into the towboat business, working for the Peter Marcy Towboat Line. In a mishap, he was thrown over the wheel of one of the tugs and severely injured. Burdick kept on working, concealing his injuries from his family. However, death finally collected its dues.

A few weeks after his death, a letter to the editor told more about Burdick and his service with the *Sarah E. Pettigrew*. The writer was especially laudatory of Burdick's devotion to his friends, and only excerpts can be used:

Aside from the Pettigrew, there were numerous other ships, about a dozen or so, laid up at the levee during the continuance of the blockade., which became food for flames when the prowess of Farragut and Bailey once more opened the lower Mississippi to the commerce of the world.

That the ships were cleared out at that time, goes without saying, so that they were flying light; but Capt. Burdick, whose hard-earned savings were invested in his ship, elected to stay by her and see that the wharf rats did not get away with anchors, sails and rigging, so that the "bonny boat" would be unable to sail when England and France recognized the new Confederacy. The great clear decks and 'tween decks would be a revelation to a person unfamiliar with nautical matters, as showing the vast capacity of a ship capable of stowing 5000 bales of the somewhat loosely compressed cotton of those days.

I am not certain that the other ships had keepers, but my impression is that Capt. Burdick had general supervision of the whole.[192]

The writer, a newspaperman, etched a word picture of what life was like in a city under war-time blockade. And he spoke of the parties held on the *Sarah E. Pettigrew* as she laid at the levee as seafarers waited out their internments. One of the participants he mentioned was "Jim" Hickey, "one of our brightest and merriest wags that Portsmouth has ever produced, Heaven rest his soul! he's dead." The letter was only signed "John."

Four years before Burdick's death, the Alabama Claims Commission settled with the owners of the *Sarah E. Pettigrew*. It was case No. 503 in the files. Daniel Marcy received $8,218; estate of S. C. Thwing, $2,054; estate of Washington Williams, $58,218; estate of Albert R. Hatch, $4,109; with interest from May 12, 1861.

The ruling set a value of $72,599 on the ship. It's interesting to note that her two Confederate shareholders, Peter Marcy and Joseph J. Nickerson, received nothing.[193]

New Hampshire

SPECIFICATIONS: 1857. Samuel Badger. Billet head, square stern. Burthen, 999 tons. Length, 176 feet; beam, 35 feet; depth, 17.5 feet. Two decks. Original owners—J. N. Tarlton, William Simes, William D. Fernald, Thomas Weeks, Oliver Wilson, J. J. Matthews, and Samuel Badger.

It seems more than a little ironic that the two ships named *New Hampshire*, and also the two named *Granite State*, were all built in Maine. Samuel Badger built the two *New Hampshire*s and the first *Granite State*. The first *New Hampshire*, built in 1837, was lost in April 1857, about the time that Badger was laying the keel for another ship, so it was appropriate to keep a good name going, and most of the owners were New Hampshire men anyway.

Unhappily, Samuel Badger never saw the *New Hampshire* in the water. The master builder died on September 27 at the age of 63, and his death closed out the troika of great shipwrights who had so long dominated construction on the Piscataqua. A newspaper comment said he was "well known as an eminent shipbuilder, enterprising citizen and christian gentleman."[194] Badger's death delayed the launching of the *New Hampshire*, and she went down the ways the next week.

Capt. Thomas Weeks took the *New Hampshire* to sea on December 3, taking along as passengers Daniel Libbey and S. M. Merrick. The *New Hampshire* went into Mobile and there loaded for Liverpool. For the next two years Weeks was in command, and the *New Hampshire*'s service was the familiar routine of working between Liverpool and Le Havre and the cotton ports. Late in 1859, Capt. W. A. Lord took her over and was master until she was lost in 1867.

Over the years, the *New Hampshire* passed through the usual travails of a sailing vessel. In 1861, on a passage from New York to Liverpool, the ship lost her second mate, Harrison T. Franklin. The poor devil was washed overboard in a heavy sea. He was "the second son of Mr. F. A. Franklin of this city. An upright young man of much promise, and his loss is severely felt by his relatives and friends."[195]

In 1863, while on passage from New York to San Francisco, the *New Hampshire* later reported the unusual circumstance of being ignored by the USS *Lancaster*, although flying a distress signal. The *New Hampshire* reached the Pacific by making some repairs herself, but she kept on leaking badly:

> Leak continued to increase, until it reached 1800 strokes per hour. The crew kept at the pumps day and night, until they were exhausted. After the most laborious of exertions by the officers and crew, the New Hampshire succeeded in getting into port on the 16th. Capt. Lord justly complains that assistance was refused him by one of our men-of-war, which passed by a short distance when his sign of distress by flying.[196]

The San Francisco paper said the *New Hampshire* was flying her flag with the Union upside down. If the incident was investigated, the report didn't reach newspapers in Portsmouth.

Once repaired in San Francisco, the *New Hampshire* went to Hong Kong carrying $110,000 in gold. From there she went to England. In February 1865, she was sold for £6,500 sterling and went under the British flag, although Lord continued as master. She went out to the East Indies again, and took on cargo at Akyab, Burma. On June 4, 1866, the *New Hampshire* put into Mauritius, leaking. The captain had to post a bottomry bond of $15,000 for repairs; the bond was payable within 20 days after her safe arrival. She arrived at Falmouth, England, on October 21, and went on to Bremerhaven, then back to Shields, England, where she was loaded for Bombay. It was her last passage. She was abandoned at sea in March 1867:

> Capt. Lord's report of the loss of ship New Hampshire, states that she sailed from Shields March 16, with a full cargo, and a crew of 23 men, for Bombay. From 22d to 25th, when in lat. 47 46 N, lon. 7 8 W, had variable winds and heavy weather.
>
> From 4 to 6 PM the wind, which was from the south, increased to a gale. At 8 PM took in the mizentopsail, and at 10 PM took in the foreroyal, a very heavy sea running at the time. At 12 midnight tried the pumps and found but little water in the ship. At 1 AM of the 26th was struck by a sea on the port side, which knocked the ship on her beam ends, and shifted the cargo, so that she lay with her starboard rail in the water. The pumps were then started, and kept going all the time, but no suck could be got. At daylight found the ship making more water than could pump, and it was concluded to try, if possible, and reach Sicily, supposed to bear E 25 miles. The ship was kept before the wind, but did not right. With everything adrift about the decks, and the lee braces foul and washed overboard, could not get to them to square the yards. At 10 AM saw a ship to windward, and finding our vessel had gone still further over, we hove to, and set a signal of distress, and there being a steamer in sight, after much delay, she bore down and spoke us, but did not come near enough for me to tell him our situation, or what I wanted, not even stopping her steam.
>
> The sea at this time running very heavily, it was thought best to try and get the ship off again, and try to reach Sicily, which was done about 11:30 AM; but, after running about twenty minutes, found it impossible to keep the ship afloat any longer, as the water was then up to lower decks. Hove to again and set signal of distress, and the ship beforementioned, then being about three miles to windward, immediately kept away for us. This was about 11:45, and proceeded to

get boats overboard. The long boat and one quarterboat were got out by noon, when we found the ship was settling down so fast that we had not time to take a single article with us, and only 15 succeeded in reaching the boats when the ship went down at 12:15, and eight of the crew with her. All efforts to save them proved fruitless, and after every search had been made, we got on board the English ship Koomah. On the 28th we were transferred to the English ship Constance, bound for London, and arrived at Gravesend on the 31st of March.[197]

Orozimbo

SPECIFICATIONS: 1858. Marcy & Pettigrew. South End. Billet head, square stern. Burthen, 890 tons. Length, 172.5 feet; beam, 33.3 feet; depth, 16.65 feet. Two decks. Original owners—Daniel Marcy, William Pettigrew, and True M. Ball, all of Portsmouth; S. C. Thwing, of Boston; Peter Marcy and Joseph J. Nickerson, of New Orleans.

Late in November 1857, the *Portsmouth Journal* noted the "general suspension of ship building." The newspaper was gratified to learn that the keel for a new ship [*Como*] had "just been laid in the yard of Messrs. Raynes & Son. So little prospect has there been for work that good carpenters, who have commanded $2 to $2.50 per day, have offered to work for 75 cents or a dollar a day. We hope the time for better wages is not more distant than the opening spring. Messrs. Marcy & Pettigrew, at their new ship yard at the South End, have just laid the keel of another ship."

The slack in shipbuilding was easily confirmed. In 1856, there had been 11 launchings of big craft; that fell off to 6 in 1857 and dropped to 4 in 1858. Various factors were responsible, among them a glut in new ships. After all, only so much cotton could be produced, and every new ship made the number of available bales smaller. And, too, the demand for transportation for immigrants was falling off. Finally, metal, steam-powered vessels were steadily increasing.

Daniel Marcy had retired from active sea duty, and the veteran master Joseph J. Nickerson took the *Orozimbo* to Boston under tow by the steam tug *Rescue*. From there, she went on to New Orleans and loaded for Queenstown. After some months away from home, she returned and was taken over by a Captain Folsom. A Captain Townsend had her in 1860, and, en route to New Orleans, the *Orozimbo* was dismasted and thrown on her beam ends off the Dry Tortugas. When she righted she had four feet of water in the hold, but made it to port. Along with the *Alice Ball*, she was interned briefly as East-port, Maine, because of her ownership. The *Liverpool Telegraph*, on May 16, 1863, reported the *Orozimbo*'s arrival at Callao and then the Chinchas, where she loaded guano for Hamburg, Germany.

At some point, the *Orozimbo* was sold in Bremen and renamed the *Nordstern*. In 1870, she was sold in Antwerp and became the *Pauline*.[198]

Como

SPECIFICATIONS: 1858. George Raynes, Jr. Billet head, square stern. Burthen, 943 tons. Length, 180.7 feet; beam, 33.4 feet; depth, 16.7 feet. Two decks. Original owners—Jonathan M. Tredick, Richard Jenness, and George W. Haven, all of Portsmouth; William Sheafe, of Boston.

The *Como* was launched on October 7 and taken to sea by a Captain Cobbs on November 8. She put into Boston and was loaded with ice for Madras. It seems that even an extensive ice trade was over for the Port of Portsmouth. Ice companies found it more expedient to ship their product by rail to Boston for storage in the big ice-houses than to send it to Portsmouth, which had poor rail connections with the interior. The *Como* took her ice to India, arriving there on April 7, 1859. She came back into Boston on January 7, 1860, and was sent to Mobile. With a cargo of cotton, the *Como* went to Liverpool, and then took a cargo to Calcutta.

She spent the Civil War years in the East Indian trade, and in 1864 was sold in Singapore for £11,000, going under the Union Jack. In 1871, loaded with railroad iron, she sailed from Cardiff, and foundered at sea on the passage. "Encountering severe gales, causing the vessel to leak badly. The crew worked until thoroughly exhausted, and were finally obliged to abandon her.... All hands were saved by the ship *Cornelius Grinnell* of New York, and taken to London."[199]

Donati

SPECIFICATIONS: 1858. Tobey & Littlefield. Billet head, square stern. Burthen, 898 tons. Length, 166 feet; beam, 34.25 feet; depth, 17.75 feet. Two decks. Original owner—Calvin Adams, of New York.

The sale of the *Donati* prompted a commentary on the slackness in the shipbuilding industry. The *Donati* had been ready for launching since the spring but didn't go down the ways until October. The vessel was named for an astronomer, G. B. Donati, who, in 1858, discovered a new comet with an orbit of 2,800 years. Calvin Adams paid $46,000 for her, so it's doubtful that Tobey & Littlefield even made expenses.[200]

The *Donati* was another rugged ship, along the lines of the *Alice Ball*. Capt. W. H. Adams of Bangor took the *Donati* to sea, headed for New Orleans with a cargo of hay and potatoes. Her passage took 17 days. She came back up the East Coast to Boston, and went back to New Orleans. She loaded and went to Liverpool, and there's no further news about her.

Harry Hastings

SPECIFICATIONS: 1858. Elbridge G. Pierce. Pierce Island. Burthen, 900 tons. Original owner—Henry Hastings, of Boston.

"Shipbuilding, though very dull, is not entirely extinct on the Piscataqua.... The ship now building at Pierce's Island for Messrs. Hastings of Boston, under the superintendence of Mr. Pierce, is nearly ready for caulking."[201] Harry Hastings had already had one ship, the clipper *Charger*, built on Pierce Island. Before that, Fernald & Pettigrew had built the clipper *Noonday* for him. Pierce was a newcomer to the Piscataqua shipbuilding scene, and he built only two, the *Harry Hastings* and the *Charger*. Coming to Portsmouth from Farmington, Maine, he confounded the local experts by making the two successful launches from Pierce Island. Prior to his arrival on the island, the floating dry dock for the Navy Yard had been built there in 1851–1852. Before the *Hastings* was launched, the *Journal* continued its pessimistic view of the industry, reporting on November 13:

> The shipping interest which is important to New England, still continues in a depressed state, and taken as a whole is absolutely losing money. On our own coasts, and in all foreign ports, freights are below paying rates, and that too notwithstanding the great cotton crop which must be carried abroad. The fact is, in the last seven years, more ships have been built than the legitimate commerce of the world demanded, and the dull times must remain till the the surplus is used up, as it will be by the partial suspension of building. So says the Newburyport Herald.

The *Harry Hastings* wasn't registered in the Portsmouth Customs District, so her exact measurements aren't in Nelson's records. However, she did leave the Port of Portsmouth on December 1, under tow by the *R. B. Forbes*. "They presented a handsome appearance as they glided down the river against the full strength of the tide — what they gained by working last Sunday remains to be seen."[202] A week earlier, November 27, the *Journal* had praised the ship's owner:

> COMMENDABLE. — It is a time honored custom to compliment the workmen upon the completion of a new ship by a treat. Henry Hastings, Esq. the owner of the new ship "Harry Hastings," just launched at Peirce's Island, exhibited excellent taste in his method; doing away with the miserable practice of furnishing drink to the workmen, by placing $75 in the hands of a dealer to furnish each of the men in his employ with a Thanksgiving turkey. His example is highly commendable, and will be more pleasantly remembered by both receivers and donor than would any "treat" in the too common acceptance of the term. For it is a treat not only to the workmen, but also to their better halves, and the cheerful little ones, who gave such heartfelt cheers at the launch of the noble ship.

George W. Tucker was master of the *Harry Hastings* when she left the Piscataqua for Boston. She didn't linger long; loaded for San Francisco, she sailed on December 15, and arrived on May 3, 1859.[203] Her time of 130 days was far from a record, but still respectable— many of the clippers didn't do much better. She made a fast turn-around, sailing on May 28 for New York and entering on September 14.[204] She had bettered her outbound passage by 30 days—very respectable. Tucker left her, and a Captain Coleman took her to London and the Far East. On December 27, 1862, the *Journal* reported that the *Harry Hastings* had sailed from Akyab on April 16 for Falmouth, England, and "has not been heard from."

Georgianna

SPECIFICATIONS: 1859. Marcy & Pettigrew. South End. Billet head, square stern. Burthen, 891 tons. Length, 174 feet; beam, 33.15 feet; depth, 16.575 feet. Two decks. Original owners—Marcy & Pettigrew, William Martin, of Portsmouth; Peter Marcy, of New Orleans; S. C. Thwing, of Boston.

Before 1859 was well under way, the *Journal*, on March 26, reprinted a lengthy article from the *Boston Courier*, that discussed the depressed state of shipbuilding. The writer carefully documented the phenomenal growth during the 1850s, tracing its causes to: (1) immigration in great numbers from Europe; (2) the discovery of gold in California and Australia; (3) the Crimean War; and (4) the unusual demand for guano. In summing up, the writer made the flat statement that "there is an excess of equipped tonnage, over and above the business demands of the world." He concluded: "the true remedy for the existing evils is a total suspension of building."

That conditions were worsening for shipbuilders can be seen in the fact that the Piscataqua yards produced only four ships in 1859, one of them a medium clipper, the *Shooting Star*—the last of the type ever launched on the river. For George Raynes & Son, the construction of the *Shooting Star* was the end of a glorious era. A few months later the shipyard was in the hands of a receiver. However, ships would again be launched from there, with William D. Fernald as the builder.

The *Georgianna* was the first of the nonclippers launched in 1859. She was followed by the *Richard III* and the second *Portsmouth*. The *Journal* reported on September 17:

> The ship Georgianna, was launched in fine style, from the yard of Messrs. Marcy & Pettigrew, near the South Mill, on Monday forenoon, and now lies at Pier Wharf, foot of Daniel street. She is about 1100 tons, and owned by Peter Marcy of New Orleans, and the builders. This is the third ship which has been launched from this yard; and there are now but two other vessels on the stocks in this harbor — a ship about 1000 tons, at Tobey & Littlefield's, Noble's Island, (for sale,) and a ship at the Badger yard, across the river.

Capt. John Salter was the only master the *Georgianna* had in her short existence. Salter took her to New Orleans, where she loaded for Liverpool. She arrived there on January 16, 1860. Returning to her home port, New Orleans, she loaded for New York. Going back down to New Orleans, she ran into a storm, lost her sails, and went on her beam ends off the Dry Tortugas. Repaired, she left New Orleans for Liverpool but was hit by lightning on November 20 north of Bermuda. She caught fire, and the crew was taken off by the *Levi Woodbury*. Insurance on the freight money and vessel was $64,000. Her cargo was valued at $210,000.[205]

Richard III

SPECIFICATIONS: 1859. Tobey & Littlefield. Billet head, square stern. Burthen, 898 tons. Length, 166 feet; beam, 34.25 feet; depth, 17.125 feet. Two decks. Original owners—Richard Hawley Tucker, Daniel Stone, Capt. J. E. Scott, and the Lenoxes.

It wasn't a Shakespearian scholar who named the *Richard III*; it was a Tucker family affair from first to last. However, a myth has been going the rounds ever since. The legend goes to the effect that Richard Holbrook Tucker's daughter-in-law, Mrs. Richard Holbrook Tucker, Jr., gave birth to a son the day the ship was launched. However, Miss Jane S. Tucker of Wiscasset, the daughter of Richard Holbrook Tucker III, insists the story isn't true, and the chronology bears her out. Her father was born on October 29, 1859, and the *Richard III*, at that time nameless, was launched on November 8. It's hair-splitting, really, because Richard Hawley Tucker, founder of the shipping industry, wrote on November 3 that he had had "Richard III" put on the stern of the new ship in recognition of the compliment.

However, the human Richard Tucker III didn't go into the shipping business; he became an astronomer and lived in California, where Jane Tucker was born.[206] Miss Tucker has told me that her father often spoke of making a voyage on the *Richard III*, and how beautiful the ship was. Unfortunately, he also saw her, 25 years later at Juneau, after she had been stripped down to a barge.

Capt. J. E. Scott departed Portsmouth on December 21 for Charleston, arriving there on January 4, 1860. Samuel G. Gardiner was mate, and the *Richard III* carried 170 tons of hay on speculation. Again, Jane Tucker has provided log extracts that give a clear picture of the long career of the *Richard III*. The ship had to wait two months for a cargo at Charleston, finally loading with 3,846 bales of Upland and 54 of Sea Island, plus rice and rosin. Freight money was £2,922. While in Liverpool, the *Richard III* was coppered. Her return cargo consisted of 130 tons of railroad iron and salt, charged to the captain's own account. Freight was £563, including primage.

Unlike the *R. H. Tucker*, the *Richard III* didn't get involved in blockade running; or, if she did, it doesn't show in her logs. When the Civil War started she was en route from Greenock, Scotland, to San Francisco, under Capt. John K. Greenough. She was carrying 1,445 tons of coal for H. N. Dickenson & Co. The ship arrived there on August 27, having taken 166 days on the passage. From San Francisco, she dropped down the coast to the Chincha Islands, but didn't get out of there until March 1, 1862, with 1,633 tons of guano at 60s. a

The Richard III *was still another of the vessels that the Tuckers of Wiscasset had built for them on the Piscataqua. Jane S. Tucker collection.*

ton, or £4,899, for Antony Gibbs & Sons. The ship put into Cork for orders, having been out 116 days, and then went on to Greenock. Her next passage was back to the Chinchas to load guano for Barcelona, Spain, at $21 a ton. From Barcelona she went to Rangoon in ballast. She loaded 1,585 tons of rice at 80s., plus another 100 tons bagged. That cargo was off-loaded at Amsterdam, and she then went to Cardiff. Samuel G. Gardiner, her long-time mate, became master, with George Franklin as mate, on the voyage to Rio de Janeiro; then George Church became master, with Alexander Jenkins as mate. Throughout the 1860s the *Richard III* roamed the world. In 1866, she took 63 Chinese passengers from Hong Kong to Singapore; it's not clear whether the passengers were charged $175 as a group or whether that was the individual fare.

In 1869, with E. H. Wood as master and Alfred Call as mate, she sailed from Charleston to Wiscasset to refit. The ship spent the summer and early fall in Wiscasset, which must have been a pleasure for the master and his oft-separated family. The *Richard III* departed Wiscasset on October 30, and arrived in New Orleans on November 26. She was there nearly three months before leaving with 3,357 bales, 1,522,193 pounds; and 1,200 staves. Freight money was $13,681.77, plus primage. She took that load to Le Havre and went to Cardiff. There she was remetaled and reclassified (as to insurance risk), and took on 1,272 tons of railroad iron for New York. From New York, she went to Savannah, departing that port on November 12, 1870, with 3,445 bales of cotton. Freight money was £3,501, plus primage.

Back and forth she went. E. H. Woods was still in command in March 1872 when the *Richard III* left New Orleans carrying a cargo with freight money of £3,461, plus primage. When she recrossed the Atlantic it was to Philadelphia, with scrap iron, pig iron, soda ash, and crates—freight money, £1,1423.

From Philadelphia, she went to Savannah under Capt. J. T. Hubbard, who would be master for the next few years. Hubbard found cargo in Charleston, not Savannah: Upland, at half an English penny; freight money was £3,648. She brought back salt. On April 25, 1873, with E. W. Reed as mate, she left Charleston with 1,735,875 pounds of cotton—freight money, £3,750. At Liverpool, the ship was again coppered, and loaded merchandise, earth ware, pig iron, some barrels of stout, and tin plate, with freight money about £1,000.

Mrs. J. T. Hubbard shipped aboard the *Richard III* on her next passage. The ship left Philadelphia, taking to Antwerp refined petroleum in casks of 42 gallons. Freight money was £3,184. She came back across to Charleston in ballast, and returned to Liverpool. Coming back, she brought salt to Gloucester, and then went to Wiscasset, arriving June 10, 1874. Her stay didn't last long; with Richard III himself on board as well as Mrs. Hubbard, she went to Liverpool. On one trip Mrs. Hubbard stayed over in Liverpool, where apparently her daughter, Fannie, was born. The ship spent the summer of 1876 at Wiscasset, and a dance was held on board. Again, in 1877, the *Richard III* was "hauled up" in Wiscasset for the summer. By 1880, the Hubbards were the parents of three children, all of whom made a summer passage in the ship.

E. H. Wood was the *Richard III*'s last commander while owned by the Tuckers. In 1881, Captain Wood went to Liverpool from Charleston with 3,672 bales of cotton. The ship came back from Liverpool in ballast, and in December 1881 hauled more cotton to Liverpool. From that port she went to San Francisco, arriving in November 1882. In ending her log extract, Miss Tucker wrote:

> Purchased by Middlemas & Boole. Changed hands several times during fifteen years of running coastwise and offshore in the Pacific. Captains James McIntyre and T. J. Connor. In 1897 converted to a barge and made trips from British Columbia to Alaska. Lost, January 1907, in Clarence Straits, Juneau.

Portsmouth

SPECIFICATIONS: 1859. John Neal. Kittery Foreside. Billet head, square stern. Burthen, 994 tons. Length, 176 feet; beam, 34.9 feet; depth, 17.45 feet. Two decks. Original owners—James N. Tarlton, T. J. Coburn, William Simes, Daniel Marcy, Thomas E. Call, William Fernald, William Preston, and John Neal.

John Neal had a ready-built shipyard at hand for constructing the second *Portsmouth*. The yard was in the estate of his father-in-law, the late Samuel Badger. Again it seems odd that so many vessels bore New Hampshire–related names, yet no square-rigger carried the name of Kittery, where they were built.

The *Portsmouth* was the last big vessel launched in the 1850s. Ships like her were possible only because of the craftsmanship that went into them. One of the skilled artisans who worked on the *Portsmouth* was Chandler Brooks, of Kittery. Brooks was apprenticed as a joiner, and he worked for William Badger through the master's last years. Brooks just kept at his trade when Samuel Badger moved to the Foreside. Other vessels Brooks worked on included the ships *Piscataqua* and *Merrimac* and the schooners *Norah* and *Mary J. Adams*. Brooks died in 1890 at the age of 87.

The *Portsmouth* didn't get clear of the Port of Portsmouth until early January of 1860, when she sailed for Mobile under Capt. Jeremiah Trefethen. She went to Liverpool, and came back into New York on August 17, 1860. Trefethen was from Kittery, and he died in New York on September 19; the body was brought to Kittery for burial. Probate records show him as owning at least 5/48 of the *Portsmouth*, which shares were paid to his heirs, after being appraised at $1,000 each.

In 1862, under a Captain Borland, the *Portsmouth* came into the Port of Portsmouth on May 7. She was one of the last of the Piscataqua-built ships ever to return to the river bringing a cargo. The *Journal* proudly announced on May 24 that the *Portsmouth* had arrived carrying 6,000 tons of salt—which, if it had been true, would probably have been the largest shipment of salt into Portsmouth until Granite State Minerals started operating. Unfortunately, the paper had to retract the statement: 6,000 hogsheads of salt was correct, "in weight not far from 1,400 tons, which is a pretty good cargo for a ship not quite a thousand tons measurement. This fine ship sailed again on Tuesday [May 27] for New York under Captain Herman A. Tarlton." She went to Cadiz and loaded salt for New York, arriving there on October 2, 1862. Tarlton was relieved in 1865 by Capt. Robert Boardman. In February 1865 it was reported:

266   Tall Ships of the Piscataqua

The ship Portsmouth, owned by Jas. N. Tarlton and others of this city, is placed among the missing, in the Boston record of marine disasters for January. The ship sailed from Navassa, about the middle of Oct. for Queenstown, since which time no tidings have been heard from her, and she is supposed to have been lost in the gale which prevailed in the vicinity of Cuba and the Banks about the 21st of October. There is a possibility of her crew having been rescued by some outward Chinaman or Pacific trader.

The Portsmouth was commanded by Capt. Robt. Boardman of this city. The chief mate was Horton Card of Newcastle. Among the seamen were Thomas Yeaton (son of Mr. Moses Yeaton) and Charles A. Weeks (only son of Mr. Charles P. Weeks) of this city, and both estimable young men. Capt. Boardman was a very capable young officer, — son of Dr. J. H. Boardman, and brother of Asst. Paymaster Boardman, who recently died on the ship Stonewall at Havana — and these bereaved families have the full sympathy of the community in their affliction. We think the losses of our city in men and money concerned in commerce was never so heavy in any year as during 1865. In fact, it seems to us we have not been called upon to chronicle so many terrible disasters during ten years previous to this one. — *Chr.*[207]

In 1883, people's memories of the *Portsmouth* were refreshed when a painting of the vessel was placed on display:

A picture placed in a window of Montgomery's music and art store last week has attracted much attention. It represents the former ship Portsmouth of this port, Capt. Herman A. Tarlton, as she appeared when hauling the wind off the Western islands to signal the bark Anglo Saxon of Portland, Me., the latter desiring to correct her longitude. The Portsmouth was a vessel of about a thousand tons, and though not a clipper was anything but a dull sailer: on the trip when the incident represented occurred, she made the passage from New York to Cadiz, Spain, in sixteen days, and the return trip to New York in nineteen, the crew on the ship's arrival in the latter port being in debt two days' wages, not having worked out the two months' advance received on shipping. The picture was painted in 1862 by M. Conti of Naples, from a sketch taken on board the ship, the vessel being carefully measured by men sent by the painter, so that her proportions might be exact.[208]

V The 1860s

In the early months of 1860, optimism was rife in the Port of Portsmouth in eager anticipation of a revival in shipbuilding—perhaps even reaching the high plateaus of 1854 and 1856. A news report said:

> In taking a run through the ship yards in this city, we find quite a revival in this branch of industry, which has been at low water mark for a year or two past. In the old yard of George Raynes, we find laid out the keel of a clipper bark of 350 tons which is to be built by Mr. William Fernald, recently of Newburyport, for Messrs. Draper & Son of Boston. She is to have a heavy frame of white oak, with hard-pine planking, and is intended for the Mediterranean trade.
>
> Messrs. Tobey & Littlefield, at Noble's Island, who have built some of the best ships ever constructed on the river, have nearly completed a beautiful ship of about 1,000 tons, for Messrs. Page, Richardson & Co. of Boston. She will be launched in the course of a week.
>
> As soon as the ways are cleared a ship of about the same size is to be built for Jonathan M. Tredick, Esq., of this city, which will be pushed forward with all convenient dispatch.
>
> Messrs. Tobey & Littlefield have also laid the keel of another 1000-ton ship, which is not yet sold. All three of these vessels will be constructed of white oak, in a most thorough manner, and will undoubtedly sustain the reputation of the builders, as reliable and successful ship builders.
>
> Messrs. Snow and Badger, at the ship yard of Marcy & Pettigrew, have on the stocks, nearly ready for launching, a

The devastating effect of the Civil War on southern shipping is clearly demonstrated by scarcity of vessels along the once-thriving Savannah waterfront. The photo was made in 1865 while the cotton trade was still depressed. Courtesy of the Library of Congress.

beautiful schooner of 130 tons, which is awaiting a purchaser.

Messrs. Neal and Matthews, at the yard of the late Capt. Samuel Badger, at Kittery Foreside, are getting out the frames for a vessel, but have not yet determined to put them up.

There is a prospect that ship building in this section will recover to some extent from the recent stagnation, and that much work will be provided for our skillful mechanics. As it is, the wages of ship's carpenters have slightly advanced, and will probably remain through the season a little higher than last year. — *Gazette*.[1]

However, realization of the hoped-for boom proved elusive. Only 14 three-masted square-rigged vessels were launched during the decade, along with 10 fairly sizable barks. Tobey & Littlefield alone built 10 of the 14 ships, 3 of them in 1860. John Neal built 1 ship. William F. Fernald built a bark, the *Fury*. In 1861, 2 ships were built; 1862, none; 1863, 3; 1864, 1; 1865, 1; 1866, 1; 1867, 2; 1868, 1; 1869, 1.

A brief news squib in March of 1861 contained none of the optimism of the previous year:

> SHIP-BUILDING IN PORTSMOUTH. — Messrs. Tobey & Littlefield, at their yard on Noble's Island, have a ship on the stocks, nearly completed. She is of about a thousand tons burthen, and we believe is for sale.
>
> Marcy and Petigrew, at their yard at the foot of Pleasant street, have recently commenced building another ship, also of about a thousand tons.
>
> These, we think, are all the vessels now in course of construction on the Piscataqua.[2]

Several factors entered into the gradual decline of Piscataqua shipbuilding, not the least of which was the constant improvement in steam-propelled vessels. Today, it would be like trying to decide whether to fly over the Atlantic in a propeller-driver aircraft or a jet. The early transatlantic steamers had had a lot of tragic accidents, costing many lives, but they were becoming safer. Great Britain was leading the way in steamship development, forcing the rest of the maritime nations to follow. That was part of the story; of more immediate damage to shipbuilding along the East Coast was the outbreak of the Civil War. A news item datelined Calcutta, July 22, 1861, emphasized the problem:

> The employment of American vessels for the present is about stopped, from the impossibility of shippers obtaining insurance, as most of the insurance companies have received orders from home to avoid them altogether until further orders, while the few that will insure are so limited as to extent and direction as to preclude any business of importance being done.[3]

Another news item in the summer of 1861 defined another aspect of the problem, at least for the Port of Portsmouth. The ship *Frank Pierce* came into the river for repairs, but she had to go on to Boston because there were no mechanics to work on her—they were all on the Portsmouth Navy Yard.[4]

Tobey & Littlefield ventured into construction of a steam-driven merchantman in 1864, an event that will be discussed in detail later. But the demand for big sailing vessels stayed minimal. On June 9, 1866, the *Journal* discussed the slack in shipbuilding:

> This is a question of no little importance, one which many are asking, — and one which requires attention in a national point of view. It is well known that the danger of merchantmen in the time of the rebellion led to the sale of many of

our ships abroad — and also that the depredations of the Confederate privateers, and the numerous wrecks and disasters, have greatly reduced the number of our ships, and placed the advantages of commerce in the hands of other nations. It was to be hoped that with the change of times our ship yards would again resource with the sound of the hammer, and ships would be seen going up wherever a yard could be found. But it is not so in New England, or elsewhere in our country. The true cause is, that the excessively high duties on the various materials necessary for ship building, and expense of labor as a secondary item, make the cost of our ships so great that they cannot come in competition with the cheaper vessels built elsewhere, and make a living business.

In former times on our river there have been a dozen vessels building at the same time, when the call for them was no greater than at present: but now we have but one, and that in the progress of slow construction. In former times on the shores of the Kennebec, thirty ships might be seen going up at the same time — now probably not half a dozen can be seen in the course of construction. The same remark applies to ship yards every where on our coast.

While the fact of the hard pressure of duties on our shipping is forbidding their construction, our neighbors down east, just on the line, are reaping a rich harvest. We have before us in a private letter from New Brunswick, a list of seventy-one vessels, measuring 47,578 tons, built this spring and now building there, of which only five are of less than 300 tons — twenty of them are over 1000 tons, and some are up to 1500 and 1600. Of these there were building at

St. John and vicinity,	29	vessels	tons	25,625
Outports,	8	"	"	2,470
North Shore,	21	"	"	11,695
Schediac,	13	"	"	7,788

On the whole coast of New England, and over our whole country, there are probably not now constructing more ships than in the little British province north of us. Ships of 1300 tons can be built there for between 40 and 50,000 dollars; while at home, under the disadvantages of the times, the cost is nearly double. They are many of them constructed of hackmatac, a cheaper material than we use, but they possess all the advantages for the carrying trade, and enter into it to supply the deficiency in our own mercantile marine, much to their advantage.

What can government do, and what is its duty to do, to change the current, and increase the means of successfully doing our own business in our own vessels? The answer is plain. Give encouragement to the builders by granting drawbacks on the material used — on the copper — the iron — the cordage, and other materials, the duties upon which are now so burdensome as to prevent progress. A change of policy in this respect would so increase the business of ship building, that government would be a gainer instead of a loser by the aid thus afforded. The matter should immediately receive attention by those who have the power to regulate it.

The U.S. House of Representatives did take cognizance of the plight of the shipbuilders in 1867 in the form of a resolution that would give the constructors a drawback on the raw materials they were using. However, the building of sailing ships—merchant ships, that is—was never to make a strong comeback. As subsequent events will show, seven more big square-riggers were built in the 1870s, but the harsh reality was that Portsmouth's heyday was over. However, that wasn't yet foreseen in May 1860, when the *Liverpool Packet* went into the water.

Liverpool Packet

SPECIFICATIONS: 1860. Tobey & Littlefield. Billet head, square stern. Burthen, 992 tons. Length, 175 feet; beam, 35 feet; depth 17.5 feet. Two decks. Original owners—Page & Richardson, of Boston.

Fifty-five years before, William Badger had built and launched a small ship, the *Liverpool Packet*, and, during the War of 1812, a British privateer of that name had raised hob with shipping along the New England coast, so the name was a familiar one to the people living in the Piscataqua region. The *Liverpool Packet* was launched on May 11 in the traditional style, "in the presence of a large number of spectators. She is built of oak, copper-fastened, treenailed and finished in the first style of workmanship. Page, Richardson & Co. of Boston own her. She is intended for their line of Boston and Liverpool packets, and will be commanded by Captain Freeman Crosby."[5]
Captain Crosby took the *Liverpool Packet* to St. John, where she loaded lumber for Liverpool. After his arrival in Liverpool, Captain Crosby wrote a letter, which was published in the *Journal* on August 30, 1860.

PORTSMOUTH SHIPS — THE LIVERPOOL PACKET. — We are justly proud of our ships, knowing that some of the best vessels afloat have been built here, and we take much pleasure in chronicling anything that is said in their praise. We have heard from the Liverpool Packet, commanded by Capt. Freeman Crosby, which sailed from here for St. John, N. B., and thence to Liverpool, in May last. A private letter received from Liverpool says: — "The Packet has been examined by all the Inspectors here, and they pronounce her good. Several ship builders have visited her, all of whom admire her model, and some of them have taken notes. The dock master says she looked nice enough to be placed in the exhibition at London." The Liverpool Packet was built here during the present year by Messrs. Tobey & Littlefield, is 993 tons per register, owned by Messrs. Page, Richardson & Co. of Boston and others, and is one of the best ships in the United States. We spoke of the beauty of her model, and the completeness of her outfit about the time of her sailing, and we are glad to learn that she has fully realized the expectations of her owners and builders, in her sailing and all other qualities.

An expected revival in immigration inspired the *Packet*'s owners to add one more vessel to their fleet in 1860, the *City of Boston*.[6] The Civil War changed the *Packet*'s service, and she went to the Orient. The *Liverpool Packet* sailed from Shanghai on September 15, 1863, and was never heard from again.[7]

Manchester

SPECIFICATIONS: 1860. Tobey & Littlefield. Billet head, square stern. Burthen, 1,066 tons. Length, 178 feet; beam, 36 feet; depth 18 feet. Two decks. Original owner—Preston Ames, of Boston.

Not much is known about the *Manchester*. She was launched in September, and, under a Captain Trask, she cleared the Port of Portsmouth on September 28, under tow by the steamer *Joseph Bell*. En route to New York, she had to seek refuge in Newport, Rhode Island. After the bad weather, she moved to New York. She cleared out of there for Liverpool, working as a packet.

Nelson listed her as captured and burned by the CSS *Alabama*, but he gave no details or source for the statement.[8]

Santee

SPECIFICATIONS: 1860. Tobey & Littlefield. Figurehead, round stern. Burthen, 896 tons. Length, 174 feet; beam, 33.25 feet; depth 16.625 feet. Two decks. Original owners—Jonathan and T. Salter Tredick.

Two vessels named *Santee* were launched on the Piscataqua within five years of each other. One, the USS *Santee,* was built on the Portsmouth Navy Yard. Tobey and Littlefield launched the other *Santee* on October 30. The *Journal* wrote on December 1:

> She now lies at the Pier Wharf [foot of State Street], nearly ready for sea, under command of that active and experienced master, Capt. William Parker. She is, we think, of different model from any ship built here — a medium clipper, and capacious. The material and workmanship are of the first order; having numerous extra bolts, and the most secure fastenings of refined iron. We may safely say that a superior ship has not been built on the river.
>
> The cabin is a handsome specimen of the skill of our home artists. The beautiful mahogany, rosewood and maple finish of the cabin was by A. T. Joy, — the painting and graining by Edward D. Coffin, — the upholstery by S. M. Dockum. The arrangement of the work was by Thomas Martin, master joiner. The cabin is about 15 feet square. In place of staterooms on each side are recesses with sofas, and light and air are admitted on each side directly into the cabin. The new arrangement is a decided improvement on the old narrow cabin.
>
> The rigging was the work of Messrs. Deering & Yeaton.

Capt. William Parker took the *Santee* to New York. Parker was then 56 years old, a veteran of more than 40 years at sea. He was in his 86th year when he died in 1889. The *Santee* departed New York on December 27, 1860, for Liverpool, arriving there on February 5.[9] From Liverpool, she went to Calcutta, taking 108 days on the passage. She was ordered to Colombo (Sri Lanka) and then back to Europe. In 1863, while on a passage from Akyab to Falmouth, England, she was captured by the Confederate raider *Conrad,* later named the *Tuscaloosa.* It was reported that she was captured on April 28, and bonded. The paper commented that the bond was a "handsome sum" because she was a vessel of nearly a thousand tons.[10] The *Journal,* a few weeks later, said the first reports were that the *Santee* had been burned, but that she was actually under bond.

The *Santee*'s next commander was Albert T. Salter, a nephew of one of the owners and a cousin to the other. Captain Salter was only in his 20s. He died in Washington, D.C., in 1905. After the Civil War the *Santee* continued in the East Indian trade. In 1867, she loaded at Calcutta for New York at $8 a ton for 100 tons of saltpeter; $13 for linseed; and other cargo at $14.50 per ton.[11] From New York she went around Cape Horn to San Francisco, taking 54 days on the passage. A Captain McGraw had her in her last years and was in command when she was lost in 1870. A news report said:

> PROBABLE LOSS OF A PORTSMOUTH SHIP. — The ship which struck the rocks off Skibbereen, south coast of Ireland, and sunk, on the 30th of December (as before reported), is supposed the Santee, of Portsmouth, N. H. She was commanded by Capt. Magraw, and was on the voyage from Guanape to Liverpool with a cargo of guano. A few things had washed ashore, and among them was a portion of an iron stove bearing the name of "Joseph Sargeant, Boston, No. 4," which leads to the supposition that the ill-fated vessel was the Santee, as her owners state that the stove used on board was of this discription. A few bags had also been found which appeared to have contained guano. The vessel was fully due at her port of destination several weeks ago. Nothing is known as to the fate of her crew.
>
> The Santee was an A1 ship of 1078 tons register built at Portsmouth N. H., in 1860, and was owned by Messrs. T. M. & T. S. Tredick.[12]

Piscataqua

SPECIFICATIONS: 1860. John Neal. Kittery Foreside. Figurehead, square stern. Burthen, 890 tons. Length, 173 feet; beam, 33.25 feet; depth 16.625 feet. Two decks. Original owners—James N. Tarlton, William Simes, Horton D. Walker, et al.

The third merchant sailing vessel to honor the fast-flowing river on which they were launched, the *Piscataqua* slid into the water on December 1. The first *Piscataqua* was built in Dover in 1804; the second in Kittery in 1852. Seven years would pass before John Neal launched another ship from his father-in-law's old yard. Neal had worked for years under Samuel Badger, and after the latter's death in 1857 he built the *Portsmouth*, which was followed by the *Piscataqua*, then the *Merrimack* in 1867. His last vessel, the *Granite State*, was in partnership with Daniel Marcy in 1877. John Neal was killed on May

10, 1898, when he was struck by a street car in Kittery. Neal was then 84 and apparently became confused, stepping back into the car after he had safely crossed the tracks.

The *Piscataqua* was taken to sea by a Captain Borland on January 6, 1861, sailing for Mobile to load for Liverpool. Sometime in 1862, the *Piscataqua* was taken over by Capt. Nathaniel G. Weeks of Greenland. She left New York in July for Liverpool. She had William Wright, of Orono, Maine, and Nathaniel M. Jewett and Everett T. Howard, of Bangor, as passengers. Also on the list was William Simes, Jr., son of one of the owners.

On June 30, 1864, the *Piscataqua* had a brush with one of the Confederate cruisers. In 1885, under Alabama Claim No. 2626, the various surviving partners were paid damages. John Neal and Daniel Marcy each received $597; Samuel Adams and John Broughton, $1,155; Oliver Wilson, James P. Bartlett, and George W. Pendexter, $577 each; William and Joseph Simes, as executors, $577; William B. Trask, as administrator, for Horton D. Walker, $1,155; William H. Hackett, administrator, $577. The total came to $8,121.[13]

In 1865, the *Piscataqua* had trouble on a passage from Cardiff to Bassein, Burma. The *Chronicle* said on August 11:

> SHIP PISCATAQUA. — We are informed by the first officer of the ship Piscataqua, before reported put into Cape Town, in distress, while on the voyage from Cardiff to Bassilan, that after Capt. Tompson was washed overboard, he assumed the full command of the ship and carried her safe into Cape Town, where he delivered her to the United States Consul. He states that the romantic story which has been published in some of our contemporaries is absolutely without foundation, and as it was calculated to do great injustice to his character, he desires an emphatic contradiction.

Nelson wrote that the *Piscataqua* ran up on the rocks at the Cape of Good Hope and became a total loss on July 20, 1865.[14]

City of Montreal

SPECIFICATIONS: 1861. Tobey & Littlefield. Figurehead, square stern. Burthen, 996 tons. Length, 178 feet; beam, 34.7 feet; depth 17.35 feet. Two decks. Original owner—Richardson and Co., of Boston.

The *City of Montreal* bears an unusual distinction: she was the last Piscataqua-built square-rigger ever to return to the Port of Portsmouth with cargo in her hold. But that was far in the future when the *City of Montreal* was launched on March 30, with the *Chronicle* offering praise: "These enterprising builders have built some of the best ships ever floated on the Piscataqua; and Richardson & Co. having purchased several of them, are, of course, satisfied of their being No. One." Not only was the *Chronicle* enthused but so was a spectator at the launching, who wrote:

> *Messrs. Editors:* — Having witnessed the launch of the new ship "City of Montreal" from the ship-yard of Messrs. Tobey & Littlefield, this morning, I cannot refrain from expressing through your columns, (if you will allow me the privilege,) my extreme delight on the occasion. As I saw the masterpiece of labor and skill glide from the spot on which she was reared, safely into the water, and then gazed with admiration upon her beautiful model and magnificent appearance, I could but congratulate her builders on their great success. This ship is owned by Messrs. Page, Richardson & Co., of Boston, and is the fourth ship launched from the yard of Messrs. T. & L. within the past year; three of which have been purchased by the above named owners.
>
> Much credit is due to these men of enterprise, who in such times of alarm and discouragement continue in their educated and legitimate business, while nearly the whole country seems paralyzed with fear.
>
> The result of their endeavors thus far is conclusive evidence that they are equal to the business in which they have engaged. If their pecuniary means at the commencement were limited, their ability was abundant, and although they have had to compete with men of fortune, yet they have, by eminent faculties, personal independence and principles of honor, continued to prosper; their ships now afloat are reflecting credit upon them; and justice requires me to say that our city is greatly indebted to them.[15]

Shortly after the launching, the *Chronicle*, on April 16, again waxed enthusiastic over the *City of Montreal*:

> THE NEW SHIP "City of Montreal," (the only thing about her which we don't like is her long name,) now lying at Pier Wharf in this city, is a beautiful craft — one of the finest ships we ever examined. She is to sail for Montreal immediately, and has been visited by many of our citizens within a few days. She was built in the most thorough manner, by Toby & Littlefield, of this city; and no care or expense has been spared, in any

department, to render her one of the best vessels afloat —
which she undoubtedly is, as well as one of the most richly
finished and furnished. The spars, &c., are from the yard of
Wm. R. Martin; the rigging was done by Deering & Yeaton; the
painting by Edward D. Coffin; the cabin work and upholstery
by A. T. Joy & Son; and each and all is excellent and elegant
— in keeping with the substantial symmetry of the hull. The
"City of Montreal" is owned by Page, Richardson & Co.; and
goes forth from her birth-place, probably, forever, — another
floating monument to the skill of Portsmouth mechanics.

As the story of the *City of Montreal* develops, it will be seen
that she was deserving of that praise. Under Capt. John Bush, the
City of Montreal left the Port of Portsmouth on April 20 and arrived in
Montreal on May 9.

On May 20, 1862, the Journal said the New York Shipping List
"notes the sale of A-1 new ship *City of Montreal*...at $60,000, bought
by Thomas Dunham and Stephen W. Cary to go in Dunham's London
Line." She began sailing the North Atlantic trade routes, and later
she was on a passage from London to Boston when her captain
became ill.[16] That was off the coast of Ireland, but the shipping notes
failed to say whether she put into an Irish port or came to Boston.
With that she disappeared from Portsmouth marine notes for more
than 30 years. In November 1898 it was reported:

> The barge City of Montreal, now discharging coal at the
> North End coal pockets, was built at this port 30 years ago.
> Her keel was laid in the old shipyard on Noble's Island, by
> Tobey & Littlefield. She was fitted out as a full-rigged ship.
> After being in the merchant business about 25 years, she was
> purchased by a coal syndicate and converted into a barge.[17]

Grimy from coal dust, the *City of Montreal* in 1898 was a far
cry from the proud sailing vessel that left the river in 1861. But she
continued working until December 26, 1909, although she never again
entered the Port of Portsmouth:

> The barge City of Montreal ashore at Plymouth as a
> result of Sunday's storm, was originally a full-rigged ship, built
> by Tobey and Company of Portsmouth in 1861. She is one of
> the last survivors of the famous old Piscataqua square-riggers.
> Ice is getting thick in the Dover river.[18]

Simla

SPECIFICATIONS: 1863. Tobey & Littlefield. Alligator figurehead, round stern. Burthen, 1,041 tons. Length, 186 feet; beam, 34.6 feet; depth 17.3 feet. Two decks. Original owners—Jonathan M. and T. Salter Tredick.

Other than the *City of Montreal*, in 1898, the *Simla* was the last of the big vessels to return to the Piscataqua; and, at that, she didn't come in with a cargo, but for repairs. Before the *Simla* was launched, it was optimistically reported that a ship of 1,000 tons burthen "is to be launched about the first of August. The figure and the stern piece by Mr. Woodbury Gerrish are very handsome specimens of carved work. The design of the former is an alligator, and needs only life to make it real. Mr. Gerrish has taken the stand formerly occupied by Joseph Henderson on Bow Street. He has already established a reputation as a carver, and will give satisfaction to those at home or abroad who may call him in this or any other department of the business."[19]

Why an alligator was chosen for the figurehead of the *Simla* will, of course, never be known. It seems a bit odd only because the *Simla* was probably named for a British outpost in the Punjab, India, and it was a hill station—scarcely the kind of country in which alligators would abound.

Capt. Timothy N. Porter took the *Simla* to sea at the end of a towline from the steamer *Charles Pearson*, bound for Boston. One reason Piscataqua vessels often went to New York or Boston under tow was the problem of recruiting crews. There just weren't enough idle seamen hanging around in Portsmouth, but they could be rounded up in the bigger ports. From Boston, the *Simla* went to Calcutta on February 10, 1864.[20] From Calcutta, she went to London and then back to the East Indies. In 1866, on a passage from Calcutta to New York, the *Simla* went ashore on Brigantine Inlet, New Jersey, on April 22. She got off, but suffered loss of her rudder, and her masts had to be cut away. She anchored in Little Egg Harbor, New Jersey.[21]

What happened next couldn't happen today, but it was approved in 1866. The *Simla* waited in Little Egg Harbor for a chance to be repaired, but the caulkers in the New York shipyards were out on strike. The strike had gone on for five weeks. "Ten thousand men are thus thrown out of employment.... The pawnshops are overrun with articles pledged by those mechanics to supply their families with the necessaries of life."[22] Two days later, the newspaper was bewailing the fact that the Navy wasn't sending any work to the Portsmouth

Navy Yard. The Tredicks were unhappy to have their big ship lying idle, and they decided to do something about it. On May 21, it was reported that the Secretary of the Navy had given permission for the *Simla* to go into dry dock at the Portsmouth Navy Yard. This was hailed by the *Chronicle*:

> We are glad to notice that Messrs. Tredick of this city have determined to bring their ship Simla, recently damaged while on her voyage to New York, around to this port for repairs, the Secretary of the Navy having consented to grant the use of the floating dry dock at the Navy Yard, in which to dock the ship. This will prove a good chance for our worthy mechanics, who will doubtless repair the ship in a better manner than it would have been done in New York, where in many instances the smallest amount of work is done for the largest price that can be charged. At this time, when work at the Navy Yard is less in demand by the Department, an expenditure of several thousand dollars upon one of our merchant ships is quite fortunate for our mechanics. The last ship, not a man-of-war, that was docked at the Navy Yard, was the British steamer North American of the Portland and Liverpool line, which was injured in approaching Portland harbor and brought here for repairs. The recent strike in New York has sent many vessels from that port to be repaired at other seaports, where it can be done cheaper and better and in as short time.

What neither the Tredicks nor the *Chronicle* nor the Navy Department reckoned with was the open sympathy that the Portsmouth Navy Yard workmen entertained for their fellows in New York. They had met and passed resolutions supporting the strike. On June 7, the Portsmouth workmen put their sympathy into action: they struck for higher wages; "and the owners not complying with their demands, the work of caulking is suspended for the present. They have been receiving $3.00 per day and struck for $4.00. A committee from the caulkers of New York visited our city on Thursday, and this is the result. We believe the strikers were mostly strangers here."[23]

Still determined, the Tredicks had the *Simla* moved into the floating dry dock at the Navy Yard. But the caulkers refused to work on her, so "40 carpenters and 19 calkers were discharged of course."[24] While the Portsmouth Navy Yard men were being fired for supporting the strike in New York, the New Yorkers went back to work without winning their fight for a ten-hour day. Eventually, the work on the *Simla* was done, and she departed from the Port of Portsmouth for the last time, heading for Cardiff on July 28.

Captain Porter commanded the *Simla* until 1870, when he asked for relief. Capt. Albert T. Salter, previously on the *Santee*, went to Spain to take over the ship. The *Simla* was used chiefly in the East Indian trade. She had pleasant passage in 1871 from Calcutta to New York, with "unusual light weather; the skysails have scarcely been in or a reef taken the entire passage."[25] But the next year was a different story. Captain Salter, who was accompanied by his wife, reported severe gales and squalls coming from Bombay to New York. Albert Salter turned the ship over to Thomas S. Salter, who sailed her into Boston in 1874 from Calcutta. That prompted the *Chronicle*'s little joke on November 28: "there may have been some old hulks in the forecastle, but the captain and the first officers were Salters."

Capt. Samuel G. Gardner, one of whose commands had been the *Richard III*, relieved Thomas Salter for one East Indian voyage, and he brought her back by way of Liverpool and New York. Capt. Albert Salter resumed command, taking the *Simla* to Europe and the East Indies in 1875.[26] Returning to the United States in ballast from Marseilles, France, the *Simla* went ashore at Barnegat Inlet, New Jersey, early in January 1877, and was a complete loss. Salvagers tried in vain to get her off, but eventually the hull was sold, along with the sails and rigging, for $2,475. The Boston underwriters approved the sale, and the purchasers were James Howard & Co. of Boston.[27]

Coronation

SPECIFICATIONS: *1863. Tobey & Littlefield. Figurehead, square stern. Burthen, 1,049 tons. Length, 183.8 feet; beam, 35 feet; depth 17.5 feet. Two decks. Original owners—Henry Wenzell, et al., of Boston.*

The *Coronation*, although not yet named, was launched in April, but it was several months before Tobey & Littlefield could find a buyer. Late in October, it was reported that the firm had "disposed of the ship launched at their yard a few months since to a Boston firm, and she is now being rigged." That item had appeared in the *American Ballot*, a Portsmouth paper, and the *Chronicle* responded in stern tones:

We are authorized and requested to state that Messrs. Tobey & Littlefield have not yet sold their fine ship; and we regret to learn that the above premature announcement caused an unknown would-be purchaser from Boston to return to the city without calling on the builders, whose A-1 ship is in the market.[28]

However, a few days later, the *Chronicle* indulged in a bit of heavy-handed humor at the expense of the figurehead being installed on the *Coronation*. The theme resounds with the political animus of the time and is a bit trying for a late-twentieth-century reader:

> CATHEADS AND COPPERHEADS. — The new ship of Tobey & Littlefield, at the Pier, has recently donned a new symbol, that might, but we presume does not, indicate that the owners were of the party designated Copperheads. "The projecting timber from which a ship's anchor is weighted" is usually ornamented with a piece of carved work, sometimes the head of an animal, a star, or shield: in this case the decoration is a large, copper-colored human face. A mere freak of the fancy, we suppose, as the ship is not yet sold; but the splendid craft is worthy of a gold figure head or cat-head.   H.

It would appear that the *Ballot*'s little scoop didn't do irreparable harm, because on November 14 the *Journal* reported the ship had been sold to Henry Wenzell, "at a price not made public. She is now being fitted for sea, and is to be called the Coronation."

On the third of December she cleared the Port of Portsmouth for New Brunswick, under a Captain Edwards. When she arrived in London on May 2, she was sold to a British firm and rechristened the *Ravensbourne*. In 1872 she was sold to a German company and became the *Atalanta*.[29]

Daniel Marcy

SPECIFICATIONS: 1863. Daniel Marcy. South End. Burthen, 1,031 tons. Length, 181 feet; beam, 35 feet; depth 17.5 feet. Two decks. Original owners—William Ross, Daniel Marcy, Richard Jenness, True M. Ball, Mary E. Pettigrew, and John Reding.

William Pettigrew, the master shipwright who had directed the construction of so many Port of Portsmouth vessels, was gone. He died in February 1863. For the time being, Daniel Marcy kept the operation going with the assistance of master builder David Badger. Pettigrew was only 52 when he died; Mary Pettigrew, his widow, held an interest in the *Daniel Marcy*. Mrs. Pettigrew died in 1882, at the age of 66. Like the *Coronation*, the *Daniel Marcy* went unsold for quite a time. The collapse of the cotton trade and the depredations by Confederate raiders made investors cautious. As it was, it was an entirely Portsmouth-organized syndicate that finally bought the ship and named her for the builder. The *Chronicle* reported on October 27:

The two splendid ships launched this week, in this city, one each from the yards of Tobey & Littlefield and Daniel Marcy, leave the stock in all of our private yards clear of ships — though a couple of smaller craft are in the course of construction, as we have before mentioned. Uncle Sam is building quite a little fleet of war vessels at the Navy Yard. *Mr. Marcy's ship was commenced two or three years ago* [emphasis added] and work was for a long time suspended on her.

There are now three new ships lying at our wharves — one belonging to the builders, Tobey & Littlefield, which is for sale; one to J. M. Tredick & Son, and one to Daniel Marcy.

May the d—l fly away with these rebel pirates, ere they catch one of these fine craft; and may these excellent specimens of Piscataqua marine architecture often return to their birth-place, to confer still greater benefits to our people.

Although Daniel Marcy had quietly given up taking to sea new vessels in which he had an interest, it was still a bit of a surprise that the first master of the *Daniel Marcy* was William Ross and not Marcy. However, besides building ships, Marcy had other engrossing interests: he was serving in the U.S. House of Representatives, and that in itself was a testimonial to the strong feeling in parts of New Hampshire against the Civil War; Marcy was a Democrat and, therefore, a Copperhead. Captain Ross took the *Daniel Marcy* to New York on January 4, 1864, where she loaded for San Francisco. The passage took 182 days, far from a good time. In September, she sailed for Hong Kong, carrying $82,000 in gold.[30] From there she went to Akyab. A letter from her first officer, dated Akyab, February 12, 1865, to the *New Bedford Standard*, was reprinted in the *Journal*. It reported the murder of the second mate, George B. Wood, Jr., only 26 years old, by a member of the crew. The *Daniel Marcy* was in the Strait of Malacca at the time. When the ship docked, the killer was sent to Calcutta to be tried and probably hanged.

The *Daniel Marcy* stayed in the Pacific and East Indian trade. In June 1870, she was at Manila and was loaded for New York. Her cargo was 825 tons of dry sugar at $11 in gold per ton ($9,075) and 100 tons of hemp at $11.25 in gold per bale.[31] In 1872, one of the Marcy sons had command of the ship and took 159 days from New York to San Francisco, experiencing heavy gales off Cape Horn. In April 1873, the *Daniel Marcy* was sold to a Boston syndicate for $57,000.[32]

In April 1877, the *Daniel Marcy*, under a Captain Bicknell, sailed from Manila for New York. A month into her passage, she was lost in the Gasper Straits. "All hands were saved. Her cargo consisted of 14,706 piculs hemp, 300 piculs sapan wood, 285 quintals indigo, and 175,000 cigars."[33] A later report said the ship went aground in a fog, stove a hole in her hull and filled with water. "At 12 o'clock the crew took to the boats, and landed at the lighthouse where they were hospitably received and provided with the necessities of life; afterward they proceeded to Singapore. Captain Bicknell stayed with the wreck to save everything possible."[34]

General Grant

SPECIFICATIONS: 1864. Tobey & Littlefield. Burthen, 1,480 tons. Length, 251 feet; beam, 34 feet; depth 23 feet. Original owners—R. B. and J. M. Forbes, of Boston.

Undoubtedly a valid argument could be made that the *General Grant* doesn't belong in a book about three-masted, square-rigged sailing vessels. The *General Grant* was primarily a steamship—the first commercial, steam-powered vessel built on the Piscataqua. The *General Grant* has to be included, if only because she was the wave of the future even as the Port of Portsmouth yards were still producing windjammers. Steam-propelled ships had been crossing the Atlantic for years, and the early ones all carried sails, or had the means to use them during the frequent breakdowns. As far back as 1851, the owners of the clipper *Typhoon* had kept Fernald and Pettigrew waiting while they debated whether to make her a sailing vessel or steamer.[35] They chose the first course, as history shows. But shipping firms were becoming more and more aware of the advantages of steam, which allowed a vessel to move regardless of the wind and tide.

British builders were going heavily into metal vessels, and increasingly into steam propulsion, although one of the most famous of the British clippers, the *Cutty Sark*, was an iron-hulled vessel. The *Cutty Sark*, incidentally, is the only clipper-type surviving, moored in a special dock at Greenwich, England. Britain, after centuries of shipbuilding, was suffering from the lack of timber, while in the United States oak was still available. By 1864, the Port of Portsmouth yards were dependent on timber being cut north of Rochester. Reuben Tilton had gangs of workmen in the woods getting out pine and white oak, and had 10,000 tons stockpiled.

Why R. B. Forbes contracted with Tobey & Littlefield can only be speculated. The firm did have a yard where really large vessels could be launched. Also, while other yards seemed to be stagnating, Tobey & Littlefield was fairly busy. Forbes ordered the ship, to his specifications, late in 1863, and she was launched on May 18, 1864. Not only was the *General Grant* unusual because she was being built for steam, but it must be remembered the Civil War was raging, and the ship was constructed so that she could be readily fitted as a war vessel.

While the *General Grant* was on the stocks, a visitor who came to Portsmouth from Salem, Massachusetts, later wrote about the ship to the editor of the *Chronicle*; his comments offer pertinent insight:

> Passing through your city a few days since, my attention was arrested by the building of a vessel at Messrs. Tobey & Littlefield's ship yard. Although a stranger, I was received and treated with the most gentlemanly courtesy. The location for a ship yard is one of the best I have ever seen. With the railroad running directly through it, every article of material is easily transported; indeed, there is every facility that could be desired for the building of ships; and I should judge, too, from the short interview, and from the workmanship being displayed in their present productions, that the right men are in the right place.
>
> I was informed that the ship, or steamer, in course of construction, was under contract with Capt. R. B. Forbes, of Boston; that she is to be a steam propellor, and so constructed that she can be used for a war vessel if needed; and, if I am allowed to express my opinion as to what is requisite for a war vessel in these times, or what is most needed by our government, I should say that this vessel, modeled as she is for speed, (for truly there can be nothing sharper) and so arranged internally to protect her boilers and motive power, differently from anything yet constructed — is completely adapted for the work, as she can either fight or run away.
>
> In noticing a structure of this kind outside the precincts of Uncle Sam, it is natural to the observer to scrutinize carefully the material and workmanship. Now, Mr. Editor, as I have seen nothing in public print in relation to the building of this vessel, I have to conclude that the proprietors of the journals in your city are ignorant of this, I may say, great curiosity; and I would most respectfully, as one who appreciates such, invite your attention to it. — [This Chronicle has spoken of this fine craft several times before. We fear H. M. S. don't take the papers. — ED. CHRON.] If it be said it is nothing new — that our government is building just such vessels continually — let me say that it is not so. Our government has not such a ship afloat or on the stocks, of such a peculiar model; and whoever will take the pains to compare the material and workmanship with that at our Navy Yards, either at Portsmouth or Boston, must admit, unless ruled by prejudice, that in every respect it

is fully equal, and I should say, not speaking disparagingly of Government work, that in many respects it is superior to that, — and it is reasonable to suppose this would be the case; for, while Government has not reputation to gain or lose, strictly speaking, these men have the high reputation gained by building some of the finest and best ships in the world to maintain.

Capt. Forbes is a gentleman of wide experience and great discernment, and is highly popular, and, doubtless, has some prominent place in view for this model craft. Hoping to see such credit as is deserving to the parties concerned in this vessel, in your columns, I am, very truly,

Yours, H. M. S.[36]

In its own article on the launching, the *Chronicle* went into some detail about the *General Grant*. One point the newspaper stressed was the sharpness of her design. She had beam of only 34 feet, yet her overall length was 251 feet. She is "very sharp in the extremities, but has good mid-ship bearings." The contract called for the ship to be rigged in Portsmouth, "after the design known as the 'Forbes Rig' with the top masts fidded [given a supporting bar] to the shaft and every necessary contrivance for housing them. Her model was fitted out under Forbes' order, to suit himself, but due credit will doubtless be given to B. J. Lawlor of Chelsea, Massachusetts, who drafted and made the moulds, should she prove successful.

"We are not aware who is making the machinery, but we understand it is nearly ready to go in, consisting of two 60-1/2 by 36-inch cylinders, for boilers of large capacity with all the modern improvements. She is calculated to spread a considerable amount of canvas, say 3,500 running yards."[37]

In the following paragraph there is a strong hint as to how Tobey & Littlefield won the contract to build the Piscataqua's first steam merchantman: "at the time of the launch one of the tug boats recently built at the Portsmouth Navy Yard was plying on the river, ready to render assistance, if necessary, she being there by the courtesy of Commodore [George F.] Pearson and to S. M. Pook, Esq., naval constructor, who made possible the building of the ship at Tobey & Littlefield." The item added that Forbes had intended to have the *General Grant* built elsewhere, but Pook talked him into Portsmouth.

In June, it was reported that the *General Grant* was lying at Pier Wharf, where she was being rigged. Once masted, sparred, and her rigging taut, she was to go to Boston for her machinery, although the engine hadn't arrived from England. A month later, she was still lying at Pier Wharf, and the same news item indicated that shipbuilding on the Piscataqua, except at the Navy Yard, had stopped.

Eventually the *General Grant* was towed to Boston, and a large party made the passage in her. Presumably she was to go into the trade with San Francisco and China. In 1866, the *General Grant*, which had been renamed the *Meteor*, was sold at auction at Grand Junction Wharf in Boston for $250,000 to a Mr. Wise of New York.[38]

What happened to her isn't clear. A ship named *General Grant* was wrecked in the Falklands in 1868, and it's a tale of a horrible ordeal for 18 months for the ten who survived. However, the description doesn't seem to fit.

It can be said, however, that the *General Grant* was the last wooden-hulled merchant steamer built on the river until World War I, when the Shattuck Shipyard at Newington produced 15 of them — but none were constructed to use sail also.

Tartar

SPECIFICATIONS: 1865. Tobey & Littlefield. Billet head, elliptic stern. Burthen, 820 tons. Length, 161 feet; beam, 33.6 feet; depth 21.3 feet. Two decks. Original owner—Robert L. Taylor, of New York.

Shipbuilding on the Piscataqua was really in slack water by 1865. Smaller vessels, mostly two-masted schooners, were being built. David D. Badger launched two at the old Marcy & Pettigrew yard. At 344 and 409 tons, these schooners would have been considered large vessels 60 years before. William F. Fernald, who was operating in the old Raynes shipyard, built three schooners in 1865, all of them over 300 tons, but only Tobey & Littlefield built a ship.

The *Tartar* was launched on March 29. She had been built strictly on speculation. Perhaps Tobey & Littlefield had a little spare money after building the *General Grant* and could afford to gamble on another. And it was a gamble. The *Tartar* wasn't sold until November, and then Deering & Yeaton rigged her. The terms of the sale weren't reported.[39]

Capt. E. A. Follansbee took the *Tartar* to New Orleans, arriving there on December 28.[40] Apparently she went from New Orleans to England, thence to Calcutta. In February 1867, it was reported that she was on the beach at Deal, and that wreckers had gone to her assistance. The crew, all of whom were ill, were rescued. In its report, the *Chronicle* used the occasion to vent some spite against Tobey & Littlefield: "She was built here in 1865 by a firm, whom, as they do not take The Chronicle, though we have given hundreds of dollars worth of advertising notices, in years past, we cannot afford to comment further."[41]

Semiramis

SPECIFICATIONS: 1866. Tobey & Littlefield. Billet head, elliptic stern. Burthen, 1,185 tons. Length, 182.3 feet; beam, 36.5 feet; depth 23.5 feet. Two decks. Original owners—John S. Pray, Thomas E. Call, Samuel Adams, et al.

Semiramis was an Assyrian queen who, after death, became a goddess in the religion of her people. Some of the names tagged onto Port of Portsmouth ships indicate, if nothing else, that the city had students of the classics in its midst. The only ship launched in 1865 was described thus:

> NEW SHIP. — We give notice to-day of the launching of the new ship, unnamed, from the yard of Messrs. Tobey & Littlefield. This ship, now in the market *for sale*, is a superior white oak built ship, of the following dimensions, viz: 183 feet in length on deck, 36 1-2 feet wide, 23 1-2 feet deep, and of about 1200 tons burthen. Her frame is of New Hampshire white oak, well seasoned before being covered. The planking inside and out is of the best quality *white oak*; and in every part the material used was of the best quality — *square bolted* and *through treenailed* from keel to gunnel. In model she is a duplicate of the ship "Coronation," built by Messrs. T. & L. in 1863; her sailing qualities and carrying capacity have therefore been proved — and she can be safely estimated to carry 1700 tons dead weight, or 2200 tons Calcutta goods on 22 feet draft water. She will rate in the first class with French Lloyds, and will be a serviceable and durable ship. She is to be immediately rigged and fitted for sea, which will take about one month. The attention of ship buyers is respectfully called to this fine vessel.[42]

The next day it was announced that the ship had been beautifully launched, which was followed by the news that the ship had been sold to Pray, Nathaniel K. Walker, Capt. Edwin A. Gerrish, Adams, et al., for $75,000. Two days after Christmas, the ship was given a name. The *Chronicle* said the *Semiramis* appeared beautiful and staunch as she laid at Pier Wharf, "ready for sea, and the object of admiration for the numerous people looking at her."[43] Earlier the paper had made the wry observation: "It is almost always said that the last ship built is the best; in this case it seems to be true. She is class A-1 with Lloyd's for nine years, and is equal in every respect to the best ships ever built on the Piscataqua."[44]

The veteran shipmaster Edwin Gerrish took the *Semiramis* to sea, assisted by the Navy's tug *Portfire*. She headed for New Orleans, carrying 90 tons of hay and 1,100 bushels of potatoes. In March, she was chartered to load cotton for Liverpool at 5-1/2 per pound (about $.12). A year later, she was again chartered to load cotton at New Orleans. Her load was 3,505 bales, or 1,632,000 pounds.[45] If the freight rate was consistent with 1867 standards, the *Semiramis* was paid nearly $20,000 for the passage. From Liverpool she went to San Francisco, and there loaded with wheat at £3 per ton. She carried away 37,000 sacks. On arriving in Liverpool, she was ordered to New York, where she loaded ordnance stores for the Mare Island Navy Yard in San Francisco.

In 1873 the *Semiramis*, along with the *Yosemite* and the *Prima Donna*—all ships managed by Capt. John S. Pray—became involved in a dispute in Liverpool. The *Semiramis* had gone into Liverpool, and it was decided to discharge part of her crew. The ship's articles had stipulated that "the undersigned are to be discharged at Liverpool, if mutually consented between the master and the seamen."[46] The U.S. consul claimed he couldn't decide such a matter, so he forced the captain to pay a total of $1,490 in gold as extra pay for each man discharged. Pray filed for a refund, and extensive hearings were held, stretching into 1875. The outcome wasn't reported.

Captain Gerrish commanded the *Semiramis* until October 1875, when she was sold to a Baltimore syndicate for $42,000.[47] The previous winter she had hauled wheat from San Francisco to Liverpool at £2.5.0 per ton, and when she came back across the Atlantic the sale took place. Within a week, the syndicate sold the *Semiramis* to an English firm for $45,000, making a neat, quick profit.[48] She was used as a passenger packet between Baltimore and Bremen. In 1890 the *Semiramis* was sold in Bremen and renamed the *Union*.[49]

Yosemite

SPECIFICATIONS: 1867. Tobey & Littlefield. Billet head, elliptic stern. Burthen, 1,153 tons. Length, 183 feet; beam, 37.2 feet; depth 23.5 feet. Two decks. Original owners—John S. Pray, et al.

The *Yosemite* scored a first right after her launching on October 29: while being taken to the Pier Wharf the next day she tripped her anchor and swung in toward Church Point. Her bowsprit struck an old house sitting on the Bow Street ledge, known as the "Pigeon Coop." The building was occupied by several families, and some of the women living in it were injured. "The unceremonious upsetting of the house caused a fire, and an alarm was given."[50] The tug *Pioneer* pulled the *Yosemite* into the Portsmouth Navy Yard's dry dock to see what damage she had suffered; there was none.[51] No other ship ever underwent that experience until May 18, 1920, when the steel steamer *Brooklyn*, launched by Atlantic Shipbuilding at Freeman's Point, got away from her tug, swung in the tide, and also bayoneted the "Pigeon Coop" with her bowsprit.[52]

For a while there seemed to be some conflict over the ship's name. Some papers spelled it *Yo Semite*, but others went with the conventional *Yosemite*. The latter prevailed.

The crew for the *Yosemite* arrived in Portsmouth on January 6, 1868, and were described as a "fine body of men."[53] Where they had been recruited wasn't said. Capt. Andrew Mack took the *Yosemite* to sea on January 11, carrying a cargo of hay to Mobile. She was taken out of the river by the *Portfire*. On her maiden voyage, she spoke with the ship *J. H. Stetson* of Wiscasset, from New Orleans for Liverpool. She supplied the *Stetson* "with fresh meat, soups, &c. Capt. sick and part of his crew. His child and two seamen had died."[54] From Mobile, the *Yosemite* went to Liverpool, and from there to San Francisco, where she loaded 34,000 sacks of wheat at £3 per ton, and was back in Liverpool by April 17, 1869. She went to New York and took on a load of ordnance material of Mare Island, San Francisco. In 1876, the *Yosemite* was at Mauritius in the Indian Ocean, having been docked, "stripped, caulked and recoppered, and is about to reload her cargo." She was bound from Manila for Boston, and 1,000 bags of sugar had already been sold because of damage from a leak, "and it is expected more will be rejected still."[55] She was carrying 9,548 piculs of hemp, 12,000 of sugar, 195 piculs of sapan wood, and 50,000 cigars.

For years she sailed the trade routes of the world. She was sold in 1877:

> We notice that the sale of the ship Yo Semite, of this port, now at San Francisco, has been consummated at $39,500. Samuel Blair is the purchaser. The ship was built here in 1867, and registers 1154 tons. Her owners were Capt. John S. Pray, William Simes, William D. Fernald, Stephen Tobey, Daniel Littlefield, Thomas E. Call, John T. French, Wm. R. Preston, Jos. Hiller Foster and others of this city, and Capt. Andrew Mack and others of Kennebunk, Me. The Yo Semite is a fine ship, and the San Francisco papers say she is in perfect order and will be used as a coal carrier. She was built by Tobey & Littlefield, a former firm that did much to add to the celebrity of Portsmouth as a ship-building place, and never launched a poor vessel.

Samuel Blair put the ship into profitable lumber trade between San Francisco and Puget Sound, under a Captain Saunders. A news item said she's "now employed in the local trade on the West Coast."[56] David A. Wasson wrote to the editor of the *Portsmouth Herald* on February 15, 1906:

> Of the magnificent fleet of square riggers launched on the Piscataqua, but five remain, and only one of these in her original condition, the bark Yosemite, launched in 1868, now owned in San Francisco and engaged in the coal trade between Australian and Pacific coast ports. The ship Dashing Wave, launched in 1853, and the bark Richard III (1859) have been within a year cut down to barges, and are now used in the Puget Sound lumber trade. On our Atlantic coast the big City of Montreal, launched as a ship in 1861, but cut down to a barge for the coal trade in 1898, is the only surviving representative of the square-rigged fleet. On the Nova Scotia coast and under the British flag may be found the Grandee, also reduced to an ignominious coal barge and in the trade between Cape Breton and Halifax. This vessel bears the distinction of being the last square-rigger owned at Portsmouth or in the state. She was launched here in 1873 and was sold as recently as 1894.

More than 40 years after her launching the *Yosemite* was still an active freighter. The *Herald*, on March 1, 1907, reported:

> The bark *Yosemite*, built at Portsmouth in 1868, and the last American survivor of the fleet of Piscataqua-built square-riggers, has been sold by her San Francisco owners to Chilean interests, and sailed Wednesday from Tacoma, Wash., for Valparaiso, under her new flag.
>
> The *Yosemite* is of 1,040 tonnage, and was formerly ship-rigged. Several of the old Piscataqua ships are said to be afloat under foreign flags in their original rigs, but under this flag there remain but the *City of Montreal*, *Dashing Wave* and *Richard III*.

Like so many of the Port of Portsmouth ships, the *Yosemite* no longer held news interest once it was sold to foreigners. But it's highly to the credit of her builders, Tobey & Littlefield, both then deceased, that the old ship could still attract a buyer.

Merrimack

SPECIFICATIONS: 1867. John Neal. Kittery Foreside. Billet head, elliptic stern. Burthen, 1,208 tons. Length, 180.6 feet; beam, 35.5 feet; depth 24.2 feet. Two decks. Original owners—Horton D. Walker, Nathaniel G. Weeks, George W. Pendexter, Edward F. Sise, John Sise, William Simes, et al.

With the launching of the *Merrimack*, the shipbuilding era was slowly winding down in Kittery. Only two more full ships would be built—one in 1873 and the other in 1877. A couple of schooners were built there in 1866—one of them, the *Mary J. Adams*, by Neal. In February 1867, there was news comment:

NEW SHIP FOR PORTSMOUTH. — I was pleased to learn by your last Journal that Horton D. Walker and others have contracted with John Neal, to build a first class white oak Ship of about 1100 tons, to be launched the coming summer. The frame for the Ship has been in dock over four years; Mr. Neal having received it soon after the Rebellion commenced.

Although several ships have been built here since the Rebellion yet this is the first contract made by Portsmouth owners, and I now hope more will soon be made. Time was, when we had and no doubt your senior editor can well recollect when there was owned in this port more than sixty sail of square rigged vessels, besides at least one hundred sail of smaller vessels. Now how does it stand? Why, we cannot number twenty sail altogether. We need some great event to move our business men, and instil into our industrial and commercial people a new life to save us from falling back any farther. No city in the United States could formerly boast of more intelligent masters and seamen than we had and nearly every family in town thought of their sailor boy on the sea.

Boston is moving, and all her first people are awake to the extension of her Commerce. Our laboring classes are loudly calling for employment and no town of its population has more capital, or is more able than ours to endeavor to recover their former standing as a Commercial people. All our mechanics are well off, many quite wealthy; now let them join others competent to manage a ship, and form companies as they do east of us; no matter how many owners, only once commence and no doubt everything will result in a profit to all concerned. W.[57]

The *Merrimack* was launched in October, and the news story said she would be commanded by Capt. Benjamin F. Jacobs, who had lately been master of the first *Granite State*. On December 7, the *Journal* commented:

> NEW SHIPS. — The beautiful and substantial ship Merrimac, Capt. Jacobs, is now ready for sea, and may be bearing away before the wind, ere our paper issues. She is bound for Savannah. Her tonnage is 1208. She is owned by Messrs. Horton D. Walker, John Neal & Co., Capt. Jacobs and others. She was built by Messrs. Neal & Co. of the best material, and her whole appearance is a graceful model of strength and beauty, with a capacity of carrying about four thousand bales of cotton.

The tug *Portfire* towed the *Merrimack* out to the open sea, where she headed for Savannah. "She was laden with hay and takes out mine host Philbrick of the Philbrick and Farragut hotels as passenger." The item then named the owners and continued, saying the ship was built by "Messrs. Neal and composed of the best material, and her whole appearance is of graceful strength and beauty. She can carry 4,000 bales of cotton. It seems a little singular that a ship built on the Piscataqua should be named for a sister river — and we suggest to the christener of this ship that he name one of the other fine vessels that he may put afloat, after old Strawberry Bank."[58]

A few days after the Jacobs took the *Merrimack* to sea, the *Chronicle* was quite excited over the efficiency of the telegraph system. The owners of the *Merrimack* were informed by wire that the ship had been aground on Elbow Key, and that the master, by then at Key West, needed instructions and money. Salvage had been awarded, and repair work was being done. One of the owners took the train to Boston and wired Jacobs at Key West to have money drawn on him. Within hours, a return wire said the bills had been met and the ship was proceeding on her passage.

In 1870, a one-sixteenth interest in the *Merrimack* was sold to Charles H. Mendum for $4,170. Mendum was probably second only to Frank Jones, the brewer, in his holdings of Portsmouth real estate. The item noted: "The Merrimack has proved a good investment for her owners, and is under the management of an efficient merchant [probably Horton D. Walker]."[59] Later that year, the *Merrimack* was wrecked:

> Ship Merrimack, Capt. Jacobs, built at this port in 1867, 1288 tons burthen, recently wrecked in the Bay of Jahdo, was insured as follows: On *vessel* — Boston $10,000; Mercantile $5,000; American $5,000; Franklin $2500; China $10,000; Boylston $5,000; Washington $10,000; Neptune $10,000;

National $7,500; New England $10,000. Total $75,000. On *freight* — Manufacturer's $5,000; Boston $5,000; Independent $5,000; India $5,000; Boston Lloyd $10,000. Total $30,000. The captain's primage is insured for $1500 in the Manufacturers'.[60]

Simple arithmetic shows that Charles Mendum made quite a bit of money on his investment—even if it did come out of a shipwreck.

Calcutta

SPECIFICATIONS: 1868. William F. Fernald. North Mill Pond. Billet head, elliptic stern. Burthen, 843 tons. Length, 163.5 feet; beam, 33.5 feet; depth 21.5 feet. Two decks. Original owner—Capt. J. Gilman Moses.

At 1867 drew to a close, three new vessels were tied up at the Pier Wharf: the bark *Quickstep*, the *Yosemite*, and the *Merrimack*. The first two were built by Tobey & Littlefield, and the third by John Neal. The news item then went on to say:

Mr. William F. Fernald, at his ship yard, North End, in this city, will in about four weeks launch a well built ship, to be owned by Capt. J. Gilman Moses and others of Portsmouth. Mr. Fernald is also building two barques for Messrs. Draper & Sons of Boston, modelled closely after their celebrated barque Fury, built by Mr. Fernald. When these vessels are completed, Mr. Fernald will have built his twenty-first vessel in the yard he now occupies, which is the one where George Raynes for so many years built his celebrated ships.

Late in December of 1859, the Raynes Shipyard had been advertised as available to a tenant.[61] George Raynes, Jr. had built the medium clipper *Shooting Star* and then put his business into receivership. William F. Fernald leased the property in 1860 and began operations, building the bark *Fury*. Through the next seven years he built only schooners and barks, many of them of good size. The three barks had total burthens of 1,143 tons and the ten schooners averaged 280 tons. Fernald never lost his lifelong interest in shipbuilding. When he died on April 11, 1895, he had stopped to watch some work being done near his old shipyard.[62]

With all his experience in building vessels, the *Calcutta* was Fernald's first venture with a full-rigged ship. She was rigged at Pier Wharf, and there took on a cargo of hay. The hay was brought over from Kittery in a schooner, which, it was explained, saved the expense of carting and tolls on the Portsmouth Bridge. Tongue in cheek, the writer said: "The cruise of the schooner was about as short as any we ever heard of, but we did not learn if the crew shipped for the voyage or for the run."[63]

With Mrs. Moses for a passenger, Captain Moses took his new ship to sea on January 31. Captain Moses kept the command only to Charleston, turning the vessel over to her working master, Joseph Shillaber. Although he yielded the quarterdeck to Shillaber, Moses wrote a report to her builder giving his impression of the new ship:

A TAUT LITTLE SHIP. — Capt. J. Gilman Moses, of the new ship Calcutta, recently built in this city by Mr. Wm. F. Fernald, writes in the following high terms of praise of the power and capacity of the vessel, and her behavior on her first voyage:

CHARLESTON, S. C., March 8th.

Mr. Wm. F. Fernald, Portsmouth, N. H. Dear Sir: — Presuming you would like to hear how the "Calcutta" performs, I thought I would drop you a line to show up the whole thing. In a few words, she is the handiest, best working and best steering ship I ever sailed in — not excepting the "City of New York." I have not yet, as I told you I should, got 300 miles out of her in 24 hours; but have made 270, and this was the only day I had during the passage for trying her sailing capacity. The weather was fearful the whole passage.

And what now most surprises me is, that she only draws 15 1-2 feet, cotton loaded; this certainly is astonishing. — I took out only 30 tons ballast; shall finish loading to-morrow, and shall have 1,200,000 pounds, hard. The Bark, Chase, has 1,076,752. I thus get a very handsome freight, about 3150 pounds Sterling, or in currency, $21,000; but the outs are fearful.

I admit I hit the market just where I wanted to, but freights are all gone to smash — one-half dues; ships arriving every day. Hope to be away by the 11th. The niggers struck for wages, and I did not stow a bale of cotton for 5 days, or I should have been at sea on the 4th; so much for the niggers. I understood the Bark broke down, but did no harm. We shall carry in number of bales, about 2800; of this, 323 are Sea Island, equal in capacity to 502 bales. I mention this, as probably you will see the clearance in the papers.

Yours, JOHN G. MOSES.[64]

Obviously this letter from Captain Moses indulges in epithets for black people not tolerated today, but it does raise a point. It's common nowadays to think of the nineteenth century pound sterling as equivalent to five dollars in U.S. currency. Yet division of the figures quoted by Moses as to the value of his freight money set the pound at $6.66.

On the *Calcutta*'s arrival at Charleston, her third mate, a man named Hurley, became first mate of a New York ship, the *Narragansett*. "We wish him a safe and speedy passage. He is the youngest mate sailing from the port of Charleston."[65] Captain and Mrs. Moses made the passage to Liverpool in the *Calcutta*.

In large part, the *Calcutta* sailed the East Indian and Pacific trade routes, turning a good profit for her owners. In 1872, she caused some concern by being more than 170 days out of Calcutta for Boston, a passage she usually ran in less than 100 days. Her provisions gone, she put into Bermuda for supplies. When she cleared out, she sprang a leak and had to put back. She discharged her cargo and repaired. In June, the *Boston Traveller* published an account of the *Calcutta*'s troubles:

> She had previously touched there for a supply of provisions and water, but when she crossed the Gulf Stream was beset by a hurricane, and while lying to was struck by a heavy sea, which caused her to leak so badly that it was necessary to scud to keep her from sinking. It was no easy matter to get sufficient sail on her to keep her from being struck upon the stern where she was before the wind, or to keep her from broaching to while scudding. More vessels have foundered by scudding than by any other incident of the sea. Not only did Capt. Robertson scud his ship successfully and manage to keep her afloat, but did so without the loss of a single spar.
>
> If the weather had been moderate he might have made an attempt to reach his destination after his ship was pumped out, but in the face of a gale such an attempt would have ended in destruction. Therefore, he prudently put away for Bermuda, where he arrived with his ship leaking badly and his crew almost exhausted.
>
> The vessel's cargo had to be discharged to stop the leak, and the part of it which was damaged was sold for the benefit of the underwriters. Capt. Robertson, who has had much experience in shipping, was ever on the alert to forward the repairs on his ship with as little expense as possible. The ship is now lying at Tudor's wharf, Charlestown. Everything from the chainplates to the trucks showed that no pains had been spared to make her as ship-shape as possible. Her lower rigging has been turned in as neatly as that of any vessel's we ever saw; and everything about her decks is all that could be

desired. Her hull does not seem to have been affected by the terrific gales she has weathered. Built of New Hampshire white oak, the best wood in the country, she is very strong, and is of a good model for carrying and sailing. She has noble breadth of beam, and fair ends, and if her bottom corresponds, is handy vessel. That she is here and not in the bottom of the Atlantic, considering the perils to which she has been exposed, reflects great credit on her commander. We often hear invidious remarks when a vessel is compelled to put into port for any cause, as if her captain ought to be omnipotent, but rarely is a gallant sailor complimented when he saves his vessel under adverse circumstances. If ever any man was entitled to credit for saving his ship and her spars, Captain Robertson ought to rank with him, and ought also to receive some token of approbation from the underwriters. He has been about forty-five years at sea, but never encountered such severe weather as he experienced on the coast this winter.[66]

In January 1875, under a Captain Tanton, the *Calcutta* "arrived at Boston on Saturday from the Philippine Islands, having made the voyage in 164 days, including a stoppage at Sandy Hook. She brought a cargo of 43,961 bags of sugar, consigned to Boston parties. When she came up to the wharf her hull and rigging were covered with ice to the height of 20 feet above her rails. Guess that vessel knew what a 'cold wave' meant."[67] In March, a share in her was sold at a price that set a value of $36,000 on the vessel. And that was followed by comment on her published in the *Charleston News and Courier*:

> The superior American ship Calcutta, of 843 tons, was cleared at this port for Liverpool, on Saturday last, by Messrs. D. Jennings & Son, with the following freight list: 62 bags of sea island cotton, weight 19,904 pounds; 2,621 bales of upland cotton, weight 1,176,901 pounds; 3,600 locust treenails and 200 tons phosphate rock. Total value of cargo $194,499. This fine ship is the property of Capt. John G. Moses, of Portsmouth, N. H., where she was constructed in 1867, and she took a freight from this port to Liverpool in March, 1868, when her cargo was 323 bags of sea island cotton and 2,304 bales of upland cotton, she then being a new vessel; and, while the number of bales of cotton is about the same as then, the weight of the bales is no doubt much greater, and she has now 200 tons phosphate rock.[68]

On November 5, 1878, the *Chronicle* reported:

Advices from Cape Town, Cape of Good Hope, dated Oct. 1st, says: "The Calcutta, ship, from Rangoon for Falmouth, was towed in here Sept. 28th, in charge of the mate, by the Georgietta Lawrence, American schooner. The mate reports that the master, Hanson, died on Aug. 6th. On Sept. 11th, during a heavy gale, the rudder was damaged. On the 19th, she spoke the Red Gauntlet from Calcutta for Liverpool, on the Agulhas Banks, and was offered assistance which was not then required. On the 22d, during another gale, the rudder was carried away. The Cape of Good Hope then bore north by west, thirty miles distant, but a southerly wind coming on, the vessel was blown to the westward. A jury rudder was rigged by hanging a spar over the stern, and the vessel again made the Cape of Good Hope on the night of the 26th, twenty-three miles off. On the 27th she spoke the Georgietta Lawrence, which, after lying by all night, took the Calcutta in tow in the morning about fifteen miles off Table Mountain, and brought her into port."

In February 1879, Captain Moses went to Liverpool in connection with the affairs of the *Calcutta*. Perhaps one of the problems was paying off the captain of the Georgietta Lawrence, who had put in a claim against the ship for $50,000. How much he did get wasn't reported, but he did have salvage money due. Over the years, Moses gradually sold off shares in the *Calcutta*. In 1879, he sold 12/64 to Vernon H. and Emma S. Brown for $2,625, which indicates a value of $14,000 for the ship. On another occasion, 1/16 went for $1,150. Captain Moses owned 1/16 when the *Calcutta* was wrecked on May 3, 1881, on the coast of South Africa. Capt. A. J. Smith was among the dead. Only the chief mate, Charles H. Freeman, of Brewster, Massachusetts, the carpenter, and one seaman lived. The mate wrote home:

I lost everything. The captain's dog was saved, and I shall try to bring him home to his brother Frank. We have only recovered five of the bodies, viz., the captain, second mate, steward and two of the foremast hands. I shall have to remain here until a Lloyds surveyor comes to the wreck from East London, and then I shall try to make my way to the nearest port and get home the best way I can. I have found some very good friends since landing, and they have done everything they possibly could to make us comfortable. We are about 40 miles from any settlement, and that is inland.[69]

William Ross

SPECIFICATIONS: 1869. Daniel Marcy. South End. Billet head, elliptic stern. Burthen, 919 tons. Length, 168 feet; beam, 34.3 feet; depth 21.9 feet. Two decks. Original owners—Daniel Marcy, et al.

There aren't many men who have had the pleasure of being master of a vessel named for themselves. That honor fell to William Ross because of his long service with Daniel Marcy. Ross lived in Portsmouth for many years, but moved to Boston in 1893. The *William Ross* was launched on July 20, the last square-rigger of the 1860s.

Captain Ross cleared out of the Port of Portsmouth on August 26, heading for St. John. She was loaded with lumber products for Liverpool, leaving St. John on September 16, and arriving in Liverpool on October 15. She left Liverpool in December for Calcutta, taking 114 days on the passage. In Calcutta the ship was loaded for Boston. Her cargo was made up of 300 to 500 bags of cutch (vellum leaves), 360 bales of gunny bags, and 300 tons measurement goods—all at $10 per ton. At the last moment about 40 chests of indigo were added, at $14 a ton. The next year, she was sent to Antwerp from Calcutta, and then to Boston.

In 1872, while at Callao, she was sold to Bryce, Grace & Co. for £12,500, and went under the Peruvian flag.[70] In 1890, the *William Ross* was sold to a German firm and renamed the *Augustina*. A Norwegian company owned her in 1894.[71]

VI The 1870s

At the end of July 1869, a news article was published which any knowledgeable reader could see was sounding the death knell for large, wooden, square-rigged sailing vessels. An excongressman from Maine made a tour of the British shipyards and docks and then penned a grim picture of the future of shipbuilding in the United States. The *Portland Press* paraphrased him:

> It is useless for our ship-builders to expect to regain the lost supremacy of wooden ships. The commerce of the world is to be carried on by steam hereafter, and the iron propellers manufactured in England are to take the place of sailing vessels, the same tonnage doing four times the work of the latter. He thinks a war with England would force the U.S. to the creation of a steam marine which might bring back our maritime supremacy — a remedy that would be worse than the disease.[1]

The truth of what the man had to say was slowly becoming obvious in the Port of Portsmouth, and before the decade of the 1870s had run its course the construction of square-riggers had ceased for all time. Eight of the big ships would be built, and two or three of them were among the biggest merchant sailing ships ever launched on the Piscataqua. As in the 1860s, shipbuilders were pleading for help from Congress to restore American commerce. Several plans were put forward. On January 21, 1871, the *Journal* published an item taken from the *Boston Advertiser*, but written by that paper's Portsmouth correspondent:

The ship owners and builders of this city are looking for some action by Congress to restore American commerce, — either to allow the registry of foreign built ships, or drawbacks to builders for the duties on imported materials. A new ship of 1000 tons has just been sold here, on stocks, including her spars, for $38,000, and the builder states her cost at $55,000. Ship-owners here assert that a vessel of the same tonnage can be built in the British Provinces for about half the money; and even if not so good a craft, the insurance office will rate her equally well. Portsmouth ship-yards and even the navy yard are almost deserted, but there is some talk of laying a new keel the coming season if congressional action favors. A ship and a schooner were sent to St. John, N. B., for repairs last season; but although the owners claim a great saving by the unpatriotic movement, as wages were from $1.50 to $1.75 per day in gold there, and good men could be hired here from $2.00 to $2.50 in greenbacks, it is difficult to see how a large saving could have been made. Parties from this city went down to oversee the work.

In 1870, only one vessel of any size was built on the river—the bark *Neptune*, 493 tons—and a 21-ton sloop. In the spring of 1871, the *Journal*, in its April 8 issue, flatly laid the blame for the depressed state of shipping on the railroads. It argued that the movement of goods, once done in ships, was now by railroad cars:

They have now become the ships of civilization, just as the camel is the ship of the desert. For look at it: — In 1860 there were in the United States 28,771 miles of railroad, and in 1870, there were 54,436 miles, an increase of more than 20,000 miles in the last ten years. In 1830 were but just 41 miles. Doubtless, at this rate, there will be 100,000 in twenty years more. And what must be the effect of this vast monopoly, but a decrease in the amount of shipbuilding and shipping!

The writer probably didn't live long enough to see his prophecy about railroad expansion come true, and how he would have marveled if he could have seen the railroads mostly a memory and airplanes and trucks as "the ships of civilization."

In 1872, with Ulysses S. Grant in the White House, Daniel Marcy, in a bid for a State Senate seat, charged that Republican indifference was destroying the shipbuilding industry. The *Journal*, ever zealous in its defense of the Republican Party, contended that all GOP efforts to revitalize shipbuilding had been thwarted by the Democrats. The *Journal* thrust its sword at a sore place for the Democrats, contending that by supporting secession, which led to the Civil War, they had helped bring about destruction of the nation's merchant fleet. It was a point hard to rebut, as Marcy himself had been one of the Copperheads. Incidentally, Captain Marcy didn't win election to the State Senate. The slow pace of shipbuilding continued, although there was a little action in 1871.

Jean Ingelow

SPECIFICATIONS: 1871. William F. Fernald. North Mill Pond. Female figurehead, elliptic stern. Burthen, 1,075 tons. Length, 177 feet; beam, 36.7 feet; depth, 23 feet. Original owners—John Gilman Moses, et al.

A SONG OF THE 20TH CENTURY.

BY JEAN INGELOW.

The city, he saith, is fairer far,
　　Than one which stood of old;
It gleams in the light all crimson bright
　　With shifting glimmers of gold,
Where be the homes my fathers built,
　　The houses where they prayed?
I see in no sod the paths they trod,
　　Nor the stones my fathers laid.
On the domes they spread, the roofs they reared,
　　Has passed the leveling tide,
My fathers lie low, and their sons outgrow
　　The bonds of their skill and pride,
　　　　Shifting, sweeping change,
　　　　　　It plays with man's endeavor,
　　　　They carved those names grown strange
　　　　　　And they said, "Abide forever."

The city, I say, lieth far away,
　　Whereunto no change may come;
It has rays manifold of crimson and gold,
　　But I cannot count their sum.
They sigh no more by its happier shore
　　Who wander, foreboding not,
Or waning away of a changeful day,
　　Or changing life and lot;

> They dream not there on earth's changing face,
>   Or mutable wind and sea —
> Thou are changeless; grant me a place
>   In that far city with Thee!
>   There record my name,
>   Father! forget Thee never
>   For Thy thought is still the same,
>   Yesterday, to-day and forever.[2]

Few vessels, if any, including the famed clipper *Nightingale*, were given more publicity in Portsmouth newspapers than the *Jean Ingelow*. The English poetess, then in her 51st year, was enjoying a large following both in the United Kingdom and the United States. The principal owner of the *Jean Ingelow*, John Gilman Moses, was a frequent visitor to England, and it was he who gave the vessel her name.

The circumstances around the construction of the *Jean Ingelow* are illustrative of the Slough of Despond into which the shipping industry was slipping. She could have been ready for sea within a few weeks after July 2, 1870, as the *Journal* reported:

> A new ship of a 1000 tons, nearly finished at Mr. Wm. F. Fernald's ship yard at North end, will be ready to launch about the middle of this month. She is a model in design and finish reflecting great credit upon her skillful builder. There are but three or four of this class of vessels of the same rate of tonnage, now building. The mercantile marine list of our country, containing for staunchness, speed and beauty the many names of Portsmouth vessels, is the most fitting tribute that could be paid our ship builders.

But the ship didn't get launched; there was little or no interest in her. In October it was reported that a buyer was being sought.[3] In December, the *Journal* said the ship was "the only one on the stocks between Bath and New York. This superior craft is still for sale. The report of a sale in the Boston papers last week was premature."

Finally, in January, came a report that the ship had been sold to a syndicate headed by former Mayor Horton D. Walker. The price was given as $36,000.[4] The *Journal* had to retract that the next week. Fernald turned them down because he claimed the ship had cost him $56,000 to build. Then Capt. John Gilman Moses put together another group and bought the ship for $38,000. A week later, with a deal apparently certain, it was announced that she "will be launched in a few days." Actually, she went into the water the day that item was published. It was reported: "just as the vessel started off her ways, the sun broke forth, appearing as if a baptism of luck."[5]

While she was being readied for sea, the newspapers enjoyed a debate over the naming of her:

> WHAT'S IN A NAME? — Well, a great deal, oftentimes; and at any rate, nobody likes to be called nicknames. The satisfactory naming of a baby is sometimes as difficult if not as troublesome as its teething; and the successful christening of a ship is no small affair. For instance take the new ship Jean Ingelow, whose name was selected after much thought and examination, by Capt. Moses, who will first take her to sea. Now this noble craft, when purchased, was ornamented with a female figure-head, and of course must have a corresponding name [Lest any hypercritical reader should object to this word female, let us say there was a figure of a woman at the prow.] The name of Harriet Hosmer was thought of, but more than one vessel bears that now; Alice Cary, but here is already a barque of that name; and so on with many others.
>
> It is the rule that whoever is allowed to name a vessel, is expected to present "her' with a suit of flags — (and all vessels are *her*, of course, whether their name be male, female or neuter.) One of the out-of-town owners expressed a desire to name this ship; but the name of his lately deceased wife, which he suggested, is already borne by two ships. And this duplicating a name, even in different countries, is often productive of great confusion and inconvenience — as also is the case with noted public horses.
>
> So at last Jean Ingelow was decided upon, — and most happily so, all agree, for no poet has sung of the sea more sweetly than she, the gifted writer and true woman. Let us give long life to England's poetess, and *bon voyage* to her beautiful American name-sake; and may the success of the latter, like the fame of the first, become worldwide.[6]

So who was Jean Ingelow? The human Jean Ingelow was born in Boston, Lincolnshire, England, March 17, 1820. Her childhood home faced the water, and it stirred in her a love for the sea. When she was 13, the family moved to Ipswich, East Suffolk, and in 1863 she went to live in London, where she spent the rest of her life. Her first poems were published in that same year, and that brought her into close touch with the great literary figures of the day. Much of her writing was devoted to children, and her *Mopsa the Fairy* was a nineteenth-century classic. She wrote several novels, none of which attracted much attention. The modern poet Stanley Kunitz called her "The High Tide of the Coast of Lincolnshire" one of the finest of modern ballads.[7] Physically, she was described as "a small woman with a gentle nervous manner, roughly hewn, almost masculine face, and the most beautiful smile in the world! She was trifle prim but this was tempered by a keen sense of humor."[8]

The *Boston Advertiser*'s Portsmouth correspondent made a detailed report, which is a valuable study of ship construction in the 1870s:

> The Jean Ingelow is of very clean and beautiful model — half clipper style — and it is thought will prove a fast sailer. She looks trim and trig as a pleasure yacht, and will stow a large cargo. She is built almost as heavy and strong as a naval vessel, and finished in handsome style; the accommodations for officers and crew are of the very best and on the most liberal scale, and the ship throughout is fitted and furnished with all the modern improvements, alow and aloft.

> The model was by Mr. Fernald, who has few equals and no superiors as a marine draughtsman and architect. The noted beautiful and swift barques, Fairy, Scud and Wasp of Boston, were designed by him and built for Messrs. Draper & Co., and the three-masted schooner Charles E. Morrison of Boston is also from his skillful hand. The frame of the Jean Ingelow is of New Hampshire white oak, which is pronounced by the chief examiner at Lloyd's to be the best of all timber for this purpose; and her outer planking and working deck are of Southern pine. She is very heavily timbered, braced and bolted; the inner frame trimmed and turned by pattern to a nicety, and the breast and after hooks the deepest we ever saw, and brought well out at the points and very firmly fastened.

> The salting of a ship is no small item, about ninety hogsheads being used between decks of the Jean Ingelow, is filling every crack and crevice left between the outer and inner boarding, by means of air-holes left for this purpose and for ventilation. Portsmouth ships have always been thus salted — an excellent plan, which is not so generally followed by builders elsewhere, and this is one reason for the superior endurance of Piscataqua-built ships over most others.

> The accommodations for officers and men are all on deck, according to the modern fashion, and are about the best we ever examined. In this regard the improvements of the age are as noticeable on ship-board as in the house, compared with those of the last generation. And it is noteworthy, too, that while the merchant marine is thus bettered for poor Jack especially on board Uncle Sam's craft he fares worse and worse as

to quarters, while the officers, in the latter case, monopolize more and more room and expense of fittings.

The spacious and airy trunk-poop contains, in the after-cabin the captain's stateroom, which is quite a good-sized apartment, neatly furnished with spring mattrass bed, lounge, &c., and lighted by the binnacle lamp at night, if desired, by sliding back a screen from the same. There is also a good state-room for the pilot, and water closet, medicine closet, &c. In the forward department or fore cabin, the mate has a fair-sized stateroom; but as he always has to keep the log, and is there-fore what might be called the ship's editor or reporter, we think he ought to have even better accommodations. Here on the opposite side of the cabin is the bread closet, a large tin-lined tank holding 2000 pounds of biscuit; and the neatest possible shelves for the crockery, little closets for stowing away oil and molasses cans, &c., &c. The water butt is an immense boiler-iron tank between decks, holding four or five thousand gallons.

The joiner work and finishing of the ship was done by Mr. Samuel Clark; and the after-cabin is handsomely finished in chestnut and curled maple pannelling with rosewood and gilt pilasters, and white and gilt cornices, oval mirror, &c. The boys have a house by themselves separate from the men, with good room and bunks for four, — a good plan. The cook's galley is large and well furnished, as the kitchen should ever be, whether afloat or ashore, and he has a private room under his own lock and key. The forecastle has bunks for ten, and is also roomy and convenient.

The ship is rigged by Mr. Joseph C. Muchmore and has Howe's rig, of Russia cordage throughout, and wire fore and aft ways. The painting is done by Mr. Josiah Grover. The furniture is from Mr. A. T. Joy's establishment. The ship's husband, or at least the gentleman whom we found in charge of the prepa-rations of the Jean Ingelow for her bridal with the ocean, in the absence of Captain Moses, was Captain John Davis, who has himself had forty-seven years' experience on shipboard, most of the time on quarterdeck, the longest term of any of the shipmasters at this port, and who tells us that he never walked so fine a craft as this before.[9]

Every little tidbit of news available about the *Jean Ingelow* was presented to its readers by the *Journal*. It was reported that she was taking on board 250 tons of stone ballast, at $1.10 per ton. By March 18 she was ready to leave, and a local poet dedicated a few lines to her:

For the Portsmouth Journal.

THE "JEAN INGELOW."

Fit name for noble ship, whose sails unfurled
   Fling their responses with each passing breeze
To her, whose strains have thrilled a listening world,
   Echoed across the seas.

From her impassioned soul, on waves of thought,
   Like the strong pulsing of the ocean's breast,
The mystic ships their golden freights have brought,
   Flinging from east to west.

Wafted with mighty power, from heart to heart,
   By words of cheer and fancies sweet and true,
Her songs have moved with Poet's subtlest art
   The old world and the new.

Deep in all natures lies a hidden fire
   Only such poet's touch can bring to light;
Just as the sea, when flood tide-winds are higher,
   Grows almost infinite.

So when with glistening eyes her name we read,
   And see the white sails spreading to the breeze,
From loving hearts will rise the prayer, "God Speed,"
   Echoed across the seas.

There was some speculation that Captain Moses would take the *Jean Ingelow* on her maiden passage, as he had done with the *Calcutta*. But that didn't prove true. The command was given to Capt. Benjamin F. Jacobs of York. Jacobs had lost his two previous commands, the last one being the *Merrimack*, but apparently there was still confidence in his seamanship. The *Jean Ingelow* left Portsmouth forever on March 23, towed by a tug to Boston.[10] She was chartered to take a cargo of ice to Calcutta. Before the ship left the Port of Portsmouth, Jean Ingelow's American publishers had Davis Brothers, Portsmouth photographers, take pictures of the ship at her mooring in the North End. Copies of the photographs were forwarded to the poetess. Also before she went out of Portsmouth, the *Providence Journal* observed:

> More fitting tribute could not have been paid to the special bent of Miss Ingelow's genius! She loves the sea; she was born near its shores; and some of her choicest imagery has been drawn from long familiarity with the ebb and flow of its

tides, the undulations of its waves, and the motion of its white-winged ships.[11]

The *Jean Ingelow* sailed from Boston to Calcutta on April 17, 1871. As early as June 1871, in anticipation of her return passage, a painting, showing her taking a pilot of New York, was executed and on display in E. H. Joy's music store in Portsmouth. On the seventeenth the *Journal* said, "it is a beautiful specimen of marine painting, artistic and picturesque, and invites attention. It is wholly original...the work of our talented artist Thomas P. Moses." In other words, Moses painted the *Jean Ingelow* before she even arrived within range of his brush. Later in September, it was reported the *Jean Ingelow* ran aground on a sand bar while going up to Calcutta on August 14. The vessel was loaded with ice and was badly strained.[12] Captain Jacobs brought the ship back to the United States and was relieved by Capt. Charles G. Shillaber, who made several voyages in her. In 1875 the *News-Courier* waxed ecstatic over the *Jean Ingelow*:

> The beauty of her lines and the attractive appearance, which have made the best class of merchantmen, built in the United States, well known the world over, can be appreciated by our citizens if they take a look at the Jean Ingelow, 1,100 tons, belonging to Portsmouth, N.H., which has just arrived here from New York. She is one of the most sightly ships that has entered this port in some time, and can be seen at the Commercial Wharves.[13]

By that time the *Jean Ingelow* was commanded by Capt. George S. Tanton, who had her for the next few years. At an auction in Portsmouth a 1/32 share in the ship was bid in by Captain Moses for $1,500, giving the vessel a value of $52,800. At the same time, a 1/32 share in the *Calcutta* went for $1,150.[14] In January 1876, the *Charleston News and Courier* reported:

> — The superior American ship Jean Ingelow, Capt. Tanton, of about 1100 tons, was cleared yesterday for Liverpool, by Messrs. D. Jennings & Son with the following valuable cargo: 393 bags sea island cotton, 2,858 bales upland cotton and 240 tons phosphate rocks — total weight of cargo, 1,422,694 pounds, value, $222,839. This first class ship is in every respect an admirable specimen of American nautical taste and skill, and with favorable gales there can be no doubt but that she will make a creditable passage to Liverpool.[15]

In April 1877 the *Jean Ingelow* sailed from New York for Java. Portsmouth's George S. Tanton was still master. The captain was a brother to the furniture maker, Harry Tanton. Other Portsmouth residents in the crew were Horace Clark, first mate; Daniel Lovell, carpenter; and Herbert E. Simpson, son of a partner in one of the city's oldest businesses, a clothing store at Bow and Market streets. It closed its doors late in 1988.

An intimation came in December 1878 that all wasn't well with the *Jean Ingelow*:

> The ship Jean Ingelow, built at this port in 1871 by William F. Fernald, and owned by Capt. J. Gilman Moses, Moses H. Goodrich, Thomas E. Call, Isaiah Wilson and others of this city, is now over two hundred days out on the passage from Cardiff to Singapore with a cargo of coal, and grave fears for her safety are entertained. Her tonnage was 1076, and she sailed under command of Capt. George S. Tanton of this city, Mr. Horace Clark being the first officer. Capt. Tanton, we are informed, married an English lady just before starting on his last trip, and his bride accompanied him on the voyage.[16]

The *Jean Ingelow*'s fate is unknown. However, an odd story was reported of how one person from Portsmouth escaped the *Jean Ingelow*'s fate—whatever it was. Herbert Simpson, who went to Java in her, and then to Cardiff, decided to leave the ship. Captain Tanton at first wouldn't let him go, but agreed after the young man's father intervened in a letter to the captain. Simpson came home from Cardiff, and then went back to sea in the steamship *Indiana*.

This sketch opened with a few lines by Jean Ingelow, and so it shall close:

> "Then I hear the water washing, never golden
>   waves were brighter,
> And I hear the capstan creaking — 'tis a sound
>   that cannot cloy.
> Bring her to, to ship her lading, brig or schooner,
>   sloop or fighter,
> With a 'pull'e haul'e, pull'e haul'e, yoy! heave,
>   hoy!"

Grandee

SPECIFICATIONS: 1873. Tobey & Littlefield. Grandee figurehead, elliptic stern. Burthen, 1,285 tons. Length, 193.6 feet; beam, 38.5 feet; depth, 23.8 feet. Two decks. Original owners—Benjamin F. Jacobs and John H. Burleigh, of South Berwick; Micajah C. Burleigh, of Somersworth; Thomas E. Call, Charles H. Mendum, Charles E. Myers, et al., of Portsmouth.

The building and launching of the ship *Grandee* brought to an end what had really grown into a shipbuilding dynasty on Noble's Island. The business had started 20 years before with the *Brother Jonathan*, and in the course of two decades the partnership built 22 three-masted, square-rigged ships; 5 barks; 2 schooners; and a brig. That was a far cry from the hundred built by Master William Badger prior to 1829, but the total tonnage was far in excess of the latter's production. Before constructing the *Grandee*, Tobey & Littlefield hadn't built a ship since the *Yosemite* in 1867—although, in that year, the firm built two barks. One of the barks, the *Quickstep*, at 820 tons, was bigger than many of the ships that had been built on the Piscataqua. In 1868 the yard produced no vessels, but in 1869 3 barks went down the ways, and in 1871 a 60-ton schooner was launched.

So, it was undoubtedly with much pleasure that the *Journal* reported on October 12, 1872:

— Messrs. Tobey & Littlefield are making preparations for the construction, at their shipyard, of a ship of about 1200 tons. She will be owned by Capt. Jacobs and others of this city, and be first class in every respect. The building of this vessel and the one now under way at Neal's shipyard, will give employment to our mechanics for some time. It is a pleasure to note the revival of this once important branch of business along the shores of the Piscataqua. Ships, we are told, are now paying the owners much better than at any time for the past dozen years.

The ship *Grandee* was launched on August 12, and a news story said that "a large number of ladies and gentlemen were on board to enjoy the novelty, as the noble vessel 'kissed the sea' a prolonged shout of applause went forth from the crowd who were present. After gracefully yielding to the single anchor, the *Grandee* was taken in tow by the steamer *Clara Bateman*, assisted by the steam launch from the *USS Plymouth*, towed to the shears at the navy yard, where her lower masts will be put in, then she will be hauled to this side and her rig-

The Grandee *was built in 1873 in Portsmouth by Tobey & Littlefield. Courtesy of Mariners' Museum, Newport News, Virginia.*

ging completed. She will then leave for Boston or New York, as her engagements may require under the command of Captain Jacobs.... The *Grandee* is one of the finest specimens of marine architecture even constructed on the Piscataqua."[17]

There was almost a note of sadness in the *Journal* item on August 30 when it was observed that the completion of the *Grandee* ended shipbuilding on Noble's Island, and that the yard and the remainder of the island would be used by the railroads for wharfage and other purposes. Noble's Island became one vast coal bunker, and the railroads changed its shape dramatically. In the past ten years Noble's Island has undergone more radical changes. It is now the site of office and residential condominiums, and each of the structures thereon bears the name of a ship built there more than a century ago. Stephen Tobey quietly retired from active life and bought a house in the Creek, in which he lived out his days. Daniel Littlefield founded a family lumber business that continued in existence on Raynes Avenue until 1988, although Littlefield himself died in 1901.

The *Grandee* sailed from Portsmouth on September 14, bound for New York, where she loaded a miscellaneous cargo for Valparaiso. As a sort of footnote, a news item remarked that a new style of steering apparatus had been installed in the *Grandee* by Michael R. Perkins of Portsmouth. Unfortunately, no details about the new gear were given.[18] The *Grandee* actually went to Callao, arriving there on February 5, 1874, a passage of 86 days, "beating the celebrated clipper ship *Aginore* by five days."[19] The value of her cargo was put at $30,000. Captain Jacobs informed the agent, Charles H. Mendum, that she was a fine sea-boat. Two years later, the *Grandee* went from New York to Callao in 69 days, the fastest passage ever on record.[20] She then went on to Pacasmayo, 200 miles farther north on the Peruvian coast. Jacobs brought her back to Hampton Roads in 86 days. Capt. Joseph R. Shillaber assumed command and took the *Grandee* from New York to Melbourne in 81 days. The ship luckily escaped serious damage from an iceberg on the passage. She actually bumped the berg but took on no water, so she cleared away, repaired, and went on with her passage.[21]

When the *Grandee* returned to New York, Captain Jacobs resumed command, and held it until 1884. In that year, a 1/32 interest in the *Grandee* was bought at auction by Charles H. Mendum for $800. The amount seems low for such a profitable ship, one that paid her shareholders a dividend after every voyage.

In 1879 Jacobs sailed from New York, heading for Japan. On November 29, 1879, the *Journal* reported:

> — The ship Grandee of this port, Captain B. F. Jacobs, arrived at Yokahama, Japan, Nov. 14, in 148 days from New York, has been chartered, by her agent in this city, to load sugar at Manilla, for New York, at $8.50 per ton, and will carry 1830 tons. The Portsmouth correspondent of the Concord *Monitor* says that several vessels have been chartered on the spot, by their captains, for the same voyage and cargo at $12 and $15 per ton, among them the ship William H. Marcy, of this port, which will carry 2200 tons, at $12 per ton. The recent rise in the price of sugar has caused freights to advance to paying rates, and managers of ships who were wise enough not to charter at low rates, will make rich returns to the owners, which will be gladly received after the ruinously low rates for the past few years.

On his voyage to the Far East in 1882, Jacobs took his wife and family with him. He also had as a passenger Thomas S. Gay of Portsmouth, a sail maker by trade, who believed a sea trip would benefit his health. Gay planned to leave the *Grandee* in Japan and come home by steamer, but he enjoyed himself so much that he made the passage home in her.

In 1884, Jacobs was having so much trouble with his vision that he yielded command to his chief mate, H. T. Evans, who had been on the ship ever since her maiden voyage. For three years all went well with the *Grandee* and her new master. At the time Jacobs gave up the ship, a painting of her was on display in a Portsmouth store.[22]

Evans brought the *Grandee* into New York in 1885, in 107 days from Hong Kong and 90 days from Angiers, Java, "thus adding a score to her reputation for making good time."[23] While on that passage, the *Grandee* spoke the ship *Baun*, from Calcutta to Demarara, carrying 600 Chinese coolies. "The *Baun* reported having a contagious disease on board and had lost 18 coolies up to that time." Things went well with Captain Evans until 1887, when sex intruded on the success story:

> The following is given us as the correct statement of the ill proceedings of Capt. H. T. Evans of the Portsmouth ship Grandee, already referred to:
>
> When the Grandee arrived in port at New York after a fine passage of ninety-four days from Hong Kong, she found an anchorage near Governor's island. Early on the following morning a passing boatman was called to the ship's side, and got the job of seeing ashore a woman who had been a part of the ship's company, though her name does not appear on any of the ship's papers. The woman was landed at a Red Hook wharf, on the Brooklyn side, but Capt. Evans landed at the Battery, where he met Capt. Jacobs and the agent of the vessel, and was ordered to dock her at Pier 47, East river.
>
> After her arrival there the business of the voyage was about to be settled, when Capt. Evans astounded all hands by a confession that he could not explain his accounts nor face the owners. He admitted that he had spred it pretty heavily in Hong Kong, and estimated that in his accounts of expenses and disbursements at that port nearly $4,000 were overcharges that he had squandered. He professed the most sincere repentance, and offered to make every effort to assist in straightening out the ship's accounts, and to make any other reparation he could. On the following Saturday the crew were to be paid off and the accounts fixed.
>
> Capt. Jacobs arrived on board the ship at the appointed time, but Capt. Evans had gone. He had packed up his dunnage and disappeared. His flight was also at the expense of the

ship, for he had money in his possession to pay the men and to pay bills, which will bring his defalcation up to about $5,000. It is supposed that he went to Europe, as he disappeared on steamer day; and it is also supposed that the woman he brought from China is the companion of his flight. The sailors all knew her as a public woman in Hong Kong, and say that the captain became infatuated with her while on a spree. He told them on board that she was his wife. She is a German woman about thirty years old, and rather good looking.[24]

Perhaps the most astounding aspect of the Evans story is that it didn't happen more often to mariners who were often gone for long periods from home—although it may have happened to others on Portsmouth ships without getting the publicity that Captain Evans's problems did. However, Captain Jacobs, who was then making his home on Middle Street in Portsmouth, spent weeks in New York straightening out the affairs of the *Grandee*. He then sent the *Grandee* to sea under Capt. Timothy H. Winn. Later she was commanded by Capt. Edwin A. Gerrish, who had commanded the ill-fated *Rockingham*. Gerrish made a voyage to the west coast of South America and returned to Boston in November 1890.

Once again, Benjamin F. Jacobs took command of his beloved ship, sailing her to Manila. His wife and daughter, Isabel, went along. They returned to Portsmouth in March 1892 and were the guests of Charles H. Mendum, the ship's manager. Mrs. Jacobs went back to sea with her husband, but daughter Isabel entered a boarding school in Boston. The *Grandee* came back to Boston in March 1893, and Jacobs reported an extremely rough passage, running into a southeast gale "approaching hurricane force, during which everything movable about the deck and a new suit of sails was lost. The ship was constantly submerged for 20 hours, lost jib boom and washed cover off the well hole, taking in large quantities of water. It is said that Mrs. Jacobs, who has accompanied her husband in his voyages for several years, will now return and take up her residence in Portsmouth."[25]

However, there was more to the story than that: the *Grandee* had been sold to the Boston Tugboat Co., and Captain Jacobs was retiring from the sea. He also moved his residence from Portsmouth to Malden, Massachusetts.[26] Benjamin F. Jacobs died in February 1903, while wintering in Pine Bluff, North Carolina; his body was brought to Portsmouth for funeral services.[27]

Later, the *Grandee* went under the British flag, and the Dominion Coal Co. stripped her and used her venerable hull for a barge. What finally happened to the *Grandee* isn't clear. On October 27, 1894, the *Journal* reported:

— The old Portsmouth ship Grandee, which a few years ago was sold to the Dominion Coal company and was converted into a coal barge, is feared to have been lost. While towing from Quebec to Sydney, C. B., on Wednesday of last week she broke away from the steamer which was towing her and all efforts to find her have proved futile. The Grandee was commanded for several years by Capt. B. F. Jacobs of this city and was generally termed the yacht of the East Indian fleet on account of her grace and swiftness.

However, in his definitive work, *American Merchant Ships*, Matthews said her home port was Sydney, Cape Breton Island (Nova Scotia), that she kept her maiden name, "and she appears listed in Canadian Registers as late as 1912."

No matter her ultimate fate, the *Grandee* was long remembered in Portsmouth, as evidenced by an item in 1884:

In one of the show windows of Montgomery's music and art store, last week was placed a picture which attracts a good deal of attention, it being a representation of the ship "Grandee" of this port, lying at anchor in Hong Kong, China. The picture is the work of a Chinese artist who has somewhat eccentric ideas regarding perspective, if we may judge from the result of his attempt to delineate the lofty hills behind and above the town of Hong Kong; but he managed to "catch on" to the ship just right, and produced an excellent likeness of one of the finest ships ever built on the Piscataqua river.

The Grandee was built in 1873 by Messrs. Tobey & Littlefield, for Capt. B. F. Jacobs and others, and was the last vessel built by that firm, though we believe Mr. Littlefield afterward constructed several smaller crafts; she registers 1295.43 tons, and for sailing and carrying far exceeds the original expectations of her owners; and under command of Capt. Jacobs — who by the way is of that energetic and thoroughly competent class of shipmasters for which this region was once famous — she has made a clipper's record for speed, though her carrying capacity was not sacrificed to sailing qualities when she was laid down.

She sailed from this port on the 20th of September, 1873; loaded in New York for Callao, Peru; and made the passage to the latter port in seventy-nine days, and from Callao to San Francisco in twenty-nine. In San Francisco she loaded with flour and wheat for Liverpool, made the passage in 118 days, and landed 1826 tons of cargo in first-class condition. In

1875 she made a trip from New York to Callao in sixty-nine days, that being the best time on record; and she has also a record of eighty-one days from New York to Melbourne, Australia, a passage not often beaten.

Frank Jones

SPECIFICATIONS: 1873. John Neal. Kittery Foreside. Full-length figurehead, elliptic stern. Burthen, 1,453 tons. Length, 199 feet; beam, 39.4 feet; depth, 25 feet. Two decks. Original owners—Daniel Marcy, Peter Marcy, William Ross, et al.

In naming this vessel, Daniel Marcy paid tribute to the steadily rising star in New Hampshire's political and industrial life. Frank Jones was parlaying the fortune he had made in brewing ale into banking, railroading, hotels, communications, and other business interests. He had been mayor of Portsmouth and, in 1874, was the successful Democratic candidate for a seat in the U.S. House, a post he held for two terms. No extant records show whether or not Frank Jones had an interest in the *Frank Jones*. However, he wasn't listed as an original investor.

It was announced in February 1872 that John Neal would build a 1,500-ton ship for the Marcy brothers, with construction to start in the spring. Shipbuilding, however, didn't move as quickly in the 1870s as it had in earlier decades, so it was August before the preliminaries could be reported: "Preparations have commenced for the building of a ship at Badger's Island, to cost $100,000. Capt. Daniel Marcy being the mover in the matter."[28]

A year later, a news report said the launching of the *Frank Jones* would take place around September 1. It finally happened on the twenty-fourth, with "a large crowd of spectators to the fine spectacle."[29] A week later, it was reported that the *Frank Jones* "has a full length figurehead of the gentleman whose name she bears. She has now been towed to Commercial Wharf." On October 2, the *Journal* eulogized the new ship:

> Wednesday afternoon the new ship Frank Jones glided from the ways of Neal's ship yard, and amid the huzzas of thousands of people who thronged every lookout in the neighborhood or floated in a hundred boats upon the river, the noble ship plunged into the water of the Piscataqua. It was a grand launch. No sooner was the vessel clear of the ways than two

immense anchors were dropped from her bows and soon brought her to a stand-still.

The steam tug Clara Bateman was ready to take the vessel in tow, and she was soon safely moored at one of the navy yard docks, where her main-mast was put in. She would then be brought over to Long Wharf to be dressed for the seas. As we have before stated, she is considered by the best judges one of the best ships that has ever been launched in these waters. It is estimated that when ready to sail she will cost about $120,000. So superior is she considered, that the naval authorities here have caused plans and specifications of her to be made for the use of the department, giving a full description of every stick of timber in the vessel.

The Frank Jones has a keel of 195 feet in length, and the ship's length over all is 210 feet. She is 26 feet deep and has a 40 feet beam. Her tonnage will be rated at about 1600. She is owned by Hon. Daniel Marcy, Captain Peter Marcy of New Orleans, Captain Wm. Ross, Jr., and Mr. John Neal. Her complement of men will be about 26, all told. She will sail under command of Capt. Wm. Ross, Jr. Capt. Ross has been with Hon. Daniel Marcy for about seventeen years, and has made successful voyages to all parts of the world. He is considered a model sea captain in every respect and will be proud of the new ship of which he is commander and part owner. His first mate is Mr. Horace Clark of this city, and his second mate Mr. Franklin Pierce Marcy of New Orleans, youngest son of Capt. Peter Marcy.

This is the eighteenth ship that has been built by Hon. Daniel Marcy since 1844. That year he built the Judah Touro. In succeeding years he has seen launched under his direction the R. D. Shepherd, Peter Marcy, Frank Pierce, Levi Woodbury, James Buchanan, Express, Henrietta Marcy, S. C. Thwing, Sarah Pettigrew, Georgiana, Orozimbo, Eloisa, Asphodel, Niobe, Daniel Marcy, Wm. Ross, and the Frank Jones.

The last is the largest vessel and best of them all. Most of these vessels have been sold, the reputation of Capt. Marcy's ships standing so high that the Niobe, Daniel Marcy and Wm. Ross were purchased in foreign ports at prices that equalled if not exceeded the cost of new ships. The F. Jones will probably be ready for sea before the close of October. — *Times*.

On November 8, the *Journal* reported:

— The splendid new ship Frank Jones sailed hence for New York on Wednesday morning, whence she goes to Liverpool with a cargo of grain. She is commanded by Capt. William A. Ross, who has two Portsmouth men as mates, Messrs. Horace Clark and Samuel Sides, both veritable sea-dogs. Master James Rand, only son of the late Alphonzo L. Rand, goes out as one of the boys. We have already given an extended description of this magnificent ship; it sufficeth to say that the "Frank Jones" is one of the noblest and most thoroughly finished vessels which has ever left these waters, as the thousands of visitors testify who have enjoyed an inspection. The vessel is owned by Capts. Daniel and Peter Marcy, Capt. Ross and others.

Although the Internal Revenue Service wasn't the "all-seeing eye" it is today, there were still tax matters to resolve. After the *Frank Jones* sailed, the town of Kittery tried to collect property taxes on her. In 1875, it was reported:

> The Town of Kittery undertook to tax the ship Frank Jones, built at Neal & Co.'s yard. While the ship was on the stocks, Mr. Neal told the Collector of taxes to take the ship and have the question settled legally. This the officer omitted to do, and now a process for the tax is issued against Mr. Neal. The larger part of the ship was owned out of Kittery, and if the owners are compelled to pay this tax it will be a hint to put up their ships on this side of the Piscataqua, and pay but one tax on their property.[30]

Arriving in New York on November 7, the *Frank Jones* was chartered for Liverpool, and loaded with 23,809 bushels of corn in bulk; 3,235 bushels of corn in bags; 13,595 bushels of wheat in bags; 299 barrels of rosin; 1,800 barrels of flour; 1,518 bags of oil cakes; 1,250 oars; 1,815 handspikes; 200 boxes of cutch; 500 sewing machines; 938 bags of cotton; 2,000 boxes of cheese; and 2,000 staves.[31] She sailed from New York on November 22 and returned in March 1874. That was her last call there. Under Capt. James M. Nichols, she made an uneventful passage to San Francisco, and left that port, in ballast, for Manila. She was being towed out when disaster struck:

> — The Portsmouth ship Frank Jones, Capt. Nichols, in ballast, for Manila, while being towed to sea on Friday last from San Francisco, parted her hawser off Fort Point and went ashore about 200 yards outside the Fort. A strong northwest wind was blowing. The tug kept too near the south shore. The hawser broke three times, and the last time the ship was close to the rocks. The pilot attempted to get sail on her, but she struck before anything could be accomplished. The vessel proved a total loss. The ship was built by Neil & Matthews at

Kittery in 1873, and owned by Daniel Marcy, William Ross and Peter Marcy, each sixteen sixty-fourths; John Neal and John F. Matthews, each five sixty-fourths; Oliver Wilson, four sixty-fourths; Chandler Brooks, two sixty-fourths. She was built under the supervision of Capt. Marcy, her dimensions being as follows: length of keel, 190 feet; length over all, 212 feet; breadth of beam, 39 feet; 2 inches; depth of hold, 25 feet, 9 inches; registered tonnage, 1453 13-100. The vessel was partly insured. The wreck was sold at auction in San Francisco on Monday, for $4750. The hull was deeply embedded in the sand, and the bottom stove in; and there was no hope of its removal.[32]

The *Journal* continued with weekly reports on the status of the wreck; on April 14:

— The ship Frank Jones, which was stranded on a sand bank below San Francisco while bound for Manila in ballast, has been stripped. An attempt to tow her afloat failed. The pilot who had charge of her at the time she went ashore has been exonerated of blame; the accident, under the circumstances, was unavoidable.

On April 21, the progress of salvage work was described:

— It appears that the ship Frank Jones is not the total loss which was at one time apprehended, and although no doubt little better than a total loss as far as the Underwriters are concerned, she is not likely to bleach her bones upon the rocky resting place of Fort Point, San Francisco. It will be remembered that this fine ship, 1454 tons register, owned by Daniel Marcy and others, of this city, and under charge of Capt. Nickles, cleared on the 29th ult. for Manila in ballast, and while being towed out to sea by the steamtug Monarch, parted her hawser and went ashore at Fort Point. After being stripped of sails, running rigging, etc. the hull was sold at auction and the Merchants' Exchange on Monday last to Capt. F. Lee for the trifling sum of $4750, and the purchaser, or those whom he represents, are striving hard to make a good thing of their bargain. A contract has been made with A. W. Von Schmidt, of Blossom Rock fame, to get her off, the contractor to pay all the expenses, and, if successful, to get two-fifth of whatever she may sell for when afloat, and earnest work has already begun. The masts and spars are being taken out, and is being put in a condition to be raised high and dry when repairs will be made and she will be launched. A week or two in dry dock and the wreck sold for $4750 will be worth $50,000.

Opinions of nautical men differ as to the probability of success. Some of them maintain that she can never be got off, while others have implicit faith in Von Schmidt's practical knowledge and his ability to carry out the job, provided only that the weather gives him a reasonable chance. At any rate, the stake is a big one and worth playing for: $50,000 for less than $5000 leaves a wide margin for expenses and profit — only what the Underwriters may say is a different matter.

On April 28 it was reported that her condition was basically the same:

— The condition of ship Frank Jones, at San Francisco, remains the same. Her lower masts and topmasts are still up, and chains have been lashed from the mast heads to the hull on the starboard side to carry out the plan of heaving her down on her broadside when the ballast has been got out. The pumps were started on Thursday, but no effect was visible, as the tide ebbed and flowed in her. A bulkhead is being constructed forward, aft of the holes in the vessel's bottom, and this, after being made water tight, will, of course, neutralize the leaks in that quarter. After the ballast is all out it is calculated that with three tugs, one on each mast, she can be easily hove down on her broadside and then towed off.

Then, on May 26, there was a fairly dispassionate analysis of the wreck and its causes:

— Of the ship Frank Jones, wrecked off San Francisco, the *Post* of that city prints the statements of the captain of the steamtug Monarch, which was towing the ship Frank Jones to sea at the time she was wrecked, and of other steam-tug captains, relative to the loss of that vessel. From this account, and the comments of the *Post*, we gather that the Pilot Board of San Francisco laid the blame for the accident on the captain of the tug, while the tug captains and the *Post* reporter considered the pilot of the ship wholly at fault. Three other vessels started for sea on the same afternoon the Frank Jones was beached, but only one of them got out, the remaining two both parted their hawsers just about where the Frank Jones parted hers; neither of these vessels — the barques Oakland and Bohemia — had a pilot on board, but each hoisted jibs, and sailed back to a safe anchorage. The captain of the Monarch asserted that if the pilot of the Frank Jones had let go the anchor when the ship's hawser parted the first time, and held on (as he could easily have done) until the steamer's hawser could have been gotten out, instead of trusting to the rotten ship's hawser a second time, there would have been no danger of wreck. All efforts to move the ship have been futile, work has now been abandoned, and the ship sold at auction for $700.

Two years after the *Frank Jones* was lost, Portsmouth residents were given a miniature reminder of her:

> — A handsome and accurate model of the Portsmouth ship Frank Jones, the work of Mr. W. M. C. Philbrick of Kittery, who was carpenter on that vessel when she was wrecked, has been on exhibition for some days at Preston's drug store. The hull is made of wood from the old Fort Point Lighthouse, and most of the spars from the ship. It is one of the finest models, of its size, we remember ever to have seen.[33]

In 1893, it was reported that "a very large painting of the ship *Frank Jones* was placed on the wall of the billiard room at the Rockingham on Friday [January 6], by Messrs. H. P. Montgomery and E. Washington Brown. The picture has been painted a long time, but has been thoroughly cleaned renovated and varnished by Brown, and forms a handsome ornament for the hall. The painting represents the ship off Boston and was painted by Stubbs. It is enclosed in a massive eight-inch gold frame, and covers a portion of the wall, 10 feet by 7-1/2 feet."[34]

The painting is today the feature attraction in the main room of the Portsmouth Yacht Club at New Castle. Barbara Becker, the third generation of her family to be associated with the Portsmouth Yacht Club, said the painting was brought along when the club moved from its original headquarters on Mechanic Street to New Castle. How it came into the possession of the Yacht Club isn't known, and it was in bad shape, but has since been reframed and restored by artist Earlene Hansen. Another and similar painting is in the Portsmouth Public Library.

Chocorua

SPECIFICATIONS: *1875. William F. Fernald. North Mill Pond. Burthen, 1,163 tons. Length, 177 feet; beam, 37.5 feet; depth, 23 feet. Original owners—Charles H. Mendum, et al.*

Mt. Chocorua stands a little to the south of the more famous Presidential Range in New Hampshire's White Mountains, yet to many it's the most beautiful peak in the Granite State. The ship's name honored one of the great chiefs of Indian legend. Chocorua ("Old Bear"), alone and unarmed, was pursued to the top of the mountain by a white scalp hunter. After unsuccessfully pleading for his life, Chocorua put a curse on the mountain and then plunged to his death. In the nineteenth century it was believed that a malignant disease in cattle could be traced to streams flowing from the south side of Mt. Chocorua.

Why Charles H. Mendum, who contracted with Fernald for the building of the ship, named her *Chocorua* isn't known. Early in June 1874 is was reported that Fernald and Mendum had contracted for a ship, along the model of the *Jean Ingelow*, "one of the finest vessels in every respect that ever left these waters."[35] Contract in hand, Fernald promptly sent gangs of ship carpenters into the woods of Stratham and Barrington to cut the white oaks needed for the new vessel.[36] By mid-July, the keel had been laid and a large supply of timber had come down from Stratham, probably by water. One workman, George W. Watkins, had a narrow escape from death when a piece of timber fell from a staging. The *Chocorua* was launched on January 4, 1875. On February 23 the *Portsmouth Times* noted:

> The new ship Chocorua was gaily dressed with bunting on Monday, in honor of Washington's birthday. Many persons visited the ship during the day to take a look at her splendid equipments and elegant finish. At 12 o'clock, per invitation of the superintendent of construction, Charles H. Mendum, Esq., a large party of gentlemen sat down to a banquet gotten up for the occasion in the spacious cabin. After attending to the wants of the inner man, the party was called to order and James P. Bartlett, Esq., chosen president. Mr. B. paid an eloquent tribute to the enterprize of the shipbuilders and also to the navigators.

In fact, Capt. Daniel Marcy took advantage of the occasion to enlighten his fellow citizens as to the problems facing shipping and shipbuilding. The reverential manner in which his remarks were reported makes it hard to believe that only a dozen years earlier Daniel Marcy had been vilified in the *Chronicle*, the newspaper now quoting him:

> — Hon. Daniel Marcy, during his sensible and practical speech at the gathering of merchants on board of the Chocorua on Washington's birthday, offered some suggestions in regard to taxes upon shipping which his experience as the leading builder and owner of ships upon the Piscataqua has given him occasion to be familiar with. Capt. Marcy spoke of the tonnage duties, and the manner in which our vessels are measured,

causing us to pay higher duties in foreign ports than vessels of like size with foreign measurements. The high valuation placed upon shipping by our local assessors was referred to.

The Capt. said that not only did our ships cost high, but the duties and charges upon this species of property were excessive. He spoke in commendation of Portsmouth ships and Portsmouth Ship-masters.

Without undertaking to judge whether, under the treaty regulations with Great Britain, it would be admirable to reduce tonnage duties, we have no doubt that something should be done in the way of relieving the other burdens complained of, and to discover what is required, should be the duty, not only of the builder and owner, but of every one who appreciates the relations of shipping to the welfare of our nation.

It would seem that while other interests have sought protection at the hands of Congress from high taxes, the shipping interests have not made the hardship complained of sufficiently understood by that body. What is needed, it seems to us, is a proper co-operation of ship builders, to the end that Congressmen may understand the necessity of fostering this important interest of our nation, one that carries our products to foreign markets and brings to our shores the fruits of other countries.

No nation can flourish, said the Captain, without commerce, and the interest of the West is to have our own ships able to carry our products abroad with equal facilities with the ships of other nations. The Little tariff bill has relieved builders in the matter of yellow metal, and now the interests of the seaboard states should be further relieved by lessening the tax on articles necessarily imported for the construction of ships, liberalizing tonnage dues and measurements, in short, encouraging the building and owning of vessels. Let the shipping interest co-operate in laying the matter properly before Congress and the country, that this feature of our nation's wealth may be encouraged and developed, and the quiet yards of New England will resound with the sound of the ship carpenters' tools, and the inland towns find a new demand for the growth of their forests.

Capt. Charles B. Matthews took the *Chocorua* out of Portsmouth on February 26, headed for New York. When leaving, she was under tow by the *Clara Bateman*, "and was saluted with parting cheers in passing the fleet at the other piers."[37] She was chartered for Callao. A news item listed all of her 30 owners:

— The fine new ship Chocorua built by Mr. William F. Fernald is owned by thirty persons, twenty-two of whom reside in this city. The *Times* gives their names as follows: Charles H. Mendum, Charles D. Matthews, William H. Rollins, Geo. W. Butler, Joseph A. Grace, Geo. W. Plumer, Alex. Robinson, Benj. W. Curtis, John R. Holbrook, Joshua Brooks, A. A. Fernald, Wm. R. Preston, George W. Pendexter, George Stott, Henry L. Garrett, Nathan F. Mathes, Samuel J. Gerrish, Chas. E. Myers, Charles E. Simpson, Robert Roberts, J. H. Morrison, Isaiah Wilson, Portsmouth; Eliza P. Philbrick, Rye; M. H. Burleigh, D. H. Buffum, Great Falls; Isaac Furber, Newington; W. H. Morton, Rollinsford; Oliver Wilson, Chandler Brooks, Augustus Spinney, Josiah W. Lewis, Kittery, Me.; Abraham Brooks, Nathaniel Staples, Eliot, Me.; John H. Burleigh, So. Berwick, Me.; J. P. Simpson, Jonathan Tapley, York, Me.; Edward W. Barstow, John E. Chase, New York.[38]

The *Chocorua* was back in New York by August 1876 and sailed soon after for Angiers, Java, arriving there on January 20, 1877. The news reached Portsmouth on February 28. Because the vessel had not been heard from in more than six months, her owners tried frantically to get more insurance on her, but the underwriters wouldn't have any part of it. News of her safe arrival brought relief for the owners. From Angiers she went to Singapore for a cargo of tin, sugar, gambier nutmeg, pepper, etc., which she brought into Boston on August 21, 106 days from Singapore. She went back out to China, and on the passage spent 10 worrisome days becalmed in one of the South Sea straits, near Sandalwood Island. Matthews reported that there were fires every night along the shore, "indicative of the reception these cannibals would have given the crew if the vessel had gone ashore. Owing to light winds and calms, she was 28 days winding through the passages, finally docking at Shanghai on April 18, 1878."[39] Again, she came back to Boston.

In January 1880 the *Chocorua* loaded for a trip to Sydney and Brisbane. She cleared at Boston on February 9. Word came from Sydney by cablegram on May 18 that Captain Matthews had died on the passage. Ethan A. Locke of Kittery, Maine, the first mate, took command and finished out the voyage. Captain Locke was still master when the *Chocorua* was wrecked on September 20, 1883:

— The ship Chocorua, Capt. Locke, built in this city in 1874, by William F. Fernald, is reported by a cable dispatch to have been lost at Balinao, Philippine Islands, previous to the 1st, while on the way from Hong Kong for Iboilo. Crew supposed to be saved, as nothing to the contrary is reported. She was probably in ballast. Vessel and freight are insured in Boston offices for $50,000. On the 15th of August she was reported at Hong Kong undergoing repairs, having been ashore in Mindora Straits on June 10th, at which time she was got off with loss of anchors, hawser, &c.[40]

Captain Locke arrived at his Kittery home in December and told the story of the wreck:

Capt. Ethan A. Locke of Kittery, master of the late ship Chocorua of this port, has arrived at his home in Maine. The disaster to the vessel happened at six o'clock P. M. on the 29th of September, the ship having sailed from Hong Kong on the 26th. A gale commenced to blow on the 29th, and by four o'clock in the afternoon the Chocorua was under short sail; and at six o'clock, just as the order had been given to ware ship, breakers were sighted ahead and on the lee bow, close aboard, and though the helm was at once put hard up the ship had hardly commenced paying off when she thumped on a coral reef nine miles from land, and hung there until she came off in fragments. A terrific sea was running, and within fifteen minutes from the time the ship struck she was full of water and going to pieces — a total wreck. About midnight the forward house was carried away by a sea, one man going with it; this was the only life lost by the disaster, the rest of the crew lashing themselves to the rigging, and passing the remainder of that night of terror in momentary expectation of having the ship break up under their feet. By daylight the sea had gone down so much that the crew were able to launch the only remaining boat, and two trips were made to the land, the last boat load reaching the beach at eight o'clock in the evening; the ship's masts were seen to fall not long after the boat left her the last time. The men were almost naked on landing, Capt. Locke being shod only with a slipper on one foot and a stocking on the other. The castaways next day reached the telegraph station at Boliano, Philippine islands, where they were kindly cared for.[41]

William H. Marcy

SPECIFICATIONS: 1875. Daniel Marcy, with David Badger. South End. Burthen, 1,607 tons. Length, 213.7 feet; beam, 41 feet; depth, 24.5 feet. Two decks. Original owners—Daniel and Peter Marcy.

While many were skeptical over the continued building of huge, three-masted sailing vessels, Daniel Marcy was willing to risk such ventures. In May 1874, it was reported that Marcy was making preparations for the construction of a large ship. There were to be two—one for each of his two older sons to command. In the execution of his plans, Marcy had as his right hand one of the ablest shipwrights on the river: David D. Badger. The ship was going to be Badger's last; when it was finished he quietly retired to his Newington farm and became a truck gardener. He was the father of Mayor Daniel Badger, the man who cleaned out Portsmouth's red-light district in 1912. Badger died March 18, 1882, at 60.[42]

The keel of the *William H. Marcy* was laid in July, and it was "the largest that had ever been laid in this city being 205 feet in length."[43] So keen was the interest in the new Marcy ship that the newspapers avidly pursued details of her construction. In February 1875, for example, it was reported:

— The ship now building at Marcy's shipyard is the largest ever put on the stocks here, being 225 feet in length, and of 1700 tons burden. There will be used in building it 473,000 feet of pine lumber, 550 tons of oak timber costing $15 per ton, 69 tons of iron, and to cover the deck it will take 5000 feet of Southern pine at a cost of $50 per M. The labor on the vessel will cost $25,000. She will be commanded by Capt. Henry L. Marcy.

Perhaps the above item is most important for telling from whence the materials for Marcy's ship were coming. Native timbers were nearing exhaustion. In April 1875, the *Chronicle* related that a large "boiler tank, weighing up to 4,000 pounds, with a capacity of 38,000 gallons of water, was put in position in the hold of Captain Marcy's new ship on Saturday morning." In May, it was reported that "six large coils of wire rigging for Marcy's new ship, made at Glasgow, Scotland, arrived here over the Eastern Railroad on Monday."[44] The increasing use of railroads to move goods was noted in the preliminary remarks about the 1870s in this chapter, and here it's shown that even shipbuilding materials were arriving by rail—not water. It's noteworthy that the veteran spar and mast maker, William R. Martin, supplied those items for the *William H. Marcy*. Where did those timbers come from? Not the woods of New Hampshire or Maine, but from the timberlands of Michigan—and by rail, of course. The importation of steel wire also indicates increasing dependency on that material for rigging a ship, especially the standing rigging. No one knows, no one will ever know, how many times the clippers and the big square-riggers had to drift to a stop in midocean and spend a day or two tightening up their rigging. Hemp stretches, steel doesn't—not much, anyway.

However, it was nearly a year before the *William H. Marcy* plunged into the water. In its prelaunching story on June 5, the *Chronicle* said:

> The splendid new seventeen-hundred-tonned ship at Marcy's shipyard will be launched to-day at high water, which will occur about half past twelve P. M. There have been fears expressed by casual observers that the floating of the vessel will be attended with some risk, and that extra precaution will be needed to avoid accident, but these anxieties are entirely groundless, as there is not a better or safer launching ground on the river. And only a walk to the yard and from there to the stern of the vessel now lying upon the stocks is needed to convince the most incredulous. In the first place, Capt. Marcy has lengthened the old ways nearly one hundred feet, so that the ship drawing, as she will, only eight and one-half feet of water, and the depth of water at her stern at high tide being ten feet or more, she will float before entirely leaving the launching ways, after which it will be an easy matter to check and control her. The material of the ship from bow to stern is of the very best, and has been selected and put in under the personal supervision of Capt. Marcy, whose experience as a shipbuilder has given him the great success and fame by which is known among ship masters and owners at home and abroad. The length of the keel of the above mentioned vessel is two hundred and five feet; breadth of beam forty-one and two inches; depth of hold from top of floors to top of lower beam, fifteen feet and six inches; height between decks eight feet and six inches; angle of dead rise five degrees; angle of entrance thirty-nine degrees; angle of clearance thirty-seven degrees; capacity seventeen hundred tons, carpenter's measurement. She is to be called the "William H. Marcy," and is owned by Peter Marcy, Esq., of New Orleans, and his brother, Hon. Daniel Marcy of Portsmouth. She will be commanded by Capt. J. T. Marcy, the second son of the builder, and as she is thus preeminently a Marcy ship, we predict for her the good fortune that has attended her owners,

that good fortune that is born of shrewd business foresight, hard labor, and a personal attention to one's affairs.

As a large crowd will be present to witness the launch, we would suggest that next to Pierce's Island there is no better point of observation than Brown's Hill, in front of the residence of H. F. Wendell, Esq.

For Portsmouth readers, undoubtedly the most intriguing part of the above account is the term "Brown's Hill." Henry F. Wendell's residence was at 2 South Street, which puts it on the rise of ground at the junction of Newcastle Avenue and South Street in present-day Portsmouth.

All the fears advanced by the local launching experts were proved unjustified. "Some 3,000 spectators being present and jamming every vantage point on Pierce Island, many of whom, as is human nature, pleasurably anticipating disaster. The spectators were everywhere, all spaces being occupied by men, women, and children at an early hour, to witness the large mass of wood and iron rush into the water. But it didn't rush at all. It simply glided down the ways, and into the channel as though it had been over the tracks a hundred times." After the ship was safely afloat, she was secured to wait for the fuller night tide to get her over to the shears wharf at the Navy Yard. She was finally tied up at one o'clock the next morning.[45]

On Tuesday, July 16, Capt. Daniel Marcy hosted friends at a luncheon on board the newly named *William H. Marcy*. The ship, under the command of Judah Touro Marcy, was scheduled to leave the Port of Portsmouth the next day. The *Chronicle* commented, in part:

> The William H. Marcy is, without doubt, the finest and most perfect embodiment of naval skill and architecture ever set afloat. She is as strong as the best of New Hampshire oak and Norway iron can make her, besides having been built by one of the best carpenters that ever handled an adze, David D. Badger. From truck to keelson excellence of construction seems to have been the prevailing idea.
>
> After partaking of the viands, the speech-making was supplemented with James P. Bartlett selected as chairman.

The *Journal*'s reporter wrote on July 17 that the speeches were "of a congratulatory order, mention being made of the courage of Capt. Marcy, whatever might be the prospects of business, to build and get a company to own ships. He was known all over the State where timber grew, and his expenditure for ship building here had done much to increase the wealth and reputation of Portsmouth.

"Capt. Marcy spoke of his love for Portsmouth and his pride in his ships and his ship masters. Thirteen ships he had set afloat, each one commanded by Portsmouth captains, and he had never been disappointed in one of these officers. He spoke of the keen enjoyment which his family connections in New Orleans always felt in returning to Portsmouth, and said the celebration of the 17th of June had done more to inaugurate an era of good feeling than could all the politicians. Cheers were given for the Captain, as we always call him; for his son J. Touro Marcy who commands the ship, and for others. The affair was pleasant one, and the tone of the remarks showed a high appreciation of the manner in which Capt. Marcy had used his means and the capital of his friend in developing the industry of Portsmouth ship building."

Unfortunately, the contemporary news accounts left unresolved one tricky question: for whom was the *William H. Marcy* named? The father of Daniel and Peter Marcy, the owners, was named Peter. One or the other might have had an early-born son who was being honored, but that doesn't check out. Richard E. Winslow III, an astute researcher, joined me in pursuit of an answer, and we both came up wanting. It could be speculated that the Marcy brothers honored a remote tribal connection, William Learned Marcy, and simply didn't have the right middle initial. William L. Marcy, 1786–1857, was a brilliant lawyer, governor of New York, and Secretary of State. Whatever, the *William H. Marcy* was so registered in the Port of Portsmouth.

The *William H. Marcy* sailed on Wednesday, the sixteenth of July, at 9:00 A.M. Such are the vagaries of wind power, the ship was only off Rye Beach in the afternoon. When she did get to New York, she was loaded with freight for San Francisco. Clearing New York on August 31, she docked in San Francisco on January 17, 1876.[46] From San Francisco, the ship went to Liverpool, probably with grain. She arrived in England on June 22, a passage of 106 days. She loaded salt for New York, and on that leg of her voyage she lost a seaman, Francis McMahon of Prince Edward Island. McMahon fell overboard while catting the anchor and was drowned.

With one round-the-world trip accomplished, the *William H. Marcy* went to sea again from New York on November 10. She arrived on the West Coast on April 9, 1877. While in the vicinity of the Falkland Islands, a severe leak developed but was kept under control by her pumps. After docking in San Francisco, the ship was surveyed, and it was ordered that she be caulked and coppered and six extra beams installed.[47] (In an aside, it should be noted that almost worldwide telegraphic communications had speeded up shipping news.) The scarcity of cargoes and her own repairs kept the *William H. Marcy* in port until November 17, when she sailed for Liverpool. She went back to San Francisco and joined the large number of ships waiting for cargoes. While the ship was idling in the harbor, Captain Marcy rescued a small boy named Peter Jensen, who had put out from Berkeley in a small skiff. The youngster's craft swamped just as Marcy's boat reached him. But it was far from the first incident of the kind in Judah Touro Marcy's life, as indicated by the *San Francisco Evening Bulletin* on February 14, 1879:

> Capt. Marcy, commanding the ship Wm. H. Marcy, which finished loading at Oakland Long Wharf, and owned by his father, has quite an enviable record as a saver of human life. He has made several voyages to this port, and on each occasion he saved the lives of one or more persons from drowning. On one occasion he saved two persons from drowning off Front street wharf. On another occasion he saved two lives off Union street wharf. Still later, two persons were saved by him from drowning off Mission street wharf. About three weeks ago he saved two boys from drowning off Goat Island. This makes a total of nine lives saved by this heroic captain in this port. The Marcy sails with her gallant commander and a cargo of wheat for Liverpool to-morrow.[48]

Finally, in January 1879, the *William H. Marcy* was chartered to carry wheat to the United Kingdom, at a rate of £1.12.6 to Liverpool or Le Havre, or £1.15 to Cork. She went to Ireland, unloading her wheat at Queenstown. During her last months in Marcy ownership, she was in the Far East and then London.

Daniel Marcy, taking his third son, George D. Marcy, with him, went to England in April 1881 and, while there, negotiated the sale of the *William H. Marcy* to a German syndicate.[49] The sale was reported in the *Chronicle* on January 18, 1882, and on February 25 the paper commented:

> Ship William H. Marcy, recently sold in London for 12,000 pounds sterling, was owned in part by Messrs. Daniel Marcy and John R. Reding of this city, and Joel Wilson of Kittery. This ship was commanded by Capt. J. Touro Marcy. She goes under the German flag, having been sold to a firm in Bremen, who have before purchased ships built under the supervision of the senior Capt. Marcy, and are especially satisfied with the quality of our Portsmouth-built ships. It seems that ships built on our river are bound to last. Every now and then the sale of some old vessel, which from its age seems to have exist-

ed long after vessels contemporaneously built have gone to Davy Jones' locker, is announced as having been built on the Piscataqua, years long gone.

It is a pity that this industry has not been kept up in Portsmouth, but while mechanics will prefer to work even a third of their time on the navy yard, to constant employment at private shipyards, at fair wages, or upon contracts for doing portions of a ship's work, there can be but little inducement for the master builder to let us hear the sound of the axe, hammer and tool of iron resounding, where now all is in a state of peaceful quiet and repose.

Daniel Marcy struck a fairly good bargain in selling the *William H. Marcy*—she brought £12,000 sterling. While Daniel Marcy was in England, he was joined by his wife and her sister, a Mrs. Chapman of Old Cambridge, Massachusetts. Also in the party were Daniel and O. E. Ross, sons of Capt. William Ross.

Granite State

SPECIFICATIONS: 1877. John Neal and David D. Badger. Kittery Foreside. Burthen, 1,683 tons. Length, 252 feet; beam, 41.5 feet; depth 24 feet. Original owners—Daniel and Peter Marcy, William Ross, and John Neal.

Undoubtedly, the tremendous size of their proposed new vessel induced the Marcy brothers to build it in John Neal's yard at Kittery Foreside. David D. Badger was induced to come out of retirement in Newington to lend a hand. Peter Marcy, who, early in life, had been a ship's carpenter, came to Portsmouth in September 1876 to take part in the planning of the ship. The brothers' proposal brought the comment: "This will be good news to the large number of carpenters of Kittery, many of whom have been out of work for a long time."[50] In December 1876, 25 men were working on the new ship, and the keel was nearly ready for the frame. Seventy tons of ship timbers were logged by S. S. Brackett off the woodlot of John Hatch in Greenland and hauled to Kittery. By April, the frame was up and presented quite a shipshape appearance. The *Chronicle* said on June 5, 1877:

On Monday the bowsprit for the new ship on the stocks at Kittery was taken from the sparyard of Mr. William R. Martin, where it was built, to be transported to Kittery. The bowsprit is of hard pine and weighs about nine tons, the truck

The next to the last full-rigged ship built on the Piscataqua River in 1877, the Granite State *is shown here after being wrecked near Land's End, Cornwall, England, on November 5, 1895. Courtesy Peabody Museum of Salem.*

on which it was mounted (one of the navy yard timber trucks) weighing about a ton; and on arriving near the draw the oxen were unhitched and the load left standing, the bridge owners refusing to take the responsibility of permitting it to cross, possibly fearing the wheels would cut through the planking, or that the heavy weight might carry one of the draws down altogether, — at any rate, they would not assume the risk of allowing the heavy laden truck to be drawn across. During the afternoon the railing of the bridge was cut away, and the heavy bowsprit tumbled overboard, making a prodigious splash as it struck, to the infinite delight of the usual crowd of overseeing small boys.

Having been tumbled into the river, the bowsprit was floated to the Foreside for installation on the vessel. By the end of June, more than a hundred men were employed in the shipyard, including the caulkers. It was speculated that "another new ship of about 1400 tons will be built there."[51] Alas, it was only speculation. In its prelaunching story on August 3, the *Chronicle* gave an exhaustive description of the *Granite State*:

> The new ship "Granite State," built at Neal's shipyard at Kittery, is the largest, and is claimed by her owners to be the best built merchantman ever put together on the Piscataqua; and after a visit to this splendid specimen of naval architecture, and carefully inspecting her under the guidance of Capts. Marcy and Ross, and Messrs. John Neal and Charles H. Downs, we are strongly inclined to consider the claim fully substantiated, and that everything which experience could suggest or the most liberal outlay secure has been done to make the noble ship as firm as she should be to do honor to her name.
>
> There has been used in the construction of the "Granite State" over 500,000 feet of yellow pine, 650 tons of ship timber, 35,000 feet of white pine, 100 tons of iron and a large amount of copper; she is very heavy fastened, and trenailed all through with the best of locust. Great care has been taken to utilize all her room to the best advantage, and throughout her accommodations are of the first order.
>
> Her length over all is 252 feet; breadth of beam, 41 feet 6 inches; depth of hold, 24 feet. She has a long floor, is sharp fore and aft, will have a very large carrying capacity, and unless her model belies her will be a fast sailer. She has a five-foot hoop running six feet forward of the mainmast, timbered up the same as a three-decked ship as far as the poop deck. There are four main keelsons sixteen inches square, fastened to the main keel with 1 1-2 inch iron; two sister keelsons each side of the main keelson, 30 by 13 inches, fastened with 1 1-4 inch iron. Her ceiling is of the best yellow pine, commencing at the floor timber heads with planks 14 by 15 inches, running up above the bilge; the remainder are 12 and 14 inches. The clamps are 10 inches, all square bolted with 1 1-4 inch iron. There are three lower deck water ways, similarly fastened. She has double beams in all her working hatchways; also double water ways on her upper deck. She is square bolted throughout, one bolt being driven out and the other in. The outside planking is of the best material and unusual thickness, and fastened in the most thorough manner.
>
> The cabin and joiner work, by Mr. C. H. Downs of this city, reflect credit on the designer and master workman; better

work has seldom been seen than in this ship. The after house is 48 feet long and 24 wide, having a pilot house in the forward end, and the main entrance to the forward and after cabins. The companionway ladder, of hard wood, on either hand leads into the forward cabin, which contains rooms for the officers, pilot room, steward's room and pantry, with bins and tanks for holding ship's stores. The forward cabin will be used as a dining saloon. The mizzen mast will be handsomely cased, and orna- mented on the forward side with the New Hampshire coat of arms in a rich frame; an armory will be built on the after side.

The after cabin will be splendidly fitted, with all the modern improvements. The finish is white, enameled doors and panels, with Webster's latest patterns of moulding and caps. The gangway entrance leading to the after cabin is fitted with a hard wood ladder mounted with brass. The after cabin saloon is 15 feet long and 11 feet wide, lighted by sky and side- lights. There are spare staterooms, bath-room, closets, etc. The furniture is to be of the latest pattern and very handsome; and not the least important article is a very large and convenient medicine chest, which will be stocked by Mr. Wm. R. Preston.

While the "after-guard" have been so carefully provided for, the seamen have not been forgotten. The forward house, 43 feet long and 19 feet wide, has in its forward part two forecas- tles for the crew, with separate entrances to each, and with fittings for stoves in cold weather. There are berths for twenty men, and the arrangements for their comfort are the best we have ever seen. Aft of the forecastle are the boys' room, and carpenter's room, carpenter's shop, (extending the whole width of the house,) and the ship's galley, which is fitted with sinks, lockers and shelves arranged with an eye to cleanliness and comfort. The boys' sleeping rooms occupy the after end of the house. The important end of good ventilation has been sought to be attained in every room in the ship which is to be occupied by human beings.

The spar work, by Mr. William R. Martin, is being done in a manner which will maintain his deservedly high reputa- tion as a mechanic. The lower masts are built of the best southern yellow pine, and heavily banded. The lengths are: fore, 79 feet; main, 82 feet; mizzen, 76 feet. The fore and main topmasts are each 51 feet long; the length of the maintopgal- lant, royal and skysailmast and pole is 67 feet. Length of main yard, 84 feet; topsail yard, 76; topgallant yard, 66; royal yard, 44; skysail yard, 34 feet. The bowsprit is 23 feet outboard and

30 inches in diameter. Her jib boom is 58 feet long. She will be fitted with double topsail yards.

The iron work is done by Mr. B. Frank Rice, the well known shipsmith of this city, and like all the rest of the work, is being done in the very best manner.

The rigging work, we regret to say, is to be done by Boston parties: not that it will not be well done, but we think our own riggers would have done it as well and as cheaply. Mr. Frank Low is the master rigger; the rigging is to be of wire, and the ship will have an extra topmast backstay to each side on all her masts, and double topgallant backstays.

She is fitted with Emerson's patent windlass, said to be the best in use, and Russell & Son's patent pumps.

Mr. John Neal is the master builder, and Mr. David Badger foreman. Capts. Marcy and Ross have given her their personal superintendence, and left nothing undone to make her as good as any ship ever built in the State of Maine, if not the best one ever built there. The "Granite State" is rated A 1 for eleven years in French Lloyds.

The owners are Messrs. Peter and Daniel Marcy and John Neal, and Capt. Ross, each owning one-fourth. She will be commanded by Capt. Ross, who has had marked success as a shipmaster for over twenty years.

It was intended to have launched the "Granite State" on Saturday, the 4th inst.; but the tide not serving right the launch has been postponed until next week, probably Wednesday or Thursday.

When launched she will be taken to the navy yard to be masted, rigged and ballasted, and will remain there until ready for sea.

The building of this vessel has given employment for many months to a large number of mechanics and laborers, many of whom would otherwise most probably have been idle much of the time; and if nothing else influenced us, the fact that she was built on the Piscataqua, and the money paid for labor distributed among our own workmen at a time of marked depression, would make us heartily wish success to the good ship "Granite State." Long may she float, and success attend all her ventures!

Further mention of David D. Badger, the construction foreman, is necessary. Few men were his equals as shipwrights. He came from Brunswick, Maine, when he was 21 and went to work for Fernald & Pettigrew on Badger's Island. During the Civil War, with the decline

John R. Holbrook had his sail loft on Market Street, near the junction with Deer. Holbrook cut and sewed many of the suits of sails bent on the Piscataquà-built ships. Among the ships he serviced was the second Granite State. *Courtesy of Strawbery Banke, Inc.*

in shipbuilding, he worked on bridges in Connecticut, but came back to Portsmouth in 1870. Daniel Marcy employed him on several vessels, including the *William H. Marcy* and the *Granite State*. After launching the *William H. Marcy*, Badger had bought a farm in Newington. However, when Daniel Marcy began planning the *Granite State*, he brought Badger out of retirement. During the construction, Badger rode six miles each way to work, six days a week; a day's work then began at sunrise and ended at sunset.

In its lengthy description of the *Granite State*, the *Chronicle* didn't mention that her sails were sewn by the veteran sailmaker John R. Holbrook. At one time or another, Holbrook made at least three suits of sails for the *Granite State*. The *Chronicle*, on August 28, said that many suits of sails were made in Holbrook's Market Street loft "in the palmy days of wooden ship building, — before England decided that ships dug out of the ground should be considered better than those grown in the woods, and bulldozed all maritime nations to her dictum. We believe that there is more canvas in the *Granite State*'s sails than in the suit of any other merchant vessel ever fitted out here."

While Holbrook was cutting and sewing sails, another veteran sailmaker, Thomas S. Gay, created "two splendid burgees, each 45 feet by 15 feet, for the ships *Paul Jones* and *Granite State*." The lettering was done by Willard J. Sampson, a painter. Gay will be remembered as the man who went as a passenger, round trip, to Japan in the *Grandee* for reasons of health. He apparently benefited from the voyage. His loft was over the old Spring Market, and long since destroyed.

When her rigging and other preparations were completed, the *Granite State* was ready for sea. It's a matter of curiosity that Daniel Marcy's eldest son, Henry L. Marcy, didn't have the command; it had been speculated he would at the time the *William H. Marcy* was given to Judah Touro Marcy. Henry L. Marcy was at sea in the bark *Quickstep*, which might be the explanation. For his officers, Captain Ross had Thomas Fitz of Boston, first mate; Samuel S. Sides of Portsmouth, second mate; Richard Burnham of Kittery, ship's carpenter; and Andrew Morine of Baltimore, steward. Four boys—one each from Concord, Eliot, Kittery, and Portsmouth—went out as apprentices.

The *Granite State* was already under charter to a Boston firm to haul ice and apples to Rio de Janeiro. Captain Ross took the ship out of Portsmouth on October 1 with two tugs handling her. Once beyond Whale's Back Light, the tug *Clara Bateman* turned back, and the *Major* went on alone. "The *Granite State* had her stay-sails set when she passed Rye Beach, and the tug was taking her along at a good rate. A number of gentlemen made the trip around in the vessel, by invitation by Captain Ross and Captain Marcy."[52] The next day, the *Chronicle* had a report on the maiden passage:

> Ship Granite State arrived in Boston at noon on Tuesday. After the Major and her tow left the lower harbor on Monday the wind freshened steadily from the southwest, a heavy sea running, and at four o'clock in the afternoon they were nearly abreast of Thacher's island lights; and during the next seven or eight hours they made hardly a mile of progress. At three o'clock Tuesday morning the wind abated, and then the steamboat took the ship along rapidly, making more from that time to eleven o'clock than had been made all the time before since starting. It was a long, hard pull for the steamer, but she did her work well.

One of the boys belonging to the ship fell from between decks to the ballast in the lower hold and was roughly shaken up, though no bones were broken; he was brought back to this city by the Major, and hopes to be all right before the ship sails. The tug made the trip back in about six hours, bringing a number of the passengers who went around in the ship.

The *Granite State* drew comment as soon as she arrived in Boston. The *Boston Post* said of her:

> The new ship *Granite State*, built at Neal's shipyard in Kittery, and now in Simpson's dry dock at Boston, is a beauty. The *Granite State* is in dock to be coppered; and we are informed that when she was taken out of the water the length of grass on her bottom was a foot in some places. As soon as she comes out of the dock she will commence loading her cargo of ice and apples for Rio de Janeiro about the 20th inst. [October].[53]

As can be safely assumed, the mere contention that the *Granite State* was the largest ship ever built on the Piscataqua—first mentioned in the August 3 *Chronicle* article above—spawned an argument. Before she even left Portsmouth, the debate was raging in the *Portsmouth Weekly*. A letter writer took the paper to task for claiming the *Granite State* was the biggest ever built, offering as his candidate for that honor the famed clipper *Sierra Nevada*, built in 1854 and registered at 1,942 tons. But that was by "old measurement." The writer argued that the *Granite State* was 228.95 feet long, 41.04 in beam, and 24 feet deep. The *Sierra Nevada* was 223 feet long, 43.6 in beam, and 27.8 in depth, which would mean, in the new measure, 1,672.90 tons—to the *Granite State*'s 1,683 tons. "So the Granite State seems a little larger." That stirred up another letter writer who came up with totally different figures for both vessels, and concluded the *Sierra Nevada* was bigger. Anyway, it's all moot now.

When the *Granite State* finally left Boston after the coppering work, she carried 2,400 barrels of apples and 1,600 tons of ice to Rio de Janeiro. Her cargo delivered, after a run of 45 days from Boston, she went to Montevideo to pick up the cargo of the ship *Golden Fleece*. While in quarantine, the *Granite State* reported the loss of a sailor to yellow fever, with a second sick. However, she sailed from Montevideo, and went around Cape Horn to San Francisco. Then came a time of patience; shipping was depressed. Great ships lingered in port, waiting for the merest suggestion of cargoes. Yet, when the *Granite State* arrived in San Francisco there was a pleasant notice of her in the *Alta Californian*:

She is, without exception, the finest-looking and the strongest ship we have ever seen. She has nice, easy lines, a fine bow, and a nice elliptic stern, and will undoubtedly sail well when she has a chance. A glance below in her cabins, shows taste and elegance. The ship's construction was superintended by Captain W. Ross, at present in command, and as he carries his family with him, the cabin has been arranged for "keeping house." It is really a perfect Paradise, and all the details show good taste in the captain and his lady. The ship looks well on deck. A glance around shows that Captain Ross takes good care of his vessel. She is unquestionably a model ship, and one of which her owners and Capt. Ross, her master, may well be proud. May his days be long in the gallant ship.[54]

It took Captain Ross, despite all the admiration for his vessel, a long time to find a cargo. Finally, in April 1879, it was reported she was loading wheat for the United Kingdom.[55] She was in port at Liverpool on September 11 and sailed for New York on the twenty-third. In November, she was advertised to sail for Melbourne on December 15 in the Pioneer Line, and it was reported "Captain Ross of the *Granite State* will leave this city this week to join his ship in New York. She is loading for Melbourne. Mrs. Ross accompanies her husband."[56] She sailed on January 4, 1880, and arrived on April 22.

The next item concerning the *Granite State* is a bit puzzling, although a plausible solution can be worked out. The *Chronicle* reported on August 24 that advices from Melbourne, dated July 14, said the *Granite State* had sailed from Melbourne, under a Captain Locke, but had to put back four days later after being aground on a reef near Port Philip Head. A government pilot was in command at the time. She had to be thoroughly recaulked, and repaired, "at an expense of over $25,000," and resumed her voyage after a month's detention. The pilot's certificate was suspended for six months. The best guess is that the pilot's name was Locke, and when on the job, the pilot is the captain. On August 25, the *Chronicle* reported:

> The disaster to the ship Granite State, of this port, previously referred to, took place as she was starting on a trip from Melbourne, Australia, for Calcutta, with horses. She took the ground at the mouth of Port Philip bay on the 13th of June, was towed off by two tugs, and was on her way back in tow when she again went aground and remained until next day, when she was taken to an anchorage, making six inches an hour. The horses and fittings were discharged and she was taken into the raving dock, where it was found that the whole of her false keel

and part of her main keel were gone, the copper badly chafed and much of it stripped off, and the ship badly strained.

The *Granite State* continued sailing in the Pacific trade through the 1880s. In April 1881, it was reported:

> — The owners of the ship Granite State, which vessel is now on her way from Australia to London, have ordered of Mr. John R. Holbrook of this city a third of a suit of sails for the ship. They are now nearly completed, and will be sent to London by steamer early next month. These sails are being made in the most careful and thorough manner by Mr. Holbrook's men, and are such as our sailmakers need not to be afraid to let their English brethren examine. The mainsail is 84 feet on the foot and 72 feet on the head. 620 yards of duck were used in its construction, and the rope is nearly all covered with canvas. The sail has six buntlines rove through bull's-eyes running round it, and four leachlines rove through bull's-eyes round the sail. There is also a top-gallant sail which is fitted like the mainsail. These lines allow the sails to be hauled up almost as close to the yards as they could be furled, doing away with a good deal of hard work. By this order the experienced owners of the Granite State have passed to Mr. Holbrook a well earned compliment for the masterly manner in which his work has in all the years of his business in this city been performed. We are quite sure that it will compare well with that of the best of the British workmen.[57]

Although the *Granite State* was getting her share of cargoes, the steady use of sailing vessels was fast ebbing. For instance, in 1883 the *Granite State* was at Seattle, in Puget Sound, having just come in from Nagasaki, Japan, in ballast. "After waiting some time, the ship accepted a sugar freight from the Philippine Islands for New York or Boston at $9 per ton, although port charges had to be paid, supplies purchased and the broad Pacific recrossed without a cargo. At what price or where should a ship be built for this sort of business?"[58] The *Granite State* made it to New York on July 1, 1884, 125 days from Manila, with a cargo of sugar and hemp, which was consigned to J. R. Livermore & Co., "successor to the house of Salter & Livermore," both of which were old Portsmouth names.[59]

At last, Captain Ross took a sabbatical. When the *Granite State* left New York on August 12, Capt. Thomas Fitz had the quarterdeck. The ship went to Hong Kong, and, on arrival there, it became the scene of a wild incident with a demented seaman. The incident was reported to the U.S. consul in Hong Kong, who duly reported it to

Washington, including the formal statement by the captain, officers, and crew:

"After dinner called all hands to break out cargo in the lower hold to find a seaman named Leon Salares, who had for the second time gone into the lower hold, where nothing but kerosene oil was stowed. This time he was well armed with sheath knives, fastened on long poles and positively refused to come up. During the last night he has had a light among the oil several times. He also threatens to burn the ship if he is not supplied with food and water. Have tried by all known means to get him to come up, have tried by promising to excuse him from all work; have tried also to capture him without harm to himself or anyone else, but he has assaulted several of the men, wounding them severely.

The chief officer he struck by throwing firewood at him. It was impossible to reach him where he was stowed without lanterns, and a naked light was dangerous. He threw firewood at the lanterns and broke the glass. All the crew and officers being anxious to secure him before another night of suspense, and the weather being rainy and squally so that the hatches had to be put down and the cases of oil were all adrift, determined to capture him for his own safety and that of the ship and cargo and all on board. Gave orders to the men to secure him and defend themselves from violence, as he was a desperate and dangerous man. After four hours work captured him alive, wounded in the mouth and left arm. He died 10 minutes after being taken up. Appearances indicate suicide, as there is a clean cut under his left ear, which must have been made by a sharp instrument. Washed the body, sewed it up carefully, hove the ship to, read the funeral service for the dead, set the flag at half mast, and buried Leon Salares. All feel greatly relieved to know that he is up from the cargo. Signed by Thomas Fitz, master, and all the officers and crew."[60]

Questions lingered on about the death of the sailor, and, on December 4, 1886, the *Journal* got into the act:

The Granite State reached Woodruff's stores last night, after a voyage of 130 days from Manilla. It is eighteen months since the ship sailed from this port for Hong Kong. Among the crew was Leon Salares, a Spaniard, a man of quiet manners and a popular fellow with his shipmates. This was his second voyage on the Granite State. There were two countrymen of his in the crew. The others were Sweeds, Danes, and Englishmen.

During the early part of the voyage southward Salares attended-
ed to his duties faithfully, but later he developed a disposition
to shirk duty, and tried to influence others of the crew to resist
the Captain's orders. He became very surly, stopping just short
of outspoken mutiny.

It was in the early part of November, 1885, that the
Granite State crossed the equator in her course around Cape
Horn to Hong Kong. The winds were unfavorable, and the crew
were required to be on deck long hours during the day and
night. On one occasion Salares defied Capt. Fritz, and said:
"This ship is a floating hell, but I won't let you kill me with
overwork." Suddenly he disappeared. Capt. Fritz caused search
to be made for him, and, not finding him, he concluded that he
had fallen overboard, and made a minute to that effect in his
log. For three says Salares was missing, and then he was
found concealed between decks. A sailor saw smoke coming out
of a hatch, and found that Salares was there with his pipe.
Salares came out and went to work again, denying that he was
ill and spurning medical treatment. For a while he was peaceful but sullen. Then he disappeared again, this time down the
forehatch, and when he was detected in his second hiding place
he threatened to kill any one who approached him.

The ship's cargo was petroleum in cases, and Salares
made his way forward and barricaded himself securely with
cases of oil. He had taken about fifteen gallons of water and
about forty pounds of bread with him into his retreat, and he
was prepared for a siege. Capt. Fritz ordered the mate and
members of the crew to bring the mutineer on deck, but when
they moved on his barricade he held up a box of matches and
threatened to set fire to the inflammable cargo before he would
be taken. The Captain was now convinced that Salares was
insane, and he was left for the night in his retreat. That was an
anxious night on shipboard, and Capt. Fritz with his wife and
daughter kept watch on deck, fearing that at any minute the
desperate man in the fore-hold might fire the ship, although
immunity from punishment was promised him if he would come
on deck. On the following day another attempt was made to
capture him.

Capt. Fritz led the men below into the hold where Salares was concealed. They crawled along over the cases of cargo,
guided by the dim light of lanterns. From his concealment
Salares shouted to the men startling threats of death if they
approached him. Finally he threw a timber at the mate, which

struck him on the bridge of the nose and injured him so that he has not yet recovered. The Spaniard stood at bay, bent on murder. Capt. Fritz climbed over the cargo to within four feet of the madman, when, with a fierce lunge, the latter struck the Captain on the left wrist with a long sheath knife bound upon the handle of a shovel, and cut the lantern from his hand. The tendons of the wrist were severed, and the falling lantern was shattered over the cases of petroleum. With presence of mind Capt. Fritz smothered the blazing wick before further damage was done, and he and his men then retreated, but not before Salares had slashed the jacket of one of the sailors with his long handled knife. It now became evident to Capt. Fritz that Salares must be taken dead or alive, and two of the sailors, armed with pistols, went below again to dare the madman's fury. Salares was concealed in the cargo, and the men were afraid to approach too nearly, because of the long-handled knife and a ditching spade, the point of which he had ground to a cutting edge. With these weapons the Spaniard in his protected position had his pursuers at a disadvantage, and so they resorted to fire-arms. In the dim and uncertain light of the hold they emptied their pistols in the direction of the crouching sailor, but without effect. When the ammunition was gone the man stole upon them stealthily, and with his sheath knife on the shovel handle stabbed sailor Sam Roberts in the eye and slashed Alex Crigg on the arm. Then with a sweeping slash of his murderous knife he struck a blow at a Spaniard who had been his friend, that would have killed him if it had not missed its aim. Retreating again, the maniac hurled a piece of wood, used in stowing cargo, at his pursuers, to disable them and break their lanterns.

The wounded men were taken on deck and cared for, and a third attempt was then made to find Salares. There was no sound in the hold when the men entered, and for a long time no trace was found of the mad Spaniard. The cargo had to be broken before he was finally discovered. He made no resistance. He was dead. He had cut his throat with the sheath knife with which he had sought the lives of his shipmates.

The body of the dead sailor was brought on deck, sewed up in canvas, and buried in the sea. For two days this one man had kept the whole ship's crew at bay and in a state of terror, for with one match he might have fired the cargo. In the space in the hold where he had barricaded himself were found the bread and water and pipe and tobacco which he had stowed away. The knife and sharpened spade were there, and with them was a whetstone, on which the edges had been made keen. All the wounded men have recovered, except the mate, who was struck in the face by a piece of timber. He left the Granite State at Hong Kong, returned to this city by another vessel, and is now in Bellevue Hospital, suffering still from the results of that injury.

After unloading in Hong Kong, and not finding a cargo, Captain Fitz went to Manila and loaded sugar for the United States. In January 1887, "a large handsome picture of the *Granite State*, of this port, was placed in one of the windows of Mongomery's Music Store.... It represents the ship under full sail, running in for an anchorage at some Chinese port, apparently Hong Kong, with a Chinese sampan towing astern and just commencing to take in her light sails. The picture was painted in China by a native artist. The *Granite State* is now at New York, loaded with oil for Shanghai and nearly ready for sea. Capt. William Ross, who will command her this voyage, will be accompanied by his wife."[61]

The *Granite State* visited both Hong Kong and Shanghai and then returned to New York. In March 1889, she had another charter to China, and Captain Ross was described as "one of the most skillful, successful of American shipmasters, and has done much to maintain the prestige of the American merchant marine."[62] When the *Granite State* put into Martha's Vineyard on her return passage, it brought much relief to her owners. She had taken 64 days from St. Helena, and her long absence was causing concern. She was carrying 11,000 bales of hemp, valued at $250,000. The run from St. Helena had been rough, and sails had split and the rudder was damaged. She was taken in tow by the *William S. Slater*, but the wind made up so quickly that she began to tow the tug and nearly went aground before reaching Boston. Her visit to Boston prompted comment by the *Boston Journal*, which was reprinted by the *Chronicle* on November 13, 1890:

Under the heading "A fine New Hampshire ship" the Boston *Journal* says:

Ship Granite State, of Portsmouth, Capt. Ross, now discharging a cargo of hemp from Manila at Constitution wharf, belongs to a city that once had its sails on every sea, but it is said that the Granite State, and one other vessel, the Grandee, due at Boston from Pisaqua, are now the only full-rigged ships afloat hailing from New Hampshire's ancient seaport. The Granite State was built at Kittery Foreside in 1877 for Hon. Daniel Marcy of Portsmouth and others, and had her masts stepped and was fitted for sea at one of the piers of the navy yard. The well-known ship Paul Jones was built in the old Raynes ship yard at the north end, in Portsmouth, the same year, and that year marked the end of shipbuilding for deep water voyages, on the Piscataqua river, which used to be as famous for the production of a superior class of vessels as the Merrrimack or the Kennebec were. A few schooners have been built at Portsmouth since 1877, but not a single square rigger since the autumn that the Granite State and the Paul Jones sailed away. The latter vessel was burned at sea near Australia some four and a half years ago, soon after completing an on ward voyage from Boston. The Paul Jones had a very handsome model and was a fast sailer. The Granite State looks almost like a new vessel, and seems fit for a good many years of active service yet. She is a large ship of 1635 tons, and a fine specimen of the American merchantman.

That apparently was the last voyage Captain Ross made in the *Granite State*. The ship was sold to a New York firm, and Captain Ross settled down to a long stay on shore. Various masters had her. A Captain Barlow arrived in New York with her on February 9, 1892. Later that year, it was reported that the ship of which Captain Edwin A. Gerrish "is master, was sighted off Cape Hatteras on the 20th inst., and will doubtless arrive in Boston in a few days." And such were the realities of life for mariners: "It will be remembered that the wife of Captain Gerrish died after his departure for Iquique [Chile], on the west coast of South America, and he is, as yet, ignorant of his wife's decease. It, therefore, falls to his daughter, Miss Brownie, to tell her father."[63] "Miss Brownie" was the little girl who had captivated the crew of the CSS *Alabama* when the raider captured and burned her father's ship *Rockingham* in 1864.

The *Granite State*, one of the greatest of the Port of Portsmouth ships, finally came to the end of her days on the treacherous rocks off Land's End, England—the grave of so many ships over the centuries. A simple navigational error did her in as she was sailing from Falmouth for Swansea with a cargo of wheat. The ship was pulled off by a tug and moved into the shelter of a cove. The wheat in her old hull began to swell as she settled in the water, and the crew took to the boats. The wreck came on November 4, 1895.

Paul Jones

SPECIFICATIONS: 1877. William F. Fernald. North Mill Pond. Figurehead. Burthen, 1,258 tons. Length, 195.2 feet; beam, 39 feet; depth 23.4 feet. Two decks. Original owners—Charles H. Mendum, et al.

The ship *Paul Jones* will ever have a place in Port of Portsmouth history, not only because she honored the "Father of the American Navy," John Paul Jones, but also because she was the last of the hundreds of three-masted, square-rigged sailing vessels launched on the Piscataqua or its tributaries.

Charles H. Mendum—merchant, land developer, industrialist —signed a contract with William F. Fernald for the construction of a ship in February 1877, and the shares were all taken before the work even started. By the end of February, Fernald had 40 carpenters at work getting out the frame, with a planned launching date of September 9. Her overall cost was expected to exceed $83,000.

Both George Raynes and his son, and then Fernald, had launched many vessels on the North Mill Pond over a span of nearly 50 years without having a problem in reaching the river. However, the coming of the railroads had changed many things, and access to the river was one of them. A drawbridge had been built to connect Noble's Island with the mainland. In July, it was discovered that the *Paul Jones* was too wide to pass through the draw. Fernald simply informed the railroad that he would have to have access to the river by August 1. (This bridge had to be opened up in 1985 to allow the inward passage of the submarine USS *Albacore* to its final resting place in Albacore Park.) The dilemma brought derisive comment from the ultrasophisticated *New York World*, which was reprinted by the Chronicle on July 21:

> A Portsmouth shipbuilder has constructed a vessel, after the fashion of Robinson Crusoe's long boat. Just as he was about completing her, an unhappy thought struck him. He went and measured the draw of the railroad bridge, and found that one ship into one draw would go no times and three feet over. Whereupon he wept, cursed his own stupidity? No; he served notice on the company that he was going to float his ship and they should take their bridge out of the road. There would be little need to dispair of that man making a way in the world.

Actually, what had happened was that minor structural changes had been made in the drawbridge since the launching of the *Chocorua* in 1874. The *Paul Jones* was only 18 inches wider, but she

The white-hulled Paul Jones *was the last square-rigged, three-masted ship launched on the Piscataqua River. She was built by William Fernald in 1877. Photo courtesy Mariner's Museum, Newport News, Virginia.*

couldn't get through. Fernald let the rail companies know his ship was going to go through, even if he had to use "force if necessary."[64] It never came to that.

The *Paul Jones* was launched at 12:45 P.M. on Monday, September 24, a month behind Fernald's predicted schedule. The launching "was witnessed by a large number of people, who were glad of so good an excuse to meet together and sun themselves on such a magnificent day. Noble's Island, the bridge [Portsmouth Toll Bridge] and the shipyard, and other points from which a good view of the launch could be obtained, and the ship herself, were liberally populated.

The launch was a fine one, the beautiful ship — for she is most decidedly a beauty — gliding off smoothly, and bringing up at the proper time and place without any mishap."[65]

As far as the problem with the drawbridge was concerned, "the *Paul Jones* laid quietly inside the Noble's Island Bridge for 24 hours after being launched. On Tuesday she was warped through the draw, towed over to the Navy Yard and placed under the shears to be masted. The beauty of her model attracts general attention."[66]

In reality, the passage of the *Paul Jones* through the draw was an amicable affair. When it came down to the nitty gritty, only a few pieces of timber, added since the exit of the *Chocorua*, had to be removed from the bridge, which the railroads did without argument. Once her lower masts were stepped at the Portsmouth Navy Yard, the *Paul Jones* was towed back across the river for more fitting out. Although the ship hadn't yet gone to sea, one investor decided to sell off his 1/32 share at auction. "The sale will allow someone to invest in a good piece of property, which, if the prospects of the moving crops are to be relied upon, will repay the owners a handsome dividend on the first voyage." The share went for $2,125 to John W. Caswell, "or at a rate of $68,000 for a ship that has cost over $83,000."[67]

Even before the launch an article was published that will sound familiar to every reader who has been a newspaper reporter:

> We are always pleased to notice any local industry, and in particular like to enlarge on Portsmouth built ships, than which the world offers none better. Acting on this, we some days ago despatched a reliable and competent reporter (the same who "wrote up" Capt. Marcy's noble ship, the Granite State,) to the Raynes shipyard, to write up in good style the ship on the stocks there; but he found no one desirous of giving him the information he required — the first time he ever failed on any such errand for us. But we are bound to have some kind of report, so we take the following brief notice, which is probably correct as far as it goes, from the Boston Traveller, which publishes it under the heading "The new ship Paul Jones:"[68]

Experience dictates the belief that Fernald and his minions were unhappy with the *Chronicle* for reprinting the piece from the *New York World*. The *Chronicle* had to resort to reprinting an article from the *Boston Traveller*:

> "Mr Fernald has on the stocks at Portsmouth, N. H., a magnificent ship of 1500 tons, which will be launched early in September. a full figure of the gallant hero whose name she bears will grace her bow, and she will be commanded by Captain Jacobs, one of the most experienced shipmasters belonging to Portsmouth. Her frame is of New Hampshire white oak,

the best white oak in the world. Her ceiling, planking, deck frames and lower decks are hard pine. She is through trenailed with locust, butt and bilge-bolted with yellow metal, seasoned with salt, and will be equipped to rate A 1 for eleven years."[69]

On September 11, the *Chronicle* reported "the figurehead of the new ship Paul Jones is in place. It is a full-length figure of the great naval hero whose name the vessel bears, and is a very handsome piece of work, although we can't say whether or no it is a good likeness of the old sailor." Although there were able wood carvers in the city, the *Paul Jones* figurehead came from Boston. On the twelfth, the *Chronicle* published a little blurb that no doubt amused readers of that day:

> "Well, I declare," exclaimed a lady from Barrington in the cars on the Dover Railroad, as they passed the Raynes shipyard: "If there ain't the 'Nathan Jones.' Landsakes, just because Frank has had a ship named for him, Nathan [Frank's older brother] must go and do just like him."
>
> Aaron Young, who happened to be in the same car with his townswoman, explained that the ship she was viewing was called the 'Paul Jones,' and not 'Nathan.' "Do tell," exclaimed the rural visitor. "They've got it all over Barrington it is the 'Nathan Jones'; come to think of it, that image (the figurehead) doesn't look as much like Nathan as it ought to, if it was taken for him."

It was the *Chronicle* that gave its readers a detailed description of the new ship, a few days after the launching:

— The new ship Paul Jones was successfully launched at noon, Monday, from the Raynes shipyard, a large concourse witnessing the "kissing of the waters." She will be immediately fitted at this port. The Paul Jones is one of the best ships built at this port, and will be an honor to our merchant marine. The vessel is of splendid model, 190 feet long on the keel and 200 feet between perpendiculars; has 39 feet extreme breadth of beam, and 23 feet 6 inches depth of hold, including 8 feet 3 inches between decks. Her keel is of rock maple, sided 16 and moulded 24 inches with one three-inch shoe. The floor timbers are 20 feet long, and the space of frames from centre to centre is 30 inches. At the gunwales the frames are nine inches. The floor timbers are fastened with yellow metal driven through and riveted on the base of the keel, and are also bolted alternately through the first tier of keelsons. She has three tiers of midship keelsons, each 15 inches square, and one tier of assistant keelsons, 16 inches square. Her frame is seasoned white oak; the planking, ceiling, deck frames and pointers pitch pine, her hook white oak, and deck knees, of hackmatack. The cabin, which will be model of comfort and richness, measures 44 feet long and 21 feet wide, finished in mountain ash and black walnut, the panels embellished with choice panel paintings in oil. Her poop is 10 feet abaft the mainmast, and 4 feet high in the clear. The forecastle is 40 feet long and 17 feet wide, containing eight distinct apartments, the ventilation being perfect. Her mainmast is 77 feet, foremast 75 feet, mizzenmast 73 feet, the poles of each being 8 feet; bowsprit 44 feet, jib-boom 30 feet, flying jib-boom 14 feet. Her fore and mainyards will be 76 feet, fore and main lower topsails 60 feet, upper topsails 62 feet 6 inches, topgallant yard 50 feet, royals 39 feet. She will have wire standing rigging, ranging from one inch to nine inches; her running rigging will be Manilla hemp, with patent Waterman blocks, and all the chain and iron work now in general use. This ship has the celebrated capstan windlass built by the American Ship Windlass Co. of Providence, R. I., with all their recently patented improvements. Mr. William F. Fernald of this city is the builder of the ship, the fullest guarantee of her excellent construction; Mr. Charles E. Hayes of Kittery did the outboard joinering, Mr. George W. Pendexter the joiner work, Mr. E. D. Coffin the painting, and Mr. A. K. W. Green the caulking, each skilled workmen. Messrs. Charles H. Mendum, B. F. Jacobs and others are the owners, and she will be commanded by Capt. Jacobs. In every respect the Paul Jones is a superior ship.

The *Paul Jones* left the Port of Portsmouth forever on November 1, with Captain Benjamin F. Jacobs, one of the shareholders, in command. The *Clara Bateman* took her downriver with river pilot Russell A. Preble in charge. Once outside Whale's Back Light, the towline was cast off, and she stood away on her own. Many of the people who had gone downriver on her found a return passage on the tug. A storm blew up, and the *Paul Jones*, being out with neither cargo nor ballast, had to take shelter in Gloucester, Massachusetts. Several Portsmouth men had been invited to go all the way "around" to Baltimore. On his return to Portsmouth, one of these lucky individuals gave the *Chronicle* a report that was far from flattering to the character of one of Portsmouth's most eminent shipmasters, B. F. Jacobs:

> The men who went around from this city to Baltimore "by the run" in the new ship Paul Jones have returned, and from them we gather the following particulars of the trip, which may be of interest: The Paul Jones left this port on Thursday, Nov. 1st, and next morning was some fifteen or twenty miles to the southward and eastward of Gloucester, Mass., and at about six o'clock bore up for that port for shelter, having taken the heavy southeast gale which blew throughout that day and Saturday. She brought up inside of Eastern Point at about eight o'clock, and glad enough the crew were to get there; for it had become evident that the ship was insufficiently ballasted, so that she could do nothing on the wind, a moderately strong breeze laying her down on her side and sliding her off to leeward like a milk-pan in a mud puddle. Being in such an unfavorable trim, it is more than improbable that she could have made Portsmouth harbor again or kept off shore during the gale, had she been unable to get into Gloucester. The ship laid at single anchor until Sunday morning, the 4th, when she towed to sea and continued her voyage; and on the following Saturday, (having in the meantime been so far off shore as to be close to the Gulf Stream, if indeed she were not once in its edge,) at about five o'clock in the evening she brought up in the Horseshoe, just inside of Cape Charles, the wind at the time blowing a gale from the northeast. Here the ship laid until Monday morning, with seventy-five fathoms of chain out on one anchor and about fifty fathoms on the other; the anchors were then weighed and she started for Baltimore in tow, arriving at her dock at about five o'clock on Tuesday evening, Nov. 13th. Owing to the lack of ballast, the ship had no chance on the trip to show what she could do as a sailer, as it was impossible to do any carrying sail worth the name, except when dead before the

wind, which is by no means a ship's best point of sailing; about eleven knots was the best she made at any time, we are told, — but she will do two or three knots better than that under favorable circumstances, unless her looks belie her greatly.

We judge from the way the crew talk that they are not great admirers of Capt. Jacobs; they speak in the highest terms of the seamanship and officer-like bearing of Capt. Henry L. Marcy, who went around in the vessel; but they appear very enthusiastic the wrong way when they speak of the ship's commander. They say that the morning after the vessel's arrival at the dock he ordered them to get their traps ashore out of her in twenty minutes, and that he turned one of the ship's boys (Walter H. Prior) adrift without any means of reaching his home, the crew having to "chip in" and pay his fare back to this city, or else leave him to take the long tramp alone and with no money to pay for food and lodging on the way.

The storm and the interruption of the passage of the *Paul Jones* to Baltimore gave occasion for all kinds of wild rumors in Portsmouth. The most conservative of the rumors was that she had gone down with all hands. The newspaper's recollection of the tale was prompted by a long passage the *Paul Jones* made two years later, which also caused concern.[70]

No public examination of the surly behavior of Captain Jacobs was ever made. Apparently some hitch in arrangements developed after the *Paul Jones* reached Baltimore; the anticipated cargo wasn't there, and she had to go to New York. Why Captain Jacobs was then replaced by Capt. Edwin A. Gerrish also went unexplained. Jacobs went back to his old ship, the *Grandee*. At the time Gerrish became master of the *Paul Jones*, the *Chronicle* listed a few of the people who were serving on her. John Wilson of Kittery was the carpenter; "a Mr. Wheaton of the same place is the ship's steward; Clarence Martin of this city is an ordinary seaman; Arthur N. Goodrich, also of this city, goes out in her in his first voyage, while one of the ship's boys is from Wells."

Captain Gerrish took the *Paul Jones* to sea on January 17, 1878, heading for China. Months later it was learned that the ship ran into heavy weather in the Indian Ocean. The storm damaged her helm and injured the master so badly he was laid up for three weeks.[71] The vessel finally reached Manila, and she sailed from that port in December 1878, arriving in New York on April 3, a passage of 117 days. The trip caused the *Chronicle* to criticize those who panicked over late ship arrivals; at that, the ship had had a rough time off Mauritius when she ran into a cyclone. Gerrish went to Batavia from New York, returning the next year to Boston. From that port, she was towed to New York, and went to Shanghai. In March of 1882, the *Paul Jones* was chartered for Angiers, Java, and Captain Gerrish's family came to New York to see him off. While there, the captain's only son, Charles W. Gerrish, contracted scarlet fever and died on the fourth. "He was 16 years of age, of exemplary habits and a general favorite. The remains were brought to this city on Monday [March 6]." His mother and sister were with him.[72] The father's ship cleared New York on the eighteenth.

Captain Gerrish's last voyage in the *Paul Jones* ended in March 1884. He had planned to take the vessel to the East Indies, but ill health prevented it. Timothy H. Winn of York, Maine, long the ship's first officer, became master. She left New York on April 11, taking as a passenger William H. Preston of Portsmouth, an apothecary who frequently supplied Port of Portsmouth vessels with medical stores. She arrived in Shanghai in September, and came back to Boston. In July 1885, she was chartered to sail from Boston to Melbourne for the Peabody Line. Captain Gerrish had intended to resume command but was still too unwell to do so. The *Paul Jones* went to sea on the seventeenth. However, Captain Gerrish did eventually resume his seafaring career. In 1894, he was in command of the bark *Freeman* when he suffered a stroke while at Manila. He returned home two years later, and spent his last years in a seaman's home on Staten Island, New York.

Captain Winn and the *Paul Jones* reached Melbourne on December 26.[73] The next word concerning her came in March 1886:

> — A cable despatch received in this city on Saturday announced in brief the burning of the ship Paul Jones, and the safety of the crew. The ship was on her way, in ballast, from Melbourne to Calcutta, and was in command of Captain Winn of Wells, Me., her old commander and part owner, Capt. Edwin A. Gerrish, having been unable to go on the last two trips, through illness. The Paul Jones was built in this city in 1877 by Wm. F. Fernald at the old Raynes shipyard, and was the last square-rigged vessel built at this port. She registered 1228 tons gross and was a fine model and a good sailer. The Paul Jones hailed from this port, where she was principally owned. She was valued at about $50,000 partly insured in Boston Companies. Mr. E. S. Fay, the largest individual owner, representing 9 of the 64 shares into which she was divided, had no insurance. Nothing at present is known as to the particulars of the loss, except that the crew are safe and at Melbourne.[74]

Before closing the story of the *Paul Jones*, and the longer chronicle of the Port of Portsmouth's contributions to the American merchant fleet, a graphic word picture from the pen of a schoolboy, William B. Sturdevant, in 1866, portrays the beauty of the last of the Piscataqua square-riggers:

> While in the graduating class of the grammar school, a large ship anchored between the East Boston Ferries, waiting for her crew. Her hull, masthead and bowsprit were pure white, her spars scraped bright and on her stern in large letters was her name, *Paul Jones* of Portsmouth, New Hampshire. She also carried a figurehead of Paul Jones in full uniform.[75]

Epilogue

ALTHOUGH THE BUILDING AND LAUNCHING of the *Paul Jones* ended the three-masted, square-rigger era, the construction of some fairly large vessels continued for a few years. They were all schooners. In 1878, William F. Fernald followed the *Paul Jones* with the schooner *M. E. Eldredge*, 298 tons, which he built for Moses L. Staples of Wells. That same year, Daniel Littlefield constructed the *Cocheco*, 220 tons, for Charles E. Walker, the coal dealer. The *Cocheco* was sold in New York in 1881. Then, in 1882, Fernald built an even larger vessel for Walker, the *Annie F. Conlan*, 561 tons. In 1883, the *Grace B. Phillips*, 590 tons, was built for a party in Taunton, Massachusetts. A year after that, Fernald launched the *Grace K. Green*, 385 tons, for Walker. In 1896, the *Grace K. Green* was in a collision with the steamer *Yorktown*, off Long Branch, Long Island, and was a total loss. Four of the crew escaped by jumping on the steamer, another had his legs crushed between the two vessels and died. The *Lizzie J. Call* was the last of Fernald's productions and the last of any size on the river, at 185 tons. She was built for Charles E. Simpson and others.

Across the river, in Kittery, the *Granite State*'s departure in 1877 signaled the end of major civilian ship construction. A news item published in May 19, 1886, put the situation in focus:

> The former shipbuilding yard of Master Samuel Badger, at Kittery, where so many fine ships were built in years long past, directly opposite the launching ways of the Franklin Ship House at the Navy Yard, is being replanted by John Neal, Esq. It produces abundant crops, the soil being rich from the decay of the vegetable substances these many years.

355

Bibliography

BOOKS

Brighton, Ray. *They Came to Fish*. 2 vols. Portsmouth, N.H. Portsmouth 350, Inc., 1973.

———. *Clippers of the Port of Portsmouth*. Portsmouth, N.H. Portsmouth Marine Society, 1985.

———. *Port of Portsmouth Ships and the Cotton Trade*. Portsmouth, N.H. Portsmouth Marine Society, 1986.

Cutler, Carl C. *Queens of the Western Ocean*. Annapolis, Md. U.S. Naval Institute, 1961.

Fairburn, W.A. *Merchant Sail*. Center Lowell, Maine. Fairburn Marine Education Foundation, 1944.

Howe, Octavius T., and Frederick C. Matthews. *American Clipper Ships*. 2 vols. Marine Research Society. Salem, Massachusetts, 1926.

Kunitz, Stanley. *British Authors of the 19th Century*.

Pickett, Gertrude M. *Portsmouth's Heyday in Shipbuilding*. New Castle, N.H. J. G. Sawtelle, 1979.

Stammers, Michael K. *The Passage Makers*. Teredo Books, Ltd. Brighton, England, 1978.

Whitehouse, Robert. *Port of Dover*. Portsmouth, N.H. Portsmouth Marine Society.

NEWSPAPERS

Liverpool Chronicle
Liverpool Telegraph
Liverpool Times
London Illustrated News
London Times
Daily True Delta (New Orleans)
Daily Picayune (New Orleans)
New Hampshire Gazette
Portsmouth Herald
Portsmouth Journal
Portsmouth Morning Chronicle
Portsmouth Oracle
Portsmouth Times
Portsmouth Weekly
Rockingham Messenger

MAGAZINES

American Neptune
Granite State Monthly
Old Eliot

MANUSCRIPTS

Portsmouth Customs Records. National Archives.

Logs of the ships *Alliance, Brother Jonathan, Mary Washington, R. H. Tucker, Richard III*, and *Samoset*. Wiscasset, Maine. In the collection of Jane Tucker.

Tucker Family Papers. Wiscasset, Maine. In the collection of Jane Tucker.

Notes

The following abbreviations are used in the notes:

American Neptune	*AmNep*
Clippers of the Port of Portsmouth (Brighton)	*Clippers*
Liverpool Chronicle	*LC*
Liverpool Telegraph	*LT*
Portsmouth Customs Records	*PCR*
Portsmouth Journal	*PJ*
Portsmouth Morning Chronicle	*PMC*
Portsmouth's Heyday in Shipbuilding (Pickett)	*Heyday*
Queens of the Western Ocean (Cutler)	*Queens*
Rockingham Messenger	*RM*

Chapter 1

1. Brighton, *They Came to Fish*, vol. 1, p. 1.
2. *Sewall's Diary*, vol. 7, p. 1.
3. Brighton, *They Came to Fish*, vol. 2, p. 17.
4. *New Hampshire Gazette*, April 23, 1774.
5. Pickett, *Portsmouth's Heyday in Shipbuilding* (*Heyday*).

Chapter 2

1. *Portsmouth Journal* (*PJ*), July 27, 1830.
2. Ibid., February 19, 1831.
3. *Portsmouth Customs Records* (*PCR*), vol. 4, p. 269.
4. *Columbia Viking Desk Dictionary*.
5. *PJ*.
6. Ibid.
7. Ibid., January 19, 1841.

8. *PCR*, vol. 4, p. 270.
9. *PJ*, September 10, 1836.
10. Ibid., June 21, 1851.
11. Ibid., November 30, 1833.
12. Cutler, *Queens of the Western Ocean* (*Queens*), p. 440.
13. Ibid., p. 448.
14. *PCR*, vol. 4, p. 163.
15. *Old Eliot*, vol. 4, no. 1, p. 42.
16. *Queens*, pp. 454, 507, 538.
17. *PJ*, May 1, 1847.
18. Ibid., September 8, 1832.
19. Ibid., January 21, 1856.
20. *Portsmouth Morning Chronicle* (*PMC*), February 17, 1857.
21. *American Neptune* (*AmNep*), vol. 4, January 1944.
22. *PCR*, vol. 4, p. 167.
23. *AmNep*, vol. 4, January 1944.
24. *PJ*, January 25, 1834.
25. Brighton, *Port of Portsmouth Ships and the Cotton Trade*, p. 137.
26. *PJ*, September 14, 1833.
27. Ibid., September 30, 1837.
28. Ibid., August 31, 1850.
29. Ibid., November 30, 1850.
30. Ibid., February 22, 1834.
31. *PCR*, vol. 4, p. 166.
32. *PJ*, March 29, 1834.
33. Ibid., June 24, 1834.
34. Ibid., January 2, 1836.
35. *Reader's Encyclopedia*.
36. *PJ*, January 31, 1835.
37. Ibid., August 26, 1837.
38. Ibid., February 1, 1840.
39. Ibid., May 3, 1843.
40. Ibid., February 20, 1847.
41. Ibid., February 22, 1834.
42. Ibid., March 8, 1834.
43. Ibid., April 26, 1834.
44. *Queens*, p. 514.
45. *PCR*, p. 271.
46. *Federal Fire Society History*.
47. *PJ*, August 12, 1837.
48. Ibid., February 21, 1846.
49. Ibid., October 6, 1849.
50. Ibid., March 30, 1839.
51. *PCR*, vol. 4, p. 272.
52. *PJ*, November 7, 1855.
53. *Queens*, pp. 504, 508, 514, 541, 542.
54. *PJ*, October 21, 1837.
55. Ibid., April 16, 1836.
56. *PMC*, January 31, 1888.
57. *PJ*, September 21, 1884.
58. *PCR*, vol. 4, p. 168.
59. *Liverpool Chronicle* (*LC*), February 26, 1859.
60. *PJ*, January 1, 1859.
61. Ibid., April 23, 1859.
62. *PMC*, August 26, 1878.
63. *PJ*, January 30, 1836.
64. *Queens*, pp. 454, 478, 514.
65. *PMC*, August 20, 1853.
66. Ibid., August 22, 1853.
67. Ibid., August 29, 1855.
68. *PMC*, February 9, 1864.
69. *PJ*, March 26, 1836.
70. Ibid., May 28, 1836.
71. *PCR*, vol. 4, p. 275.
72. *PJ*, February 11, 1837.
73. Ibid., January 28, 1837.
74. *PCR*, vol. 4, p. 275.
75. *PJ*, September 15, 1838.
76. Ibid., February 6, 1841.
77. Ibid., March 20, 1852.
78. *PCR*, vol. 4, p. 274.
79. *PJ*, October 14, 1839.
80. Ibid., September 14, 1840.
81. Ibid., February 5, 1842.

82. Ibid., June 23, 1838.
83. Ibid., July 18, 1846.
84. *PMC*, October 6, 1853.
85. *PJ*, December 2, 1837.
86. *Queens*, p. 324.
87. *PJ*, February 4, 1854.
88. *PCR*, vol. 4, p. 272.
89. *PJ*, November 14, 1846.
90. Ibid., October 12, 1844.
91. Ibid., July 17, 1847.
92. *PCR*, vol. 3, p. 220.
93. *PJ*, December 26, 1846.
94. Ibid., January 2, 1847.
95. *PCR*, vol. 4, p. 171.
96. *PJ*, November 3, 1838.
97. Ibid., May 23, 1840.
98. *PCR*, vol. 4, p. 171.
99. *PJ*, March 24, 1849.
100. *PCR*, vol. 4, p. 171.
101. *PJ*, January 19, 1839.
102. *PMC*, January 24, 1879.
103. *PJ*, September 26, 1840.
104. Ibid., July 16, 1836.
105. Ibid., July 30, 1842.
106. Ibid., November 18, 1843.
107. Ibid., November 15, 1845.
108. Ibid., April 18, 1846.
109. *PMC*, March 31, 1853.
110. *Queens*, pp. 502, 503, 510.
111. *PMC*, September 18, 1856.
112. *PJ*, November 16, 1839.
113. Ibid., November 2, 1844.
114. Ibid., October 28, 1848.
115. *LC*, August 31, 1861.
116. Ibid., June 27, 1863.
117. *PMC*, February 9, 1864.
118. Ibid., February 9, 1885.
119. Ibid., September 11, 1856.
120. *PJ*, June 6, 1858.
121. Ibid., October 21, 1843.

Chapter 3

1. *Heyday*, p. 3.
2. *PJ*, September 19, 1840.
3. Ibid., January 2, 1847.
4. Ibid., September 16, 1847.
5. Ibid., January 2, 1847.
6. Ibid., May 16, 1846.
7. Ibid., December 19, 1846.
8. Ibid., April 12, 1851.
9. *PCR*, vol. 4, p. 173.
10. *PJ*, September 12, 1840.
11. Ibid., January 2, 1847.
12. Ibid., October 12, 1844.
13. Ibid., April 17, 1853.
14. Ibid., September 5, 1840.
15. Ibid., September 26, 1840.
16. *PMC*, November 16, 1852.
17. *AmNep*, vol. 4, January 1944.
18. *PJ*, March 27, 1841.
19. Ibid., April 17, 1841.
20. Ibid., August 2, 1846.
21. Ibid., January 30, 1847.
22. Ibid., September 11, 1841.
23. Ibid., July 23, 1878.
24. Brighton, *Clippers of the Port of Portsmouth (Clippers)*, pp. 70–77.
25. *PJ*, February 27, 1847.
26. Ibid., August 13, 1847.
27. *Liverpool Telegraph (LT)*, January 26, 1850.
28. *PMC*, September 14, 1853.
29. Ibid., May 15, 1855.
30. *PMC*, January 21, 1860.
31. *PJ*, September 24, 1842.
32. *Queens*, p. 405.
33. Ibid., January 15, 1848.
34. Ibid., December 1, 1849.
35. Ibid., May 9, 1857.
36. Ibid., November 20, 1841.
37. Ibid., November 27, 1847.
38. Ibid., December 18, 1847.

39. Ibid., May 14, 1842.
40. Ibid., March 6, 1847.
41. Ibid., August 6, 1842.
42. Ibid., September 10, 1842.
43. Ibid., November 12, 1842.
44. Ibid., October 21, 1843.
45. Ibid., November 25, 1848.
46. Ibid., December 2, 1848.
47. Ibid., December 16, 1848.
48. Ibid., December 2, 1843.
49. *PCR*, vol. 4, p. 176.
50. *PJ*, August 17, 1844.
51. Ibid., September 14, 1844.
52. Ibid., September 21, 1844.
53. Ibid., August 16, 1846.
54. *Rockingham Messenger* (*RM*), November 11, 1847.
55. *PJ*, November 9, 1844.
56. *AmNep*, vol. 1, January 1941, p. 48.
57. *PJ*.
58. Ibid., October 24, 1845.
59. *Queens*, pp. 405, 514.
60. *PMC*, November 7, 1854.
61. Stammers, *Passage Makers*, p. 169.
62. *Daily True Delta*, New Orleans, January 19, 1854.
63. *PJ*, June 28, 1845.
64. Ibid., August 29, 1846.
65. Ibid., March 29, 1862.
66. Ibid., August 29, 1846.
67. Ibid., September 5, 1846.
68. *Queens*, pp. 382, 504, 526.
69. *AmNep*, vol. 4, January 1944.
70. *PJ*, December 5, 1846.
71. Ibid., January 23, 1847.
72. *PMC*, October 2, 1890.
73. *PJ*, May 27, 1848.
74. Ibid., October 1, 1853.
75. Ibid., December 11, 1859.
76. *LT*, July 1, 1863.
77. *Daily True Delta*, August 15, 1846.
78. *PJ*, August 15, 1848.
79. Ibid., October 24, 1846.
80. Ibid., October 31, 1846.
81. *AmNep*, vol. 11, October 1951.
82. *PJ*, November 21, 1846.
83. *PCR*, vol. 4, p. 179.
84. *PJ*, July 16, 1847.
85. *Clippers*, pp. 96–99.
86. *PMC*, July 16, 1885.
87. *PJ*, September 25, 1847.
88. Ibid., October 2, 1847.
89. Ibid., November 13, 1847.
90. Ibid., December 2, 1848.
91. Ibid., November 11, 1848.
92. Ibid., January 31, 1852.
93. *PCR*, vol. 4, p. 180.
94. *PJ*.
95. Ibid., November 6, 1847.
96. *PCR*, vol. 4, p. 279.
97. *RM*, October 7, 1847.
98. *Queens*, pp. 384, 517, 526.
99. *PJ*, August 18, 1849.
100. *PCR*, vol. 4, p. 279.
101. *PJ*, January 8, 1848.
102. *PMC*, July 7, 1853.
103. Ibid., July 18, 1861.
104. *PCR*, vol. 4, p. 282.
105. *PJ*, September 21, 1861.
106. Ibid., March 8, 1873.
107. Ibid., October 23, 1873.
108. *RM*, November 11, 1847.
109. *PJ*, December 13, 1855.
110. *PMC*, March 4, 1879.
111. Ibid., November 10, 1885.
112. *Daily Picayune*, New Orleans, January 11, 1886.
113. *RM*, July 20, 1848.
114. Ibid., September 7, 1848.
115. *PJ*, February 12, 1864.
116. Ibid.

117. *Queens*, p. 504.
118. *PJ*, February 23, 1850.
119. Ibid., May 26, 1855.
120. Ibid., September 2, 1848.
121. Ibid., August 3, 1848.
122. Ibid., October 9, 1852.
123. *PCR*, vol. 4, p. 184.
124. *RM*, August 31, 1848.
125. *PJ*, April 26, 1851.
126. *PMC*, September 19, 1856.
127. Ibid., June 1, 1861.
128. Ibid., August 11, 1866.
129. *PJ*, December 30, 1848.
130. Ibid., February 10, 1849.
131. Ibid., April 14, 1849.
132. *PCR*, vol. 4, p. 282.
133. *PJ*, March 10, 1849.
134. *PJ*, April 10, 1849.
135. Ibid., November 3, 1849.
136. *Queens*, p. 382.
137. *PMC*, April 9, 1862.
138. *LT*, January 4, 1864.
139. *PJ*, October 8, 1864.
140. *PCR*, vol. 4, p. 186.
141. *PMC*, July 28, 1855.
142. Ibid., January 30, 1856.
143. Ibid., February 16, 1856.
144. *PJ*, September 29, 1849.
145. *PCR*, vol. 4, p. 282.
146. Stammers, *Passage Makers*, p. 354.
147. *PJ*, November 1, 1845.
148. Ibid., October 27, 1849.
149. Ibid., November 5, 1889.
150. Ibid., March 2, 1861.
151. Ibid., June 27, 1863.
152. *PMC*, January 20, 1879.
153. *PJ*, October 6, 1849.
154. Ibid., December 1, 1849.
155. February 16, 1850.
156. Ibid., June 13, 1863.
157. Ibid., April 18, 1864.
158. Ibid., December 1, 1849.

159. Ibid., October 25, 1853.
160. *PMC*, October 17, 1853.
161. *PJ*, November 5, 1853.
162. *PMC*, September 19, 1855.
163. Ibid., March 21, 1864.

Chapter 4

1. *Heyday.*
2. *Queens*, pp. 378–79.
3. *PMC*, October 1, 1880.
4. *Greyhounds of the Sea*, p. 304.
5. *LC*, October, 1862.
6. *PMC*, March 1, 1882.
7. Ibid., May 2, 1882.
8. *PJ*, August 3, 1850.
9. Ibid., September 14, 1850.
10. Ibid., September 28, 1850.
11. *Queens*, p. 328.
12. *PJ*, February 1, 1851.
13. Ibid., July 19, 1851.
14. *Clippers*, p. 28.
15. *PJ*, April 2, 1853.
16. Ibid., September 26, 1863.
17. Ibid., March 30, 1867.
18. Ibid., July 19, 1851.
19. Ibid., March 13, 1852.
20. Ibid., June 17, 1854.
21. *LC*, October 20, 1867.
22. *PCR*, vol. 4, p. 191.
23. *PJ*, January 14, 1854.
24. *PMC*, October 6, 1855.
25. Ibid., November 24, 1855.
26. *PJ*, November 23, 1861.
27. Ibid., December 21, 1861.
28. Ibid., March 15, 1862.
29. Ibid., December 27, 1851.
30. Ibid., February 7, 1852.
31. *PMC*, May 17, 1854.
32. *PJ*, May 27, 1854.
33. Brighton, *Portsmouth Ships and the Cotton Trade*, p. 84.
34. *PJ*, July 10, 1852.

35. *PMC*, February 8, 1853.
36. *PJ*, February 11, 1854.
37. Ibid., June 1, 1954.
38. *PCR*, vol. 4, p. 202.
39. *PJ*, March 6, 1897.
40. Ibid., May 8, 1852.
41. *PMC*, March 12, 1895.
42. Ibid., January 12, 1853.
43. *PJ*, October 7, 1853.
44. *PJ*, July 31, 1852.
45. *PMC*, August 16, 1852.
46. Ibid., January 12, 1853.
47. Ibid., October 26, 1855.
48. *PJ*, March 19, 1859.
49. *LC*, October 22, 1859.
50. *PJ*, March 15, 1862.
51. Ibid., November 14, 1863.
52. *PMC*, June 1, 1865.
53. Ibid., September 4, 1852.
54. Ibid., October 30, 1852.
55. *PJ*, December 11, 1852.
56. *Queens*, p. 320.
57. *PMC*, September 28, 1882.
58. *PJ*, January 1, 1853.
59. *PMC*, February 7, 1853.
60. Ibid., October 11, 1853.
61. Ibid., February 16, 1855.
62. Ibid., May 4, 1855.
63. Ibid., February 20, 1863.
64. *PJ*, September 24, 1864.
65. *PMC*, November 27, 1852.
66. *PJ*, December 18, 1852.
67. *PCR*, vol. 4, p. 91.
68. *PJ*, January 7, 1865.
69. *PMC*, July 23, 1853.
70. *PJ*, September 24, 1853.
71. *LC*, December 13, 1861.
72. Ibid., November 7, 1864.
73. *LT*, December 18, 1864.
74. *PJ*, April 19, 1873.
75. Ibid., December 10, 1853.
76. *Clippers*, p. 127.
77. *PMC*, September 17, 1858.

78. *PJ*, October 23, 1858.
79. Ibid., November 29, 1862.
80. *PMC*, December 14, 1869.
81. Ibid.
82. *PCR*, vol. 4, p. 205.
83. *PMC*, September 24, 1855.
84. Ibid., September 7, 1854.
85. *Queens*, pp. 349, 372–73.
86. *PJ*.
87. Ibid., September 29, 1860.
88. Ibid., August 11, 1854.
89. Ibid., September 23, 1854.
90. *PMC*, January 22, 1855.
91. Ibid., August 18, 1854.
92. Ibid., September 21, 1854.
93. *PJ*, January 2, 1856.
94. Ibid., June 9, 1861.
95. Ibid., November 9, 1861.
96. Ibid., March 14, 1863.
97. Ibid., February 6, 1864.
98. Ibid., September 8, 1866.
99. Ibid., September 23, 1871.
100. Ibid., April 25, 1874.
101. *AmNep*, vol. 3, January 1943.
102. *PMC*, December 2, 1853.
103. *PCR*, vol. 4, p. 295.
104. *PMC*, August 2, 1856.
105. *PJ*, June 16, 1859.
106. *PMC*, June 17, 1859.
107. *PJ*, November 10, 1855.
108. *PMC*, February 17, 1862.
109. Ibid., April 22, 1862.
110. Ibid., February 9, 1872.
111. Ibid., August 13, 1872.
112. Ibid., April 24, 1884.
113. *AmNep*, vol. 4, January 1944.
114. *PJ*, September 22, 1855.
115. Ibid., June 23, 1860.
116. *PCR*, vol. 4, p. 213.
117. *PJ*, May 24, 1856.
118. *PMC*, June 25, 1856.

119. *PCR*, vol. 4, p. 214.
120. *PJ*, November 17, 1877.
121. *PMC*, February 29, 1856.
122. Ibid., May 30, 1856.
123. *PJ*, November 14, 1874.
124. Ibid., October 30, 1875.
125. Ibid., February 19, 1876.
126. Ibid., August 24, 1877.
127. *PMC*, August 31, 1855.
128. *PJ*, November 26, 1859.
129. *PMC*, July 9, 1856.
130. Ibid., August 9, 1856.
131. Ibid., November 30, 1856.
132. *AmNep*, vol. 4, January 1944.
133. *PMC*, June 10, 1856.
134. Ibid., June 21, 1856.
135. Ibid., June 29, 1856.
136. Ibid., January 31, 1857.
137. *PJ*, July 11, 1857.
138. *PMC*, February 2, 1863.
139. *PJ*, January 7, 1865.
140. Ibid., December 30, 1865.
141. Ibid., May 25, 1872.
142. *PMC*, February 3, 1876.
143. Ibid., September 29, 1876.
144. Ibid., September 24, 1856.
145. Ibid., October 2, 1856.
146. *PJ*, April 19, 1862.
147. *AmNep*, vol. 3, June 1943.
148. *PJ*, August 2, 1856.
149. Ibid., October 28, 1856.
150. Ibid., June 19, 1858.
151. Ibid., February 20, 1860.
152. *LC*, August 14, 1861.
153. *PJ*, November 15, 1856.
154. *PMC*, January 7, 1856.
155. *PJ*, January 17, 1856.
156. Ibid., April 25, 1868.
157. Ibid., September 23, 1871.
158. Ibid., October 7, 1871.
159. Ibid., November 29, 1856.
160. Ibid., March 14, 1857.
161. Ibid., March 19, 1864.
162. Ibid., April 2, 1864.
163. Ibid., May 7, 1864.
164. Ibid., January 9, 1867.
165. Ibid., October 12, 1867.
166. *PMC*, December 23, 1876.
167. *PJ*, December 30, 1876.
168. Ibid., January 21, 1860.
169. *PMC*, July 17, 1861.
170. *Clippers*, p. 97.
171. *PJ*, October 5, 1861.
172. *AmNep*, vol. 11, October 1951.
173. *PMC*, December 4, 1867.
174. Ibid., April 27, 1868.
175. *PCR*, vol. 4, p. 313.
176. *PJ*, April 18, 1857.
177. Ibid., February 12, 1858.
178. Ibid., January 29, 1859.
179. Ibid., December 26, 1874.
180. *PMC*, September 30, 1857.
181. *PJ*, October 10, 1857.
182. *AmNep*, vol. 8, July 1848.
183. *PCR*, vol. 4, p. 314.
184. *PJ*, April 25, 1857.
185. *PMC*, September 30, 1857.
186. Ibid., October 5, 1857.
187. *PJ*, April 25, 1857.
188. *AmNep*, vol. 11, October 1951.
189. *PJ*, July 27, 1861.
190. Ibid., September 18, 1861.
191. Ibid., July 3, 1860.
192. *PMC*, August 12, 1887.
193. Ibid., October 16, 1883.
194. *PJ*, October 3, 1857.
195. Ibid., October 12, 1861.
196. Ibid., October 24, 1863.
197. Ibid., September 29, 1867.
198. *PCR*, vol. 4, p. 219.
199. *PJ*, April 8, 1871.
200. Ibid., October 16, 1858.
201. Ibid., October 30, 1858.

202. Ibid., December 4, 1858.
203. Ibid., June 2, 1859.
204. Ibid., September 17, 1859.
205. Ibid., December 29, 1862.
206. *American Merchant Ships*, p. 275.
207. *PJ*, February 10, 1865.
208. *PMC*, April 3, 1883.

Chapter 5

1. *PJ*, May 5, 1860.
2. Ibid., March 9, 1861.
3. Ibid., September 1, 1861.
4. Ibid., August 24, 1861.
5. Ibid., May 12, 1860.
6. *Queens*, p. 344.
7. *PJ*, April 9, 1864.
8. *PCR*, p. 318.
9. *PJ*, February 25, 1861.
10. *LT*, September 26, 1863.
11. *PMC*, February 5, 1868.
12. *PJ*, February 19, 1870.
13. *PMC*, March 14, 1885.
14. *PCR*, vol. 4, p. 220.
15. Ibid., March 27, 1861.
16. *LC*, February 1, 1862.
17. *PMC*, November 21, 1898.
18. *Portsmouth Herald*, December 29, 1909.
19. *PJ*, July 11, 1863.
20. *PMC*, February 20, 1864.
21. *PJ*, April 28, 1866.
22. *PMC*, May 12, 1866.
23. Ibid., June 8, 1866.
24. Ibid., June 15, 1866.
25. *PJ*, June 24, 1871.
26. Ibid., July 10, 1875.
27. *PMC*, January 26, 1877.
28. Ibid., October 24, 1863.
29. *AmNep*, vol. 3, January 1943.
30. *PJ*, October 8, 1864.
31. *PMC*, June 29, 1870.

32. *PJ*, April 19, 1873.
33. *Portsmouth Times*, June 9, 1877.
34. *Portsmouth Weekly*, August 4, 1877.
35. *Clippers*, p. 70.
36. *PMC*, May 21, 1864.
37. Ibid., May 24, 1864.
38. *PJ*, September 8, 1866.
39. Ibid., November 18, 1865.
40. Ibid., January 15, 1866.
41. *PMC*, February 16, 1867.
42. Ibid., October 9, 1866.
43. Ibid., January 7, 1867.
44. Ibid., December 22, 1866.
45. Ibid., March 28, 1867.
46. Ibid., February 10, 1874.
47. Ibid., October 29, 1875.
48. Ibid., November 5, 1875.
49. *PCR*, vol. 4, p. 322.
50. *PMC*, October 3, 1867.
51. Ibid., November 4, 1867.
52. Brighton, *They Came to Fish*, vol. 2, p. 371.
53. *PMC*, January 7, 1868.
54. *PJ*, February 8, 1868.
55. *PMC*, January 1, 1876.
56. Ibid., September 11, 1877.
57. *PJ*, February 16, 1867.
58. *PMC*, December 10, 1867.
59. Ibid., March 5, 1870.
60. Ibid., October 22, 1870.
61. *PJ*, December 31, 1859.
62. *PMC*, April 12, 1895.
63. Ibid., April 12, 1895.
64. Ibid., March 17, 1868.
65. Ibid., February 25, 1868.
66. *PJ*, June 1, 1872.
67. Ibid., January 30, 1875.
68. *PMC*, April 24, 1875.
69. Ibid., October 1, 1881.
70. *PJ*, October 12, 1872.
71. *PCR*, vol. 4, p. 324.

Chapter 6

1. *PJ*, July 31, 1869.
2. Ibid., August 10, 1872.
3. Ibid., October 1, 1870.
4. Ibid., January 7, 1871.
5. Ibid., January 21, 1871.
6. Ibid., March 18, 1871.
7. Kunitz, *British Authors of the 19th Century*, p. 322.
8. Ibid.
9. *PJ*, March 11, 1871.
10. Ibid., March 25, 1871.
11. Ibid.
12. Ibid., September 30, 1871.
13. *PMC*, December 21, 1875.
14. *PJ*, February 27, 1875.
15. Ibid., January 29, 1876.
16. Ibid., December 21, 1878.
17. Ibid., August 16, 1873.
18. Ibid., August 13, 1873.
19. Ibid., March 21, 1874.
20. Ibid., March 9, 1876.
21. *PMC*, April 18, 1877.
22. Ibid., May 12, 1885.
23. Ibid., March 3, 1885.
24. Ibid., April 22, 1887.
25. Ibid., March 25, 1893.
26. Ibid., April 24, 1893.
27. *Portsmouth Herald*, February 16, 1903.
28. *PJ*, August 3, 1872.
29. Ibid., September 27, 1873.
30. Ibid., March 6, 1875.
31. Ibid., December 6, 1873.
32. Ibid., April 7, 1877.
33. *PMC*, June 23, 1879.
34. Ibid., January 7, 1893.
35. *PJ*, June 6, 1874.
36. Ibid., August 8, 1874.
37. *Portsmouth Times*, February 26, 1875.
38. *PJ*, March 27, 1875.
39. *PMC*, May 11, 1878.
40. Ibid., October 4, 1883.
41. Ibid., December 15, 1883.
42. *PJ*, March 18, 1882.
43. Ibid., July 25, 1874.
44. *PMC*, May 29, 1875.
45. Ibid., July 7, 1875.
46. Ibid., January 20, 1876.
47. Ibid., April 28, 1877.
48. *PJ*, March 8, 1879.
49. Ibid., May 7, 1881.
50. Ibid., September 9, 1876.
51. Ibid., June 23, 1877.
52. *PMC*, October 2, 1877.
53. Ibid., October 10, 1877.
54. Ibid., August 3, 1878.
55. Ibid., April 11, 1879.
56. Ibid., December 10, 1879.
57. Ibid., April 30, 1881.
58. Ibid., December 29, 1883.
59. Ibid., July 4, 1884.
60. Ibid., April 30, 1886.
61. Ibid., January 27, 1887.
62. Ibid., March 21, 1889.
63. Ibid., April 20, 1892.
64. Ibid., July 14, 1877.
65. Ibid., September 25, 1877.
66. Ibid., September 26, 1877.
67. Ibid., October 29, 1877.
68. Ibid., September 3, 1877.
69. Ibid., November 3, 1877.
70. Ibid., October 8, 1879.
71. Ibid., August 6, 1878.
72. *PJ*, March 11, 1882.
73. *PMC*, December 31, 1885.
74. Ibid., March 27, 1886.
75. *AmNep*, vol. 1, January 1941.

Index

A. Zerega & Co., 126

Abandonments, *America*, 111; *Bremerhaven*, 184; *Constantine*, 162; *Frank Pierce*, 194-196; *Goodwin*, 84; *Judah Touro*, 109; *Matilda*, 115; *New Hampshire*, 256-257; *Samuel Badger*, 179-181; *Siam*, 127; *St. Albans*, 233; *See also* Shipwrecks

Abbott, G., 96

Abbott, John W., 58

Abelino, 51

Achilles, 155

Adams, Calvin, 258-259

Adams, Ebenezer Gilman, Capt., 43-46, 76-77, 243

Adams, John Quincy, 13

Adams, Nathaniel, Capt., 3

Adams, Nathaniel, (historian), 3

Adams, Samuel, 176, 202, 275, 287

Adams, Thomas A., 64, 67

Adams, W.H., Capt., 259

Adelaide Bell, 197

Aginore, 311

Alabama, 92-93

Alabama Claims Commission, 254

Alabama, CSS, 9, 46, 92, 117, 204, 242, 244, p245, 246-247, 272, 344

Albacore, USS, 345

Albania, 84-85

Albert Gallatin, 156-158, 159

Alden, Captain, (of the *Anna Decatur*), 223

Alexander, 12-13, 218

Alger, Captain, (of the *Sagamore*), 239

Alice Ball, 241-244, 258, 259

Alice Bell, 242

Alice Tarlton, 122

Allaire Works, 198

Allen, Captain, (of the *Solon*), 27

Alliance, 7, 47-48, 116

America, 109-111, p110, 241

America, HBM, 4

American Ice Company, 22

American Merchant Ships (Matthews), 314

American Ship Windlass Co., 349

Ames, Preston, 272

Amesbury, 4

Anderson, Robert, Major, 250

Andrew, Captain, (of the *Charles*), 67

Anglo Saxon, 266

Ann Parry, 2

Anna Decatur, 112, 223-225

Annie F. Conlan, 355
Annie Sise, 204, 236-238
Antony Gibbs & Son, 263
Apollo, 15-17, p16, 149
Aprosince, 55
Arabella, 60, 91-92, 94
Arago, 242
Archelaus, 5, 24, 118
Arethusa, 64-65
Arkwright, 215-218
Arno, 64
Ashbridge's Line, 38
Asphodel, 316
Atalanta, 281
Athens, 73-75, 136
Atkins, Edwin, 129
Atkinson, Mrs., 164
Atlantic Shipbuilding, 289
Augustina, 298
Australian, 107, 115
Azor, 181

Badger, Daniel, 325
Badger, David, 281, 334; *William H. Marcy*, 325-330, 335, 336
Badger, David D., 286; *Granite State*, 330-334, p331, p335
Badger, Samuel, 6, 7, 12, 38, 81, 124, 255, 265, 267-268, 274, 355; *Adelaide Bell*, 197; *Alabama*, 92-93; *Albania*, 84-85; *Albert Gallatin*, 156-158; *Alliance*, 47-48, 116; *Apollo*, 15-17, p16; *Charlotte*, 17-18, 25, 60; *Chatsworth*, 206-208; *Clara*, 94-96; *Ella E. Badger*, 226-227; *Epaminondas*, 96-97; *Franconia*, 78-79, 84; *Globe*, 171-172; *Granite State*, 202-205, 211, 255; *Hibernia*, 132-135, 151; *Huron*, 57-58; *India*, 21-22; *James Buchanan*, 228-230; *James Montgomery*, 182-184; *Martha*, 94, 96; *Mary Hale*, 143-145; *Mary Pleasants*, 104; *Matilda*, 115; *Milo*, 15, 25, 28-29; *New Hampshire*, 254-

257; *Norman*, 46-47, 59; *Pontiac*, 58-62; *Sabine*, 172-174; *Samuel Badger*, 179-181, 230; *S.C. Thwing*, 222-223, 230; *Solon*, 27-28, 30, 47; *William Penn*, 122-124
Badger, William, 5-6, 11, 149, 241, 271
Badger's Island, 12, 56, 63, 81, 234, 241
Bailey, Salter & Marcy, 130
Bailey, Thomas D., 176, 211
Baines & Co., 146
Baines, James, 146
Baker, George, Capt., 172, 190
Ball, John, 12
Ball, Thomas, 35
Ball, True M., 228, 232, 241, 242, 251, 257, 281
Bannockburn, 77
Barker, Jonathan, 176
Barlow, Captain, (of the *Granite State*), 344
Barnabee, Lewis, 57
Barnabee, Willis, 57
Barnes, John, Captain, 224, 225
Barnes, Lewis, 33, 34, 35, 36
Baron Bareaux, 133
Barstow, Edward W., 124, 323
Barstow, Edwin A., 125
Barstow, G.W., Capt., 124
Bartlett, James P., 275, 321, 327
Bartol, George, Jr., Capt., 48
Barton, George S., 229
Baun, 312
Beals, Silas, 219
Beatrice, 207
Becker, Barbara, 320
Bedford Galley, 3
Beecher, Laban S., 78
Belcher, George, 201
Bell, Andrew W., Jr., 78
Bell, Isaac, 197, 215
Bell, Isaac, Jr., 236, 237
Benson, John, 248
Benson, William, 35

Berwick, 3, 5, 11

Berwick, 18-21, 149

Bicknell, Captain, (of the *Daniel Marcy*), 282-283

Biddle, Nicholas, 53

Bigelow, Charles H., 20

Bigelow, Francis W., 168

Bigelow, Tyler, 92, 93

Bigler, James, 129

Billings, Samuel, Capt., 203, 226, 227

Black Diamond Line, 124

Black, John, 215

Black Star Line, 134

BlackBall Line, 146

Blair, Samuel, 289, 290

Blanchard, J., Rev., 83

Blood, A., 220

Blood, Edward, 221

Blue Ball Line, 134

Blunt, Charles B., 146

Boardman, George C., Capt., 57

Boardman, Isaac H., 220, 221

Boardman, J.H., 151

Boardman, J.H., Dr., 229, 266

Boardman, John H., 57, 156, 223

Boardman, Peter, 196

Boardman, Richard, 131

Boardman, Robert, Capt., 265-266

Bogue, Ruel B., 20

Boiling Rock, 229-230

Bombay, 143

Bombay and Bengal SS Co., 143

Borland, Captain, (of the *Piscataqua*), 275

Borland, Captain, (of the *Portsmouth*), 265

Boru, Brian, 133

Boston Tugboat Co., 313

Bowne, J.Q., Capt., 104

Boyd, George, xx, 4, 6

Boyd, William, 4

Boyd-Meserve Yard, 22

Brace, Thomas, 53

Bracket, S.S., 330

Bradford, Henry, Capt., 48, 183

Bremerhaven, 184

Brewster, Charles W., 87, 175

Briard, Captain, 153

Briard, Charles, Capt., 238

Briard, William A., Capt., 36

Bright Brothers, 146

Brighton, Ray, 3, 7, 12, 81, 159

Brilliant, 246

Brinda, 184

Brooklyn, 289

Brooks, Abraham, 226, 323

Brooks, Chandler, 265, 318, 323

Brooks, Joshua, 323

Brother Jonathan, 7, 124, 199-201, p200, 309

Broughton, Daniel, 219

Broughton, John, 275

Broughton, Noah, 201, 219

Brown, E. Washington, 320

Brown, Emma S., 297

Brown, Georgia, 240

Brown, Henry S., Capt., 38, 221

Brown, James, 116

Brown, John, 199

Brown & Joy, 78

Brown, Peter, 83

Brown, Vernon H., 297

Brown, Willard, 148

Brown's Hill, 327

Bruce, Captain, (of the *Bonnockburn*), 77

Bryce, Grace & Co., 298

Buchanan, James, 228

Buffum, D.H., 323

Bunting, Richard L., Capt., 160

Burdick, James H., Capt., 230, 252-254

Burke, Alexander, 83

Burleigh, John H., 309, 323

Burleigh, M.H., 323

Burnham, Richard, 336

Burton, Joshua, 157

Bush, John C., Capt., 194-196, 277

Butler, George W., 323

Butler, J.H., 232
Byzantium, 109

Caesar, 39
Calcutta, 293-297
Calhoun, 186
Call, Alfred, 263
Call, Thomas E., 265, 287, 289, 308, 309
Calvert, C.W., 35
Cameron, R.W., 126
Capitol, 93
Card, Horton, 266
Caroline Augusta, 40
Cary, Stephen W., 277
Caswell, John W., 347
Catharine, 113
Cathedral, 207
Caulkins, David, 126
C.B. Stevens, 178
C.E. Walker & Co., 60
Centurion, 125-126
Chadwick, John, 20
Chandler, Edward, 18, 19
Chapman, George W., Capt., 117, 205, 248-249
Chapman, Mrs., 117, 330
Charger, 259
Charles, 51, 59, 65-67, 113
Charles E. Morrison, 304
Charles Lambert, 196
Charles Pearson, 278
Charleston & Chattanooga Railroad, 79
Charlotte, 17-18, 25, 60
Chase, 294
Chase, Charles H., 73
Chase, John, 18, 19, 26, 236
Chase, John, Capt., 73, 136, 137, 197
Chase, John E., 323
Chase, Salmon P., 242
Chase, Theodore, 46, 92, 93
Chase, William F., 137
Chatsworth, 206-208
Cheeven, Charles, Capt., 154

Chick, James H., Capt., 29, 73, 97
Child, Arthur, Capt., 145, 146
Chincha Islands, 43-46
Chocorua, 320-324, 345, 346
Church, George, 263
City of Boston, 272
City of Montreal, 275-277, 290
City of New York, 181
Civil War, 9, 101-102, p268, 269, 334-335; *Alabama*, 92-93; *Alice Ball*, 242-243; *America*, 111; *Arkwright*, 216-217; *Athens*, 74; *Finland*, 101-102; *Frank Pierce*, 191-194; *Governor Langdon*, 211; *Granite State*, 204; *John Cumming*, 46; *Jummna*, 226; *Kate Prince*, 231; *Levi Woodbury*, 171; *Nicholas Biddle*, 54; *Peter Marcy*, 132; *Piscataqua*, 275; *R.D. Shepherd*, 114; *R.H. Tucker*, 250; *Rockingham*, 245-246; *Sarah E. Pettigrew*, 252
Clara, 94-96
Clara Bateman, 309, 316, 322, 336, 350
Clark, Horace, 308
Clark, Horace D., 316, 317
Clark, Samuel, 202, 305
Clark, Thomas B., Capt., 32, 50, 63
Clark, W.J., 117, 249, 250-251
Clay, Reverend, 44-46
Cleaves, Samuel, 38, 39
Clement, Zenas, 229
Clippers of the Port of Portsmouth (Brighton), 7, 81, 159
Cluney, John, 201
Coal trade, 73
Cobb, Matthew, 196
Cobb, Samuel H., 116
Cobbs, Captain, (of the *Como*), 258
Coburn, T.J., 265
Cocheco, 355
Cocheco Mills, 16
Cocheco River, 50
Coffin, Anne Cushing, 66

Coffin, Charles, 59, 65
Coffin, Edward D., 273, 277, 349
Coffin, Horatio, 59, 65, 84, 143
Coffin, T., Jr., 151
Coffin, Thomas Sheafe, Capt. 65-66
Colcord, J.C., 148
Coleman, Captain, (of the *Harry Hastings*), 260
Colorado, 213-215
Colson, Captain, (of the *Alice Ball*), 243
Columbia, 63, 143
Columbus, 118-122
Comet, 172
Commander-in-Chief, 221
Commercial Line, 75
Como, 257, 258
Congress, U.S., 299-230, 322
Connor, Thomas, 199
Connor, T.J., 264
Conrad, 273
Constance, 257
Constantine, 160-161, 162
Constellation, 140
Constitution, 120, 121
Consul, 88
Conti, M., 266
Cook, Henry, Captain, 22, 151, 220, 221
Coolidge, John T., 22
Coombs, Edward, 126
Copperheads, 281, 282, 301
Coppering, 17
Corbett, Samuel D., 41
Cornelius Grinnell, 155, 258
Coronation, 280-281
Coster, Captain, (of the *Danube*), 136-137
Cotton trade *See* Triangle trade
Coues, Samuel E., 7, 21-22, 31, 33, 37, 49, 82, 83, 87
Cox, Joseph E., 226
Crabtree, William, Capt., 146
Crane, Elisha C., 38
Crescent City Line, 85

Crimean War, 261
Criterion, 149
Crocker, Captain, (of the *Swordfish*), 76
Cromwell, John T., Capt., 174
Crosby, Freeman, Capt., 271-272
Crowell, Ambrose, Capt., 84-8
Crusader, 157
Cufferty (*Arkwright* rigger), 218
Culdrey, William E., Capt., 160
Cumming, George B., 31, 33, 41, 53, 82, 111, 174, 175
Cumming, John, 31, 33
Cumming & Son, 54
Curran, Adam, 83
Currier, Albert, 221
Currier, Joseph B., Capt., 191
Curtis, Benjamin W., 323
Cushing, Charles, 26, 38
Cushing, Seth, 196
Cutler, Carl, 37
Cutts, Eastman, 113

D. & A. Kingsland Co., 120, 125, 154
Dame, John, 148
Daniel Marcy, 281-283, 316
Danube, 136-137, 151
Dashing Wave, 7, 117, 218, 241, 290
Davis, Alex G., Capt., 211
Davis Brothers, 306
Davis, James, 208
Davis, John, Capt., 182, 215, 216-217, 236, 305
Davis, John S., Capt., 82-84
Davis, Mrs., 83
Day, John, 139
Debman, Solomon, 90
Decatur, Anna, 223
Decatur, John P., 223
Deering & Yeaton, p141, 277, 286
Deland, Tucker, 126, 127, 138, 139
Democratic Party, 189, 190, 228, 301-302
Dennett, John S.D., Capt., 182
Deshon, Dan, 50

Destebecho, Peter, 171, 172
Devil fish, 75-76
Devine, Thomas, 122
Devonshire, 136
Dispatch Line, 20, 47
Dockum, Samuel M., 148, 175, 178, 273
Dominion Coal Co., 313-314
Donati, 258-259
Donati, G.B., 259
Donohue, Justice, 129
Dorothea, 181
Dover, 3, 5, 11
Downs, Charles H., 332
Dramatic Line, 186
Draper & Co., 304
Draper & Sons, 267, 293
Dromahair, 126
Dulles, J., Rev., 172
Dun fish, 1
Dunham, Thomas, 277
Dunn, Edmund, 111
Duran, Richard, 199
Durant, Francis, 199
Durham, 5, 11
Duryea, Richard, 160
Dwight, William L., Capt., 25, 42, 46, 59, 75

Eagle Speed, 118, 234-236, 238, 239, 241
East India Trade, 179, 184; *Albania*, 85; *Alice Ball*, 243; *Annie Sise*, 237; *Calcutta*, 295; *Charles*, 66; *Granite State*, 338-343; *Isaac Newton*, 50; *James Montgomery*, 183; *John Huron*, 149; *North Atlantic*, 153; *Paul Jones*, 351-352; *Pontiac*, 62; *R.H. Tucker*, 251; *Rockingham*, 245-246; *Sabine*, 172-174; *Siam*, 127; *Simla*, 278
Edmonston, Charles, 21
Edwards, Captain, 281
E.F. Sise & Co., 25, 29, 74, 90, 108
Eldredge Brewing Co., 113

Eldredge, Heman, Jr., 113
Eliot, Maine, 5, 127, 196
Elizabeth, 3
Elizabeth Hamilton, 5, 125, 127-130, 230
Elizabeth Hanscom, 196
Ella E. Badger, 226-227
Eloisa, 316
Elwyn, Elizabeth Langdon, 210
Emblem, 101
Emerald, 38
Emery, James W., 229, 246
Emigration Commissioners, 104
Emily Caroline, 13
Emily Farnum, 60, 216, 246
Empire, 97-100, 140
Empire Line, 111, 121, 154
Empire State, 5, 140-143, 154
England, John, Rev., 82-83, 84
English and Brandon, 201
Enoch Train & Co., 206
Epaminondas, 73, 96-97
Eudocia, 143
Evans, H.T., Capt., 312-313
Exeter, 3, 5, 11
Express, 178, 230, 242, 316

Faderneslandet, 150-151
Fairy, 304
Falkland, 3
Farland, James, 20
Farmer, Sarah J., 128
Fashion, 120
Fay, E.S., 352
Federal Fire Society, 31
Fejee Mermaid, p6
Felicity, 4
Ferguson, Timothy, 18, 19, 25-26
Fernald, A.A., 323
Fernald, Frederick William, 6, 7, 12, 81, 106, 251, 267, 268; *Arabella*, 91-92, 94; *Colorado*, 213-215; *Columbia*, 63; *Columbus*, 118-122; *Danube*, 136-137, 151; *Empire*, 97-100, 140; *Empire State*, 140-143;

Frank Pierce, 177, 188-196, p189, 228; *Germania*, 161-165; *Goodwin*, 82-84; *Governor Langdon*, 208-212; *Harriet Rockwell*, 33-37; *Hope Goodwin*, 174-176; *Isaac H. Boardman*, 220-221; *John Haven*, 147-151; *Judah Touro*, 105-109, 113; *Levi Woodbury*, 19, 169-171, p170, 174, 183, 188, 228; *New Hampshire*, 40, 56-57; *Peter Marcy*, 116, 130-132, 151; *Piscataqua*, 176-179, p177; *R.D. Shepherd*, 113-114; *Robert Parker*, 75-77; *Samoset*, 115-118, 120, 200; *Thomas Perkins*, 54-55, 151; *Western World*, 154-156

Fernald & Pettigrew, 334; *See also* Fernald, Frederick William; Pettigrew, William

Fernald, William D., 232, 254, 261, 265, 289

Fernald, William F., 8, 286, 294; *Calcutta*, 293-297; *Chocorua*, 320-324; *Jean Ingelow*, 301-308, 321; *Paul Jones*, 344, 345-353, p346, 355

Ferry (*Samoset* second mate), 116

Fessenden, Charles B., 67

Fields, James T., 39

Finland, 94, 100-102

Fires, *Adelaide Bell*, 197; *Arabella*, 92; *Commander-in-Chief*, 221; *Danube*, 137; *Finland*, 102; *Flora McDonald*, 169; *George Raynes*, 168-169; *George V*, 169; *Georgianna*, 261; *Isaac Newton*, 50; *Kalamazoo*, 87; *Mary Kingsland*, 70-71, 72-73; *North Atlantic*, 153; *Robert Parker*, 76-77; *Rockingham*, 246; *Ruthelia*, 26; *Venice*, 90-91

Fishing industry, 1-2

Fitz, Thomas, Capt., 336, 339-343

Flanders, Charles, 20

Fleetford, 204

Fleetwood, 197

Flora McDonald, 169

Florida, CSS, 54

Flying Eagle, 60, 207

Folger, T.P., Capt., 124

Follansbee, E. A., Capt., 286

Folsom, Captain, (of the *Orozimbo*), 257

Forbes, J.M., 283

Forbes, R.B., 283-285

Forbes Rig, 285

Forest King, 127

Fortitude, 38-40

Fortuna, 107

Fosdick & Charlock, 70

Foster, Andrew, 85

Foster, Joseph Hiller, 289

Foster's Patent Deck-Reefing Gear, p180

Fowler, William C., 224

Fox, Edward, 20

Francis, John T., 46

Franconia, 78-79, 84

Frank, John, 132

Frank Jones, 315-320

Frank Jones Brewery, 113

Frank Pierce, 112, 177, 188-196, p189, 228, 269, 316

Franklin, 51

Franklin, F.A., 255

Franklin, George, 263

Franklin, Harrison T., 255

Fredson, Calvin R., 201

Freeman, 352

Freeman, Charles H., 297

Fremont, John C., 228

French, Francis M., Capt., 184, 185, 198

French, John, 202, 226

French, John T., 289

Friend, Antonia, 240

Frisbee, Ichabod, 248

Frost, Benjamin, 218

Frost, William S., Capt., 117, 205

Fuller, David S., Capt., 234, 235

Fuller, E.N., 229

Furber, Isaac, 323
Furness Abbey, 172
Fury, 268, 293

Gager, I.B., 31
Gallatin, Albert, 157
Gallia, 162
Gardiner, Samuel G., Capt., 204, 262, 263, 280
Gardner, William P., 102
Gardner, William R., Capt., 103
Garrett, Henry L., 323
Gay, Thomas S., 311-312, 336
General Grant, 283-286
General Harrison, 17
George III, King, 4
George Raynes, 165-169, p166
George Raynes & Son; *Arkwright*, 215-218; *Mary Washington*, 247-248
George V., 169
Georgia Line, 42
Georgianna, 260-261, 316
Georgietta Lawrence, 297
Germania, 161-165
Gerrish, Charles W., 352
Gerrish, Edwin A., Capt., 54, 239, 241, 245-247, 287-288, 313, 344, 351-352
Gerrish, Helen "Brownie", p245, 247, 344
Gerrish, Samuel, 148
Gerrish, Samuel J., 323
Gerrish & Son, 78
Gerrish, Woodbury, 278
Gibbs, John, Capt., 83
Gillespie, David, Capt., 126
Gleason & Henderson, 234-235
Glendoveer, 51, 81, 87-88
Glendower, Owen, 87
Glidden, William, Capt., 83
Glidden & Williams, 165, 167
Glidden, W.T., 145
Globe, 171-172
Glover, Charles G., Capt., 31

Goddard, John F., 17
Gold Rush, 7-8, 159, 261; *Apollo*, 16; *Charlotte*, 18; *Harriet Rockwell*, 37; *Martha*, 96; *Nestor*, 14
Golden Fleece, 337
Goodrich, Arthur N., 351
Goodrich, I.D., 78
Goodrich, Moses H., 308
Goodwin, 82-84, 204
Goodwin & Coues, 78
Goodwin, Frank, 225
Goodwin, Ichabod, 7, 21-22, 31, 33, 37, 43, 49, 82, 83, 87, 111, 174, 175, 212, 213, 223
Goodwin, William, 99
Gorham, Josiah, Capt., 207
Gorilla, 87
Gorman, N., Capt., 18
Governor Langdon, 208-212
Grace B. Phillips, 355
Grace Darling, 197
Grace, Joseph, 15-17
Grace, Joseph A., 323
Grace, Joseph, Capt., 29, 171
Grace K. Green, 355
Grace, William D., 29
Graffey, John, 83
Grandee, 290, 309-315, p310, 336, 351
Granite State, 143, 154, 202-205, 211, 255, 274, 292, 330-344, 355
Granite State Minerals, 2, 265
Grant, Ulysses S., 300
Graves, Joseph, 26
Green Acre, 128
Green, A.K.W., 349
Greenleaf, S.N., Capt., 220
Greenough, John, 48
Greenough, John K., Capt., 117, 219, 262
Greer, William E., 101
Grover, Josiah, 305
Groves, James, Capt., 157-158, 218, 219
Guano trade, 43-44, p193, 207, 261

Hackett, William H., 211, 246, 275
Hackett, William H.Y., 42, 203, 229
Hale, Samuel, 56, 63
Haley, John B., Capt., 47, 63, 149, 172, 213-214
Hall, Henry, 22
Hallet, Jonathan, 20
Hallett, U.S. Commissioner, 243
Hamilton, Captain, (of the *James Montgomery*), 183
Hamilton, Captain, (of the *Kate Prince*), 232
Hampton, 4
Hanscom, Isaiah, 196
Hanscom, Samuel, 196
Hanscom, William, 18, 25, 127, 196
Hansen, Earlene, 320
Harbinger, 37
Harding, R., Capt., 128, 207
Harding, Samuel, Capt., 148-149
Harding, Samuel, Jr., 17, 19-20
Harper, Thomas, 108
Harrat, Charles, 99, 131, 178
Harrat, John, 176
Harratt, C., 148, 175
Harriet & Jessie, 21, 83
Harriet Rockwell, 33-37, 251
Harris, Benjamin, 196
Harris, G., 146
Harris, J., 146
Harris, Theodore J., 33, 34, 35, 36
Harris, Thomas A., Capt., 66
Harry Hastings, 259-260
Hartford, 72
Haselton, I., 148
Hastings, Harry, 259-260
Hatch, Albert R., 229, 251, 254
Hatch, John, 330
Hathaway, William, Capt., 24
Haven, Alexander, Capt., 42-43
Haven, Alfred, 147
Haven, A.W., 229
Haven, George W., 147, 148, 172, 213, 258
Haven, John, 15, 28-29, 58, 59, 91, 92, 147

Hayes, Charles E., 349
Hayes, John, 206
Hayes, Lieutenant, 90
Healey, William P., Capt., 42, 113, 227
Heintzenan, S.P., Capt., 90
Helen Mar, 37
Hempstead, Captain, (of the *Elizabeth Hamilton*), 129
Hendee, Thomas W., Capt., 173
Henderson, Joseph, 278
Henderson, Robert, Jr., 66
Henrietta Marcy, 232-233, 242, 316
Henry, 51-53
Henry Clay, 186
Hibernia, 132-135, 151
Hickey, Captain, (of the *Peter Marcy*), 132
Hickey, Jim, 254
Hickey, Joshua W., Capt., 233, 241, 242
Hiern, Charles A., Capt., 53, 54
Higgens, John, 35
Hill, Charles, 96
Hill, George S., Capt., 186-187
Hindoo, 37-38
Hitchcock, J.C., 122
H.N. Dickenson & Co., 262
Holbrook, John R., 323, 335-336, p335, 339
"Hollins' turtle", 72
Holt, Edwin, Rev., 183
Holt, Taylor, 183
Hope Goodwin, 174-176
Horn, Captain, (of the *Chatsworth*), 208
Howard, Everett T., 275
Howe's patent, 216
Hoyt, Mr., 229
Hubbard, Fannie, 264
Hubbard, J.T., Capt., 264
Hubbard, J.T., Mrs., 264
Hughes, John, 199
Hunt, Albert, 27
Hunter & Co. 83

Hunter, James, 83
Hurley (*Calcutta* third mate), 295
Huron, 57-58, 204
Hurricane, 172
Hussey, Franklin H., 20
Hutchinson, Robert, 48

Ice trade, 131-132, p131, 178-179, 258
Ida, 22
Ida Raynes, 216
Ilsley, Hosea, 78
Immigrants, 7, 60-61, 86, 91, 121, 261, 272; *See also* Packet ships; Names of individual packet lines
Independence, 44-45
India, 21-22
Indiana, 308
Ingelow, Jean, 301-302, 303-304, 308
Iris, 149
Isaac Allerton, 59, 67-69
Isaac H. Boardman, 220-221
Isaac Newton, 49-50
Isles of Shoals, 1
Ivanhoe, 54
Ivy, 253

Jackson, B.R., 249
Jackson, Henry F., 67
Jackson, Sam, 218
Jacobs, Benjamin F., Capt., 203-204, 292, 306, 307, 309, 310, 311, 313, 314, 347, 349-351
Jacobs, Isabel, 313
James Baines & Co., 104
James Browne, 145-146, 147, 151
James Buchanan, 228-230, 316
James Guthrie, 181
James Howard & Co., 280
James Montgomery, 182-184
Janus, 25
Jean Ingelow, 301-308, 321
"Jean Ingelow" (poem), 306
Jenkins, Alexander, 263
Jenness, John S., 64, 78

Jenness, Peter, 241, 251
Jenness, Richard, 26, 29, 32, 64, 179, 180, 188-196, 222, 228, 229, 234, 258, 281
Jennings & Son, 296, 307
Jensen, Peter, 329
Jersey, 138-139, 151
Jewett, J.W., Capt., 34-35
Jewett, Nathaniel M., 275
Jewett, Sarah Orne, 18
Jewett, S.W., 20
Jewett, Theodore F., 18, 19, 20, 25-26
Jewett, Thomas, 18, 19
J.H. Stetson, 289
J.M. Tredick & Son, 282
John Colby, 145
John Cumming, 31, 41-46, 76
John Fraser & Co., 48
John Hale, 121
John Haven, 145, 147-151, 154
John Jay, 89
John Rutledge, 164, 165
John Taylor, 85-86, 91, 227
Johnson, Jeremiah, 53, 99, 120, 131, 148, 175
Johnson, John, 85
Jones, Albert, 223
Jones, Frank, 292, 315
Jones, John Paul, 345
Jones, Martin Parry, 230
Jones & Mendum, 238, 244
Jones & Son, 25, 64, 79, 97, 128, 179, 180, 230, 234, 238, 241, 244
Jones, Thomas, Capt., 79, 128, 130, 230-231
Jones, William, 64, 78, 94, 127, 128, 130, 156, 179, 180, 199, 230, 234, 238, 244
Jones, William, Jr., 27
Jones, William P., 64, 78, 94, 118, 127, 128, 130, 156, 223, 229
Joseph Bell, 272
Josephine, 128, 196
Joy, Alfred T., 133

Joy, A.T., 139, 273, 277, 305
Joy, E.H., 307
J.P. Proutz, 171
J.R. Livermore & Co., 339
Judah Touro, 105-109, 113, 316
Judge Shaw, 128, 196-197
Jumna, 225-226
Juno, 83

Kalamazoo, 86-87, 91
Kangaroo, 211
Kate Hunter, 31, 75, 111-113, 175
Kate Prince, 128, 172, 230-232
Kaven, 172
Kearsarge, USS, 246-247
Kelley, N., Capt., 125
Kelly, David, 35
Kelly, James, 199
Kennard, Captain, 84
Kennard, Edward, Capt., 64-65
Kennard, James, Capt., 24, 25, 52
Kennard, John, 56
Kennedy, James, 199
Kennedy, Stephen, 199
Kenney, Hampti, 99
Kermit Line, 99
Keyser, Captain, (of the *Henrietta Marcy*), 233
Kindrick, Alfred, 47
King Philip, 143-144
Kingsland, A.C., 69
Kingsland, Daniel, 69
Kingslands, 86, 97, 109, 118, 140, 154, 155; *See also* D. & A. Kingsland Co.
Kittery Foreside, 15, 28, 81, 268, 315, 330
Kittery, Maine, 208
Kittredge, George W., 228, 229
Knapp, Captain, (of the *Sagamore*), 240
Kneeland, Henry, 22
Knight, Eben, Capt., 121
Knight, Moses, 66
Knight, S.C., 54

Knight, William R., 20
Knowlton, Ammi L., 173
Knowlton, J., 175
Knowlton, John, 78, 131, 148, 176, 229
Koomah, 257
Kunitz, Stanley, 303

Ladd, Alexander, 4, 51
Ladd, Alfred, 97
Ladd, Eliphalet, 4-5, 24
Ladd, Henry, 4, 51
Ladd, H.H., 229
Ladoga, 205, 212-213, 233
LaGrange, 38
Laighton, Joseph, 245
Lambert, William, Capt., 27, 49-50, 96-97
Lancashire, 48-49
Lancaster, USS, 255
Lane, Asa T., Capt., 219
Langdon, John, Governor, 209
Langdon, Mary, 209
"The Launch" (poem), 23
Lawlor, B.J., 285
Lawrence, Joseph I., Capt., 37
Lawrence, Joseph J., Capt., 111, 187, 199
Leach, Joseph W., Capt., 191-194
Leach & Walton, 131
Lear, Tobias, 1
Lee, F., Capt., 318
Lemoyne & Bell, 236, 237
Lennox, P., 248
Lennox, William, 250
Lennox, W.P., 248
Levi Woodbury, 169-171, p170, 174, 183, 188, 190, 261, 316
Leviathan, 198
Lewis, Josiah W., 323
Libbey, Daniel, Capt., 38-39, 40, 255
Libbey, H., Mrs., 232
Libbey, Hannah, 38-39
Libbey, Henry L., Capt., 172-173, 231

Littlefield, Daniel, 7, 199, 289, 310;
  See also Tobey & Littlefield
Littlefield, Edwin F., 85
Livermore & Co., 339
Liverpool Line, 186
Liverpool Packet, 271-272
Lizzie J. Call, 355
Llewellyn, D.H., Dr., 247
Locke, Ethan A., Capt., 323-324, 338
London Line, 277
Lord, William A., Capt., 39, 255-256
Lotus, 179
Lovell, Daniel, 308
Low, Frank, 334
Lowry, Captain, (of the *Huron*), 58
Lycurgus, 149
Lydia, 50, 60
Lydston, Thomas, 38
Lyman, John P., 39, 78
Lyman, P.P., 137
Lynch, Francis, 199
Lynch, Frank, 199
Lynch, John, 199

Mack, Andrew, Capt., 289
Macoduck, Samuel, 160
Maffitt, John, 54
Maguire, Isaac, 240
Maldon, 104
Mallett, John, Capt., 85
Maloney, Daniel W., 134
Maloney, Ray, 67-68, p68
Manassas, 72-73
Manchester, 272
Mandarin, 172
Manguera, 207
Mansfield, Charles, Capt., 127
Marcy, Daniel, 8, 105, 106, 108, 113,
  114, 120, 131-132, 242, 274, 275,
  321-322; *Alice Ball*, 241;
  Chatsworth, 206-208; *Daniel
  Marcy*, 281-283; *Frank Jones*, 315-
  320; *Frank Pierce*, 188-196, p189;
  Georgianna, 260-261; *Germania*,
  162; *Granite State*, 330-344, p331,

  p335; *Henrietta Marcy*, 232-233;
  James Buchanan, 228-230; *Levi
  Woodbury*, 169-171, p170; *Oroz-
  imbo*, 257-258; *Portsmouth*, 265-
  266; *Sarah E. Pettigrew*, 230,
  251-254; *S.C. Thwing*, 222-223;
  William H. Marcy, 325-330, 335,
  336; *William Ross*, 298
Marcy, Daniel, Mrs., 192
Marcy, Franklin Pierce, 316
Marcy, George D., 233, 329
Marcy, Henrietta Priest, 233
Marcy, Henry, 233
Marcy, Henry L., Capt., 192, 325,
  326, 336, 351
Marcy, Judah Touro, Capt., 233, 326,
  327, 328, 329, 336
Marcy, Katherine Tredick, 233
Marcy, Peter, 105, 113, 130, 222,
  228-230, 232, 241, 242, 251, 257,
  260; *Frank Jones*, 315-320; *Gran-
  ite State*, 330-344, p331, p335;
  Levi Woodbury, 169-171, p170;
  William H. Marcy, 325-330, 335,
  336
Marcy & Pettigrew, 267-268, 269
Marcy, Samuel, 146, 222
Marcy, William Learned, 46, 328
Margarita, 101
Maria, 90
Marion, 204
Marr, John, 18-19
Martha, 15-16, 50, 94-96
Martin, Captain, (of the *Jumna*),
  225-226
Martin, Clarence, 351
Martin & Fernald, 131, 175
Martin, Francis, 114
Martin, Thomas, 78, 99, 131, 148,
  175, 178, 273
Martin, William, 78, 97-98, 232, 260
Martin, William R., 277, 325, 330,
  333
Mary C. Porter, 249
Mary Hale, 143-145, 151

Mary J. Adams, 265, 291
Mary Kingsland, 69-73, 87
Mary Pleasants, 104
Mary & Susan, 204
Mary Washington, 247-249
Maryland, 237
Mathes, John F., 202, 226
Mathes, Nathan F., 323
Matilda, 107, 115
Matthews, Charles B., Capt., 322
Matthews, Charles D., 323
Matthews, J.J., 254
Matthews, John F., 318
Mayhew, Captain, (of the *Harriet Rockwell*), 35
McCerran, Robert, Capt., 69, 87
McCerrin, Robert, Capt., 118, 120, 121
McCobb, Daniel M., Capt., 117
McDonald, Alan, 199
McGraw, Captain, (of the *Santee*), 274
McHenry, A.R., 122
McIntyre, James, Capt., 264
McKown, Samuel W., 21
McLane, Priscilla Palfrey, 31, 216
McMahon, Francis, 328
McNulty, Edward, 203
M.E. Eldredge, 355
Means, L.G., Capt., 243
Means, Mrs., 244
Mechanics Shipbuilding Co., 212-213, 232
Melcher, George, Capt., 244-245
Melcher, Woodbury, 245
Melville, Captain, (of the *Wellington*), 36
Melvin, M., 195
Mendoza, 239-240
Mendum, Charles H., 292-293, 309, 311, 313, 320, 321, 323, 345
Merchants' Line, 20
Merrick, S.M., 255
Merrill, Nathaniel W., Capt., 48
Merrimac, 265

Merrimack, 274, 291-293, 306
Mervin, Commodore, 44-46
Meserve, Nathaniel, xx
Meteor, 286
Mexican-American War, 100
Michaels, Anthony M., Capt., 104, 122, 123-124
Miller, James F., Capt., 38
Miller, John H., 113
Milo, 15, 25, 28-29
Minkius, Seymour, 20
Minna, 184
Mississippi, 72
Mobile, 223
Mobile, Alabama, p80
Monarch, 318, 319
Montgomery, 101, 102
Montgomery, H.P., 320
Montgomery, James, 182
Moore, Thomas, 35
Mopsa the Fairy (Ingelow), 303
Morine, Andrew, 336
Morning Glory, 212, 233
Morrison, J.H., 323
Morse, J.B., 220
Mortimer Livingston, 124-125, 126
Morton, W.H., 323
Moses, John Gilman, Capt., 14, 108-109, 155, 293-297, 301-303, 305, 306, 308
Moses, Levi, 103
Moses, L.M., Capt., 26
Moses, Mrs., 294, 295
Moses, Thomas P., 307
Moulton, Daniel, 8, 212-213, 233
Moultrie, 205-206
Moultrie, William, 205
Muchmore, Joseph C., 305
Muggs, John, 20
Mugridge, John, 55, 56
Mugridge Yard, 33, 54
Mulford, Captain, (of the *Nicholas Biddle*), 54
Murphy (*Annie Sise* sailor), 237
Mutinies; *Annie Sise*, 237; *Governor*

Langdon, 211; *John Cumming*, 44-46

Narragansett, 295
Nason, Augustus, 20
Nathan, Henry, 48
Neal, John, 8, 202, 226, 268, 274-275, 355; *Frank Jones*, 315-320; *Granite State*, 330-344, 355; *India*, 21; *Merrimack*, 291-293; *Piscataqua*, 274-275; *Portsmouth*, 265-266
Neal, William, 12, 22, 30-31, 37, 38
Nelson, George, 31, 47, 96
Neptunas, 182
Neptune, 300
Nestor, 13-14, p14
New Hampshire, 40, 56-57, 211, 254-257
New Hampshire, USS, 93
New Line, 31, 91, 104, 132, 176
New Orleans, 139
New Orleans Packet Line, 20
New Plan, 101-102
New World, 120, 121
Newell, Captain, (of the *Syren*), 158
Newmarket, 5
Niantic, 17
Nicholas Biddle, 53-54
Nichols, James M., Capt., 317
Nickerson, Joseph J., Capt., 114, 170, 171, 222, 232, 233, 251, 254, 257
Nightingale, 128, 196, 203
Niobe, 316
Noble's Island, 7, 8, 11, 199, 212, 310
Noble's Island Bridge, 345-347
Noonday, 220, 259
Norah, 265
Nordstern, 258
Norman, 46-47, 59
North America, 198
North Atlantic, 151-154
North Mill Pond, 4, 12, 345
North Star, 198

North Wind, 172
Norton, Jacob, 151

Ocean Rover, 205
Ocean Star, 249
Ocean-Monarch, 120, 121
Odell, Lory, 229
Odiorne, Thomas, 148
Odiorne's Point, 2
Olafwyk, 89
Old Town of Berwick (Jewett), 18
Oliphant, D.W., 125
Oliphant, R.M., 125
O'Quinn, Edward, 199
Orient, 184-188, 198
Oriental, 143
Orion, 172, 173
Orleans, 17
Orleans Line, 70
Oronoco, 5, 11, 50-51
Orozimbo, 257-258, 316
Othello, 218-220
Owen, U.S. Commissioner, 237

Pacific Guano Company, p193
Pacific Steam Navigation Co., 219
Packet Line, 18, 47, 132
Packet ships, 7, 14, 120-121; *See also* Names of individual ships and lines
Pactolus, 11, 25-26, 30
Page, Richardson & Co., 267, 271, 275, 276
Paine, William, Capt., 57-58
Palfrey, Ken, 68
Palfrey, Kennard, 31, 216
Palfrey, William, 31, 216
Panther, 204
Parker, William, Capt., 17, 58, 59-60, 91-92, 207, 273
Parrott, William F., 153, 225
Parsons, Albion B., 112
Parsons, Isaac D., Capt., 75
Parsons, John D., 215
Parsons, John W., Dr., 46

Parsons, Mary Augusta, 46
Parsons, William H., Capt., 32-33, 87-88, 111, 112, 174, 175-176, 223
Patriotic Line, 186, 198
Patten, George, Dr., 25
Patterson, William, Capt., 31-32
Paul Jones, 241, 336, 344, 345-353, p346, 355
Paul, Stephen, 177
Pauline, 232, 258
Payne, John A., Capt., 58
Peabody, A.P., Rev., 32
Peabody Line, 352
Pearson, George F., 285
Peck, Hiram N., 100, 104
Peirce, Joshua W., 136, 172, 197
Peirce, Mark W., 89, 136
Pelican Line, 172
Pendexter, George W., 176, 202, 208, 210, 275, 291, 323, 349
Penhallow, John P., Capt., 94-95
Penhallow, Pearce W., Capt., 25, 165-168, 239
Penhallow, Thomas W., 24, 25, 94
Pennsylvania, 124, 125
Perkins, Michael R., 311
Perkins, Thomas H., 55
Peter Marcy, 116, 130-132, 151, 316
Peter Marcy Towboat Line, 253
Pettigrew, Mary E., 281
Pettigrew, Sarah E., 251
Pettigrew, William, 8, 81, 106, 221, 241, 281; *Colorado*, 213-215; *Columbus*, 118-122; *Danube*, 136-137, 151; *Empire State*, 140-143; *Frank Pierce*, 177, 188-196, p189, 228; *Georgianna*, 260-261; *Germania*, 161-165; *Governor Langdon*, 208-212; *Hope Goodwin*, 174-176; *Isaac H. Boardman*, 220-221; *John Haven*, 145, 147-151; *Judah Touro*, 105-109, 113; *Levi Woodbury*, 169-171, p170, 174, 183, 188, 190, 228; *Orozimbo*, 257-258; *Peter Marcy*, 130-32, 151;

Piscataqua, 176-179, p177; *R.D. Shepherd*, 113-114; *Samoset*, 115-118, 200; *Sarah E. Pettigrew*, 230, 251-254; *Western World*, 154-156
Phelps, A.A., 83
Philadelphia Line, 146, 239
Philadelphia & New Orleans Line, 37-38
Philadelphia Packet Line, 217
Philbrick, Eliza P., 323
Philbrick, W.M.C., 320
Phoebe, 231
Pickering, McLauren F., Capt., 223-224, 240
Pickett, Gertrude, 7, 118
Pickett, Samuel, Capt., 36
Pierce, Elbridge G., 8, 259
Pierce, Franklin, 169, 188-191
Pierce Island, 34, 327
Pierce, Joshua W., 73
Pierce, Mark W., 73
Pigeon Coop, 288-289
Pike, Captain, (of the *Henrietta Marcy*), 233
Pike (worker on *Mary Kingsland*), 71
Pilgrims, 2
Pingree & Johnson, 54
Pioneer, 289
Pioneer Line, 338
Piscataqua, 176-179, p177, 211, 265, 274-275
Piscataqua Basin, 3
Planet, 12
Pleasants, Samuel, 91, 104, 176
Plumer, George W., 323
Plymouth Cordage Company, 139
Plymouth, USS, 309
Pocahontas, 2
Polk, James K., 94
Pontiac, 58-62
Pontiff, 22-24, 30
Pook, Samuel, 33, 54, 55
Pook, S.M., 285
The Pool, 1

Port of Dover (Whitehouse), 50
Port of Portsmouth Ships and the Cotton Trade (Brighton), 3, 12
Porter, Commodore, 72-73
Porter, Timothy N., Capt., 278, 280
Portfire, 288, 289, 292
Portsmouth, 30-31, 104, 211, 261, 265-266, 274
Portsmouth Athenaeum, 3, 78, 92, 96
Portsmouth Bridge, 5, 11, 171
Portsmouth Marine Laboratory, 33
Portsmouth Marine Railway, 17
Portsmouth Marine Society, 24
Portsmouth Navigation Co., 17
Portsmouth Navy Yard, 11, 194, 269, 273, 278-279, 285, 347
Portsmouth Pier, 60
Portsmouth, Portland & Saco Railroad, 52
Portsmouth Shipbuilding Co., 232, 244
Portsmouth Toll Bridge, 346
Portsmouth Yacht Club, 320
Portsmouth's Heyday in Shipbuilding (Pickett), 118
Powers, James, 226
Pratt, Lieutenant, 90
Pray, John S., Capt., 287, 288, 289
Pray, Samuel, 12, 13, 21, 27
Preble, Russell A., 350
Pressed hay, 66
Preston, William, 265
Preston, William H., 352
Preston, William Rantoul, 52-53, 289, 323, 333
Prima Donna, 288
Prior, Henry, Capt., 197
Prior, Walter H., 351
Pritchard, E.G., Mrs., 232
Proctor, Captain, (of the *Anna Decatur*), 225
Prompt, 136
Providence, 205

Queens of the Western Ocean (Cutler), 37
Quickstep, 293, 309, 336

Railroad, 17, 52, 79
Raitt, James, 78
Rand, Alphonzo L., 317
Rankin, 237
Ravensbourne, 281
Raynes Avenue, xx
Raynes, Charles, 81, 106, 107; *America*, 109-111, p110; *Arabella*, 91-92; *Columbia*, 63; *Empire*, 97-100, 140; *Goodwin*, 82-84; *Matilda*, 107; *Robert Parker*, 75-77
Raynes & Fernald; *Arabella*, 91-92; *Goodwin*, 82-84
Raynes, George, xx, 5, 6, 7, 12, 81, 189, 220, 267, 293; *Alexander*, 12-13; *Arkwright*, 215-218; *Athens*, 73-75; *Centurion*, 125-126; *Charles*, 51, 65-67; *Constantine*, 160-161, 162; *Finland*, 100-102; *George Raynes*, 165-169, p166; *Glendoveer*, 51, 81, 87-88; *Harbinger*, 37; *Harriet & Jessie*, 21, 83; *Henry*, 51-52; *Hindoo*, 37-38; *Isaac Allerton*, 59, 67-69; *Isaac Newton*, 49-50; *James Browne*, 145-146, 147; *Jersey*, 138-139, 151; *John Cumming*, 41-46, 76; *John Taylor*, 85-86, 91; *Kalamazoo*, 86-87, 91; *Kate Hunter*, 111-113; *Lancashire*, 48-49; *Mary Kingsland*, 69-73, 87; *Mortimer Livingston*, 124-125, 126; *Nestor*, 13-14, p14; *Nicholas Biddle*, 53-54; *North Atlantic*, 151-154; *Orient*, 184-188, 198; *Pontiff*, 22-24, 30; *Portsmouth*, 30-31; *Rockingham*, 5, 24-25, 30, 59; *Siam*, 126-127; *Susanna Cumming*, 31-33, 50, 59; *Thomas Wright*, 102-103; *Venice*, 89-91, 94; *Webster*, 198-199, 218
Raynes, George, Jr., 8, 200, 293;

Annie Sise, 236-238; *Como*, 257, 258; *Jumna*, 225-226; *Mary Washington*, 247-249
Raynes, Nathaniel K., 113, 146, 229
Raynes Shipyard, p161
R.B. Forbes, 225, 230, 260
R.D. Shepherd, 113-114, 182, 316
Rea, William, 252
Reattenburg, William, 20
Red Gauntlet, 160
Red Rover, 177
Red Z Line, 126
Reding, John R., 281, 329
Reed, E.W., 264
Regular Line, 49
Remick, Jacob, 11, 64
Republican Party, 228, 300-302
Rescue, 257
Revolutionary War, 4
R.H. Tucker, 247, 249-251
R.H. Tucker & Co, 47
R.H. Tucker & Sons, 115
Rice, Alexander, 13
Rice, Arabella, 91
Rice, B. Frank, 334
Rice, John, 47
Rice Memorial Library, 91
Rice, Robert, 15, 17, 28-29, 58, 59, 78, 91, 147, 148, 149, 172
Rice, Samuel, Capt., 91
Rice, T.J., 13
Rice, William A., Capt., 49, 75, 82
Rich, Abraham 96
Richard III, 261, 262-264, p263, 290
Richardson, Captain, (of the *Sagamore*), 240
Richardson, Watson & Co., 123, 124, 132
Richardson's Line, 134
Richmond, 94
Ricker, Charles, 248
Ricker, Clinton, 214, 215
Ricker, Moses D., Capt., 126, 149
Ricker, Moses G., Capt., 214, 215
Ricker, Mrs., 214, 215

Riley, John, 50
Rindge, Daniel, 209
Rindge, John, 177
Rita Norton, 213
Ritchie, 63
Roads, 2
Robert Harding, 149, 207
Robert Minturn, 156
Robert Parker, 75-77, 104, 177
Roberts, Charles, 20
Roberts, Edmund, 51
Roberts, Robert, 323
Roberts, Thomas, Capt., 196
Robertson, John, Capt., 217, 295
Robinson, Alexander, 323
Robinson, W.F., Capt., 47-48
Rockhampton, 146
Rockingham, 5, 24-25, 30, 59, 244-247, 313, 344
Rockingham Ice Co., 178
Rockwell, Harriet, 33
Rodgers, Captain, (of the *Beatrice*), 207
Rogers, Frederick W., 132
Rogers, Robert, Capt., 50-51
Rollins, Charles H., Capt., 143-145
Rollins, H., 78
Rollins, Ichabod, Capt., 56, 63, 143-145
Rollins, William H., 323
Ropes, William, 212
Roscius, 111
Roscoe, 208
Rose Ellis, 137
Rose, George, 222
Ross, Mrs., 338, 343
Ross, O.E., 330
Ross, William, 281, 298
Ross, William A., Capt., 317
Ross, William, Capt., 282, 330, 336-339
Ross, William, Jr., Capt., 316
Rowe, J.W., Capt., 111
Royal Navy, 3
Rundlett, G.H., 229

Rushton, Mr., 122
Russell, John A., 14
Russell, Joseph G., Capt., 140, 143
Russell, J.T., Capt., 97-100
Russell & Sons, 334
Ruthelia, 26, 30, 38

Sabine, 172-174
Sable Island, 29
Sagamore, 118, 238-241
Salares, Leon, 340-343
Salt, 2, 186
Salter, Albert T., 273, 274, 278, 279, 280
Salter, Charles H., Capt., p10, 32, 89, 132, 133
Salter, Edwin E., Capt., 149-150
Salter, Henry P., 57, 94, 149
Salter, James S., Capt., 179-181
Salter, John E., Capt., 51-52, 156, 157, 241, 261
Salter & Livermore, 339
Salter, Thomas S., 280
Samoset, 7, 115-118, 120, 200, 241
Sampson, A., Capt., 132
Samuel Badger, 179-181, 230
Samuel Gerrish & Son, 148
Santee, 60, 273-274
Santee, USS, 273
Sarah E. Pettigrew, 230, 251-254
Sarah Long Bridge, 5
Sarah Newman, 243
Sarah Pettigrew, 316
Sargent, Judge, 228
Saunders, Captain, (of the *Yosemite*), 290
Saunders, Oscar, 219
Sawyer, Albert F., 168
S.C. Thwing, 222-223, 230, 316
Scott, Daniel, 168
Scott, J.E., Capt., 262
Screamer, 76
Scud, 304
Sea Serpent, 7, 160, 165, 167
Sears, Sherburne, Capt., 67

Semiramis, 287-288
Semmes, Raphael, Capt., 246-247
Severn, 154
Sewall, Samuel, Judge, 2
Shackford, William, 56
Shah Allum, 21
Shallop, 2
Shattusk Shipyard, 286
Shaw, Lemuel, 197
Sheafe, Daniel, 65
Sheafe, Jacob, 4
Sheafe, James, 4
Sheafe, Samuel, 59, 65, 84, 143, 213
Sheafe, Thomas, 4
Sheafe, William, 258
Shenandoah, 183-184, 231
Shepherd, Rezin D., 105, 113-114, 120
Sherburne, Captain, (of the *John Haven*), 149
Shillaber, Charles G., Capt., 307
Shillaber, Joseph R., Capt., 294, 311
"Ship Ella E. Badger" (poem), 226-227
"Ship James Buchanan" (poem), 229-230
Shipbuilding, 2-7, 11-12, 59, 269-271, 299, 300
Shipwrecks, *Alabama*, 93; *Alice Ball*, 244; *Annie Sise*, 238; *Apollo*, 17; *Arethusa*, 64-65; *Berwick*, 19-20; *Brother Jacob*, 201; *Calcutta*, 297; *Charles*, 67; *Chatsworth*, 208; *Chocorua*, 323-324; *Clara*, 95; *Colorado*, 214-215; *Columbus*, 122; *Como*, 258; *Daniel Marcy*, 283; *Eagle Speed*, 236; *Empire*, 100; *Epaminondas*, 97; *Fortitude*, 39; *Frank Jones*, 318-320; *Glendoveer*, 88; *Governor Langdon*, 211-212; *Granite State*, 344; *Henry*, 52; *Hibernia*, 135; *Isaac Allerton*, 67-68; *James Buchanan*, 230; *Jersey*, 139; *John Rutledge*, 164; *Mary Hale*, 144-145; *Mary Pleasants*,

104; *Mary Washington*, 249; *Merrimack*, 292-293; *Milo*, 29; *Mortimer Livingston*, 125; *Moultrie*, 206; *New Hampshire*, 56; *Orient*, 187-188; *Piscataqua*, 275; *Pontiac*, 62; *Pontiff*, 24; *Portsmouth*, 266; *Richard III*, 264; *Rockingham*, 25; *Samoset*, 118; *Santee*, 274; *Simla*, 280; *Southerner*, 171; *Susanna Cumming*, 33; *Webster*, 199; *Western World*, 155-156; *William Penn*, 124; *See also* Abandonments
Shiverick, David, 50
Shooting Star, 261
Shores, James F., Jr., 32
Siam, 126-127
Sides, Samuel S., 317, 336
Sierra Nevada, 205, 239, 337
Simes, John D., 64, 73, 78, 79, 89, 136, 197, 236, 237
Simes, Joseph, 137, 275
Simes, Stephen, 24, 25
Simes, William, 202, 226, 254, 265, 274, 275, 289, 291
Simes, William, Jr., 24, 25, 275
Simla, 278-280
Simpson, Charles E., 323, 355
Simpson, Herbert E., 308
Simpson, J.P., 323
Sims, Thomas, 35
Sise, Ann, 236
Sise, Charles Fleetford, Capt., 236-237
Sise, Edward F., 21, 73, 74, 89, 136, 197, 215, 229, 236, 291
Sise, John, 291
Sise, Shadrach H., 13
Sise, William H., Col., 60
Skillings and Whitney Brothers, 224
Slater, Charles D., Mrs., 149
Smith, A.J., Capt., 297
Smith, Edward, 131, 133, 134, 139
Smith, Frank, 297
Smith, Jeremiah G., Capt., 115
Smith, John, 78, 99, 103, 248

Smith, Nathaniel A., 121
Smith, R., 220
Smith & Swasey, 131, 148
Snow, Samuel, Capt., 22, 96, 267-268
Solon, 27-28, 30, 47
Somersworth, 5, 11
A Song of the 20th Century (Ingelow), 301-302, 308
Southerner, 171
Sparks, David C., 249
Spaulding, Lyman, Capt., 38, 49
Spavin, Robert, 47
Spencer, Robert Trail, 90
Spinney, Augustus, 323
Spofford & Tileston, 184, 185, 186, 198-199
St. Albans, 233
Stammers, Michael, 104, 146
Standish, Myles, 2
Stanley John, 243
Staples, Leonard S., 234
Staples, Moses L., 355
Staples, Nathaniel, 323
Star of Hope, 212-213, 233
State Fish Pier, 2
Stathem, Mr., 122
Stavers, John, 26
Stimpson, Charles W., 118, 234, 238, 241
Stockman, John, 85
Stone, Daniel, 115, 206, 249, 262
Stone, William P., Capt., 210
Stott, George, 323
Stuart, Charles, 97-98
Stubbs (painter), 320
Sturdevant, William B., 353
Sullivan, Captain, (of the *Annie Sise*), 237
Susanna Cumming, 31-33, 50, 59
Swallowtail Line, 160
Swasey & Rowell, 175, 178
Swordfish, 76
Symes, Captain, (of the *Finland*), 101
Syren, 158

Talbott Co., 218

Tallahassee, 31

Tanton, George S., Capt., 296, 307, 308

Tanton, Harry, 308

Tapley, Jonathan, 323

Tarlton, Herman A., Capt., 265, 266

Tarlton, James N., 122, 169, 170, 171, 254, 265, 266, 274

Tarlton, J.H., 202, 226

Tarlton, Lewis, Capt., 226, 227

Tarlton, Thomas, 122

Tartar, 286

Taylor, J.D., 125

Taylor, John, 3

Taylor & Merrill, 48, 53, 54, 58, 85, 112

Taylor, Robert, 41

Taylor, Robert L., 48, 286

Telegraph system, 292

Tessier, Captain, (of the *Alliance*), 48

Thayer, George, Capt., 42

Third Line, 37, 70, 99, 111

Thomas H. Perkins, 7

Thomas Perkins, 54-55, 151, 251

Thomas Wright, 102-103

Thompson, Bernard, 132

Thompson, Jacob W., Capt., 89, 127, 148

Thompson, Robert W., 20

Thompson, William W., Capt., 15, 28-29

Thomson, David, 2

Thorndean, 227

Thornton, Matthew, 209

Thwing, S.C., 182, 222, 232, 251, 254, 257, 260

Tilton, Reuben, 283

Tinkham, D.W., 219

Tinkham, Dwight F., 48, 249

Tinkham, Mrs., 219

Tobey, James, 107; *America*, 109-111, p110

Tobey & Littlefield, 7, 8, 115, 124, 159, 267, 268, 269; *Alice Ball*, 241-244; *Anna Decatur*, 223-225; *Brother Jonathan*, 199-201, p200; *City of Montreal*, 275-277; *Coronation*, 280-281; *Donati*, 258-259; *General Grant*, 283-286; *Grandee*, 309-315, p310; *Kate Prince*, 172, 230-232; *Liverpool Packet*, 271-272; *Manchester*, 272; *Moultrie*, 205-206; *Othello*, 218-220; *R.H. Tucker*, 247, 249-251; *Richard III*, 262-264, p263; *Santee*, 273-274; *Semiramis*, 287-288; *Simla*, 278-280; *Tartar*, 286; *Yosemite*, 288-290, 293; *See also* Littlefield, Daniel; Tobey, James; Tobey, Stephen

Tobey, Stephen, 7, 199-200, 289, 310; *See also* Tobey & Littlefield

Tom Thumb, 16

Toppan, Christopher S., 46, 92, 93, 156

Torrey, Thomas, 67

Touro, Abraham, 105

Touro, Judah, 105-106, 113

Townsend, Captain, (of the *Orozimbo*), 257

Townshend, Charles H., 162-164

Trade Wind, 172

Train Line, 167, 175, 207, 217

Trajan, 37

Transit, 35

Trask, Captain,(of the *Manchester*), 272

Trask, William B., 275

Treadwell, Captain, (of the *Pontiac*), 62

Treadwell, Captain, (of the *Sagamore*), 239, 240

Tredick, Jonathan M., 57, 58, 59, 91, 92, 147, 148, 150, 172, 213, 258, 267, 273, 278, 279

Tredick, T. Salter, 273, 278, 279

Tredick, T.M., 274

Trefethen, James P., Capt., 75-76

Trefethen, Jeremiah, Capt., 265

Trevett, Joshua, 219
Trevor, J.D., 83
Triangle trade, 3-4, p80; *Adelaide Bell*, 197; *Albania*, 85; *Glendoveer*, 88; *Henry*, 51-52; *Huron*, 57; *John Haven*, 149; *Kalamazoo*, 87; *Oronoco*, 50; *Pontiac*, 60
Tripe, Richard, Capt., 18
Tripe, Seth M., Capt., 20-21
Tripp, Elisha, p173
Trist, Consul, 86
Triton, 2
Triumphant, 172
Tucker, George Wallace, Capt., 60-62, 219, 238, 260
Tucker, Jane S., 47, 116, 117, 201, 205, 219, 248, 262
Tucker, Joseph, Capt., 48, 116-117, 200-201, 249-250
Tucker, Mary, 249
Tucker, R.H., 47, 115, 205, 247-248, 249-251
Tucker, R.H., Jr., 247, 248, 249
Tucker, Richard H., Capt., 218-219
Tucker, Richard H., Jr., Capt., 47
Tucker, Richard Hawley, 7, 199-201, 262
Tucker, Richard Holbrook, 262
Tucker, Richard Holbrook, III, 262
Tucker, Richard Holbrook, Jr., Mrs., 262
Tucker, Richard, Jr., 249
Turner, Maxine, Dr., 101
Tuscaloosa, 273
Typhoon, 7, p10, 32, 89, 174, 177, 283

Underwriter, 187
Union, 288
Union Company, 244
Union Line, 124, 126
Unlucky ships, 71-73

Valentine, William, 203
Van Ness, Captain, (of the *Empire*), 100

Van Voorst, Justice, 129
Venice, 89-91, 94
Von Schmidt, A.W., 318-319

Waldron, Richard, 2
Walker, Charles E., 148, 355
Walker & Co., 60
Walker, C.W., 117
Walker, Horton D., 39, 176, 202, 205, 208, 210, 226, 274, 275, 291, 292, 302
Walker, Nathaniel K., 176, 210, 287
Wallace, Thomas, 243
Walsh, Peter, 199
War of 1812, 271
Warren & Thayer, 207, 239, 248
Washerwoman Shoal, 67
Washington, Mary, 248
Wasp, 304
Wasson, David A., 290
Watkins, George W., 321
Wattlesworth, Charles, 35
Weare, Samuel, Capt., 70, 109-111, 118, 119
Webb, Eckford, 198
Webster, 186, 198-199, 218
Webster, Daniel, 198
Weeks, Charles A., 266
Weeks, Charles P., 266
Weeks, Elizabeth, 203
Weeks, Myra, 203
Weeks, Nathaniel G., Capt., 58, 203, 204-205, 237, 275, 291
Weeks, Nathaniel J., Capt., 84
Weeks, Thomas, 176, 254
Weeks, Thomas, Capt., 255
Weeks, Thomas M., Capt., 177, 210
Weeks, Thomas N., Capt., 75
Wellington, 36
Wendell, Abraham Q., 78
Wendell, Daniel D., 78
Wendell, George P., Capt., 178, 179
Wendell, H.F., 239, 327
Wendell, Jacob, 179
Wendell, Mehetable, 179

Wentworth, Joshua, 147
Wentworth, Mark H., 232, 238
Wenzell, Henry, 280, 281
Western World, 154-156, 161
Whale's Back, 16
Whaling vessels, 2, p3
Whatcheer, 174
Wheaton, Mr. (*Paul Jones* ship steward), 351
White, A.H., 151
White Falcon, 231
Whitehouse, Robert, 50
Whitlock, William, 161
Whitman, Captain, (of the Venice), 90-91
Whitney, Elisha, 50
Wild Pigeon, 184
Wilkens, Lieutenant, 247
William E. Roman, 151, 160
William H. Kinsman & Co., 211
William H. Marcy, 311, 325-330, 335, 336
William Jones & Son, 79
William Penn, 122-124, 201
William Ropes & Son, 212
William Ross, 298, 316
William Russell, 49
William S. Slater, 343
Williams, Henry L., 126, 127, 138, 139
Williams, Washington, 188, 228, 229, 241, 251, 254
Williamson, James, 21
Williamson, John, 199
Wilson, Isaiah, 308, 323
Wilson, Joel, 329
Wilson, John, 351
Wilson, Oliver, 254, 275, 323

Wilson, Robert, 19
Wilson, W.H., 145
Wincelau & Co., 213
Winn, Timothy H., Capt., 313, 352
Winslow, Richard E., III, 328
Wise, Daniel, Jr., 25
Wise, George, 25
Wise, Mr., (owner of the *Meteor*), 286
Witch of the Wave, 172, 184
Wm. P. Jones & Co., 118
Wood, D.H., Capt., 162-164
Wood, E.H., Capt., 263-264
Wood, Enoch, Capt., 46-47, 92, 93
Wood, George B., Jr., 282
Wood, Mrs., 164
Woodbury, Levi, 169, p170
Wootton, John, Capt., 104
Wright, William, 275

Yeaton, John, 220, 234, 238, 239, 241
Yeaton, Moses, 266
Yeaton, Thomas, 266
Yorktown, 355
Yosemite, 288-290, 293, 309
Young, Aaron, 348
Young, Samuel, Capt., 171

Z Line, 128
Zeimira, 213
Zerega, A., 126
Zerega & Co., 57
Zittlesen, John, 160